The Tzetel Katan

זה הקטן
גדול יהיה

The Tzetel Katan

The Short Note

*Inspiration for a Holy Life
by the Chasidic Master
Rabbi Elimelech of Lizhensk*

Including prayers, teachings and
advice compiled from numerous
classic seforim

Collected and arranged by
E. S. Zisman
Jerusalem 5775

Copyright © 2015 by Eliezer Shaul Zisman

ISBN 978-1-60091-379-2

All rights reserved. No part of this book may be reproduced or transmitted in any form or by any means (electronic, photocopying, recording or otherwise) without prior permission of the copyright holder or distributor, except in the case of brief quotations used in reviews and articles.

BOOK DESIGN: Renana Typesetting
COVER DESIGN: Ben Gasner Studio

Questions and comments pertaining to this book can be directed to:
Tel: 02-627-3911
tzk43912@gmail.com

DISTRIBUTED BY:
Israel Bookshop Publications
501 Prospect Street
Lakewood, NJ 08701

Tel: (732) 901-3009
Fax: (732) 901-4012
www.israelbookshoppublications.com
info@israelbookshoppublications.com

Printed in Israel

DISTRIBUTED IN ISRAEL BY:
Shanky's
Petach Tikva 16
Jerusalem
+972-2-538-6936

DISTRIBUTED IN AUSTRALIA BY:
Gold's Book and Gift Company
3–13 William Street
Balaclava 3183
+613-9527-8775

DISTRIBUTED IN EUROPE BY:
Lehmanns
Unit E Viking Industrial Park
Rolling Mill Road,
Jarrow, Tyne & Wear NE32 3DP
+44-191-430-0333

DISTRIBUTED IN SOUTH AFRICA BY:
Kollel Bookshop
Northfield Centre
17 Northfield Avenue
Glenhazel 2192
+27-11-440-6679

Preface

The *Tzetel Katan* of Rabbi Elimelech of Lizhensk is one of the most famous handbooks for *avodas Hashem* ever written, and one of the greatest legacies left to us by a Chasidic Master. It seeks to purify and elevate its readers spiritually and emotionally, and is filled with holy and practical advice on how to deepen one's love and fear of God. Some of this advice is easy to fulfill, and is applicable to everyone, each person according to his level. Other passages seem more difficult, at first; a fact that has led some people to believe that the holy words of the *Tzetel Katan* were meant only for individuals on a high spiritual level. However, this is not true. Rabbi Elimelech's insights have an amazing power to inspire every person to come close to God. In fact, simply reading the words each day is a spiritual practice that can purify a person and enable him to fulfill their teachings. Each and every passage of the *Tzetel Katan* is like a burning coal, which can set a person's heart aflame. And even if a person cannot reach those levels immediately, by slowly trying to follow its advice – even once a week or once a month – he will find that his life is changing for the better, and that his love and fear of God are growing. It's known that even simple people reached extremely high levels of spirituality by following the words of the *Tzetel Katan* and reading it daily (as R. Elimelech himself recommends). This is an aspect of *na'aseh v'nishmah* – by doing what we can, we will come to a deeper understanding of the teaching, and ultimately, a higher connection with God.

Each night, after reciting the Midnight Prayer and Kabbalistic meditations, my teacher, the holy Kabbalist, Rabbi Chaim Shaul HaKohen Dweck, would fulfill the words of the *Tzetel Katan* (§10). I would read it to him, before we began our studies, and he would listen until the end, in a joyful spirit and in great spiritual rapture. Once, he remarked to me: "Blessed is God, who gave us Rabbi Elimelech of Lizhensk and his *Tzetel Katan*."

Rabbi Yeshayahu Zelig Margolios, *Kumi Roni*

יחיאל מיכל טווערסקי
בְּאַאמו"ר הרה"צ כמוהר"ר יעקב ישראל זצללה"ה מהאָרנאָסטייפאל

Rabbi Michel Twerski

בס"ד

Tuesday, parshas Chukas, 5775

To all Jews everywhere, who long to serve Hashem:

I was recently presented with a copy of an important work – an English translation of the *Tzetel Katan*, by my holy and pure ancestor, the renowned Tzaddik, Rabbi Elimelech of Lizhensk ztz'l. The author asked for my approbation regarding the accuracy and appropriateness of the translation.

It's known that the *Tzetel Katan* is one of the most sacred chasidic texts, and is based upon the holiest and most exalted principles of Torah. For hundreds of years, these words of fire have been considered the holy of holies among the Jewish Diaspora, and in the courts of all the Tzadikim, so that anyone who considers himself a "chasid" should be intimately familiar with its holy words.

Today, however, a new generation of *Baalei Teshuva* has arisen, who long to hear Hashem's word, and deeply desire to ascend the ladder of holiness whose "head is in heaven." Unfortunately, though, many important works are still inaccessible to them, and they have to struggle greatly with *loshon hakodesh*, which is still a foreign language to them, and in which they stumble and stutter. Therefore, the author of this volume has been inspired to invest significant time and money for the benefit of all these individuals, by translating the *Tzetel Katan* into English, so that all these thirsty souls can now quench their thirst from its words.

Honestly, the heavy communal responsibilities that rest upon my shoulders did not allow me to read each page of the book as carefully as I would have liked. However, I looked through the whole thing, and everywhere I stopped, I found it to be sensitively and accurately done. And, as our Sages have said, we can rely on the assumption that a Torah Scholar will never let something unfinished or incorrect to result from his efforts.

Therefore, I am happy to offer my own humble approbation to all the others: May this English translation of the *Tzetel Katan* become available to many. This is especially the case, seeing that the author has added a wonderful commentary that clarifies and expands upon R. Elimelech holy words, thus making them easier to understand. This is addition to the meaningful prayers that the author has also added here, that arouse the heart to Hashem.

Thus, we offer our gratitude and support to R. Eliezer Shaul Zisman, and all who helped him in this holy endeavor. In the merit of this mitzvah, may they merit abundant blessing and success in everything that they do. And may the merit of the holy R. Elimelech of Lizhensk stand for them and all their offspring, until the arrival of our righteous redeemer, may it be soon in our days.

In respect and honor,

Yechiel Michal, the son of our Rabbi, the Tzaddik, R. Yaakov Yisroel of Hornsteipel

---

Congregation Beth Jehudah • 2100 N. 52nd Street •
Milwaukee, WI 53216 • ph. 414 442-5730 • Fax 414 442-6167

מאיר אלטר הלוי הורוויץ
בן לכ"ק מרן אאמו"ר מבוסטון זצללה"ה זיע"א
עיה"ק ירושלים תובב"א
The Bostoner Rebbe of Yerushalayim
ב"ה
ב' ניסן תשע"ה

Haskomoh

The Tzetel Katan, of one of my ancestors the Holy Rabbi Elimelech of Lizhensk זצ"ל זיע"א needs no present day approbation.
This Haskomo in written in recognition of the work of Rabbi Eliezer Shaul Zisman נ"י in explaining and collecting the teachings of the recognized leader of Chassidus after the Holy Besht זצ"ל and the Holy Maggid זצ"ל the work of the Holy Rebbe Reb Elimelech of Lizhensk זצ"ל.
This unique well written and well presented work adds contemporary insight into the *Tzetel Katan*, of the Holy Rebbe Reb Elimelech of Lizhensk. In addition it contains an outstanding collection of stories, practices and prayers that will inspire the reader to strive to serve Hashem purely and wholeheartedly. My father the Bostoner Rebbe ZT"L felt it most important to make the works of Chazal and even the latest commentaries available to the English speaking Public. Certainly the work of Rabbi Elimelech, who himself writes in the *Tzetel Katan* that its words should be translated so that they are understood fully merits this undertaking.
May Hashem grant that the author successfully distribute this work so that the light and the wisdom of Chassidus may be appreciated by others. The *Tzetel Katan* helps a Jewish Neshomoh learn how to satiate their souls thirst for spirituality. Such knowledge leads to a Jewish life full of torah and personal striving to achieve that which Hashem wants of us, and can facilitate our ability to serve our creator so that we may merit redemption speedily.
Many young people express their inability to 'make contact' with Hashem. The *Tzetel Katan* was written by the Holy Rebbe Reb Elimelech especially to inspire people to follow these Holy paths, and thereby ascend in their service of Hashem. The prayers included here help a person to learn how to pour out his heart to Hashem.l
Rabbi Eliezer Shaul Zisman נ"י has my blessings that his efforts to increase the awareness of the closeness of Hashem in this world through the light of Chassidus meet with great success. May the merit of the Holy Rebbe Reb Elimelech ZT"L stand him in good stead and cause a new light to shine on Tzion, with the building of the Beis HaMikdash and the coming of our righteous Moshiach.

המצפה לישועת ה' ולהרמת קרן התורה וישראל

TRANSLATION OF SECONDARY HASKOMOH:
I agree with the words of Rabbi Horowitz, shlit"a. It's clear that this work will be of benefit to the public.

Rabbi Shmuel Kamenetsky

~~ *Approbations* ~~
From the Hebrew (see end of book)

- The book is a remarkable collection of stories, practices and prayers that can inspire the reader to serve God purely and wholeheartedly. Rabbi Elimelech himself writes in the *Tzetel Katan* that the reader should translate its words into Yiddish – meaning, into any language that he understands – in order to benefit from them. May God help the author to distribute his book widely, and may the light of true wisdom and of Chasidus spread out, and may its wellsprings flow afar, until we reach the time of grace and deliverance. (Rabbi Yitzchak Meir Morgenstern, Rosh HaYeshivah, Yeshivah Toras Chochom, Jerusalem)

- My dear friend, Rabbi Eliezer Zisman, previously published this amazing work in Hebrew, which is a collection of teachings, prayers, stories and practices surrounding the *Tzetel Katan*, by the holy Rabbi Elimelech of Lizhensk. I support and bless his efforts to increase the awareness of God in the world, through the light of Chasidus, and may the merit of the holy Rabbi Elimelech help him, and may we see a new light shine on Tzion, with the building of the Beis HaMikdash and the coming of our righteous Moshiach. (Rabbi Chaim Uri Brizel, Yeshivah Sha'ar HaShamayim, Jerusalem)

- Although it is superfluous to speak of the greatness of the teachings of the holy Rabbi Elimelech of Lizhensk, let us express our gratitude to Rabbi Eliezer Shaul Zisman, for his precious collection of teachings and insights, published as a commentary on the *Tzetel Katan*. For these are the things that a person should do and live by. Now he is inspired by a wonderful goal – to publish his book in English. I therefore support his efforts – for his other published works have been well received by Rabbanim – and I offer him my blessings, to continue his blessed endeavors and spread his wellsprings afar, in order that the Torah may be exalted. May Hashem's Name be sanctified and beloved through him, with joy, health and length of days. (R. Aron David Neustadt, Rav of Congregation Khal Chasidim, Jerusalem)

- This is a very special collection, drawn from the words of the great Tzaddikim of the past. Its words are hewn from fire and are like burning coals. They can greatly inspire and encourage a person in his service of God. The way in which the teachings and prayers surround the *Tzetel Katan* is very valuable. (Rabbi Yaakov Meir Stern, Member of the Rabbinical Court of Rabbi Shmuel Wosner *shlit"a*, Bnei Brak)

לעילוי נשמת
אברהם חיים זאב בן אסתר ינטה ביין
In Loving Memory of my dear friend
Avraham Chaim Bein a.k.a. "ACE"
תנצב"ה

לעילוי נשמת
יוסף בן אמלי מנדיל'
In loving memory of
Joseph Mandil
תנצב"ה

לעילוי נשמת
יצחק בן מרים טליו
In loving memory of
Issac Telio
תנצב"ה

לעילוי נשמת אליהו בן חנה
וסוליקה בת שמחה אביצרור

In loving memory of
Eliyahu and Soulika Abisror

תנצב"ה

לעילוי נשמת מרדכי בן עללא אסתר
ודבורה בת קריינדל ווינער

In loving memory of
Markus and Dorothy Weiner

תנצב"ה

Table of Contents

Introduction	xiv
The Life of Rabbi Elimelech of Lizhensk	xvii
The Gate of Prayer	1
The Tzetel Katan	13
The Mitzvah of Kiddush Hashem	73
Hanhagos Ha'Adam	79
Stories and Teachings	
The Tzetel Katan	134
Hanhagos Ha'Adam	159
Be Strong and Don't Give Up!	189
Glossary	207
Bibliography	210
Hebrew Prayers (starting from back of book)	
Hebrew Approbations	ג
The Prayer of Rabbi Elimelech	יא
Prayer for Sanctifying God's Name, by the Shlah HaKadosh	יד
Prayer of Repentance by Rabbeinu Yonah	טו
Prayer over Torah Study from Sha'arei Tzion	טז
Prayers for the Tzetel Katan	יט
Prayers for Hanhagos Ha'Adam	מא

Introduction

Blessed is God, who has not withheld His kindness from us, and who sends us Tzaddikim in every generation to instruct us in the way of God, in order that we may find true happiness and blessing in our lives. This is especially true in these days, before the coming of the Moshiach, when we have been blessed with the teachings of the holy Baal Shem Tov, who taught how each and every person can come close to God. The fire of Chasidus that he lit almost three hundred years ago continues to burn in our time, and has spread around the world. It has been passed down to us through the Baal Shem Tov's followers and their disciples, the great Tzaddikim, whose written works continue to inspire us until today.

Among the greatest of these Tzaddikim was the holy Rabbi Elimelech of Lizhensk, whose book, *Noam Elimelech*, is one of the most famous Chasidic texts. He also left us numerous practices and pieces of advice, which can greatly enhance our *avodas Hashem*. These are collected in the holy works *Tzetel Katan* and *Hanhagos HaAdam* ("Paths to Perfection"), which are translated in this book.

Out of my great love for these teachings, and my desire to help people appreciate their beauty and applicability, I also collected other, related teachings of Rabbi Elimelech and his disciples, and used them to frame and enhance the teachings of the *Tzetel Katan*. My hope is that when the reader sees how inspiring these teachings and practices are, he will be moved to follow them, to the best of his ability.

Rabbi Kalonymous Kalman Epstein, a disciple of Rabbi Elimelech, wrote (*Maor VaShemesh, Ki Setze*):

> People must know that the main battle against the evil inclination takes place during prayer. For even if a person studies a great deal of Torah, performs mitzvos, and donates his time and money to the poor, the evil inclination will not fully oppose him; for these actions are no real threat to it. However, when a Jew pours out his heart to God in prayer, the evil inclination

attacks him unceasingly and disrupts his thoughts. For such prayers cut to the evil inclination's very essence, and can defeat it, more than all the mitzvos.

Therefore, in addition to all the stories and teachings collected here, we have also added numerous prayers, which relate to Rabbi Elimelech's teachings. These are drawn from several works, particularly *Likutey Tefilos*, by Rabbi Nosson of Breslov (Rabbi Nachman's chief disciple), and from the works of the "Chida" – Rabbi Chaim Dovid Azulai, about whom Rabbi Elimelech once said: "There is a great Tzaddik in Italy, whose holy writings are eradicating all the heretical books found there. If only the hearts of the Jewish people were devoted to his writings, they wouldn't budge so much as an inch from their faith in God" (*Ohel Elimelech*, §281). With these prayers, the reader can pour out his heart to God and beseech Him to draw him close to His service. These prayers appear in English beneath the text of the *Tzetel Katan*, and in their original Hebrew, toward the end of the book.

It is also known that it is impossible to reach any level of holiness without God's help. Tzaddikim have spoken of the importance of praying over the topics that we study, so that the holy concepts should not remain as mere ideas, but should enter our hearts. I believe that if we truly pray to God to bring us close to Him, we will be able to fulfill all the holy practices that are recorded in this book. As Rabbi Elimelech himself said: "If a person cries out to God for a long time, beseeching Him to be able to serve Him, God will answer his request. But it takes more than a few days."

To make the teachings of the *Tzetel Katan* even more relatable, we have included a section of stories about great Tzaddikim of the past; for stories about Tzaddikim can inspire a person to serve God. Scattered among the stories, you will also find several short teachings related to each section, which were not included with the text of the *Tzetel Katan* itself.

Finally, at the end of the book, I added a section entitled "Be Strong and Don't Give Up!" which contains several helpful pieces of advice that can aid a person in his *avodas Hashem*.

I would like to thank the following individuals for their contribution to this project. First and foremost, Rabbi Eliyahu Abisror, for his vision, dedication, encouragement and patience that made this work a reality. It is in his merit that this project was conceived and realized. I would also like to thank Dr. Julian Ungar for his suport, advice and guidance in the preparation of this volume. May the merit of the holy Rabbi Elimelech protect them and their families, and may they see much joy from their children and children's children.

I would like to thank Rabbi Eliezer Shore, for his careful and dedicated translation, Rabbi Moshe Mykoff, for his fine editing work, Rabbi Chaim Kramer, of the Breslover Research Institute, for allowing me to use excerpts from his excellent English translations, particularly *The Fiftieth Gate* (*Likutey Tefilos*), and *Advice* (*Likutey Etzos*).

Above all, I would like to thank my wife, a true *eshes chayil*, in whose merit I have been able to devote myself to Torah study for many years, as well as to writing this book and others. As Rabbi Akiva said: "All that is mine, is hers." May it be God's will that we merit a long and good life together, and raise our children with joy, happiness and contentment. And may we see our children and our children's children going in the way of God.

In conclusion, I raise my voice in praise and thanks to the Creator, for the great kindness he has shown me my entire life, for allowing me to study Torah, and to publish this book.

May we see the coming of the righteous Moshiach, speedily in our days, and the fulfillment of the verse: "The deliverers will ascend Mount Tzion… and the kingship will be God's" (*Ovadiah* 1:21).

Eliezer Shaul Zisman
Jerusalem
5775/2015

The Life of Rabbi Elimelech of Lizhensk

Rabbi Elimelech Weissblum of Lizhensk was one of the greatest Chasidic masters of the 18th century. He lived at a time when the Chasidic movement was beginning to flourish and spread across Eastern Europe. He and his brother, Rabbi Zushia of Anipoli, were among the closest students of Rabbi Dov Ber, the Maggid of Mezeritch – the chief disciple of the Baal Shem Tov. After the Maggid's passing, Rabbi Elimelech moved to the town of Lizhensk, Poland, where he attracted a large following, and devoted himself to teaching and helping the community. To chasidim, he is known simply as "the Rebbe, Reb Melech," and is widely considered to have been the father of Polish Chasidus. His great influence and personal holiness also gained him the name "the Second Baal Shem Tov."

Personal Life

Rabbi Elimelech was born in 1717 (5477), in a little village near the town of Tykocin, Galicia, to Rabbi Eliezer Lipa Lipman and his wife, Mirel. Rabbi Eliezer was a successful merchant, who devoted himself to charity and good deeds, and often hosted numerous poor people at his table. According to one story, Rabbi Eliezer and his wife once hosted a group of vagabonds and beggars. They fed them, and allowed them to wash themselves from the dirt of the road. Among the group was a particularly unpleasant looking individual, whose body was covered with sores and blisters. Unable to wash even his hands and face, Mirel helped him, taking extra care not to cause pain to his wounds. Before the beggars left, the sickly beggar blessed Rabbi Eliezer and his wife. "In reward for your kindness, I bless you to have a son who is like me." The couple was shocked. However, years later, after Rabbi Elimelech was born and his light began to shine, they realized that the beggar had been a hidden Tzaddik, whose blessing had come true.

Rabbi Elimelech and his older brother, Zushia, studied Torah together and became accomplished scholars. Already, in their youth, they delved into the Kabbalistic mysteries of the Zohar and the writings of the Arizal. Later, in their thirties, they spent eight years traveling across the Polish countryside in self-imposed exile. This practice was allowed them to identify with the Shechinah – the Divine Presence – that is also in exile, and to speed its redemption. As they wandered from town to town, they spread Torah and inspired people to repent and mend their ways. During this time, they lived a life of hardship, poverty, penance and fasting – an ascetic approach that Rabbi Elimelech would maintain his entire life. However, he later instructed his followers not to imitate his practices, as they would not help them attain their spiritual goals. As he wrote in *Noam Elimelech*: some Tzaddikim reach perfection through fasting; others, through eating and drinking.

Toward the end of his wandering, while in his early forties, Rabbi Elimelech joined Rabbi Zushia in the town of Mezeritch, and the two brothers entered the Maggid's inner circle of disciples. The Maggid was the great organizer of the Chasidic movement, and sent his students across Europe to found Chasidic synagogues and communities. After the Maggid passed away in 1772, Rabbi Elimelech returned to Poland, where he attracted thousands of followers. He was known for his great modesty, humility, holiness and the exceptional love and self-sacrifice he showed for every Jew. His followers sought out his advice and blessings and, above all, absorbed his path of repentance, self-improvement and spiritual growth.

Rabbi Elimelech's first wife, Sprinza, was the daughter of Rabbi Aaron Rokeach Margolios. She bore him several children, though she herself died prematurely. After her passing, Rabbi Elimelech married Gittel, the daughter of Rabbi Yaakov Margolios. Rabbi Elimelech's oldest son was Rabbi Elazar, named after his mother's uncle, Rabbi Elazar Rokeach. His other children were Rabbi Eliezer Lipa of Chemelnick, Rabbi Yaakov of Maglanitza, Mirish and Esther Ethel.

His Teachings

Rabbi Elimelech's most famous book, *Noam Elimelech* (Lemberg, 1787), is one of the greatest works of the Chasidic movement, and has been reprinted countless times, in numerous editions. It was transcribed by his son, Rabbi Elazar, from his father's public sermons, and approved by Rabbi Elimelech. For secret reasons, though, it was not published until after Rabbi Elimelech's passing. The book is divided into sections following the weekly Torah portion. Its major theme is the role and centrality of the Tzaddik in the Chasidic community. Thus, it is known as *Sefer shel Tzaddikim* – The Book of the Righteous (as opposed to the *Tanya*, which is known as *Sefer shel Beinonim* – The Book of the Intermediates). To Rabbi Elimelech, the Tzaddik is a bridge between heaven and earth; he uplifts his chasidim to God, and draws spiritual and material blessing down into the world. The Tzaddik is not just a spiritual giant, who lives in the upper worlds, he is the leader of his flock. He lives both above and below simultaneously, both clinging to God and caring for the needs of his people. At times, he must even fall from his high level, in order to unite with his community and draw down blessings upon them.

Rabbi Elimelech also wrote a short prayer to be said before the regular daily prayers (found here on page 202). The *Tzetel Katan* was found among his manuscripts, and first published in the back of the book *Arba'a HaRashim* (Lemberg, 1849), by Rabbi Aryeh Leib of Lańcut, a disciple of the Seer of Lublin and the Maggid of Koznitz. In addition, Rabbi Elimelech composed several famous Chasidic melodies, which are sung until today.

Rabbi Elimelech's Disciples

Most of the great Chasidic masters of Poland were disciples of Rabbi Elimelech; among them, Rabbi Yaakov Yitzchak Horowitz – the Seer of Lublin; Rebbe Menachem Mendel of Rimanov; Rabbi Yisroel Hopsztajn – the Kozhnitzer Maggid; Rabbi Avraham Yehoshua Heshel – the Apter Rav; Rabbi Kalonymous Kalman HaLevi Epstein of Crakow – author of *Maor VaShemesh*; Rabbi Tzvi Elimelech Spira of Dinov – author of *Bnei Yisaschar*; Rabbi Naftali Tzvi of Ropshitz; Rabbi Dovid of Lelover, and Rabbi Moshe Leib Erblich of Sassov. It was through these great Tzaddikim that Chasidus spread throughout Poland and Galicia.

It is said that when Rabbi Elimelech's time to leave this world arrived, he passed on his spiritual strengths to four of his disciples: to the Seer of Lublin, he bequeathed his holy vision; to the Kozhnitzer Maggid, he bequeathed the spirit of his heart; to Rabbi Menachem Mendel of Rimanov, he bequeathed the soul of his mind, and to Rebbe Avraham Yehoshua Heshel of Apt, he bequeathed his power of speech.

His Passing

Rabbi Elimelech passed away on the 21st of the month of Adar, 5547 (1787). Before he died, he promised that anyone who visits his grave will be delivered from his troubles, and will not depart from this world without repenting of his misdeeds. He is buried in Lizhensk and his grave is visited yearly by thousands of chasidim from around the world, especially on the anniversary of his death.

The Gate of Prayer

Today, before the coming of Moshiach, the main form of service is prayer.

Rabbi Chaim Vital

Praying for Spirituality

During the time of the Temple, there was a God-fearing Kohen who was careful to perform all of his good deeds in secret. He had ten children: six boys and four girls. Each day, he would bow down in prayer and beg God for mercy, that none of his children ever commit a sin or be guilty of unseemly behavior.

It's said that by the time that Kohen died, he merited to see his children and grandchildren serve as Kohanim Gedolim and young Kohanim in the Temple for a period of more than fifty years. (*Tanna d'Bei Eliyahu*, chap. 18)

A person can pray without reservation to become wise in serving God, for no accusing forces can stand against such prayers. (*Avnei Zikaron*, §563)

> Moshe said to the Jews, "You ingrates! When God said to you: 'If only their hearts would be like this, to fear Me and to keep all My commandments always' (Devorim 5:26), you should have answered: 'God, You give us such a heart!'" However, Moshe did not tell them this until forty years later. (Avodah Zarah 5b)

Tosafos (citing Rashi) explains that Moshe himself did not remember to tell this to the people until forty years later. Why, then, did he become angry with them? The answer is that Moshe did not lack the fear of God, and did not need to pray for it, when God made His statement. However, the Jewish people did need to pray for it. Because they had already sinned several times, such as with the Golden Calf and the spies, they should have thought about what God was saying to them at the time.

This contradicts what many people think – that only great Tzaddikim should occupy themselves with prayers and supplications to God; whereas young people, or coarse and lowly people, should not. Yet, according to Tosaphos, Moshe did not need this prayer, since he was a great Tzaddik, but he was upset with the Jewish people for not praying. They knew that they were on a low level, which is the very reason that they should have fortified themselves and begged God to grant them the fear of Him, so that they would not sin again.

The Maharsha comments on this that even though the Sages said: "Everything is in God's hands except for the fear of Heaven," it is obvious that even the fear of Heaven is in God's hands, as well – to rectify and uplift a person's heart. Indeed, there are many verses that support this idea.

From here we see how much God desires each and every Jew to pray to Him to instill in his heart the fear of Heaven. (Introduction to *Histapchus HaNefesh*)

The Greatness of Prayer

One should pray over everything, at all times, and particularly on special occasions.

"Never forget the greatness of prayer," writes Rabbeinu Bachaya (*Devorim* 11:13). "Prayer has the power to alter the course of nature, save one from harm, and annul harsh decrees."

Certainly, this is true of every heartfelt prayer, spoken in moments of crisis, with deep faith in God. It is even truer when a person offers his prayers *before* trouble comes his way (*Sanhedrin* 44b), because such prayers have a much greater power to annul negative decrees. For example, before a joyous event – such as a wedding or *bris milah* – one should pray that no negative repercussions or *ayin hora* arise to disrupt the joy of the occasion (*Shevet Mussar* 20:14).

This principle of "praying first" applies to even the simplest act. The famous Rabbi Eliezer Ziskind, author of *Yesod v'Shoresh HaAvodah*, would offer a short prayer before beginning *Birchas HaMazon*: "Save me, my Creator, from any disturbances during Grace after Meals; let no one disrupt me during the prayer." To Rabbi Ziskind, even as simple an act as not being interrupted during *Birchas HaMazon* deserved a prayer of its own.

> It's said that when the father of the Tzaddik Rabbi Dovid of Lelov would sing Shabbos songs and reach the words "May we see our children and grandchildren involved in Torah and mitzvos," he would repeat them with such intensity that he would almost pass out. In the merit of these prayers, his son grew up to be the holy Rabbi Dovid of Lelov.

Prayer not only annuls harsh decrees, but is also the source of all spiritual and material blessings. Rabbi Simchah Bunim of Pashischa said that the way to have all one's material needs met, as well as to cling to God at all times, is to accustom oneself to pray for all things, big and small. One needn't don tallis and tefillin for this, nor sequester himself in a private room. Wherever you are – in the market, at home – you can entreat God. (As long as the area is clean, as the verse states: "Your camp shall be holy" (*Devorim* 23:15).) God will certainly hear and answer your prayers, and you will find yourself constantly attached to the Holy One.

> The famous Rabbi Naftali Tzvi Berlin, head of the Volozhin Yeshivah, once found his talmid, Rabbi Shimon Shkop, sitting and crying. Rabbi Naftali asked him the reason. Was he hungry? Did he need a new pair of shoes? (Rabbi Shkop was very poor at that time.)
>
> "I'm not crying about that," answered Rabbi Shimon. "Rather, I just learned a very difficult Rashbam on masechta Bava Basra, daf 29, and I don't understand it."
>
> The Netziv replied: "I also worked long and hard to understand that Rashbam, to no avail. So I went to the grave of Rabbi Chaim of Volozhin and asked God to open my eyes so that I might understand it." (*Shaal Aviecha VaYagedcha*, part 3, p. 18)

A person should pin all his hopes on God, and pray to Him for his every need – great or small. Nothing should be left out. The main point is, whatever you do during the day, you should pray to God to help you succeed and that He lead you along the straight and proper path. (*Ya'aros Devash*, part 1:1)

> Before becoming a Chasidic Rebbe in his own right, Rabbi Mendel of Riminov was a disciple of Rabbi Elimelech of Lizhensk. He would spend long periods of time in Lizhensk – half a year or more – praying and studying with his Rebbe. For his part, Rabbi Elimelech took care of all of Rabbi Mendel's needs, and hosted him at his meals each day.
>
> One day, Rabbi Mendel thought to himself: "Since my Rebbe is seeing to all my material needs, why should I pray for food?"
>
> Shortly after, master and disciple sat down to a meal. The servants of Rabbi Elimelech brought each guest a plate of food, but forgot to bring Rabbi Mendel a fork. Everyone started eating, except Rabbi Mendel.
>
> "Why aren't you eating," Rabbi Elimelech asked him.
>
> "I don't have a fork," he answered.

"You see," replied Rabbi Elimelech, "one must pray to God even for a fork, not to mention bigger things."

From that time on, Rabbi Mendel was careful to pray to God for everything he needed. (*Ohr Elimelech* 124)

Bessarabian Wine

Once, the Baal Shem Tov asked his disciple, Rabbi Dovid of Mikalov, to travel to Bessarabia and oversee the preparation of a large amount of wine, which was to be manufactured according to the strictest kashrus standards.

Rabbi Dovid traveled to Bessarabia for the months of Elul and Tishrei, and supervised each and every detail of the wine's production. He didn't miss a step – from the moment the grapes were picked until the wine was finally poured into the vats. Each stage was carried out according to the highest level of kashrus.

By the time he was ready to return to Medzhibuz, the rainy season had begun. The roads were muddy, making travel almost impossible. The return journey was immensely demanding – particularly because Rabbi Dovid did not want to take his mind off of the wine for even an instant. Finally, he arrived in Medzhibuz and parked his wagon in front of the Baal Shem Tov's shul. Joyfully, he ran inside to inform his master of his return.

At the very moment, a Cossack – in the employ of the local land baron – rode by on his horse. His job was to prevent the smuggling of alcohol into the province. When he saw the barrels of wine on the wagon, he started screaming, "Illegal alcohol! Illegal alcohol!" Rabbi Dovid stepped outside, where the Cossack promptly ordered him to open all of the barrels. The man put his hand into each one and drew out a bit of wine to taste. As a result, all the wine on the wagon became forbidden (due to the prohibition of *yayin nesach*). Only when the Cossack was satisfied that it was wine, and not alcohol, did he ride away.

Rabbi Dovid was heartbroken. All of his hard work for nothing! Tearfully, he returned to the Baal Shem Tov. "Rebbe, tell me please, why did I deserve such a terrible punishment?"

"It's true that you guarded the wine with your whole heart," the Baal Shem Tov answered him. "Unfortunately, at the same time, you forgot about the True Guardian, as the verse states: "If God will not guard a city, its watchman keeps his vigil in vain" (*Tehilim* 127:1). You didn't pray to God to help you guard the wine. For that reason, it seems, you were punished." (*Hischazkus b'Tefilah l'Hashem*, p. 104)

Rabbi Elimelech's Prayer

The Origin of the Prayer

It's known that this holy prayer can ward off all accusing forces and lift up our prayers to God. Its origin is lofty and holy, as Rabbi Yisachar Dov Ber, the great *Sabba Kaddisha* of Radoshitz, related, in the following story:

As a child, Rabbi Yisachar Dov Ber once visited Lizhensk, to spend time with the holy Rabbi Elimelech. While standing outside the Rebbe's home with a number of older chasidim, he noticed several extremely tall men hurrying to the Rebbe's house. They were so tall that they had to stoop down to enter the doorway. Rabbi Elimelech greeted them, and immediately shut the door after they entered. It all happened so fast that the chasidim were unable to see their faces. Curious as to who these visitors might be, the chasidim decided to wait there until they left, to catch a glimpse of them. However, to their surprise, when the tall men emerged, they walked away so quickly that all they could see were their backs. The chasidim realized that something unusual had occurred, and decided to ask Rabbi Elimelech the identity of his visitors.

Several of the elder chasidim approached the Rebbe and asked him to explain the incident. He replied as follows:

"When I realized that most people can no longer concentrate on their prayers, whether due to a lack of time, a lack of understanding, or the daily pressure of making a living, it occurred to me to compose a new, shorter version of the prayers, which everyone could say. However, the Men of the Great Assembly (who arranged the daily prayers millennia ago) caught wind of my intention. They came and asked me not to follow through with the plan, or change even a single prayer from its original version. I discussed the matter with them, and they suggested that I compose a new prayer to be said *before* praying. This would help all those who are unable to concentrate on their prayers."

"This is the prayer of Rabbi Elimelech that is printed at the beginning of many *siddurim*," the *Sabba Kaddisha* concluded.

The Prayer of Rabbi Elimelech of Lizhensk

May it be Your will, Hashem our God, and God of our fathers, who heeds the voice of entreaties, and mercifully hears the prayers of His people Yisroel, to prepare our hearts, establish our thoughts, and make our prayers fluent in our mouths. Lend Your ear to the prayers of Your servants, who plead to You with cries for help and with a broken spirit. For You are the merciful God, abundantly compassionate, with great loving-kindness. Forgive and pardon and grant atonement to us and to all Your people Yisroel, for all that we have sinned and transgressed against You. For You know that we did not intentionally disobey the words of Your mouth and the words of Your Torah and mitzvos, God forbid, but only succumbed to the evil inclination, which constantly burns within us, without rest, until it arouses in us a desire for this fallen world and its vanities. It constantly confuses us, even when we stand before You, praying for our very souls; it disturbs our prayers and our thoughts with its schemes and devices. We cannot withstand it! Our minds and hearts have become very weak, and all the troubles, hardships and constant pressures have crippled our ability to bear it.

But You, O God, are compassionate and gracious. Fulfill the promise that You made through (Moshe), Your faithful servant: "I will be gracious to whom I will be gracious, and show compassion upon whom I will show compassion" (*Shemos* 33:19). And as our Sages have said: "...even to a person who is unfit and unworthy" (*Berachos* 7a). For Your way is to bestow goodness upon both the wicked and the good. For You know our cries, our pains, and our laments over not being able to worship You and truly and sincerely attach our hearts to You. Woe to our souls! Woe to us so much, our Father in Heaven!

Now, please awaken Your great mercy and loving-kindness toward us, to cast out and eliminate the evil inclination from within us. Rebuke it! Tell it to leave us; to cease enticing us and pushing us away from Your service! Let no evil thoughts arise in our hearts, God forbid, neither when we are awake, nor asleep, and especially when we stand before You in prayer, when we study Your Torah, and when we fulfill Your commandments. Let our thoughts then be truly clear, pure, strong and sincere, as is Your beneficent will for us.

Awaken our hearts, the hearts of all Your people Yisroel, and the hearts of all who join us and desire our company, to unify You in truth and in love, to serve you sincerely, as is acceptable before Your Throne of Glory. Set our faith in You firmly in our hearts constantly, without stop, and may it be bound securely, like an unmovable peg. Remove all the barriers that separate us from our Father in Heaven, and save us from every obstacle and mistake. Do not abandon us, nor forsake or shame us. Be with our mouths when we speak, with our hands when we work, and with our hearts when we think. Our Father in Heaven, Merciful God, may our hearts, thoughts, words and actions, even every movement and feeling – those we are aware of and those we are not, the revealed and the hidden ones – be united and directed toward You, in truth and sincerity, free of all improper thoughts, God forbid. Purify our hearts and sanctify us. Sprinkle upon us purifying waters and cleanse us in Your love and compassion. Plant unceasing love and fear of You in our hearts, at all times and in all places. When we walk and when we sit, when we lie down and when we rise, let Your holy spirit constantly burn within us. For we constantly rely upon You and upon Your greatness, Your love and Your fear, Your Written and Oral Torah, the revealed and concealed, and upon Your commandments – all in order to unify Your mighty and awesome Name.

Keep us from ulterior motives, from arrogance, anger, small-mindedness, depression, tale-bearing, and other bad traits – from everything that detracts from Your holy and pure service, which is so dear to us. Shine Your holy spirit upon us, so that we may cling to You. May we long for You constantly, ever more and more, and may You raise us up level after level, until we reach the level of the holy forefathers, Avraham, Yitzchak and Yaakov. And in their merit, may You hear our prayers and answer them when we beseech You, whether on our own behalf, or on behalf of another of Your people Yisroel, whether for an individual or a group. May You rejoice and take pride in us, and may we bear fruit above and set roots below.

Do not recall our sins; especially, the sins of our youth. As Dovid HaMelech said: "Do not remember the sins and transgressions of my youth." Rather, transform our sins and transgressions into merits. Draw down upon us, from the World of Repentance, the desire to return to You and to repair the blemish we have caused to Your holy and pure Names.

Save us from the jealousy that exists between people. Let us not feel jealous of others, and let others not be jealous of us. On the contrary, let us appreciate the virtues of our friends, and not see their shortcomings. Let us all speak to each other in a way that is upright and pleasing to You, and let there be no feelings of hatred and resentment among friends, God forbid. Strengthen our bond to You, in love, for our main intention is only to give You satisfaction – as is revealed and known to You. And if we lack the wisdom to truly direct our hearts to You, then teach us, so that we might truly know Your beneficent will.

Above all else, we beseech you, O God, who is full of mercy, to accept our prayers compassionately and willingly. Amen, may it be Your will.

Prayer of Repentance
by Rabbeinu Yonah

O God, I have sinned, I have committed iniquity, I have transgressed. I have acted [wrongly] in different ways, from the day I entered this world until today. But now, my heart has raised me up, and my spirit has brought me forth to return to You in truth, with a good, whole heart, with all my heart, my soul and my might. That I should admit [to my sins] and abandon them, casting away all my transgressions, and making a new heart and spirit for myself, that I may be quick and careful in the fear of You. For You are Hashem, my God, who opens His hand in repentance, and helps those who come to purify themselves: Open Your hand and receive me in perfect repentance before You! Help me to become strong in my fear of You, and assist me against the Accuser who attacks me with guile, and seeks to kill my soul. Let him not rule over me. Keep him far from my 248 limbs, and cast him into the depth of the sea. Rebuke him, so that he not stand on my right side to accuse me. Do it, that I may walk in Your precepts. Remove my heart of stone, and grant me a heart of flesh. Please Hashem, my God, hear the prayer and supplication of Your servant, and accept my repentance. May no sin or misdeed obstruct my prayer or my repentance. May an advocate come before Your Throne of Glory to intercede on my behalf and bring my prayers before You. And if I have no advocate, due to my many and great sins, may You Yourself open a path beneath Your throne of glory, and accept my repentance, so that I do not return empty handed from before You, for You hear prayers.

Prayer Over Torah Study
from Sha'arei Tzion

Behold, I desire to study, in order for my learning to lead me to action, to proper character traits, and to knowledge of the Torah – for the sake of the union of the Holy One and His Shechinah, in fear and in love, in love and in fear, to unite the Name Y-H with the Name V-H in a perfect union in the name of all Yisroel, and to raise the Shechinah from the dust.

May it be Your will, Hashem our God and God of our fathers, to purify our spirits and souls. May the pleasantness of the Lord our God be upon us, and the work of our hands establish for us, and the work of our hands establish it.

הנהגות טובות מהרב הקדוש בוצינא קדישא • ארכנ"ו
מה' אלימלך זצקללה"ה נב"ט מק"ק ליזענסק:
אלה הדברים אשר יעשה אותם האדם וחי בהם:

א בכל עת ורגע שהוא פנוי מן התורה • ובפרט שהוא יושב בטל לבדו בחדר או שוכב על מטתו • ואינו יכול לישן • יהי' מהרהר במצות עשה זו של וקדשתי בתוך בני ישראל • וידמה בנפשו ויציר במחשבתו כאלו אש גדול ונורא בוער לפניו עד לב השמים • והוא בשביל קדושת השי"ת שובר את טבעו ומפיל את עצמו להאש על קידוש השי"ח ומחשבה טובה הקב"ה מצרפה למעשה • ונמצא שאינו שוכב ויושב בטל. רק מקיים מ"ע דאורייחא:
ב בפסוק ראשון של ק"ש וברכה ראשונה של שמונה עשרה יהרהר כנ"ל • ועוד יכוין אם יענו אותו כל אומות העולם בכל עינויסקשים ויפשטו עורו הכשרו להכחיש ח"ו ביחודו יסבול כל היסורים ולא יודה ח"ו להם • ויציר בדעתו ומחשבתו כאלו עושין לו כנ"ל • ובזה יצא ידי חיוב ק"ש וחפילה כדין:

FIRST PRINTING OF THE TZETEL KATAN, LEMBERG, 1849

The Tzetel Katan

The Short Note

"Blessed is God, who gave us
Rabbi Elimelech of Lizhensk
and his Tzetel Katan."

Rabbi Chaim Shaul HaKohen Dweck

The Tzetel Katan
THE SHORT NOTE

INSPIRATION FOR A HOLY LIFE

1 Whenever you are not studying Torah – especially, when you are sitting idly, alone in your room, or lying on your bed unable to sleep – you should have in mind the mitzvah "I shall be sanctified among the *Bnei Yisroel*" (*Vayikra* 22:32). Imagine in your heart and picture in your mind that before you is a great and awful fire burning all the way to heaven, and you – in sanctification of God's holy Name – overcome your natural fear and throw yourself into it.

God will consider your good intention as if you had actually done it. In this way, you are never merely lying or sitting around idly, but always engaged in fulfilling a positive mitzvah of the Torah.

PRAYERS

Master of the World, in Your great strength and abundant mercy, help me focus all the power of my thoughts on the act of true self-sacrifice – until I can vividly imagine various types of death and afflictions, until my senses are annulled and I can feel the very pain and suffering of death, as if I was dying for the sake of Your great and holy Name. Let there be no difference between my thoughts and my willingness to die, and actual death itself – until I reach the point that I feel my soul is about to leave me, and I have to refrain from thinking a bit, so that I do not actually die, God forbid; for You do not want me to die before my time.

In Your beneficent will, help me and teach me how to be truly *ready* to die, with love, for the sanctification of Your Name. (*Likutey Tefilos* 1:87)

COMMENTARY

Living with Self-Sacrifice

The main thing is to unite God's great Name, in truth. Which means to be willing to die in affirmation of His honor and holiness. For this reason, the Torah enjoins us to recite *Kerias Shema* morning and evening – for in

צעטיל קטן
מרבינו הקדוש הרבי ר' אלימלך מליזענסק זצלל"ה

אֵלֶּה הַדְּבָרִים אֲשֶׁר יַעֲשֶׂה אוֹתָם הָאָדָם וָחַי בָּהֶם:

א בְּכָל עֵת וָרֶגַע שֶׁהוּא פָּנוּי מִן הַתּוֹרָה, וּבִפְרָט שֶׁהוּא יוֹשֵׁב בָּטֵל לְבַדּוֹ בְּחֶדֶר אוֹ שׁוֹכֵב עַל מִטָּתוֹ וְאֵינוֹ יָכוֹל לִישָׁן, יִהְיֶה מְהַדְהֵר בְּמִצְוַת עֲשֵׂה זוּ שֶׁל וְנִקְדַּשְׁתִּי בְּתוֹךְ בְּנֵי יִשְׂרָאֵל, וִידַמֶּה בְּנַפְשׁוֹ וִיצַיֵּר בְּמַחֲשַׁבְתּוֹ כְּאִלּוּ אֵשׁ גָּדוֹל וְנוֹרָא בּוֹעֵר לְפָנָיו עַד לֵב הַשָּׁמַיִם, וְהוּא בִּשְׁבִיל קְדֻשַּׁת הַשֵּׁם יִתְבָּרֵךְ שׁוֹבֵר אֶת טִבְעוֹ וּמַפִּיל אֶת עַצְמוֹ לְהָאֵשׁ עַל קִדּוּשׁ הַשֵּׁם יִתְבָּרֵךְ, וּמַחֲשָׁבָה טוֹבָה הַקָּדוֹשׁ בָּרוּךְ הוּא מְצָרְפָהּ לְמַעֲשֶׂה, וְנִמְצָא שֶׁאֵינוֹ שׁוֹכֵב וְיוֹשֵׁב בָּטֵל, רַק מְקַיֵּם מִצְוַת עֲשֵׂה דְּאוֹרַיְיתָא:

→○ COMMENTARY ○←

that declaration of God's Unity, we give over our lives to His great Name. At that moment, a person should actually imagine that he is sacrificing his life in order to affirm God's Unity. This is the path of Tzaddikim. (*Noam Elimelech, Vayechi*)

Even greater than sacrificing one's life for the sake of God is "*living* with self-sacrifice" for the sake of God. (*Bikurei Aviv*, in the name of the Seer of Lublin)

God does not desire payments or offerings. He does not want a person to kill himself or forfeit his life. God creates myriad souls each and every minute: Why, then, would He need the soul of a sinner?

Rather, God seeks a person who devotes his whole heart and soul to Him *while he is alive*, at each and every moment; someone who refrains from indulging in his deepest physical desires, but rather presents them as an offering of love to God....

Likewise, when you study Torah or pray, you should push yourself beyond your personal limitations. Even if you find yourself dozing off, you should force yourself as best you can to rise and praise God... And when you study Torah, you should ignore any natural weaknesses you may feel, and push yourself beyond your ability, with utter devotion. This is like the story of Rava. Once, while studying Torah, Rava inadvertently squashed his fingers until they bled – yet, he felt nothing (*Shabbos* 88a). This is how a person should conduct himself in every aspect of worship....

You should also give charity beyond your means and ability. When you come across a poor person, give him everything that you have, and don't worry about leaving anything for yourself. If you do this, God, whose love is great, will consider it as though you have offered your very life. In fact, this is even greater than if you had actually sacrificed

2 When reciting the first verse of *Kerias Shema*, or the first blessing of the *Shemoneh Esrei*, you should have in mind all that we wrote above. Furthermore, you should imagine that even if the entire world were to subject you to the harshest tortures, and strip the very flesh off of your body in order to make you deny God's Oneness, you would willingly bear it all and not concede to them. You should actually imagine that they are doing this to you, as we explained above.

If you can do that, then you have truly fulfilled the obligation of *Kerias Shema* and prayer.

 PRAYERS

[Master of the World]: In Your great mercy, help me to always be able to give over my very life to sanctify Your Name, truly, and at all times. Especially, may I recite the *Kerias Shema* before bed with total self-sacrifice and devotion. And may I fully accept in my mind and heart, with true and full intention, to give myself over to death in sanctification of Your Name. May I burn with the fire of love, and overcome my negative inclinations, in order to sacrifice my body, soul, and all that I have, for the sanctification of Your great, holy and awesome Name. (*Likutey Tefilos* 1:95)

Master of the World: I am ashamed to ask for this thing. Never once have I slept in a holy way, or recited the Bedtime *Kerias Shema* in holiness and purity, because of the negative thoughts that rise in my heart and push me away. Please have mercy on me, and grant me the gift of Your own great holiness. Sanctify my mind, so that I may fall yourself on the altar; for a person can offer up his life only once, whereas in this case, you annul your strongest desires at each and every moment. This requires tremendous fortitude and causes great anguish to those who practice it thoroughly.

The Sages tell us that when a poor man brought a meal-offering, God accepted it as if he had offered up his very life, as the verse says: "When a soul brings an offering..." (*Vayikra* 2:1; *Toras Kohanim*). In other words, since this little bit of meal may have been all he had to stave off his hunger, by offering it to God, he offered his very soul. (*Be'er Mayim Chaim, Ki Sisa*)

ב בְּפָסוּק רִאשׁוֹן שֶׁל קְרִיאַת שְׁמַע וּבְרָכָה רִאשׁוֹנָה שֶׁל שְׁמוֹנָה עֶשְׂרֵה יְהַרְהֵר כְּנִזְכָּר לְעֵיל, וְעוֹד יְכַוֵּין אִם יְעַנּוּ אוֹתוֹ כָּל אוּמוֹת הָעוֹלָם בְּכָל עִנּוּיִים קָשִׁים וִיפַשְּׁטוּ עוֹרוֹ מִבְּשָׂרוֹ לְהַכְחִישׁ חַס וְשָׁלוֹם בְּיִחוּדוֹ, יִסְבּוֹל הַיִּסּוּרִים וְלֹא יוֹדֶה לָהֶם חַס וְשָׁלוֹם, וִיצַיֵּיר בְּדַעְתּוֹ וּמַחֲשַׁבְתּוֹ כְּאִלּוּ עוֹשִׂין לוֹ כְּנִזְכָּר לְעֵיל, וּבָזֶה יָצָא יְדֵי חִיּוּב קְרִיאַת שְׁמַע וּתְפִלָּה כַּדִּין:

→o PRAYERS o←

asleep thinking about the holy and pure words of Your Torah. May I repent over all that I have done before I go to sleep – especially any damage that I caused during that day. May I recite the *Kerias Shema* in holiness and with total self-annulment, for the sake of Your Name. May I completely annul myself, and shut my eyes to the illusion of this world. Rather, may I attach my thoughts to the World to Come, which is the ultimate goal. By doing so, may I annul all the desires, confusions, and suffering of this world, until I come to realize that everything is truly good. And may I annul all the harsh judgments from the world, so that it will *truly* be good. Thus, may I fulfill the verse: "If you lie down, you shall not be afraid; and when you lie down, your sleep shall be sweet." (*Tefilos HaBoker*, p. 61)

→o COMMENTARY o←

Praying with Self-Sacrifice

When distracting thoughts make it hard for you to concentrate on your prayers, remember that you would be willing to die for the sanctification of God's Name – for even sinners are willing to do this (as has happened many times in the past). This sense of self-sacrifice will enable you to concentrate fully on the words. You should always pray in this spirit of self-sacrifice. (*Likutey Etzos, Tefilah* 66).

A person who prays with such intensity that he literally "kills" himself in his prayers, should realize that if extraneous thoughts still enter his mind, they do so in order to be elevated, and it is precisely then and there that he needs to exert his greatest efforts – in order to elevate the sparks of holiness. (Ibid. 34)

When to Offer Your Life

When you recite the words of the *Shemoneh Esrei*: "Our God and God of our fathers. God of Avraham," you should willingly offer up your life for

3 You should likewise keep these thoughts in mind whenever you eat, or when you fulfill your marital obligations. As soon as you begin to feel physical pleasure, you should imagine what is written above. You should immediately declare – verbally and in your heart – that you would have greater pleasure and joy in fulfilling the commandment of "I shall be sanctified," as we explained, than in the physical pleasure you are now experiencing, since it derives from the leprous skin of the Serpent.

Thus you should say: "Even if murderers were to grab me in the midst of eating or marital relations and torture me [to make me deny God's unity], I would be happier to sanctify God's Name than to enjoy this physical pleasure."

Make sure, however, that you say this honestly, with words that are deeply rooted in your heart, and with complete sincerity. Don't try to deceive yourself, as if you could fool Heaven, God forbid.

PRAYERS

Help us sanctify ourselves in great holiness, as is fitting for Your people, Yisroel, whom You have chosen in love. Be with us always. Deliver us and help us be holy [even] in those things that are permissible to us. May we break our lower desires, and rise to ever greater levels of holiness, until we become included in Your own supernal holiness – according to your Your beneficent will. Amen. (*Sefer Kedusha, Otzar Tefilos Yisroel*, vol. 3, p. 221) the sanctification of God's holiness. On the word "*Elokeinu* – our God," have in mind that you are ready to die for the unity of God's Names Y-H-V-H and Ado-nai; and on the words "God of our fathers," concentrate on uniting the Names Y-H-V-H and *Eheyeh*.

When you say the words "*Shema Yisroel*," you should imagine that someone is torturing you and stripping the skin off your flesh, yet you willingly bear it [to sanctify God's Name]. I heard from Rabbi Elimelech that you should imagine throwing yourself into a huge, raging fire in order to fulfill the mitzvah of "I will be sanctified among the Children of Yisroel" (*Vayikra* 22:32) – that is, you would gladly be burnt alive or experience some other torture, for the sake of fulfilling this positive commandment. (*Darchei Tzedek* 1:8)

ג גַּם בִּשְׁעַת אֲכִילָה וְזִיוּוּג יְכַוֵּין כְּנִזְכָּר לְעֵיל, וּכְשֶׁיַּתְחִיל לְהַרְגִּישׁ תַּעֲנוּג גַּשְׁמִי יְצַיֵּיר בְּמַחֲשַׁבְתּוֹ כְּנִזְכָּר לְעֵיל, וְתֵיכֶף וּמִיָּד יֹאמַר בְּפִיו וּבִלְבָבוֹ שֶׁיּוֹתֵר הָיָה לוֹ תַּעֲנוּג וְשִׂמְחָה בַּעֲשִׂיַּית מִצְוַת עֲשֵׂה שֶׁל וְנִקְדַּשְׁתִּי בְּאוֹפֶן הַנִּזְכָּר לְעֵיל מֵהַרְגָּשַׁת תַּעֲנוּג גַּשְׁמִי הַזֶּה שֶׁהוּא מֵהַצָּרַעַת מַשְׁכָא דְחִוְיָא, וְכָךְ יֹאמַר: וּרְאָיָה לַדָּבָר שֶׁיּוֹתֵר הָיָה לוֹ תַּעֲנוּג וְשִׂמְחָה בַּעֲשִׂיַּית מִצְוַת עֲשֵׂה שֶׁל וְנִקְדַּשְׁתִּי בְּאוֹפֶן הַנִּזְכָּר לְעֵיל שֶׁאֲפִילוּ הָיוּ חוֹטְפִין אוֹתוֹ רוֹצְחִים בְּאֶמְצַע אֲכִילָה וְזִיוּוּג לַעֲשׂוֹת לוֹ הָעִנְיָנִים קָשִׁים הָיִיתִי מְשַׂמֵּחַ אֶת עַצְמִי עַל קִידּוּשׁ הַשֵּׁם יִתְבָּרֵךְ יוֹתֵר מִתַּעֲנוּג גַּשְׁמִי הַזֶּה, אַךְ יִזָּהֵר שֶׁיִּהְיֶה דּוֹבֵר אֱמֶת בִּלְבָבוֹ וְשֶׁיִּהְיֶה אָז בִּשְׁעַת מַעֲשֶׂה תָּקוּעַ עַל לוּחַ לִבּוֹ בְּתוֹכִיּוּת וּבִפְנִימִיּוּת הַלֵּב בֶּאֱמֶת גָּמוּר, וְלֹא יַשְׁטֶה אֶת עַצְמוֹ לִהְיוֹת כְּגוֹנֵב דַּעַת עֶלְיוֹנָה חַס וְשָׁלוֹם:

PRAYERS

TO BE SAID BEFORE EATING:

Behold, I am coming to eat and drink in order to be healthy and strong, so that I can serve the Blessed One. I am ready to fulfill the commandment to recite blessings before and after eating food. If I eat bread, I am ready to fulfill the commandment to wash my hands and recite the accompanying blessing, to make the blessing over the bread, to dip a piece in salt, to discuss Torah at the table, to wash my fingers after eating and to recite the Grace after Meals – all in order to bring pleasure to my Creator and to rectify each thing in its supernal root.

"May the pleasantness of the Lord our God be upon us, and the work of our hands establish for us, and the work of our hands establish it." (*Beis Tefilah* 3)

May it be Your will, my God and God of my fathers, in Your great compassion and love, to help me completely break my desire for food, so that I always eat and drink in great holiness and purity, at the right time, and the right amount, according to Your truly beneficent will. May I constantly draw upon myself the holy feeling of awe that can descend upon a person when he eats, so that I sit at my meal in great fear and awe of You. (*Likutey Tefilos* 2:38).

───⇾○ COMMENTARY ○⇽───

The Holiness of Eating

When a Tzaddik prays, he is certainly attached to God with pure, clear and holy thoughts. When he eats, however, he trembles at the thought that this physical act might lower him and sever his connection to holiness. Thus, while eating, a Tzaddik strives even harder to sanctify himself and cling to God with great spiritual attachment. It turns out that a Tzaddik is holier when he eats than when he prays. For most people, it is the opposite; they sanctify themselves in prayer, more so than when they eat. (*Noam Elimelech, Korach*)

One Meal with Proper Intention

By properly consuming even one meal – during the week or on Shabbos – that is, eating selflessly, with the desire to channel all of your lower cravings into the service of God, you can uplift all the food that you have eaten the entire week. This is like the Kabbalistic approach to prayer, in that a single prayer offered with proper intention uplifts all the unfit prayers of an entire year. For eating, like prayer, resembles and is a form of sacrifice. And, like sacrifices, where atonement for one transgression brings about atonement for another, similar transgression (*Shabbos* 71a), so too, one act of eating uplifts another one, to be just like it.

Likewise, a single act done with spiritual enthusiasm and proper intention, for the sake of Heaven, can uplift all the mundane actions that you have ever done. (*Pri Tzaddik, Kuntress Es HaOchel* 1:8)

Eating Selflessly

"Do not indulge too freely in a meal that you enjoy" (Gittin 70a).

A person should eat for the sake of God. If he finds himself enjoying his food too much, it means that he is no longer eating selflessly. He should then restrain himself and break his desire, until he feels he can eat again with proper intention. Only then should he return to his meal. (*Divrei Emes, Re'eh*)

One need not completely refrain from foods that one enjoys, for it is enough to avoid that which the Torah prohibits. However, in the middle of eating, while you are still hungry, you should stop and leave something over – for the sake of God. This will prevent you from sinning, and remind you of your love of God.

The same applies to every worldly pleasure: You should never satiate yourself. And in matters of the "holy covenant" (marital relations), you should restrain yourself even in what is allowed. (*Yesod HaTeshuvah* of *Rabbeinu Yonah*)

Refraining from Eating is like Fasting

When you are in the middle of a meal that you enjoy and want to finish, stop before the end. Offer your desire to God as penance for your sins. God will consider this small act like a fast and an act of atonement. It will be considered like a sacrifice, and your table will be an actual altar upon which you killed your evil inclination. (*Tziporen Shamir* §65)

This is the Table before God

Rabbi Aharon of Belz asked the following question: In the after-blessing for *mezonos* (cakes, crackers, etc.), we recite the words: "We will bless You for the food in holiness and purity." Why do we recite these words only in this short blessing, and not in the long blessing following a regular meal?

The answer is that eating is a very high and holy act. So much so, that the verse compares a table to the altar, and the act of eating to the offering of sacrifices.

Thus, just as the pious men in Talmudic times would prepare themselves for an hour before praying, in order to recite the words with perfect, holy and pure intention, so should one prepare himself for a meal, in order to eat it in holiness and purity.

Now, when one wants to break bread, he first has to spread the tablecloth, then set the table with plates and silverware, then wash his hands for the bread, and make the blessing. All this is a type of preparation, so that he will naturally eat in holiness.

However, no specific preparations are necessary to eat a piece of cake, and thus, doing so might actually damage one's spiritual level. Therefore, in the after-blessing for cake, we ask God to consider our eating to have been "in holiness and purity." (*Sichos b'Avodas Hashem*, p. 111)

4 In everything you do in this world, be it Torah study, prayer, or the performance of the commandments, you should accustom yourself to say the following: "Behold, I perform this action for the sake of the union of the Holy One and His Shechinah, to give pleasure to the Creator, blessed is He."

If you accustom yourself to say this from the depths of your heart, you will eventually begin to feel a great illumination in the words.

PRAYERS

Our Father in Heaven, Compassionate God, help us unite our hearts, thoughts, words, and all of our deeds and emotions – those that we are aware of and those that we are not – so that they are all directed to You, truly and sincerely, free of all improper thoughts. Purify our hearts and sanctify us. Sprinkle upon us pure water and purify us with Your love and your mercy. Plant a constant love and fear of You in our hearts, at all times and in all places – when we walk and when we sit, when we lie down and when we rise. May Your holy spirit burn constantly within us; for we constantly rely upon You and Your greatness, Your love and fear, Your written and Oral Torah, the revealed and hidden, and on Your commandments – all for the sake of uniting Your great and awesome Name. (*From the prayer of Rabbi Elimelech of Lizhensk*)

TO BE SAID EACH MORNING, BEFORE PRAYER:

For the sake of the union of the Holy One and His Shechinah, in fear and in love, in love and in fear, to unify the Name Y-H and V-H in a perfect union in the name of all Yisroel, behold, I accept upon myself His divinity, may He be blessed, and the fear and love of Him – for I am a servant of God. And I will fulfill the commandment to "love your fellow as yourself," for I do love every single Jew, like my own soul.

I am ready to fulfill the commandment to study Torah, as well as the commandments of *tzitzis* and tefillin. I am ready to fulfill the commandment of *Kerias Shema* and the morning prayer, and all the commandments that are connected to and included in them and similarly, all the mitzvos.

I do this in order to please my Creator, and not to receive any reward. And my intentions are according to the understanding of Rabbi Shimon bar Yochai.

ד בְּכָל הַדְּבָרִים שֶׁבָּעוֹלָם, הֵן בַּתּוֹרָה, הֵן בַּתְּפִלָּה, הֵן בְּמִצְווֹת מַעֲשִׂיּוֹת, יַרְגִּיל אֶת עַצְמוֹ לוֹמַר בָּזֶה הַלָּשׁוֹן: הֲרֵינִי עוֹשֶׂה זֹאת לְשֵׁם יִחוּד קוּדְשָׁא בְּרִיךְ הוּא וּשְׁכִינְתֵּיהּ לַעֲשׂוֹת נַחַת רוּחַ לְהַבּוֹרֵא יִתְבָּרַךְ שְׁמוֹ, וְיַרְגִּיל אֶת עַצְמוֹ לוֹמַר זֹאת בְּתוֹכִיּוּת הַלֵּב, וּבְהֶמְשֵׁךְ הַזְּמַן יַרְגִּישׁ הֶאָרָה גְדוֹלָה בַּאֲמִירָה זוּ:

PRAYERS

I accept upon myself the Torah's 613 commandments, and all the commandments of the Rabbis – in all of their details.

O gracious God, in Your great compassion, save me from my evil inclination, and allow me to serve You in truth. So may it be Your will, Amen!

"May the pleasantness of the Lord our God be upon us, and the work of our hands establish for us, and the work of our hands establish it." (*Kaf Achas, p. 220*)

For the sake of the union of the Holy One and His Shechinah, in fear and in love, in love and in fear, to unify the Name Y-H and V-H in a perfect union in the name of all Yisroel, behold, I perform this mitzvah in order to repair its supernal root in the heavenly structure, with all its details and rectifications, to fulfill the will of my Creator, who commanded me to do it, in order to please Him; to raise up the Shechinah – the fallen sukkah of Dovid – and restore the crown to its former glory; to cause spiritual outflow and abundant blessing in all the worlds, and to repair all the sparks that have fallen into the impure forces of evil, whether because of me, or because of other members of Your people, Yisroel; to rectify all 613 commandments that are included in this mitzvah, and to bring about a unification of the four letters of the Holy Name; and to purify my soul, that it should initiate a lower arousal through this mitzvah.

Let no sin, misdeed or bad thought obstruct this mitzvah, and may it ascend favorably before He who commanded it, to awaken His love. May I fulfill this mitzvah wholeheartedly, selflessly, with great longing and joy, without coarseness or foreign thoughts, in all its details, according to the law of Your holy Torah, and according to Your beneficent will.

May the words of my mouth and the thoughts of my heart find favor before You, my Rock and my Redeemer. (*Mishpot Tzeddek al Tehilim*)

─── ⇒○ COMMENTARY ○⇐ ───

"For the Sake of the Union..."

Remember the Shabbos day, to sanctify it. (Shemos 20:8)
Safeguard the Shabbos day, to sanctify it. (Devorim 5:12)

According to the Talmud, the words "Remember" and "Safeguard" were heard simultaneously (*Shavuos* 20b). This implies that both "Remember," which refers to speech, and "Safeguard," which refers to thought, must *both* be holy and pure. A person who thinks about performing a mitzvah should also express in words his desire to fulfill it. He should say: "For the sake of the union of the Holy One and His Shechinah."

Thus, the verse states: "Man does not live on bread alone; rather, he lives by all that comes forth from the mouth of God" (*Devorim* 8:3). That is, when a person states, with *his own* mouth, that he is doing something for the sake of God – from that, "he lives," for this is the essence of a person's life. (*Noam Elimelech, Bo*)

"...in the Name of All Yisroel"

The verse states: "There is not a righteous man on earth who does good and does not sin" (*Koheles* 7:20). However, if that is true, how can anyone ever do a holy act, since his limbs have been blemished by the sins he committed? How could the sanctity of that action ever rest upon him?

The answer lies in connecting oneself with the entirety of the Jewish people. For there is a spiritual world called *Kol Yisroel* (All of Yisroel), which is a perfect, faultless world – since the Jewish people, as a whole, are completely righteous, as the verse says: "Your people are all Tzaddikim" (*Yeshayahu* 60:21).

Therefore, even if an individual may sometimes sin, the totality of Yisroel is holy forever, and beyond the reach of any negative, accusing forces. Its image – known as "*Adam Kadmon*" (Primordial Man) – is forever engraved Above, where sin has no power at all.

When a person connects to that totality, his physical limbs become attached to wholeness and are thus rectified with a supernal holiness. For this reason, before each act of worship or prayer, we say: "For the sake of the union of the Holy One and His Shechinah... in the name of *all* Yisroel." For then, we can fulfill that mitzvah or that act of worship. (*Noam Elimelech, Devorim*)

Raising our Actions and Thoughts to God

The moment a person thinks holy thoughts, he becomes a "vessel" for the supernal Chambers of Holiness, which are the source of these thoughts. And when he thinks sinful thoughts, he becomes an unclean "vessel" for the Chambers of Impurity, from where all impure thoughts originate. The same applies to speech and action.

---→o COMMENTARY o←---

A person should make an accounting of all of his thoughts, words and deeds – from the day he was born, until the present – to determine if they derive from the side of holiness or from the side of impurity; the latter being all the thoughts, utterances and actions that he did not dedicate to God. (*Sefer HaTanya*, chap. 29)

Living With God's Name

Everything that God created in the world, He created for His glory, as it says: "Everything that is called by My Name, I have created for My glory; I have formed it and I have made it" (*Yeshayahu* 43:7). God created man and placed within him His Name, Y-H-V-H. The last letter *hey* is the *nefesh*; the letter *vav* is the *ruach*; the first letter *hey* is called the *neshamah*, and the *yud* is the *neshamah* of the *neshamah*. The *yud* and *hey* are called Father and Mother, and the *vav* and *hey* are called Son and Daughter.

Just as God created the holy *ruach* and *nefesh*, so He created a *ruach* and *nefesh* from the "left side" – the side of evil. And just as wine rests on dregs, so the "enlightened" soul sits upon the "animal" soul, as Shlomo HaMelech said: "Who knows that the spirit of man ascends upward and the spirit of the beast descends down into the earth" (*Koheles* 3:21), for God did not put His Name on the Side of Impurity.

The *yud* also corresponds to Elimelech, and the first *hey*, to Naomi. The final *hey* corresponds to Ruth, and the *vav* to her husband (Machlon). This is the meaning of "May the pleasantness (*noam*) of the Lord our God be upon us, and the work of our hands establish for us, and the work of our hands establish it" (*Tehilim* 90:17). For when a person does good in this world, God's Name, Y-H-V-H, rests upon him; but if not, it departs from him. (*Zohar, Midrash Ruth* 75a)

When a person gives a coin to a beggar, he unifies God's holy Name, Y-H-V-H. The coin corresponds to the letter *yud*. His five fingers correspond to the letter *hey*. His outstretched arm corresponds to the letter *vav*, and the five fingers of the beggar's hand correspond to the last letter *hey*. This forms the letters of God's Name in their proper order and draws down great mercy from Heaven.

However, this only happens when the giver offers the money first, before the beggar puts out his hand. But if the beggar asks first, the letters of God's Name are arranged in a different order. This is the meaning of the verse: "If there will be a needy person among you... you shall open your hand to him" (*Devorim* 15:7–8). That is, you should open your hand first, and not wait for him to ask you, so that God's holy Name is formed in its correct order. (Baal Shem Tov, *Mevaser Tzedek, Re'eh*)

5 When a bad character trait begins to stir in you, God forbid – one which you face habitually – be it obstinacy, pride, laziness, idleness that leads to boredom, or similar things – you should immediately say, with all of your might: "HaCana'ani, HaChiti, HaEmori, HaPrizi, HaChivi, v'HaYivusi v'HaGirgoshi," and you will be saved.

You should also learn to restrict your field of vision; that is, not to look beyond your immediate perimeter, even when you are home, and all the more so when you are in the synagogue, the study-hall, or walking outside. If you happen to see a woman – even your own wife – or young children, and the like, you should picture the Name Ado-nai (אדנ״י) before you.

---⟶○ PRAYERS ○⟵---

Prayers for Self-Refinement

FOR HUMILITY:

Guard us from ulterior motives, from pride, from anger, from pettiness, from depression and talebearing, and from other bad character traits – from everything that interferes with Your holy and pure service, which is so precious to us. Grace us with Your holy spirit, so that we may cling to You. May we always long for You, more and more. And may we ascend level after level, until we reach the level of our holy forefathers, Avraham, Yitzchak and Yaakov. May their merits stand by us, so that You always hear and answer our prayers – whether for ourselves, or for another member of Your people, Yisroel; whether for one person or many. May You rejoice and take pride in us, and may we bear fruit above and take root below. *(From the prayer of Rabbi Elimelech of Lizhensk).*

Unite our hearts to love and fear Your Name with a burning and heartfelt repentance that grows in us constantly. May we cling to You always, and may we distance ourselves from all negative and forbidden traits, especially pride, anger, pettiness and arrogance. May we recognize our low level, and may our souls be like dust to all. Give us the strength to keep our mouths from sinning and our eyes from looking at empty vanities. Remove our stubborn hearts, and may foreign and negative thoughts never confuse us; rather, may we cling to You always. May we distance ourselves from laziness and

ה כְּשֶׁיַּתְחִיל לְהִתְעוֹרֵר בּוֹ מִדַּת דַּעְתּוֹ חַס וְשָׁלוֹם מִמִּדּוֹת רָעוֹת שֶׁהוּא רָגִיל בָּהֶם כְּגוֹן עַקְשָׁנוּת וּבוֹשֶׁת שֶׁל גַּאֲוָה וְעַצְלוּת וּבְטֵלָה הַמְּבִיאָה לִידֵי שִׁעֲמוּם וְכַיּוֹצֵא בָּהֶם יֹאמַר תֵּיכֶף וּמִיָּד בָּזֶה הַלָּשׁוֹן וּבְכָל כֹּחוֹ: "הִכְנַעְנִי הַחִתִּי הַפְּרִזִּי הַחִוִּי וְהַיְבוּסִי וְהַגִּרְגָּשִׁי", וְיִנָּצֵל, וְיַרְגִּיל אֶת עַצְמוֹ לְצַמְצֵם רְאִיָּתוֹ שֶׁלֹּא לְהִסְתַּכֵּל חוּץ לְדַ' אַמּוֹת אֲפִילוּ בִּהְיוֹתוֹ בְּבֵיתוֹ וּבִפְרָט בְּבֵית הַכְּנֶסֶת וּבְחֶדֶר שֶׁלּוֹמֵד בּוֹ וּבְדֶרֶךְ הִלּוּכוֹ בַּחוּץ וּבְהִזְדַּמֵּן לְפָנָיו אִשָּׁה אֲפִילוּ אִשְׁתּוֹ וּבָנָיו הַקְּטַנִּים וְכַיּוֹצֵא יְצַיֵּיר לִפְנֵי עֵינָיו הַשֵּׁם אדנ"י:

PRAYERS

depression, and may we rejoice in Your mitzvos and in our lot in life. Let us place our trust in You always, and be quick to worship You. Be in our hearts when we think, our mouths when we talk, and our hands when we serve You. Our King, refine us with Your good advice, so that we may walk upon the path of the pious, and keep the way of the righteous. And may we do that which is good and just in the eyes of God and man. (*Beis Tefilah* 5)

[Please, God], may I never deviate from Your will or from Your mitzvos, in the slightest, not now or ever. May I completely erase my pride, so that I do not become haughty over all those things that engender pride, such as wisdom or good deeds, strength or wealth. May I feel humble and low in all of these areas, without any feelings of pride or greatness at all. For I know, O God, that I am a boor, and lack all those things. "I am more ignorant than any person, and lack human understanding." I don't have an ounce of physical or spiritual strength, and my home is devoid of any wealth. I possess neither wisdom nor strength, neither material wealth nor the spiritual wealth of good deeds. (*Likutey Tefilos* 1:14)

FOR ZERIZUS:

May I merit to enliven my mind and soul through *zerizus*, and reduce the time that I sleep each night, on account of my laziness. Let me always be quick to serve You, so that I grasp whatever Torah and mitzvos I can immediately, without delay or sluggishness. For I realize that time and nature's laws do not really exist; rather, You run the entire world with Your providence. For God's providence reveals itself primarily when we realize that He transcends time and place. Through my faith in all of this, may I merit the miracles and wonders that You will do for us, which transcend the laws of nature entirely. And may we draw down Your perfect providence, from the aspect of the World to Come. (*Tefilos HaBoker* p. 48)

[Please, God] in Your great compassion and loving-kindness, may we draw close to true Tzaddikim, and see their shining faces, which can redeem our poor souls from the pit of immoral desires, depression, laziness and all evil traits. In your loving-kindness, may we break all of these desires, so that we long only for You and for Your service. May we be quick to serve You, and may we always be happy and positive, without laziness or depression. May we rejoice in You, and serve You with joy and positivity from all that we have, and always be happy. (*Likutey Tefilos* 1:4)

---- COMMENTARY ----

Dealing with Bad Character Traits

And God said to Avram: Leave your land, your birthplace, and your father's house, and go to the land that I will show you (Bereishis 12:1).

"Leave…your birthplace." That is, a person must leave behind his bad character traits; for one bad trait always gives birth to another, just as one sin leads to another.

"…and your father's house." These are the bad traits that are part of a person inherently, which he received from his father. One must [first] leave them behind. Then, they can be brought into the domain of holiness. (*Noam Elimelech, Lech Lecha*)

The main thing is to break all your negative character traits – hatred, anger, jealousy, lust – and then, to elevate them. This can bring you to a very high level, until you have lofty visions and come to serve God with great passion and spiritual attachment. (*Noam Elimelech, Shemos*)

The Problem with Pride

One way to rid yourself of pride is to celebrate the festivals with joy; as lavishly and effusively as you can afford. (*Likutey Etzos, Ga'avah v'Anavah* 22)

Know, my friend, that there are subtle forms of pride that are easily overlooked – unless a person is wise enough to search them out. Pride is a type of idolatry, which must be dug up and uprooted, as it says (referring to an *ashera*): "One who uproots an idol must dig up its roots" (*Avodah Zarah* 45b). To do less is to imagine that one is free of pride, and is even

HaCana'ani, HaChiti

"You should immediately say, with all of your might: "HaCana'ani, HaChiti…"

Perhaps the reason for this is as the *Bnei Yisaschar* writes (*Mamarei Chodshei Kislev-Teves, mamar 4, Hallel v'Hodaah*, in the name of the Seer of Lublin), that the seven nations conquered by Yisroel are the seven *sefiros* of the *Sitra Achra*, the Side of Evil (corresponding to the seven *sefiros* of holiness), in the following order: HaCana'ani – *Chesed*; HaChiti – *Gevurah*; HaEmori – *Tiferes*; HaPrizi – *Netzach*; HaChivi – *Hod*; HaYivusi – *Yesod*; HaGirgoshi – *Malchus*.

WE CAN FURTHER EXPLAIN THIS, AS FOLLOWS:

- **Cana'ani** is related to the word *hachna'ah* – "humility." However, this is a sort of meekness that originates from the forces of evil (*kelipos*). It is opposite the ideal state, in which a person's heart is "lifted up in the way of God" (*Divrei HaYamim* 17:6).
- **Chiti**, from the word *chet* – "fear" (חת). This causes a person to constantly fear that his repentance is not effective.
- **Emori**, from the word *emor* – "speak." This force does not stop speaking to a person for a minute, trying to subtly entice him and trap him in various types of sin.
- **Prizi**, from the word "unwalled" (as in "unwalled cities" – ערי הפרזות). This relates to the trait of wantonness; that is, when a person does not seek to be bound to his Creator, but imagines that he can do whatever he desires.
- **Chivi**, from the Aramaic word for "snake" (חיוא). It schemes like the primordial Serpent, first trying to seduce a person to sin. Then it bites him repeatedly [with negative feelings of guilt and remorse].
- **Yivusi**, from the word "to trample" (as in *Tehilim* 60:14). It seeks to trample and annihilate a person from this world and the next.
- **Girgoshi**, from the word *girushin* – "divorce." It constantly floods a person's mind with foreign thoughts in order to break his connection to God and prayer. In addition, when a person is in the middle of doing a mitzvah, it suddenly wants to kill him, and applies various schemes and evil thoughts to prevent him from completing his deed.

These are the forces of impurity that a person must be wary of. (*Madanei Melech* on *Tzetel Katan*, 5)

―――→○ COMMENTARY ○←―――

pious in some areas, when, in reality, a person remains arrogant.

The following is a type of pride that is relevant to an average person. From this example, you can derive the rest.

A person becomes depressed because he has succumbed to improper thoughts, and as a result does not apply himself to his Torah studies, since he knows that Torah must be studied in purity.

Actually, this is a subtle form of pride, for this person fails to acknowledge his true spiritual level. He thinks of himself as being special, and that he knows best how to serve God. If he admitted his true level – that he never really abandoned his low desires for this world – he wouldn't dare pursue spiritual levels that are relevant only to those lofty individuals upon whom God calls. At the very least, he should fulfill the edict: "You shall not follow after your heart and after your eyes." (*Sur MeRa*, p. 33)

The Importance of *Zerizus* (Alacrity)

A person is most enthusiastic at the beginning – the beginning of the day, the beginning of study.

Embrace the trait of *zerizus* very much. Rise quickly from your sleep, since you have been renewed and have become a different person, with the power to produce and create. This is similar to the trait of the Holy One, blessed be He, who creates worlds. Whatever you do, do it quickly and with enthusiasm, for you can serve God with all things. (*Tzavaas HaRivash*, 20)

Leaving Lethargy Behind

"They traveled from Refidim and camped in the Sinai desert. And they traveled from the Sinai desert, and came to Kivros HaTa'avah" (Bamidbar 33:15–16).

The evil inclination leads you away from the good path by first making you lazy and apathetic. If you do not fight back, by acting quickly and enthusiastically, but are slow getting up in the morning to serve God, you will eventually become lax in Torah study, which will lead to all sorts of forbidden desires, God forbid.

Therefore, you must do everything possible to acquire the trait of *zerizus*. Then, you will run to study Torah, which will teach you how to avoid harmful desires and improper actions.

This is the meaning of the verse: "They traveled from Refidim" – that is, they distanced themselves from "*rafeh yadayim*" (weak hands; i.e. lethargy); "and they camped in the Sinai desert" – they labored at Torah.

Afterward, however: "They traveled from the Sinai desert," which means that they no longer needed

―→∘ COMMENTARY ∘←―

any special tactics to overcome their evil inclinations in order to study Torah, for these were necessary only at first. By then, the words of Torah had become sweet to them, and, having made the words their own, they were able to study without interference. Then the Torah itself taught them how to break their lower desires. Thus, the verse continues: "and they camped at *Kivros HaTa'avah*" (The Graves of Desire). Meaning, they killed their negative desires. (*Maor VaShemesh, Masai*).

Idleness

"It's not the mouse that steals, but the hole that steals" (Arachin 30a).

It is important not to leave any empty spaces in the middle of your day. You should always know what you are doing next, be it studying Torah, performing a mitzvah, or any other clearly definable act; even resting, if you need to refresh yourself.

This is the meaning of "It's not the mouse that steals, but the hole that steals." It is not the evil inclination that makes you sin, but your free time. (Eliezer Shaul Zisman)

Be careful not to waste even a single hour in meaningless activity, for time is very precious – it passes and never returns. With each passing hour, a person's life is shortened, for no man dies suddenly; rather, he passes away a little at a time…. My beloved child, try not to interrupt your studies needlessly; do so as little as possible, for the punishment for this is very severe. (Other than in cases like that of Rabbah, who would begin his lessons with a joke, in order to open his students' hearts to the Torah – *Shabbos* 30b). (*Rachamei HaAv, Bitul*)

The Benefits of Humility

- Arrogance leads to poverty. (*Likutey Etzos, Ga'avah v'Anavah* 3)
- When a person is so humble that he is literally nothing, he can attain Torah and greatness at the same time. Otherwise it is hard for the two of them to coexist. (Ibid. 24)
- When a person is arrogant, it is a sign that he will have problems. The opposite is also true: A humble and lowly person will come to great honor. (Ibid. 25)
- If things are not going well for you, you should realize that it is due to your own pride. You must repent and lower yourself, until you are at the level of *"mah"* – "What?" Then things will again go well for you. (Ibid. 32)

6 If you have an illicit thought, God forbid, you should say several times: "You shall beware of everything evil" (*Devorim* 23:10). At that moment, you should think about Chazal's teaching, that a man should avoid illicit thoughts by day, so as not to come to impurity at night. Do not let the impure thought dwell in your mind, God forbid, so as not to defile the Supernal Intellect.

---- PRAYERS ----

Master of the Universe: You know the shame and pain of the downcast. Remember the preciousness of my poor soul. Take pity on me in Your tender kindness. Help me, strengthen me and encourage me. Sanctify me with Your exalted holiness. Let Your holiness and purity be drawn down upon me, so that from now on I will be able to guard myself against all improper thoughts, against mental confusion, and especially against skepticism and sinful thoughts of any kind. Let my thoughts always be holy, clear and free of all impurity. (*Likutey Tefilos* 1:5)

---- COMMENTARY ----

Avoiding Improper Thoughts

Does the Holy One deal unreasonably with his creatures by ordering them not to have desires (As in the Ten Commandments.)? How can He command something that is beyond a person's control; for desires arise in a person's heart even against his will.

It would seem, then, that a person is never punished for thoughts that arise spontaneously, but only for those that he willingly dwells upon. In other words, when an illicit desire suddenly enters a person's mind, he must reject it. Only if he continues to think about it *after* he realizes that it is forbidden, does he transgress the prohibition of following after his desires. (*Derech Pikudecha, prohibition* 38)

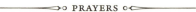

A person is not punished for a sudden lust or unholy thought that arises in his mind that he is unable to prevent; only if he turns it over in his mind. (*Sefer HaMidos, Hirhurim* 1, 46)

Turning Our Thoughts to Holiness

You should remember the 613 commandments in everything that you see. That is, you should immediately think about the mitzvah connected to that thing (provided you are in a clean place).

For instance, when you see a human being, you should think: "You shall love your neighbor as yourself."

When you see your friend's money or house, you should think: "You shall not covet," or think about the mezuzah that is affixed there, or the mitzvah of making a fence around

ו כְּשֶׁיָּבֹא לוֹ חַס וְשָׁלוֹם מַחֲשָׁבָה רָעָה מְנִיאוּף יֹאמַר כַּמָּה פְּעָמִים:
"וְנִשְׁמַרְתָּ מִכֹּל דָּבָר רָע", וִיהַרְהֵר אָז בְּדַרְשׁוֹת חֲכָמֵינוּ זִכְרוֹנָם
לִבְרָכָה שֶׁדָּרְשׁוּ עָלָיו שֶׁלֹּא יְהַרְהֵר אָדָם בְּיוֹם וְיָבֹא לִידֵי קֶרִי בַּלַּיְלָה,
וְלֹא יַנִּיחַ חַס וְשָׁלוֹם לִשְׁהוֹת הַמַּחֲשָׁבָה רָעָה בְּמוֹחוֹ שֶׁלֹּא לְטַמְּאוֹת
שֵׂכֶל הָעֶלְיוֹן חַס וְשָׁלוֹם:

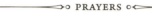

PRAYERS

"I called with all my heart; answer me, O Lord; I will keep Your statutes. I called to You; save me and I will keep Your testimonies. I rose before dawn and cried out; I hoped for Your word. My eyes preceded the night watches, to speak of Your word. In your faithful love, O Lord, hear my cry; sustain me, as is Your way. Those who pursue wickedness draw near; they are far from Your Torah. You are near, O Lord, and all Your commandments are true. "Of old, I knew of Your testimonies, that You have established forever." May it be Your will, my God and God of my fathers, to remove from me impure desires and evil thoughts, a frivolous attitude and an attraction to meaningless activities, a depressed nature and an inclination to falsehood, a misguided attitude and a destructive and poisonous spirit, a feverish, confused, and impure spirit, and an inclination to anger, jealousy, competitiveness, heresy, arrogance and destructiveness. Please, God, remove them all from me. Amen. (*Shomer Yisroel*, p. 320)

COMMENTARY

the roof. Whatever you see, you should immediately bring to mind the mitzvah that is connected to it. This will save you from improper thoughts. (*Darchei Tzedek* 73)

If the evil inclination tries to convince you to sin, you should say several times out loud the verse that speaks of that prohibition. This will remove your desire. The inverse of this is true as well, concerning mitzvos and good deeds. (*Tzidkas HaTzaddik* 98, in the name of the Arizal)

Sin Brings Bad Thoughts

Every sin creates an impure force (*kelipah*), God forbid. As long as that force of evil is in the world, a person will have evil thoughts related to that sin. A person must repent in order to destroy that force from the world. (*Noam Elimelech, Pinchas*)

A person's sins cause him to have extraneous thoughts and defile his mind, God forbid. (Ibid., *Emor*)

COMMENTARY

Holy Thoughts

Thought is exceedingly high – higher than everything else that a person considers important: such as vision, the sense of hearing, etc. Thought is able to reach and grasp very lofty things. This is why you must be very careful about what you think. (*Likutey Etzos, Machshavah* 21)

Improper Thoughts Weaken the Mind's Holiness

When a person is born, his mind is limited. As he begins to apply his mind to serving God, it grows slowly. However, if a person brings foreign thoughts into his mind – which are known as "external knowledge" – the holiness of his mind becomes weak, according to the place he allowed in his mind for that foreign knowledge. Then, all the worst character traits start to converge and attach themselves to this foreign knowledge. (*Likutey Etzos, Da'as* 26)

God Rejoices When We Act in Holiness

God's main pleasure and joy is when we act in holiness, with pure thoughts. (*Noam Elimelech, Emor*)

Torah Study Annuls Bad Thoughts

It is proper for a person to overcome his natural inclination [for physical desires] and act with extra holiness – having pure thoughts and a proper outlook – in order to be saved from them. For desire exists only in a heart that is devoid of Torah. (Rambam, *Mishneh Torah, Isurei Biyah* 22:20; *Shulchan Aruch, Even HaEzer* 25:1)

⁂

A person who studies the weekly Torah *parshah*, each day, with Rashi, will certainly be saved from committing any serious sin that day. (*Elef Ksav*, in the name of Rabbi Yissacher Dov of Belz)

Spiritual Purity

Talking to one's friends about their spiritual struggles and giving them encouragement in their search for God is a remedy for a nocturnal emission. (*Likutey Etzos, Bris* 9)

⁂

Giving charity in secret rectifies nocturnal emission. (Ibid. 53)

⁂

A person who experiences a nocturnal emission should recite the following ten psalms on the same day: Psalms 16, 32, 41, 42, 59, 77, 90, 105, 137, 150. One who recites these psalms on the same day need have no further fears about the harm such an emission can cause. Any damage will certainly be repaired through doing this. It is a very great *tikun*. (Ibid. 68)

⁂

Thinking about your own original Torah insights is effective for eliminating undesirable thoughts. (*Sefer HaMidos, Hirhurim* 13)

---— COMMENTARY ○—

Paths of Atonement

- Answering "*Amen, yehei shemei rabbah*" with all of your strength, in a loud and strong voice, until your limbs tremble, as well as answering Amen after each and every blessing.
- Carefully observing the Shabbos, with all its stipulations and specific details; that is, to put great effort into learning the laws of Shabbos in order to understand them well, and by reviewing them many times in order to be an expert in all the laws.
- Concentrating intensely on the "Song of the Sea," in the morning prayers, and reciting it loudly and joyfully, as though you have just been redeemed from Egypt.
- Remaining silent and forbearing in the face of insult, rejoicing in your suffering, and keeping in mind that "God instructed him to curse" (*Shmuel 2, 16:10*). (That is, the person is only a messenger from God.) This is in order to atone for your sins.
- Listening eagerly to the discourses of a Torah scholar that speak to your heart. Private, personal prayer. (Rabbi Moshe Teitelbaum, *Hanhagos HaTzaddikim*, §4)

God Delights in a Person Who Withstands a Test

It's important to remember the following: If God tests you in matters of spiritual purity, it is clear that you have the potential to reach great heights in this very area, more than most other people. For this is precisely why God is testing you: so that you work on yourself with all of your might, and reach complete holiness.

Rabbi Tzadok HaKohen writes (*Tzidkas HaTzaddik* 44 and 49) that a person who is overwhelmed by physical desires should not become depressed and feel that he is inherently flawed, for the opposite is true; he has the potential to develop a powerful love of God and a desire for the truth. Not only that, he can become pure and clean in the very area in that he stumbled repeatedly before. By restraining himself from sin, he not only repairs his earlier transgression, measure for measure, but also rectifies his very soul.

From here we learn that a person who feels challenged in the area of personal holiness and spiritual purity should know that God, in His great love and compassion, is sending him a loving message from heaven. "My precious and beloved child," He is saying: "I have given you the ability to attain even higher levels of holiness, which is the greatest way to serve Me. It is precisely you whom I have chosen to be My holy emissary in this world, so that I will be extolled by you in all the worlds – surpassing even the service of the holy angels." (*Sichos b'Avodas Hashem*, p. 78)

7 If a person accidentally sees something indecent, God forbid, such as animals or birds mating, or a handbreadth of a woman's [hair or skin] that should be covered, or one's wife when she is in a state of impurity, or similar things, he should immediately recite the verse: "Do not follow after your heart" (*Devorim* 15:29), so as not to defile his mind, God forbid.

―――――∞ PRAYERS ∞―――――

[Master of the world], help us to guard our eyes from seeing anything evil. May we use our eyes to see only holy things. For the eyes of a Jew are lofty and exalted, and constantly behold great and awesome things. If our eyes were pure, we would know great things, simply in what we already see. Please, then, let us guard our eyes, and sanctify them with the utmost holiness, and may we see wondrous and awesome things. (*Tefilos v'Tachanunim* 59)

―――――∞ COMMENTARY ∞―――――

Guarding Your Eyes

A person who sinned with his eyes can repair them by crying over his sins, as it is written: "Rivers of water flowed from my eyes because they did not keep Your Torah" (*Tehilim* 119:136). The verse does not say: "because *I* did not keep Your Torah"; rather, because my eyes did not keep the Torah. (*Sha'arei Teshuvah, sha'ar rishon* 15)

The difficulty one experiences in guarding one's eyes is considered like a fast. (*Avodas Penim* 3:11)

The Root of Jewish Suffering

The "sin of youth" – which is the most heinous crime in the Torah – is the cause of all Jewish suffering and of all the harsh decrees that we face. Furthermore, all the ups and downs a person experiences in life are based on one's level of spiritual purity (*kedushas habris*).... This sin starts off sweet, but ends in bitterness, leading to depression and dissatisfaction, which robs a person of joy in life... On the other hand, guarding the Covenant, guarding one's eyes, not touching that which is prohibited, and avoiding forbidden newspapers or books brings happiness, confidence, and joy in life. Furthermore, the gates of Torah and fear of God open for him. (*Yisroel Kedoshim* p. 238, in the name of Rabbi Shmuel Wosner, *Shevet Ha-Levi*, 4:160)

Accustoming Oneself Slowly

A person who finds it hard to overcome his negative inclination should accustom himself gradually to guarding his eyes. He should make a commitment to act with purity for just one day. Let him do this

ז

כְּשֶׁיָּבֹא חַס וְשָׁלוֹם לְיָדוֹ בְּהִזְדַּמְּנוּת כְּנֶגְדּוֹ הִסְתַּכְּלוּת דְּעָה חַס וְשָׁלוֹם כְּגוֹן בְּהֵמָה וְחַיָּה אוֹ עוֹף שֶׁנִּזְקָקִין זֶה לָזֶה אוֹ טֶפַח מְגוּלָּה בְּאִשָּׁה בִּמְקוֹם עֶרְוָה אוֹ בְּצוּרַת אִשְׁתּוֹ נִדָּה בִּמְקוֹם עֶרְוָה וְכַיּוֹצֵא בָּהֶן יֹאמַר תֵּיכֶף וּמִיָּד הַפָּסוּק: "וְלֹא תָתוּרוּ אַחֲרֵי לְבַבְכֶם", וְלֹא יְטַמֵּא אֶת שְׂכְלוֹ חַס וְשָׁלוֹם:

PRAYERS

[Please, God], let me constantly sanctify my eyes, and never gaze at anything that will spiritually damage my vision. May I look only at Your Torah, Your true Tzaddikim, and at everything that sanctifies the eyes, until they become completely and truly holy and pure. May I fix all that I have damaged with my eyes. In Your mercy, help me and protect me from harming my sense of sight, God forbid, so that the light of my eyes will never dim. "Even until old age and hoary hairs, do not forsake me!" Protect the light of my eyes always, so that I may study Your Torah day and night, banishing sleep from my eyes yet not suffering from that at all. And may my eyes shine like the sun and the moon. (*Likutey Tefilos* 1:51)

COMMENTARY

immediately – today! – which is the aspect of "Today, if you will heed My voice" (*Tehilim* 95:7). Afterward, he can commit to doing it yet another day. Slowly, he will accustom himself to living properly, for "one mitzvah leads to the next."

This is only hard at first, as Chazal say: "All beginnings are difficult." Afterward, a person will find it pleasant, as the Talmud states, that if a person avoids sinning and overcomes his evil inclination two or three times, the Holy One Himself will guard him from then on, as the verse states: "Behold, God does all these things twice or thrice with a man" (*Iyov* 33:29). (Israel Kedoshim, p. 238)

The Power of Trust

If you want to guard your eyes, you should strengthen your trust in God. For instance, if you need to meet someone, you should trust that God will help you find him; thus, you do not needlessly look around [in the street]. Thus, it is written: "He will save a person with downcast eyes" (*Iyov* 22:29). That is, the Holy One cares for the needs of a person who guards his eyes. (*Shomer Emunim*, part 1, *HaBetachon v'Hischazkus* chap. 6).

A father who guards his eyes will merit raising his children without suffering. He will merit healthy and successful children. (*Imrei Kodesh*, in the name of *Rabbi Uri of Strelisk*, §38)

8 Train yourself not to speak to anyone, save out of great necessity – and even then, you should keep your words to a minimum, weighing them carefully to ensure that they do not contain any trace of falsehood, flattery, gossip, tale-bearing, belittlement of others, or self-aggrandizement, God forbid. Train yourself to follow Chazal's principle: "Teach your tongue to say, 'I don't know.'" And when people who are careless in this speak to you about frivolous matters, you should use any means possible to avoid the conversation. And if you cannot, you should offer the briefest answers possible, no more than is absolutely necessary.

―――――∽○ PRAYERS ○∾―――――

May it be Your will, Master of the World, Compassionate and Gracious One, that I guard myself today and every day from speaking or hearing slander and gossip. May I be careful never to speak against any individual, and all the more so, against the entire Jewish people, or any part of them; which is a very great sin. May I never cast aspersions on Your righteousness and justice, for that is the most grievous sin of all. And may I never utter words of falsehood, flattery, contention, anger, pride, spite, mockery, or anything else forbidden. Let me not sit among scorners, nor become proud or angry even in my heart, nor think badly about any Jew.

May I speak only about things that pertain to my body and my soul, and may my every action, word and thought be for the sake of Your Name.

O Father in Heaven! Let me guard my ears and eyes, today and every day, from hearing or reading slander and gossip, contentious words, trivialities, and everything forbidden. As for everything that I have heard or read that is not according to Your will, please help me to forget it. Help me to never hear or read anything improper, even unintentionally, or under duress. May my ears and eyes be sanctified, to hear and see only mitzvos. (*Chofetz Chaim, Etzah v'Soshiah*, §8)

―――――∽○ COMMENTARY ○∾―――――

Avoiding Lashon Hora

A common problem today concerns people who are overly pious, observing *halachic* strictures such as eating glatt kosher meat, or only *shemurah* matzah, or avoiding cooked or fried matzah, etc. While some of these people deserve praise for this, other, more superficial individuals, imagine this to be the essence of piety, when in reality, they lack piety altogether.

For not only do these people fail to repent over the sins or their

ח יַרְגִּיל אֶת עַצְמוֹ שֶׁלֹּא יַתְחִיל לְדַבֵּר לְשׁוּם אָדָם זוּלַת לְצוֹרֶךְ גָּדוֹל הַהֶכְרֵחַ לוֹ, וְאַף הַהֶכְרֵחַ יְדַבֵּר בִּדְבָרִים קְצָרִים מְאוֹד מְנֻפָּה בְּשָׁלֹשׁ עֶשְׂרֵה נָפָה, שֶׁלֹּא יִהְיֶה בְּדִיבּוּרוֹ שׁוּם שֶׁקֶר חַס וְשָׁלוֹם וְשׁוּם חֲנִיפָה וְשׁוּם לְשׁוֹן הָרַע וּרְכִילוּת וְשׁוּם הַלְבָּנַת פָּנִים וְלֹא שׁוּם הַרְאוֹת מַעֲשָׂיו לִבְנֵי אָדָם, וְיַרְגִּיל אֶת עַצְמוֹ בִּכְלָל שֶׁאָמְרוּ חֲכָמֵינוּ זִכְרוֹנָם לִבְרָכָה: "לְמוֹד לְשׁוֹנְךָ לוֹמַר אֵינִי יוֹדֵעַ", כְּשֶׁמְּדַבְּרִים אֵלָיו בְּנֵי אָדָם אֲשֶׁר אֵין נִזְהָרִים מִלְּדַבֵּר דְּבָרִים בְּטֵלִים יַשְׁמִיט אֶת עַצְמוֹ מֵהֶם בְּכָל כֹּחוֹ וּבְכָל מִינֵי תַּחְבּוּלוֹת, וּכְשֶׁלֹּא אֶפְשָׁר לוֹ לְהִשָּׁמֵט מֵהֶם בְּשׁוּם אוֹפֶן עַל כָּל פָּנִים יְקַצֵּר מְאוֹד בָּזֶה שֶׁמֻּכְרָח לְהָשִׁיב לָהֶם:

→o PRAYERS o←

My God, guard my mouth from speaking slander, gossip or any other form of blemished speech, so that I will not express a single tainted word about any Jew in the world. Guard my tongue from evil and my lips from speaking falsehood. Protect me from being harmed by anyone else's blemished speech, such as slander; or from being ambushed by the sinful speech of prideful people, heaven forbid. Help me and all Yisroel guard ourselves from blemishes in speech, so that we will sanctify our mouths constantly. Guard us from pride. Free Your Shechinah, which descended into exile as a result of the flaw of pride that comes in consequence of the sin of slander, Heaven forbid. Have compassion on me for the sake of Your Name. Help me from this moment on to rectify all this. Guard me from the grievous sin of slander, and from every type of flawed speech. Guide me to sanctify the speech of my mouth with every sort of holiness. (*Likutey Tefilos* 1:58)

→o COMMENTARY o←
---

youth, they continue to transgress the Torah by speaking libelously about others whose greatness they cannot even touch. They mistakenly think they can tell the difference between good and evil, and that they are smart enough to discern truth from falsehood.

And even if they are correct, who gave them permission to transgress the prohibition of *lashon hora*, whose punishment is severer than the three cardinal sins – idolatry, adultery and murder? The fact that they think they can speak badly of others only reveals their attachment to their own transgressions and immature desires. Their bad words about others speak only badly about themselves. (*Sur MeRa*, p. 25)

⇢○ COMMENTARY ○⇠

Dovid HaMelech exclaimed to the Holy One: "Master of the World! When [my enemies] study the laws of Leprosy and Tents, they jeer at me and say, 'Tell us, Dovid, what is the death penalty of one who seduces a married woman?' 'Death by strangulation,' I reply. 'Yet such a person still has a portion in the World to Come. Not so, one who shames his neighbor in public: He has no portion in the World to Come.'" (Bava Metziah 59a)

Studying "Leprosy" means that they were engaged in speaking *lashon hora* (which causes leprosy). This is despite the fact that they were studying the tractate of "Tents," which alludes to one's death (that is, the laws of impurity from contact with the dead). Ideally, remembering our ultimate end should awaken in us a sense of humility, as the Sages have said: "Be exceeding humble, as the hope of man is with worms" (*Pirkei Avos* 4:4). This is the ideal antidote for *lashon hora*. (*Ohel Elimelech*, §243)

Not Humiliating Others

So shall you say to Yosef, "Please, forgive your brothers' transgression and their sin, for they did evil to you. Now please forgive the transgression of the servants of the God of your father" (Bereishis 50:17).

Chazal say that if a person sins against his fellow and repents, he must still appease him to gain forgiveness (*Yoma* 85b). Despite the fact that Yosef's brothers asked him for forgiveness, we do not find a verse that states that he actually forgave them. Even though it states that he "comforted them and spoke to their hearts," it does not say that he forgave them. This suggests that they died still guilty of their transgression.

Indeed, their punishment was stored away, to be carried out much later, upon the Ten Martyrs [of the Roman period]. (*Rabbeinu Bachaya, Vayechi*)

Humility Regarding One's Accomplishments

Lead me in Your truth, and teach me, for You are the God of my deliverance; for I have hoped in you (Tehilim 25:5).

Dovid HaMelech prayed never to become conceited in his service of God. Rather, he asked God to help him understand how everything is really from Him; that it was *He*, in His compassion, who led Dovid on the path of truth. This is the meaning of "Lead me in Your truth…for You are the God of my deliverance." [That is, You God have helped me in all this, for you are the God who helps]. (*Noam Elimelech, Miketz*)

→o COMMENTARY o←

Humility is the root and source of everything holy; it is the foundation of everything. It is referred to as *ekev*, as in "The reward for humility (*ekev anavah*) is the fear of the Lord (*Mishlei* 22:4). *Ekev* also means "the heel of the foot" – for the foot supports the entire body. Thus, there should be an element of humility in everything a person does. (Ibid, *Ekev*)

Speaking Frivolously

Do not speak too much about unnecessary things. God grants each person a fixed amount of words to use during his lifetime: Why should you shorten your life by speaking about things that are neither a mitzvah, nor absolutely needed? This is what Shlomo HaMelech said in *Shir HaShirim* (5:6): "My soul went out when he spoke." In other words, God says: "The soul which I gave man leaves him when he speaks." (*Hanhagos HaTzaddikim*, Rabbi Mendel of Linsk, 53)

∾

"A man has joy with the response of his mouth" (*Mishlei* 15:23). The word "response" – *maaneh*, מענה – is related to the word "affliction" – *inuy*, ענוי. That is, when a person afflicts his mouth by not speaking unnecessarily, he attains joy – namely, the love of God. (*Ohel Elimelech*, §262)

∾

People waste time from Torah because they are irresistibly drawn after empty talk. The desire to talk about trivial matters or mock and belittle things is extremely strong – even though a person derives no physical pleasure from the act at all.

This is because for every act that a person does, he receives a [corresponding] spirit from Above. This spirit does not rest until it performs further, similar acts below, be they mitzvos or sins. This is the meaning of "One mitzvah begets another, and one sin begets another" (*Pirkei Avos* 4:2). Furthermore, the spirit that is drawn down corresponds to the value of the mitzvah or the sin. Torah study – which is the greatest of all commandments – has a great power to draw down a holy spirit, whereas the reverse applies to idle chatter and derisive speech, which are the very opposite of Torah. This is why people take such great pleasure engaging in them, more than any other sin. (*Biur HaGra, Mishlei* 1:23)

Rectifying One's Speech

A person who wants to rectify the spiritual blemishes in his speech should stay up all Thursday night studying Torah. If he cannot remain awake the whole night, he should recite the entire book of Psalms on Shabbos, without interruption. (*Vechay Bohem*, p. 76, in the name of Rabbi Mordechai of Chernobyl)

9 Immediately upon waking, you should accustom yourself to say: "I give thanks to You, living and eternal King, for mercifully restoring my soul within me; Your faithfulness is great." You should also say, joyfully, even in your own language: "Blessed is the supernal God, who has given me this mitzvah of tzitzis, which surrounds me, and the mitzvah of washing the hands in the morning, to remove the impure spirit and hard, impure force from my two hands." Your heart should be full of joy when you say this. You should also make a commitment to minimize your speech, as I mentioned above, in section 8.

PRAYERS

May we merit washing our hands each morning until we can "raise our hands to our hearts, to our Father in Heaven" (*Eichah* 3:41). And may I fulfill the verse: "Lift your hands in the holy place and bless God"; that is, may I purify the twenty-eight sections of my hands and raise them up to the level of my consciousness, so that I know that God alone runs the world, and that there are no binding laws of nature. May I subdue and uproot the force of Amalek in the world, which is the source of all heresy. And by washing and raising our hands, may we overcome all atheism; for this is the main way to defeat the *Sitra Achra*. (*Tefilos HaBoker*, p. 43)

COMMENTARY

The Joy of Mitzvos

The Arizal revealed to his disciples the reason that he merited grasping such deep secrets and mysteries of Torah, experiencing a revelation of Eliyahu HaNavi and attaining Divine Inspiration: It was on account of the great joy he felt when performing the mitzvos. (*Sefer Charedim*, Introduction)

If a person believed that his prayers and Torah study were actually causing an outflow of blessing to all the worlds, he would serve God with joy and fear, and out of deep gratitude. He would be careful with his every action and make sure he said every word [of prayer] correctly. For a human being is "a ladder on the earth, with its head in heaven," and every gesture and word, each goal and effort makes a mark Above. Certainly, he would be careful to do everything for the sake of Heaven.

Some people ask: "Am I important enough to rectify the upper and lower worlds, or that all my actions have an effect Above?" However,

→ COMMENTARY ↜

ט יַרְגִּיל אֶת עַצְמוֹ תֵּיכֶף וּמִיָּד כְּשֶׁיִּתְעוֹרֵר מִשֵּׁינָתוֹ יֹאמַר: "מוֹדֶה אֲנִי לְפָנֶיךָ מֶלֶךְ חַי וְקַיָּם שֶׁהֶחֱזַרְתָּ בִּי נִשְׁמָתִי בְּחֶמְלָה רַבָּה אֱמוּנָתֶךָ", וְיֹאמַר אֲפִילוּ בִּלְשׁוֹן אַשְׁכְּנַז בְּלֵב שָׂמֵחַ: "בָּרוּךְ אֵל עֶלְיוֹן אֲשֶׁר נָתַן לִי מִצְוֹת צִיצִית אֵלֶּה אֲשֶׁר אֲנִי מְסוֹבָב בָּהֶן, וּמִצְוַת נְטִילַת יָדַיִם שַׁחֲרִית לְהַעֲבִיר רוּחַ רָעָה וְהַקְלִיפָּה הַקָּשָׁה מֵעַל שְׁתֵּי יָדַיִם שֶׁלִּי", וְיִרְאֶה שֶׁיִּהְיֶה לִבּוֹ מָלֵא שִׂמְחָה בְּאָמְרוֹ כנ"ל וִיקַבֵּל עָלָיו הַגֶּדֶר שֶׁל מִיעוּט הַדִּיבּוּר הַנִּזְכָּר לְעֵיל סִימָן ח':

PRAYERS

May it be Your will, our God and God of our fathers, to willingly and compassionately receive this mitzvah of *tzitzis* that we perform as though we have fulfilled it in all its details and with all the spiritual rectifications that it accomplishes, and as if we had in mind all the proper intentions, and fulfilled all 613 commandments that are connected to it. In the special merit of the mitzvah of attaching *tzitzis* to the four corners of our garment, may You gather in our exiles from the four corners of the world and bring us joyfully to our land. Help us to remember, guard and fulfill all of Your commandments, and to completely repair our souls in this lifetime. And may we merit wearing the spiritual garment for our souls in the World to Come. (*Beis Tefilah*, §9)

COMMENTARY

such an attitude merely allows an individual to follow his base desires. The truth is that every person can actually cling to God through his good deeds, as it is written: "You shall go in His ways" (*Devorim* 28:9). For by being compassionate below, one awakens the attribute of compassion Above, in all the worlds. (Rabbi Yaakov Yosef of Polnoye, *Toldos Yaakov Yosef, Ekev*)

Nothing helps a person attain enlightenment like the joy of performing a mitzvah. Spiritual attachment, Godly vitality, and joy from prayer and tefillin – these are the very life of holiness. (*Sur MeRa*, p. 36)

More than for anything else, the Chofetz Chaim took himself to task for not fulfilling the mitzvos with enough joy. (Heard from Rabbi Tzvi Hirsh, grandson of the Chofetz Chaim)

You should perform the commandments with so much joy that you do

———⇾o PRAYERS o⇽———

Help me fulfill the mitzvah of *tzitzis* in all its fine details and with all the inner intentions of the mitzvah, together with the 613 mitzvos with which it is bound up. Protect me with the holy fringes of the *tzitzis* and save me from all forms of immorality. Help me sanctify myself at all times by drawing Your holiness upon me, and in this way, save me from the "promptings of the Serpent" – the blandishments of all the people who would like to tempt me and induce me to turn aside from the path of truth, whether from evil motives or not. Help me draw the light of the true wisdom of the Tzaddikim upon myself through putting their teachings and guidance into practice. Bring me to the truth, and never let a word of falsehood cross my lips. (*Likutey Tefilos* 1:7)

The Joy of Mitzvos

May it by Your will, Hashem my God and God of my fathers, to lovingly help me merit great joy, true joy, in serving You, as it is written: "Serve Hashem with happiness, and rejoice with trembling." Bring me to fulfill all the mitzvos with a happiness and joy that come from the mitzvah itself. While engaged in each mitzvah, let me rejoice over the fact that You have lovingly given me the privilege of performing this mitzvah.

———⇾o COMMENTARY o⇽———

not even want any reward for them in the World to Come. You only want God to bring you another mitzvah as a reward for this one, because your joy is in the mitzvah itself. (*Likutey Etzos, Simchah* 2)

Try to be as happy as you can. Search for your good points in order to make yourself happy. If for no other reason, you can be happy that you are a Jew and God did not make you a non-Jew. If you genuinely realize the true implications of this you will find joy without limits. And nothing will be able to spoil it, because God Himself made it so. Get into the habit of saying out loud and with all your heart: "Blessed be our God

who created us for His glory and separated us from those who are in error etc." No matter what you may go through you will always be able to take heart from this and be happy all your life. (*Likutey Etzos, Simchah* 29)

It is a great mitzvah to be happy at all times. Be determined to keep away from depression, and aim to be happy constantly. Happiness is the remedy for all kinds of diseases, because many illnesses are caused by depression. You must be resourceful in order to make yourself happy. Often you must do something a little bit crazy in order to make yourself happy. (Ibid. 30).

———→○ PRAYERS ○←———

Let all my joy be from the mitzvah alone, and not from the thought of the reward I will receive in the World to Come, not to speak of any honon or other extraneous benefits I anticipate from other people, or other mundane advantages of any kind. Let my entire joy be from the mitzvah itself. Let my World to Come be in the actual performance of the mitzvah, so that I will have no wish for any reward for the mitzvah in the Next World. Let my reward be that You will grant me another mitzvah, as taught by our Rabbis: "the reward for a mitzvah is a mitzvah." (*Likutey Tefilos* 1:5)

———→○ COMMENTARY ○←———

The Fruit of Depression

You should avoid depression as much as possible, for it leads to a host of other sins. Depression first increases a person's desire for food (we see this empirically, that depressed people tend to overeat), which, in turn, draws other types of desires in its wake. (*Maor VaShemesh, Behaloscha*)

The evil inclination is less interested in the actual sin than in the depression that a person falls into after committing it. (*Rabbi Nachum of Chernobyl, Az Tis'chazek*, §364)

The Greatness of *Tzitzis*

In every generation, there is one mitzvah that needs to be rectified more than all the others. In our generation, this is the mitzvah of *tzitzis*. (*Noam Elimelech, Noach*)

As soon as you wake up in the morning, take the holy *tzitzis* in your hand and contemplate the greatness of the Creator. You should feel great fear and awe of Him – a genuine and exalted fear. Do not fulfill the mitzvah of *tzitzis* simply out of habit. (*Be'er Moshe, Bereishis*, in the name of Rabbi Zushia of Anipoli)

Carefully observing the mitzvah of *tzitzis* provides protection against the "Serpent's counsel," which is evil advice. One who fulfills this mitzvah carefully will be guided solely by the Tzaddikim. (*Likutey Etzos, Etzah* 2)

Washing the Hands

There is a tradition attributed to Rabbi Zushia of Anipoli *zt"l*, that a person should not walk four *amot* (about six feet) in the morning without first washing his hands. Indeed, a person should not even stand on his feet before washing his hands. This is alluded to in the verse: "He *stands* on a way that is not good; he does not reject evil" (*Tehilim* 36:5). (*Igra d'Pirka*, §9)

10 Be very diligent in your set program of Torah study, which you should begin immediately after rising from sleep and having recited the Midnight Prayer. Never remove the *Tzetel Katan* from whatever book you are studying – even for a moment. Whenever you sit down to study, recite *Tefilas HaShov*, which begins: "Please, God..." as well as the prayer over Torah study found in the *Sha'arei Tzion* prayerbook, which begins: "I desire to study...." Try as best as you can not to interrupt [your studies], even with other thoughts – except for thinking about this *Tzetel Katan*, which should always be before you, for the light within it will help you to improve.

⟶o PRAYERS o⟵

Loving God, help us study and meditate on Your holy Torah constantly, day and night, in holiness and purity – us, our children and our children's children; and let us never forget the Torah. Don't let the Torah ever cease to be heard from our mouths or the mouths of our descendents. (*Likutey Tefilos* 1:12)

I remembered Your Name in the nights, O Lord, and I kept Your Torah. I rose at midnight to thank You for Your righteous judgments. I rose early, while it was still night, and I cried out, hoping for Your word. My eyes preceded the watches, to speak of Your word. You heard my voice; do not hide Your ear from my sighing or from my crying.

Master of the World, full of compassion and love, have mercy on me, and help me rise each night at midnight. Let me wake from my sleep and overcome my tiredness. Let me return to You in perfect *teshuvah*, and recite the midnight prayer with a truly broken heart – to mourn over the destruction of the Temple, and to pour my heart out over my sins against You, from the days of my youth until today; for my own sins have prolonged the exile. Please, send me pleasing words and prayers from heaven, that I may appease You. And may I also find in myself points of goodness. (*Tefilos HaBoker* p. 3)

May I be worthy to recite the midnight prayer each night, and to pour out my heart to You, as well. May I find myself and all my concerns in the *kinos* and psalms of the midnight prayer, so that I am not merely reciting the words over what happened in the past, but also over all

י יִזָּהֵר מְאֹד בְּהִתְמָדַת הַלִּימוּד שִׁעוּרִין כְּסִדְרָן תֵּיכֶף וּמִיַּד אַחַר קוּמוֹ מִשְּׁנָתוֹ וְאֶחָד וְאֶחָד אָמְרוּ תִּיקוּן חֲצוֹת וְהַצֶּעטִיל קָטָן לֹא יָזוּז מֵהַסֵּפֶר שֶׁלּוֹמֵד בּוֹ אֲפִילוּ שָׁעָה אַחַת, בְּכָל פַּעַם שֶׁיֵּשֵׁב אֶת עַצְמוֹ לִלְמוֹד וְאַחַר שֶׁיֹּאמַר תְּפִלַּת הַשָּׁב הַמַּתְחֶלֶת "אָנָּא הַשֵּׁם" וְכוּ' וּתְפִלַּת הַתַּלְמוּד תּוֹרָה בְּסֵפֶר שַׁעֲרֵי צִיּוֹן הַמַּתְחֶלֶת "הִנְנִי רוֹצֶה לִלְמוֹד", יִרְאֶה בְּכָל כֹּחוֹ שֶׁלֹּא לַעֲשׂוֹת שׁוּם הֶפְסֵק אֲפִילוּ בְּמַחְשָׁבָה אַחֶרֶת זוּלַת מַחְשֶׁבֶת הַלִּימוּד וּמַחְשֶׁבֶת הַצֶּעטִיל קָטָן שֶׁהוּא לִפְנֵי עֵינָיו כִּי הַמְאוֹר שֶׁבָּהּ יַחְזִירֵנוּ לְמוּטָב:

PRAYERS

that is happening to me now, down to the smallest detail. (*Tefilos v'Tachanunim* p. 79)

Teshuvah and the Light of Torah

Master of the World! I tremble in fear to begin studying the holy Torah. For how can a mouth as blemished as mine speak words of the holy Torah, and how can eyes, impure like mine, look into the holy Torah, or my ears, which have listened to *lashon hora*, hear the holy Torah, or my mind, which has been sullied by forbidden thoughts, think about the holy Torah? I fear that You will say to me: "Wicked man, why do you recount My statutes, and mention My covenant with your mouth?"; for the offerings of the wicked are an abomination. I fear that I have lost hope in God. Yet, my heart tells me: "Why do you sleep? Rise and cry out to your God. For He longs to show mercy, and does not desire the death of the wicked, but only his return, that he may live."

God, not in my own merit do I plead to You, but in Your great mercy alone. For You are a forgiving King, and Your right hand is outstretched to accept penitents. May it be Your will, my God and God of my fathers, to open a path beneath Your throne of glory, and accept my repentance and my prayers. Have mercy and forgive me for all the sins I have committed, from my youth until today – whether in this incarnation or in a previous one. Do not cast me away empty-handed. In Your great compassion, hear my prayers. For You hear the prayers of all. Put my tears in Your flask. May the words of my lips and the thoughts of my heart be pleasing to You, God, my Rock and my Redeemer. (*Tefilah l'Moshe, Otzar Tefilos Yisroel*, vol. 3, p. 50)

―――――◦ PRAYERS ◦―――――

Please, God, let my Torah study be an elixir of life. Let my learning bring me back to You in genuine, perfect *teshuvah*. Let it restore my youth like the eagle, and give me back the times I have spent in such intense darkness. From now on, let the merit and power of the holy Torah shield me and protect me from every kind of sin and transgression and from all wrongdoing, both when I am actually engaged in my studies, and at times when I have to interrupt them. Let the merit and power of the Torah give me constant protection and save me from every kind of sin and wrongdoing, just as You have informed us through Your holy Sages, who said that "the Torah shields and protects both while one is engaged in it and at times when one is not." Let my Torah study bring a flow of holiness and purity into me, and from now on let me sanctify and purify myself the way You want me to – for my own good. (*Likutey Tefilos* 1:12)

―――――◦ COMMENTARY ◦―――――

The Benefits of Diligent Study

The power of the Torah is very great, and one who labors in it continuously will be able to perform miracles, even without knowing any Kabbalistic meditations. The main thing is to study the codes of Jewish law until you know how to issue legal rulings. In previous eras, there were many leading sages who were able to perform miracles merely by virtue of their devotion to Torah study day and night. (*Likutey Etzos, Talmud Torah* 77)

Interrupting Torah Study

A person who defiles his mouth with impure speech causes all of his Torah and prayers to become impure. This includes someone who interrupts his Torah study needlessly. He "sits outside the camp [of holiness]." Even worse, he will be severely punished for this. For if a person brings a gift to a great king, but offers it in an ugly container, his gift will only make the king angry. (*Vechay Bohem*, p. 224, in the name of the *Shlah*)

The great scholar, Rabbi Zelig Reuven Bengis *zt"l* said that the most productive period of his studies was when he was in the Volozhin Yeshivah, on the long winter nights, following the evening prayers, from 5:00 p.m. until 2:00 a.m. Then, the students studied nine hours straight, without interruption, and made great progress in their studies. (*Hi Sichasi*, p. 112)

Advice for Waking at Midnight

The following practices can help a person to wake at midnight:

- Bringing Jews back to Torah observance.
- Giving charity without knowing the recipient, and without the recipient knowing that you gave it.
- Reading the daily passages [of *Chok l'Yisroel*] with fear and love of God, while wearing tefillin. Your intention then should be to draw upon yourself fear of God from the letter *yud*; the love of God from the letter *hey*; the merit of Torah – namely, of the verses you are reciting – from the letter *vav*; and the merit of the mitzvah of tefillin from the last letter *hey*.
- Laying tefillin with the following intentions in mind:
  - The four parchments of the head tefillin correspond to God's Name Y-H-V-H.
  - The 21 times this Name of God appears in them corresponds to the four letters of the Name E-H-Y-H (whose numerical value is 21)
  - The four compartments of the head tefillin also correspond to the Name E-H-Y-H.
  - Have in mind, as well, that the four letters of the Name Y-H-V-H correspond to the four Names *Av, Sag, Mah* and *Ban* (ע״ב, ס״ג, מ״ה, ב״ן); and that all four of these expansions of God's holy Name actually derive from the three letters Y-H-V alone, aside from the final letter *hey*.
  - The four paragraphs written on the parchment of the hand tefillin correspond to the four letters of the Name Y-H-V-H, and contain four Names Y-H-V, though not expanded, while the 21 times God's Name is written in them correspond to the Name E-H-Y-H. The actual box of the arm tefillin corresponds to the Name A-D-N-Y, as is explained in *Sha'ar HaTefilos*, by the Arizal.

Whoever fulfills these practices every day will merit receiving God's help to rise at midnight. (*Minhagei HaAri, Tikun Chatzos* 8)

⁌

When you say the blessing *Hashkivenu*, and the blessing *Hamapil* (in the bedtime *Kerias Shema*), ask God to help you wake at midnight. (*Birchat Chaim* 10:8)

───○ COMMENTARY ○───

The Importance of Midnight

Rabbi Elimelech of Lizhensk would go to sleep early each night. He explained that Torah study and prayers only ascend after midnight. Thus, from the time of the evening prayers until he awoke from his sleep [at midnight], he would not speak a word to anyone. (*Kedushas Noam Elimelech*, p. 82)

Some people stay awake until midnight, recite the *tikun chatzos* prayer, and then go to sleep. However, this practice is not correct, for it warps all the channels [of Heavenly blessing]. The time to sleep is before *chatzos*. This is a form of worship in its own right. Afterward, one should rise at *chatzos*, which is a time of Divine compassion and favor. For when the Holy One delights in the Garden of Eden, after *chatzos*, one should not be sleeping. (*Birchas Chaim* chap. 10, §4)

11 Accustom yourself to praying with all your might, in a strong voice that draws your attention to your words. During both the morning and evening prayers, you should face the wall and look into your prayerbook without glancing around, from the beginning of the prayers until the end. When the prayer leader repeats the Shemoneh Esrei out loud, you should look into your prayerbook and answer "Amen," after each blessing, with all of your strength. During the Torah reading, you should listen carefully to each and every word, as though they were reading the Megillah. While in the Beis HaKneses, act as though your were mute, both before and after the prayers, until you leave for home.

───○ PRAYERS ○───

God in heaven, everything is revealed to You, and You know the great confusion we experience while praying. We have no one to rely upon but You. Have mercy upon us and deliver us from every improper and confusing thought, from now and forever. May our thoughts be always pure, clean, and holy, especially when we pray, so that not a single improper thought enters our minds. May our prayers never feel like a burden. Deliver us, so that we can pray to You with all our heart and soul, with great concentration, in holiness and purity, in fear and in love. May our thoughts and our words of prayer be fully

COMMENTARY

The main devotion of a Jew is to get up every night for the midnight prayer. (*Likutey Etzos, Chatzos* 6)

Teshuvah before Torah Study

The essence of repentance is to feel genuine regret in your heart, to verbally confess [your sins to God], to abandon the sin, and to make a commitment never to do it again nor return to your folly. Self-affliction is necessary only to purify the body and soul, and wash away the [spiritual] stains.

Before every prayer, Torah study session or mitzvah, you should repent in your heart, so that the action is not wasted, by enlivening the forces of impurity (*kelipos*), God forbid.

May God help us return to Him in truth. (*Sur MeRa*, p. 23)

יא יַרְגִּיל אֶת עַצְמוֹ לְהִתְפַּלֵּל בְּכָל כֹּחוֹ וּבְקוֹל הַמְעוֹרֵר הַכַּוָּנָה לְהִדָּבֵק הַמַּחֲשָׁבָה לְדִיבּוּר, וּפָנָיו אֶל הַכּוֹתֶל בְּתוֹךְ סִידּוּר הַתְּפִלָּה בַּבּוֹקֶר וּבָעֶרֶב, וְלֹא יִסְתַּכֵּל לִצְדָדִין מִתְּחִלַּת הַתְּפִלָּה עַד סוֹפָהּ, וּבַחֲזָרַת הַשְּׁלִיחַ צִבּוּר הַשְּׁמוֹנָה עֶשְׂרֵה יְעַיֵּין בְּסִידּוּר לַעֲנוֹת אָמֵן בְּכָל כֹּחוֹ עַל כָּל בְּרָכָה וּבְרָכָה, וּבִשְׁעַת קְרִיאַת הַתּוֹרָה לְהַטּוֹת אָזְנוֹ עַל כָּל דִּיבּוּר וְדִיבּוּר מֵהַקּוֹרֵא כְּקוֹרֵא אֶת הַמְגִילָּה, וְלַעֲשׂוֹת עַצְמוֹ כְּאִלֵּם בְּבֵית הַכְּנֶסֶת אֲפִילוּ קוֹדֶם הַתְּפִלָּה וְאַחֲרֶיהָ עַד הֲלִיכָתוֹ לְבֵיתוֹ:

PRAYERS

united, so that we do not utter a single word without intention and concentration. May we be worthy to pray to You with true self-sacrifice, and may You give us strength to subdue, cast out and erase all foreign thoughts, so that we can completely take our minds off of them. And may our thoughts be always holy and pure. (*Otzar Tefilos Yisroel*, vol. 2, p. 493)

May I serve You with truth, faith and simplicity. May I engage in Torah learning and prayer with intense feeling, and invest all of my strength and all the thoughts of my heart and mind into each word of prayer. May I believe with perfect faith that the world is filled with Your glory, and that when we pray, You stand before us and take heed of our every word. May I know before whom I stand: the King of kings,

PRAYERS

the Holy One, blessed be He. As a result, may I experience fear and awe of You. May I have profound intention in my every word of prayer, and never lose my focus. And may my mind not stray from focusing on the meaning of the words and be free of all superficial and foreign thoughts. Rather, may I connect my thought to my words of prayer with a strong, inseparable bond. (*Likutey Tefilos* 1:84)

Have mercy on me, for the sake of Your Name. Deliver me, help me, and strengthen me, with Your great might, that I may put every ounce of my strength into prayer, and constantly pray to You with great force, until all the prideful, selfish and foreign thoughts within me are annulled and lose their ability to disturb my prayers. Rather, may

COMMENTARY

The main vitality of a Tzaddik comes to him through prayer, through which he clings to the Creator. (*Noam Elimelech, Vayechi*)

In today's generation, before the coming of Moshiach, the main form of worship is prayer. (*Sefer HaTanya, Kuntress Acharon*, p. 162, in the name of Rabbi Chaim Vital)

Concentration during the *Amidah*

A person who wants to know if his deeds are pure and honest should examine his prayers. If he can concentrate during the entire *Amidah*, reciting all the blessings without extraneous thoughts, he knows that he is a Tzaddik. This is the meaning of the verse: "The refining pot is for silver and the furnace for gold, and a man according to his praise" (*Mishlei* 27:21); that is, according to his prayers. (*Sefer Charedim*)

Uniting Your Thoughts and Your Words

"If Esav comes and strikes one camp, the remaining camp will escape" (Bereishis 32:9).

That is, even if [the evil inclination] attacks the camp of my thoughts, by confusing them, "the remaining camp will escape." That is, through the one camp I have left – which is my power of speech – I can recoup and regain the first camp, which is my thoughts. (*Noam Elimelech, Vayishlach*)

Some people pray with *kavanos*, the Kabbalistic meditations on Divine Names. However, in our time, that is not really necessary. Indeed, I heard from the holy Rabbi Elimelech of Lizhensk, that one should not pray with *kavanos*. The reason to pray from the Arizal's version of the prayerbook is because the Name Y-H-V-H is written out fully. (*Maor VaShemesh, Ekev*)

PRAYERS

I be able to cast them out and completely remove them from having any contact with me, so that they are completely unable to enter my mind, and my prayers become pure, proper, pleasing and acceptable to You. (*Likutey Tefilos* 2:43)

Answering "Amen"

Master of the World! You know that I am mere flesh and blood, unable to answer "Amen" with full concentration and according to its mystical meaning. May it be Your will that my intention to do so be joined with the intentions of those remaining few people who know how to concentrate and answer "Amen" properly. (*Otzar Tefilos Yisroel*, vol. 2, p. 535)

COMMENTARY

True Prayer

The Serpent (the evil inclination) convinces a person to pray for his own needs: "Give me health! Give me livelihood!" and so on. You must overcome this inclination and to try to pray without any intention for personal benefit. Pray as if you did not exist in this world at all. Then, you will attain the light that was hidden away for the righteous. (*Likutey Etzos, Tefilah* 27)

By studying the codes of Torah law, a person can achieve true prayer, which emerges from the heart with complete sincerity. If a person really knew and believed wholeheartedly that the entire world is filled with God's glory, and that God stands over him while he is praying and hears his every word, he would be scrupulous about saying them in the correct way and praying with total concentration and devotion. But people's hearts are split, and they do not feel this reality with all their heart. Instead their hearts are filled with questions and doubts – because it is in the heart that the evil inclination fights its battle. Now the legal codes set forth the final decision of the law after all the arguments between the Sages. These arguments are really the source of the turmoil stirred up by the evil inclination, because even that which is unholy derives its vitality from the realms of the holy. The legal codes represent the resolution of conflict, and therefore studying them resolves the turmoil in the heart at its root. Then one can pray as one should – wholeheartedly and truthfully. (*Likutey Etzos, Tefilah* 57)

Facing the Wall

A person should face the wall during prayer. For the word "wall" – *kotel* (כותל) – alludes to the unification of God's two Names: Y-H-V-H and Elokim. This is because the Name Y-H-V-H has a numerical value (*ge-*

———→∘ COMMENTARY ∘←———

matria) of twenty-six – כו, while the letters תל have the same *gematria* as five times the Name Elokim – אלהים. A person should have in mind to completely unify these two Names when he prays, and to sweeten the harsh Judgments (alluded to by the Name Elokim) with loving-kindness (alluded to by the Name Y-H-V-H). He should likewise intend to include and encompass the left side in the right. (*Be'er Mayim Chaim, Bechukosai*)

Answering "Amen"

The reader's repetition of the *Amidah* creates a greater spiritual union than the silent *Amidah*. This is because we answer "Amen" after each blessing, which has the numerical value of God's two Names combined: Y-A-H-D-V-N-H-Y (יאהדונהי). This union is not formed when a person prays silently. For even though a person pronounces God's Name Y-H-V-H as A-D-N-Y, nonetheless, the two Names are not fully merged.

The word "Amen" itself hints to the unification of these two Names. Thus, the union [created by the reader's repetition] is higher. (*Madanai Melech*)

12 You should constantly imagine – especially when you are reading this *Tzetel Katan* – that someone is standing beside you and exhorting you to follow all its practices, down to the smallest detail. If you accustom yourself to doing this, you will eventually feel a tremendous awakening in your soul – a burning fire and a Godly flame.

———→∘ PRAYERS ∘←———

Master of the World! May I long to serve You so much that I can immediately find myself in the words of every *sefer* that I study; that is, may I recognize my own lowness and become deeply inspired and motivated to serve You from everything that I learn. May I study all the holy books, and derive from them good advice, and great inspiration and encouragement to serve You, at every moment, in a way that fits my personality, my spiritual level, and everything that happens to me. May the verse be fulfilled in me: "Behold, I come; In the scroll of a book it is written about me" – that is, may I feel that every book I study was written specifically *for me* and speaks precisely to me and about all that I am going through. Then, I will know that I truly long to fulfill Your will, as it is written: "O God, I desired to do Your will and have Your Torah within my heart." (*Tefilos v'Tachanunim*, p. 26)

The Reader's Repetition

All the laws that apply to prayer and the Shemoneh Esrei also apply to the reader's repetition; especially since this repetition is even holier than the silent Amidah. One should not speak, arrange his business, or walk around at that time. The Arizal wrote that during the reader's repetition, all the mystical rectifications that were accomplished during the silent Amidah are accomplished again, on a higher level.

Rabbi Chaim Vital writes that the main form of service in the era before Moshiach – the period we are in now – is prayer. For this reason, the evil inclination makes every effort to prevent a person from concentrating in prayer, such as by distracting him with people coming in or out of the room, or similar things. Then, God takes no delight in him, as his service is lacking. All this occurs because a person wants to know everything that is going on, and see everyone coming and going, who they are, and where they sit, etc.

A person should hold back from looking around, and not gaze beyond his immediate surroundings. Perhaps, then, he will be able to pray with concentration, without extraneous thoughts. (*Vechay Bohem*, p. 207)

יב יְצַיֵּר בְּמַחֲשַׁבְתּוֹ תָּמִיד וּבִפְרָט בִּשְׁעַת קְרִיאַת הַצֶּעטיל קָטָן הַזֶּה כְּאִלּוּ אִישׁ אֶחָד עוֹמֵד סָמוּךְ לוֹ וּמְעוֹרֵר אוֹתוֹ בְּקוֹל רַעַשׁ גָּדוֹל לְקַיֵּם כָּל הַנְהָגוֹת אֵלּוּ, וְאַל יַפִּיל שׁוּם דָּבָר אַרְצָה אֲפִילוּ נְקֻדָּה קְטַנָּה וּכְשֶׁיַּרְגִּיל עַצְמוֹ כָּךְ אֲזַי בְּמֶשֶׁךְ הַזְּמַן יָבֹא עָלָיו הִתְעוֹרְרוּת גָּדוֹל מִצַּד נִשְׁמָתוֹ רִשְׁפֵּי אֵשׁ שַׁלְהֶבֶת יָ"הּ:

COMMENTARY

The Image of Rabbi Elimelech

Based upon a statement of the Jerusalem Talmud, that a person should imagine that the author of a Torah teaching is standing in front of him [when he studies that teaching], we can say that one studying the *Tzetel Katan* should actually picture Rabbi Elimelech of Lizhensk encouraging him to fulfill all its precepts. For his holy lips are moving in the grave (see *Sanhedrin* 90b), and can greatly inspire a person, if he is worthy. (*Madanai Melech*)

13 Tell your spiritual mentor, or even your trusted friend, all the improper thoughts you have that are against the holy Torah, which the evil inclination brings to your mind and heart during Torah study and prayer, when you lie on your bed, or in the middle of the day. Don't conceal anything [from him] out of embarrassment, for by relating and giving voice to these things, you break the power of the evil inclination, making it unable to overcome you to the same degree at a later time. Additionally, you may receive good advice from your friend on how to follow God's way. This is an amazingly effective practice.

PRAYERS

Speaking to one's Teacher or Friend

Master of the World! May our souls be purified by studying Your holy Torah, which is like fire, as it says: "Is not My word like fire?" And may we be cleansed of every sort of blemish – inside and out. May we be worthy of purifying and sanctifying our minds, so as not to think vacuous or forbidden thoughts, and may You sanctify and purify us, until we become a vessel for Your holy Shechinah. May we always be able to find good advice, understanding, and original and authentic ways to serve You. May we find in Your Torah the proper way to fix our souls and the path to serve You. Help us encounter Tzaddikim, who are Your servants, and good friends, to learn from them the ways of Your Torah and Your holy and true service, free of all falsehood, God forbid. (*Otzar Tefilos Yisroel*, vol. 3, p. 57)

COMMENTARY

Drawing Close to Tzaddikim

"The Kohen shall go outside the camp, and he shall look and see that the leprous mark has healed" (Vayikra 14:3).

"...go outside the camp" – that is, a Tzaddik must leave his own [high] level and descend to the low level of the person who has left the camp of the Divine Presence, and whose sins have separated him from holiness.

"and he shall look" – that is, the Tzaddik will set his holy vision and thoughts on the person, *"and see that [he] has healed."* That is, the person becomes healed precisely because the Tzaddik has looked at him. (*Noam Elimelech, Metzora*)

יג לְסַפֵּר בְּכָל פַּעַם לִפְנֵי הַמּוֹרֶה לוֹ דֶרֶךְ הַשֵּׁם וַאֲפִילוּ לִפְנֵי חָבֵר נֶאֱמָן כָּל הַמַּחֲשָׁבוֹת וְהִרְהוּרִים רָעִים אֲשֶׁר הֵם נֶגֶד תּוֹרָתֵינוּ הַקְּדוֹשָׁה אֲשֶׁר הַיֵּצֶר הָרַע מַעֲלֶה אוֹתָן עַל מוֹחוֹ וְלִבּוֹ הֵן בִּשְׁעַת תּוֹרָה וּתְפִלָּה הֵן בְּשָׁכְבוֹ עַל מִטָּתוֹ וְהֵן בְּאֶמְצַע הַיּוֹם, וְלֹא יַעֲלִים שׁוּם דָּבָר מֵחֲמַת הַבּוּשָׁה, וְנִמְצָא עַל יְדֵי סִיפּוּר הַדְּבָרִים שֶׁמּוֹצִיא מִכֹּחַ אֶל הַפּוֹעֵל מְשַׁבֵּר אֶת כֹּחַ הַיֵּצֶר הָרַע שֶׁלֹּא יוּכַל לְהִתְגַּבֵּר עָלָיו כָּל כָּךְ בְּפַעַם אַחֶרֶת, חוּץ עֵצָה הַטּוֹבָה אֲשֶׁר יוּכַל לְקַבֵּל מֵחֲבֵירוֹ שֶׁהוּא דֶרֶךְ הַשֵּׁם וְהוּא סְגוּלָה נִפְלָאָה:

PRAYERS

Have mercy on me, O Master of Mercy, great in counsel and mighty in deeds. May I always be able to accept the advice of the true Tzaddikim and upright people of the generation, who derive all their advice from the holy Torah that they received from their own teachers, the true, holy Tzaddikim. May I draw close to them in truth, and receive from them advice regarding everything in the world – whether in the area of serving God, in business, or in other activities. May I ask them about them all, and benefit from their advice and resourcefulness. May their holy wisdom shine in me, and as a result, may great loving-kindness flow down upon me, sweetening and annulling all the harsh judgments that befall me in the world. And may I receive a complete deliverance, at all times, as it is written: "Deliverance is in a multitude of counselors." (*Likutey Tefilos* 1:117)

COMMENTARY

"You shall appoint a king over you, whom the Lord, your God, shall choose... and he shall write for himself two copies of this Torah on a scroll... and he shall read it all the days of his life, so that he may learn to fear the Lord, his God, and keep all the words of this Torah and these statutes...." (Devorim 17:15–19)

Even if a person has learned the entire Torah and all the holy books of our Sages, he still can not fully repent or remove all the barriers between him and God if he does not attach himself to the Tzaddikim and holy people of his generation.

I heard from the saintly Rabbi Elimelech, that a person should choose one Tzaddik and make him

COMMENTARY

his teacher. Yet the question remains: how does one choose?

If you see a Tzaddik who follows the holy Torah in everything he does, without relying on any leniencies in Scriptural or Rabbinic laws; if his heart burns with the flames of spiritual unifications, and his thoughts are reflected in his actions – your should choose him as your teacher.

This is the meaning of "You shall appoint a king over you" – for the Rabbis are considered like kings (*Gittin* 62a).

"Whom the Lord, your God, shall choose" – in other words, whom should you choose as your Rabbi and teacher?

"He shall write for himself two copies of this Torah." According to Rashi, the king carried one of these scrolls with him throughout the day, while the other he stored in his treasury. That is, the fire of Torah burns with love and fear in the Tzaddik's heart (his treasury), and his thoughts are manifest in his actions (i.e. throughout the day). (*Maor Va-Shemesh, Shoftim*)

Guarding Your Thoughts

You should pray with every ounce of your strength, putting all your energy into the words. This is the aspect of "All my bones will say, 'O God, who is like You?'" (*Tehilim* 35:10).

You should concentrate fully on the words that you are saying, and force out all foreign thoughts from your mind, because every type of confusing thought, and all the doubts

---

14 Be extremely careful to review this *Tzetel Katan* at least once a day. Translate each word into your own language. Make it an inviolable practice to study chapter sixteen of the *Reishis Chochmah* before marital relations, as well as the practices of the Arizal. If time permits, you should read chapter seventeen of *Reishis Chochmah*, as well. Consider this an inviolable rule.

COMMENTARY

Holy Relations

"Rabbi Chama ben Rabbi Chanina said in the name of Rabbi Yitzchok: Whosoever sets his bed between north and south will have male children" (Berachos 5b)

This is because the Menorah stood on the south side of the Temple chamber, and the Showbread Table stood on the north. By arranging

COMMENTARY

and questions a person has during the day, enter one's mind during prayer. Therefore, you must make a tremendous effort to overcome all these confusing thoughts. (*Likutei Shoshanim*, p. 42)

When irrelevant, distracting thoughts enter your mind during prayer, you should simply ignore them. Concentrate on your prayers, and think carefully about the words you are saying. Don't look back to see if the thoughts have left you, for they will go away by themselves. Even if the same thought comes again and again, simply remain firm and refuse to pay any attention. Just concentrate your mind on the words of the prayer you are saying at the time. In the end the irrelevant thought will simply go away. (*Likutey Etzos, Tefilah*, §84)

When you find it hard to concentrate properly on your prayers because of irrelevant thoughts and distractions, remind yourself that you would certainly be ready to die in sanctification of God's Name – for even the sinners of Yisroel have sacrificed themselves for this. This sense of self-sacrifice will enable you to bind your thoughts to the words of the prayers and pray with total concentration. Even if you are completely unable to pray, you should push yourself, at least, to pray simply, like a child in school. Say a few words in total simplicity, and listen well to what you are saying. (*Likutey Etzos, Tefilah* 66)

יד יִזָּהֵר מְאֹד וּמְאֹד לַחֲזוֹר לִפְעָמִים בְּכָל מֵעַת לְעֵת זֶה הַצֶּעטִיל קָטָן, וִיפָרֵשׁ כָּל תֵּיבָה וְתֵיבָה בְּלָשׁוֹן אַשְׁכְּנַז, וְזֶה יִהְיֶה לוֹ חֹק וְלֹא יַעֲבוֹר מִלִּלְמוֹד קוֹדֶם הַזִּוּוּג פֶּרֶק ט"ז בְּרֵאשִׁית חָכְמָה וְהַנְהָגוֹת הָאַרִ"י זִכְרוֹנוֹ לִבְרָכָה, וְאִם יִשָּׁאֵר לוֹ פְּנַאי יִלְמוֹד גַּם פֶּרֶק י"ז מֵרֵאשִׁית חָכְמָה הַנִּזְכָּר לְעֵיל וְזֶה יִהְיֶה לוֹ חֹק וְלֹא יַעֲבוֹר:

COMMENTARY

one's bed in this fashion, one will recall the Beis HaMikdash, and pray that his children will be both successful in Torah (symbolized by the Menorah), and affluent (symbolized by the Showbread). As a further result, a person will remember to sanctify himself [during marital relations] so that his children will indeed be deserving of all this. (*Talmidei Rabbeinu Yonah, Berachos* 5b, in the name of Rabbeinu Yonah)

15 When sitting down to a meal, before washing your hands, recite the *Tefilas HaShov* of Rabbeinu Yonah z"l. Then, after you have eaten some bread, say the following: "For the sake of the union of the Holy One and the Shechinah, I do not eat in order to have physical enjoyment, God forbid, but only to keep my body healthy and strong to serve God. Let no sin, transgression, evil thought, or physical pleasure prevent the unification of the Holy One [and the Shechinah], which results from [uplifting] the sparks of holiness in this food and drink."

───── PRAYERS ─────

Father in Heaven, help me and save me, that I may break my desire for food. May I eat a minimum – only as much as I need to live – and may I do so in holiness and purity, for the sake of Your Name, alone. (*Otzar Tefilos Yisroel*, vol. 3, p. 221.)

Loving God, bring me to eat in holiness and purity, with no physical desire whatever. Give me the power to arouse the light of the twenty-eight holy letters of Creation which are clothed in everything in the world, until all my enjoyment of everything I eat or drink comes only from the light of the holy letters contained in it. Through this, give me

───── COMMENTARY ─────

Teshuvah Before Eating

You should say the following, whenever you eat: "Master of the World, may I eat in holiness, and may my intentions be for Your sake. And save me from excess eating and drinking." Two or three times during your meal, you should pause to look in *seforim*, or to think about Torah that you heard from your Rabbi or in his name. And every time, you should pray in your mind: "Master of the World, help me and teach me to do Your will, and save me from the evil inclination." (*Midrash Pinchas, Hanhagos Rabbi Shmuel Valtzis*, §17, 18)

Today, a person's table can atone for him like the altar in the Temple, as the Talmud says on the verse: "This is the table before God" (*Berachos* 55a on *Yechezkel* 41:22). Therefore, just as people would repent and cry bitterly over their sins before bringing their sacrifices, so that their offering not be considered "a slaughtering of the wicked" (*Mishlei* 15:8), so should a person repent before beginning to eat...

This explains the connection between two identical words in the Torah: "And the man [Eliezer] came into the house... and [food] was *put*

טו קוֹדֶם נְטִילַת יָדַיִם לַאֲכִילָה יֹאמַר תְּפִלַּת הַשָּׁב שֶׁל רַבֵּינוּ יוֹנָה זִכְרוֹנוֹ לִבְרָכָה, וְאַחַר אֲכִילַת הַמּוֹצִיא יֹאמַר בָּזֶה הַלָּשׁוֹן: "לְשֵׁם יִחוּד קוּדְשָׁא בְּרִיךְ הוּא וּשְׁכִינְתֵּיהּ אֵין אֲנִי אוֹכֵל לַהֲנָאַת גּוּפִי חַס וְשָׁלוֹם רַק שֶׁיִּהְיֶה גּוּפִי בָּרִיא וְחָזָק לַעֲבוֹדָתוֹ יִתְבָּרַךְ שְׁמוֹ" וְאַל יְעַכֵּב שׁוּם חֵטְא וְעָוֹן וְהִרְהוּר רַע וְתַעֲנוּג גַּשְׁמִי אֶת הַיִּחוּד קוּדְשָׁא בְּרִיךְ הוּא עַל יְדֵי נִיצוֹצוֹת קְדוֹשׁוֹת שֶׁל הָאֲכִילָה וְהַשְּׁתִיָּה הַזֶּה",

---

➤ PRAYERS ○←

a good heart: let my heart radiate with great holiness through enjoying and being nourished only by the light of the letters that powered the act of creation and are contained in all things. (*Likutey Tefilos* 1:19)

May I eat in great holiness and purity, only in order to maintain my body. May I reduce my inborn desires and make due with only a little food, so that I will resemble those Tzaddikim who eat only to satiate their holy souls, as it is written: "A Tzaddik eats to satisfy his soul." Please, help me eat in such great holiness that I become satiated from the light of my soul, and delight in God – to be satisfied and delight in the pure, holy, and supernal lights. May I merit "beholding the pleasantness of God, and visiting His chambers." And may we fulfill the verse: "God will continually guide you, to satisfy you with the

---

➤ COMMENTARY ○←

before him to eat" (*Bereishis* 24:32-33), and the verse: "And Yosef died... and was *put* in a casket in Egypt" (Ibid 50:26). These are the only two places in the Torah where the word וישם is used.

Apparently, whenever someone offered Eliezer food, he would repent and imagine the day of his death, as Avraham Avinu had taught him to do. (*Rachmei HaAv, Achilah*)

Eating in Holiness

When you eat, imagine that the food is *terumah*, *ma'aser*, or *bechoros*, the tithes which the Kohanim and Leviim ate in great holiness and purity. (*Noam Elimelech, Re'eh*)

Every Jew, even the greatest Tzaddik, must suffer a certain amount of pain each day. Indeed, the deeper his understanding and attachment to God, the greater the pain he must endure. But eating in holiness and with the fear of God can help to sweeten this pain somewhat and prevent it from becoming overpowering. (*Likutey Etzos, Achilah* 20)

Whenever you eat or drink, remember that the taste in your mouth – when you chew and swallow – is the inner holiness and holy sparks of that food, and that by eating, chewing and digesting, you are extracting the food's holiness so that it does not become waste and nourish the "Externalities" (the forces of evil). Then, your soul will derive benefit from the inner holiness [of the food], while the remaining waste will be expelled to the "Externalities." At that moment, you should resolve to relieve yourself as soon as you feel the need, and not allow feces and urine to remain inside your body for even an instant, as they pollute your thoughts and defile your soul.

Furthermore, when you eat, picture the letters מא"כל (*ma'achal* – food) in Ashuris (Torah script), and have in mind that these letters have a numerical value of 91 – the same gematria as the Names Y-H-V-H and A-D-N-Y combined (יאהדונהי).

---→o PRAYERS o←---

purity of your soul" – until we can purify all the levels of our souls, constantly, and be satiated by the Supernal Illumination. (*Likutey Tefilos* 2:5)

May it be Your will, Lord my God, and God of my fathers, to save me from even a trace of anything forbidden, especially that which

---→o COMMENTARY o←---

"How do they separate the First Fruits? A man goes down to his field and sees that a fig has formed. He ties a string around it... and declares 'This is the First Fruit.'" (Mishnah Bikurim 3:1)

I heard from Rabbi Elimelech of Lizhensk [a homiletic interpretation of this statement]: "A man...sees that a fig has formed" – that is, if a burning desire to eat forms within him, he should "tie a string around it." In other words, he should prevent the desire from overwhelming him by remembering that he is mere flesh, and that one day he will be sprouting up grass. (*Maor VaShemesh, Ki Savo*)

Redeeming the Sparks of Holiness

In every created thing, and in all types of food, there are sparks of holiness. These constitute the taste, smell and quality of the food, so that the more sparks that it contains, the better the taste and the smell.... For this reason, it is forbidden for a person to take physical pleasure from

וִיכַוֵּין כְּשֶׁהוּא אוֹכֵל דָּבָר מָה שֶׁהַטַּעַם שֶׁהוּא מַרְגִּישׁ בְּפִיו בִּשְׁעַת לְעִיסָה וּבִשְׁעַת גְּמִיעָה הִיא פְּנִימִיּוֹת הַקְּדוּשָׁה וְנִיצוֹצוֹת הַקְּדוּשָׁה הַשּׁוֹרָה בְּמַאֲכָל אוֹ בְּמַשְׁקֶה הַהוּא, וְעַל יְדֵי הָאֲכִילָה וְהַטְחִינָה בְּשִׁינַיִים וְהָאִצְטְמוּכָא נִבְרָר הַפְּנִימִיּוֹת מֵהַמַּאֲכָל שֶׁלֹּא יֵעָשֶׂה מוֹתָר לְהַשְׁפִּיעַ לְחִיצוֹנִים, וְאָז נַפְשׁוֹ נֶהֱנִית מֵהַפְּנִימִיּוֹת, וְהַפְּסוֹלֶת נַעֲשֶׂה מוֹתָרוֹת וְנִדְחֶה אֶל הַחִיצוֹנִים, וִיקַבֵּל אָז בְּמַחֲשַׁבְתּוֹ שֶׁתֵּיכֶף וּמִיָּד כְּשֶׁיַּרְגִּישׁ שֶׁיִּצְטָרֵךְ לִנְקָבָיו לֹא יִשְׁהֶה אֶת הַפְּסוֹלֶת בְּקִרְבּוֹ לְטַמֵּא חַס וְשָׁלוֹם אֶת מוֹחוֹ וּלְשַׁקֵּץ אֶת נַפְשׁוֹ לְהַשְׁהוֹת אֶת הַצּוֹאָה וְהַשֶּׁתֶן בְּקִרְבּוֹ אֲפִילוּ רֶגַע אֶחָד, וְגַם יְצַיֵּיר לְפָנָיו בִּשְׁעַת אֲכִילָה הָאוֹתִיוֹת "מַאֲכָל" בִּכְתָב אַשּׁוּרִית וְיַהַדְּהֵר שֶׁעוֹלָה צ״א כְּמִנְיָן הוי״ה בְּשִׁילוּב אדנ״י:

———→o PRAYERS o←———

eating and drinking. And save me from all illness, which results from eating and drinking. Let me sort out and reveal all the sparks of holiness that are attached to everything that I eat and drink, and may I draw down light, holiness and blessing into all that I consume. (*Beis Tefilah* 3)

———→o COMMENTARY o←———

them (without a blessing), for do to so is to desecrate something holy, as there is nothing more consecrated than this (*Berachos* 35a).

However, when a Jew makes a blessing on that which is fit for him to eat – with pure intention, spiritual attachment and love and fear of God – he uplifts the holy sparks to their lofty and holy source, and draws down blessing to all the worlds. This is hinted at by the word for "blessing," *bracha*, which is related to the word for "pool," *breicha*. This alludes to the mystery of the stream that draws down blessing to all the worlds.

For that reason, the person making the blessing deserves to eat that particular food or drink, and it becomes his; for he uplifted the holy sparks that are in it to their source, and drew down an even greater amount of beneficence. (*Ohev Yisroel, Naso*)

There is nothing physical in this world whose life-force and vitality do not derive from the holy sparks from the upper worlds. (*Noam Elimelech, Toldos*)

In all that you do, your intention should be for the sake of the Creator. Through this, you redeem the sparks of holiness. (*Noam Elimelech, Behar*)

16 Human beings are created in this world only so that they might break their natural inclinations. Therefore, a person should strive to fix his personality traits when he is eighteen years old, as I will explain.

For instance, a person who is naturally stubborn, should break this trait by doing precisely the opposite of what comes into his mind to do, for forty consecutive days. Similarly, a person who is innately lazy should practice doing everything quickly, for forty days; whether on the way to bed at night or getting out of bed in the morning. He should dress quickly, wash his hands and relieve himself, and, immediately after studying from a *sefer*, go quickly to the synagogue to pray.

───────⇢○ PRAYERS ○⇠───────

Master of the Universe! Living God and King of the world, the Joy of Yisroel: Have mercy on me for the sake of Your Name, and save me from the depression and laziness that ruin me, which have caused me to lose time from Torah study, prayer and so much goodness, and which brought me to what it has brought me. For the holy Sages have told us that the main bite of the Serpent is depression and laziness, may God save us! Have compassion upon me, You, who are full of compassion, and save me from now on from these bites. Grant me life, and I will live. "Bring joy to the soul of Your servant, for to You, O God, I have lifted up my soul. Let me hear joy and gladness; may the bones that you have broken rejoice." May I study Your Torah always, and serve You with alacrity, enthusiasm, and joy; for it is fit to rejoice in Your service and in Your holy Torah, which are our lives and the length of our days, forever – in this world and in the next. Everything else is vanity and without substance, for "What does a man gain for all his labors under the sun?" – aside from Torah, prayer and holy service. (*Likutey Tefilos* 1:128)

───────⇢○ COMMENTARY ○⇠───────

Breaking Negative Traits

A person who wants to break a negative trait should conduct himself in exactly the opposite way. For instance, if he is inclined to anger, he should work on being compassionate. If he is arrogant, he should humble himself completely – one trait contrasting the other. And if he is stingy, which is a terrible trait, he must work to overcome it.

Then, when he fixes his personality traits and can act properly for the rest of his life, he will be happy in this world and fortunate in the World to Come. (*Noam Elimelech, Tzav*)

טז הָאָדָם לֹא נִבְרָא בָּעוֹלָם רַק לְשַׁבֵּר אֶת הַטֶּבַע, לָכֵן יְזָרֵז אֶת עַצְמוֹ לְתַקֵּן מְדוֹתָיו בִּשְׁנַת שְׁמוֹנָה עֶשְׂרֵה דַּוְקָא כְּמוֹ שֶׁאָבֵאֵר, כְּגוֹן מִי שֶׁנּוֹלָד בְּטֶבַע שֶׁל עַקְשָׁנוּת יְשַׁבֵּר אֶת טִבְעוֹ אַרְבָּעִים יוֹם רְצוּפִים לַעֲשׂוֹת דַּוְקָא לְהֵיפֶךְ מִמַּה שֶׁיַּעֲלֶה בְּמַחְשַׁבְתּוֹ, וְכֵן מִי שֶׁבְּטֶבַע עָצֵל יַרְגִּיל אֶת עַצְמוֹ אַרְבָּעִים יוֹם רְצוּפִים לַעֲשׂוֹת כָּל דָּבָר בִּזְרִיזוּת הֵן בְּהוֹלֵךְ לִשְׁכֹּב עַל מִטָּתוֹ הֵן לָקוּם בַּבּוֹקֶר מִמִּשְׁכָּבוֹ הֵן בִּזְרִיזוּת לִבִישַׁת בְּגָדִים וּנְטִילַת יָדַיִם וּלְנַקּוֹת אֶת גּוּפוֹ וְלֵילֵךְ בִּזְרִיזוּת לְבֵית הַכְּנֶסֶת תֵּיכֶף אַחַר קוּמוֹ מֵהַסֵּפֶר וְכַיּוֹצֵא בָּהֶן,

---
→○ PRAYERS ○←

Master of the Universe! Help me acquire holy *zerizus* – to perform every holy act quickly, and never push it off till tomorrow. Especially, when I need to wake up – whether at midnight or in the morning – may I do so with *zerizus*, in holiness. And may I fulfill the words of our Sages: "Strengthen yourself like a lion to get up in the morning to serve your Creator," and "As soon as you awake, you should rise quickly to serve your Maker."

Master of the Universe! Your eyes are upon the faithful. May it be that by getting up quickly in the morning, I strengthen my own faith in You, and spread the faith and knowledge of You to everyone in the world. And through this, may I crown You over my entire body, and over the entire world. (*Tefilos HaBoker, p. 9*)

→○ COMMENTARY ○←

It is impossible to completely break your natural inclinations; instead, you should elevate and sanctify them. For instance, a person who gets angry should redirect his petty and trivial shows of emotion into indignation toward the wicked. The same applies to every trait – it should be redirected toward holiness.

Ultimately, a person will come to such a high level that he is totally divorced from these lower inclinations. His inborn negative qualities will never surface in him again, for everything has been greatly sanctified. (Ibid.)

Improper character traits are the root of all sins. It is because of bad *midos* that a person transgresses God's will. (*Noam Elimelech, Tazria*)

If you want to fulfill a mitzvah perfectly, you must first sanctify and refine your negative traits, such as pride, jealousy, hatred, anger, etc. The more refined your personality, the more valuable will be your mitzvos.

It is impossible for your mitzvos

Likewise, someone who is naturally shy, in a bad way, should train himself to pray in a loud voice and energetically for forty days, in order to fulfill the verse: "All my bones will say, ['O God, who is like You?']" (*Tehilim* 35:10). He should say the blessing over the Torah in a loud voice, doing so until Heaven helps him remove this negative form of embarrassment. Similarly, a person who is unable to speak clearly and concisely should practice listening to his own words for forty days, whether he is speaking of mundane or holy things, and when he is studying [Torah]. This is because practicing anything makes it second nature. So too, someone who by nature is lax in his studies should practice studying more than he normally does, for forty days, and each time he should begin by looking into my *Tzetel Katan*. Thereafter, Heaven will help him break his bad personality traits more and more, until they are gone.

―――――――⟿○ PRAYERS ○⟽―――――――

Acquiring Holy Boldness

Loving God, let me understand how to strike the right balance and go about my life with bold determination, yet without brazen arrogance of any kind. Let me only assert myself for the sake of Your Name, in order to genuinely serve You. Save me from the harsh, bitter torments of hell that are the punishment for insolence. Shameless people ultimately fall into hell without anyone to help them. Merciful God, have pity on me! Save me from any form of brazen arrogance, and from the stubbornness of my body. Inspire me with true holy daring and determination, and give me the courage to stand up against the arrogant people who want to distance others from the truth and demoralize those genuinely seeking to follow the paths of holiness. Let me be bold as a leopard

―――――――⟿○ COMMENTARY ○⟽―――――――

to be free of all dross unless your character is also completely pure. (*Likutey Shoshanim*, at the end of *Noam Elimelech*, "*Ki ner mitzvah*")

Rising Quickly in the Morning

Every God-fearing Jew who seeks to serve Him should rise like a lion each morning, when God returns his soul to him, in order to serve Him in holiness, through Torah study or prayer. We saw how Rabbi Elimelech would awaken with a great shout and declare to himself: "Shame on you for wasting your time sleeping!" (*Ohel Elimelech*, §48, from *Maor VaShemesh, Tetzave*).

וְכֵן מִי שֶׁטִּבְעוֹ בַּיְשָׁן מֵחֵלֶק שֶׁל בּוּשָׁה רָעָה יַרְגִּיל אֶת עַצְמוֹ אַרְבָּעִים יוֹם לְהִתְפַּלֵּל דַּוְקָא בְּקוֹל רָם וְכֹחַ תְּנוּעַת אֵבָרָיו וּלְקַיֵּם כָּל עַצְמוֹתַי תֹּאמַרְנָה, וּלְבָרֵךְ עַל הַתּוֹרָה בְּקוֹל רָם עַד שֶׁיַּעַזְרוּהוּ מִן הַשָּׁמַיִם לְהָסִיר הַבּוּשָׁה הָרַע מִמֶּנּוּ, וְכֵן מִי שֶׁאִמְרֵי פִיו אֵינָם עוֹלִים יָפֶה וּמְסֻדָּר מֵחֲמַת הֶרְגֵּל טִבְעוֹ וּכְלֵי הַדִּבּוּר שֶׁלּוֹ, יַרְגִּיל אֶת עַצְמוֹ אַרְבָּעִים יוֹם לְהַטּוֹת אָזְנוֹ לְהַדִּבּוּרִים הַיּוֹצְאִים מֵאֵלָיו הֵן בְּמִילֵי דְעָלְמָא וְהֵן בְּמִילֵי דִשְׁמַיָּא הֵן בִּשְׁעַת לִימּוּד כִּי הֶרְגֵּל שֶׁל כָּל דָּבָר נַעֲשֶׂה שִׁלְטוֹן, וְכֵן מִי שֶׁטִּבְעוֹ אֵינוֹ מַתְמִיד בְּלִימּוּדוֹ יַרְגִּיל אֶת עַצְמוֹ גַּם כֵּן אַרְבָּעִים יוֹם וְיִלְמוֹד יוֹתֵר מֵהֶרְגֵּל שֶׁלּוֹ וְיִסְתַּכֵּל בְּכָל פַּעַם קוֹדֶם הַלִּימּוּד בְּצֶעטִיל קָטָן שֶׁלִּי וּמִשָּׁם וְאֵילָךְ מִן הַשָּׁמַיִם יַעַזְרוּהוּ לִהְיוֹת מוֹסִיף וְהוֹלֵךְ בִּשְׁבִירַת מִדּוֹת הָרָעוֹת עַד תֻּמָּם:

→○ PRAYERS ○←

against them, and help me overcome them, bringing them down to the dust, breaking and utterly destroying them. Let me always be bold and determined in serving You. (*Likutey Tefilos* 1:22)

Kind and loving God, inspire me with holy boldness so that when I pray I'll always have the courage to throw shyness aside. Don't let me feel embarrassed in front of You. Let me have no inhibitions at all about asking You to bring me to the highest of levels in Your service. Bring me close to You in every way. Work miracles and wonders to raise me up from the lowest degradation to the most exalted levels of holiness. Bring me quickly to the highest levels of holiness until I reach the ultimate perceptions of Your Godliness on the level of the

→○ COMMENTARY ○←

"They seek Me daily and wish to know My ways" (Yeshayahu 58:2).

When a person realizes that the evil inclination will constantly try to ensnare him for the seventy or so years of his life, and that the battle against it will continue for a very long time, he may start to feel heavy and lethargic, for he cannot imagine himself fighting so long and being saved.

The best way to push away this heaviness is by realizing that yesterday is gone and tomorrow is still uncertain. As Ben Sira says (*Yevamot* 63b): "Do not wait for tomorrow, for no one knows what it will bring. Perhaps it will come, but you may no longer be here. It follows that you are concerning yourself with a world that is not even yours."

―――――∘ PRAYERS ∘―――――

true prophets and Tzaddikim, who were always rising from level to level. (*Likutey Tefilos* 1:30)

Guard My Mouth

Compassionate Father! Have mercy on me, and grant me the trait of silence, so that I am careful never to engage in idle chatter, and all the more so, never to say anything that is forbidden. In the merit of Rabbi Shimon ben Gamliel, Rabban Yochanan ben Zakkai, Rabbi Meir, Rav Huna, Rabbi Yitzchak, and Rabbi Yehudah ben Shushan – Tzaddikim who were extremely careful with their power of speech – may I, too, learn this trait and restrain my tongue – other than for words of Torah and prayer. May the words of my mouth and the thoughts of my heart be acceptable to you, God, my Rock and my Redeemer. (*Mishpot Tzedek*, §8)

O God and God of our fathers, help me and guard me from speaking evil. Don't let me ever misuse my power of speech. Don't let a single bad remark about any Jew ever leave my mouth. Don't let me harp on other people's faults. Put it into my heart to always search for all the good and positive points that are to be found in every single Jew, even the most lowly. Let me make every effort to dig down until I find merit even in the most insignificant. Be with me at all times and help me discover something good in everyone. Let me always judge all people positively. Compassionate God, save me from the terrible sin of slander and tale-bearing, which is equal in its severity to the three worst sins in the Torah – idolatry, adultery and bloodshed; for slander is equal to all three of them. (*Likutey Tefilos* 1:38)

―――――∘ COMMENTARY ∘―――――

Actually, the main war against the evil inclination takes place only on a single day. When you wake up in the morning, you should think of yourself as a new creation, with just that day to serve God and avoid the evil inclination. It is not so hard for a person to control himself for only one day. It is easy to serve God enthusiastically for only one day. And when you wake up the next day, you should think the same thing, again. It turns out that for your entire life, you will be serving God only one day at a time, free of all heaviness and lethargy. (*Arvei Nachal, Bereishis*)

Measuring Your Words

A person is unable to concentrate in prayer because of the empty concerns that are rooted in his heart. Silence, on the other hand, greatly enhances one's fear of God; for it is impossible to fear God when one's heart is constantly broadcasting information. (*Likutey Shoshanim*, p. 52)

―――――⇒o PRAYERS o⇐―――――

Becoming Diligent

Help me labor at Your holy Torah constantly, day and night. Open my mind and let my eyes see the light of Your Torah. Grant me a clear, pure intellect with which to study Your holy Torah. Give me a rapid grasp of everything I study. Let nothing in the world have any power to distract me and throw me off course during my study-sessions – whether irrelevant thoughts, or fantasies about the vain pleasures of this world, or confused and distorted ideas about my studies themselves and how to approach them. Help me fight off all such distractions and confusion while studying. Let me rapidly cover plenty of ground with clear understanding. Let me start and finish all the books of the holy Torah, both the Written and the Oral Torah, and go through them again and again many times (*Likutey Tefilos* 1:15)

My King and my God – to You I pray! Please, God, in Your great mercy, save me, so that I may study Your holy Torah, selflessly, with great diligence. May I meditate on Your Torah day and night. And may you be with me always, to help and deliver me, so that the words of the Torah never become base and darkened in my mouth.... Rather, may I study the Torah in great holiness and purity. May I annul all my base physicality while I am studying, in a way that lets me feel in my heart and mind the sweetness, pleasantness, spirituality, the refinement and the depths in Your holy Torah. For You alone know the great sweetness, pleasantness, and spirituality in the words of Your holy and pure Torah, as it is written: "They are more precious than gold, than the finest gold, and sweeter than honey and the "drippings of the honeycomb." (*Likutey Tefilos* 1:111)

―――――⇒o COMMENTARY o⇐―――――

Whoever guards his tongue merits having a holy spirit rest on him, for the less a person talks, the closer he comes to holiness. (Ibid, in the name of *Midrash Pinchas*)

You should speak only about those things that are absolutely necessary for your physical and spiritual well-being. Before you say anything, consider whether it is absolutely necessary, and, if not, don't say it, even if you are in doubt – not until you are sure that you must, such as in matters as obtaining food and drink, etc. (Ibid, in the name of *Maggid Meisharim*)

A person is given a limited amount of words to speak in his life, and if he speaks about mundane things, he uses them up. This is the meaning of: "My soul went out when he spoke" (*Shir HaShirim* 5:6). This is even truer when it comes to speaking things like gossip or slander. (*Derech Pikudecha, mitzvos lo taseh* 34)

⟶○ COMMENTARY ○⟵

Diligence in Torah study

If you want to devote yourself to Torah study unflaggingly, be careful never to speak against a single Jew. Do your best to seek out merit and worth in every Jew. Even if a particular individual seems to you to be wicked, you should still make an effort to find some good points in him. Then he will no longer be wicked! When every Jew is lovely and pleasant in your eyes, you will be able to apply yourself to Torah study continuously. (*Likutey Etzos, Talmud Torah* 69)

The study of the holy Zohar can fill you with enthusiasm for all your Torah studies. The very language of the Zohar is precious and can inspire you to serve God. (Ibid., *Talmud Torah* 70)

Be extremely tenacious in maintaining your daily commitment to Torah study, and be steadfast in not allowing the various situations that arise to cause you to break your schedule. Never forget Rambam's words (*Mishneh Torah, Talmud Torah* 1:5): "Every single Jew, whether rich or poor, healthy or sick, young or aged and infirm, even a pauper who has to

---

17 Whenever you are not involved in Torah study or prayer, you should learn to commit to memory those passages that people need to know by heart, such as *Tikun Rachel* and *Tikun Leah*, *Tefilas HaShov*, the Blessing over the New Moon, *Berich Sh'mei*, *Al HaKol*, and *Modim d'Rabbanan*. You should also think about the positive mitzvah "I will be sanctified..." as written above (section 1).

⟶○ COMMENTARY ○⟵

The Shlah writes (*Sha'ar HaOsiyos*): "I discovered a manuscript from Rabbi Moshe Cordovero, in which he relates that an old man taught him how to nullify [improper] thoughts. One should repeatedly say the following verse: 'A fire shall burn continuously on the altar; it shall not go out' (*Vayikra* 6:6)."

It's clear to me that the old man was Eliyahu HaNavi, though Rabbi Moshe Cordovero did not want to reveal this, in his great humility. Therefore, if a sinful or empty thought enters your mind, be careful to say the verse many times. It seems to me that you should also recite the verse: "I hate those who harbor iniquitous thoughts, but Your Torah I love" (*Tehilim* 119:113). You should say it with fervor, and be as strong as a lion.

I think that it is good for a person to accustom himself to saying these

———⇒○ COMMENTARY ○⇐———

beg for charity, or a man with many family obligations, is required to set fixed times for Torah study, day and night – as it says (*Yehoshua* 1:8): "You shall meditate on it day and night."

There are those who say that the words "to set fixed times" – *keviyut itim* – are related to the verse "For God will... rob those who rob them (*v'kova et koveihim*)" (*Mishlei* 22:23). That is, you should steal time from all of your mundane activities in order to study Torah each and every day. (*Hadracha shel Rabbi S. Tefilinsky*).

The main thing is studying correctly, with full concentration. This means focusing completely on the matter at hand; not looking at the clock or drinking tea, not flipping through seforim, or even noticing your hunger, tiredness, or similar distraction. Your thoughts should be fully concentrated on your study. Your head should be in the Gemara. The hours you study should be full and focused, and you should not spend them like someone who was simply passing through. The main thing is to study what you enjoy, for then you will be able to apply yourself even more to your studies, and find the greatest success, joy and satisfaction. (*Yair Nesivos*, p. 13, in the name of the Rebbe of Gur, shlit"a)

יז בְּכָל עֵת שֶׁהוּא פָּנוּי מֵהַתּוֹרָה וּמֵהַתְּפִלָּה יִלְמוֹד אֶת עַצְמוֹ בְּעַל פֶּה דְּבָרִים הַצְּרִיכִים לוֹ כְּגוֹן תִּיקוּן רָחֵל וְתִיקוּן לֵאָה וּתְפִלַּת הַשַּׁב וּבִרְכַּת לְבָנָה וּבָרִיךְ שְׁמֵיהּ וְעַל הַכֹּל וּמוֹדִים דְּרַבָּנָן, וִיהַרְהֵר בְּמִצְוֹת עֲשֵׂה שֶׁל וְנִקְדַּשְׁתִּי וְכוּ' כַּכָּתוּב לְעֵיל:

———⇒○ COMMENTARY ○⇐———

verses constantly, whenever he is not occupied with studying Torah. Even if other people are around, he can still whisper them – as long as the place is clean, and it is permissible to mention words of Torah there.

I found it written (*Tanna d'Vei Eliyahu Zuta*, chap. 2) that even if a person is not versed in Chumash or Mishnah, but simply sits the whole day and reads the verse: "And Lotan's sister was Timnah" (*Bereishis* 36:22), he still receives rewarded for studying Torah.

It's written in *Yeshuos Yaakov* that there really is no difference between the verse "And Lotan's sister was Timnah" and "*Shema Yisroel*" (as Rambam writes), because every letter of our holy Torah contains awesome and wondrous secrets, as the Zohar and Ramban teach. Certainly, it has the power to purify one's thoughts. (*Birchas Chaim*, chap. 4, §41, 42)

ספר

שני לוחות הברית

זמרות טהורות · מפנינים יקרות · חבור על שתי תורות · בכתב
ובעל פה מגיני מסורות · ערוכות וסדורות · מהגבור בגבורות · איש
האלהי בוצינא קדישא מרא דארעא דישראל · החכם השלם בכל
המדות והחכמות · גלויות וסתומות · הגאון . אשר שפעת יפעת אור
תורתו · זרח בכל התפוצה · מקצה אל קצה · כבוד מהר"ר ישעיה
במהר"ר אברהם הלוי זצ"ל · ממשפחת הורוויץ · הספון וטמון
במנוחתו בארעא קדישא · ונשמתו בגנזי מרומים תחות
כורסיה דעתיקא קדישא:

וברכה לראש משביר · נאור וכביר · בן המחבר · ענף עץ אבות הנשר הגדול בעל
כנפים הפורש כנפיו לתימן שם החכמה והמדע · ותבונה אבן ראשה אבן פנה החסיד
ועניו הגאון הגדול מופת דורנו כמהר"ר שעפטל סג"ל נר"ו · אב"ד ור"מ דק"ק פוזנא
והגליל יצ"ו · אשר נתן לבו ונפשו להביא ספר הנכבד הזה לדפוס להאיר עיני חכמים
באור יקר · המנהיר ומזהיר מזוהר · ספר הקדש הזה כאשר יחזו עיני מישרים · כישאל
איש בתומים ואורים:

ובצל החכמה בצל הכסף הם שלשה מטיבי צער האחים הקצינים בני איש אחד הסגות כהר"ר מנחם מענדל ז"ל אשר
נדבה רוחם והזילו הון יקר מכיסם למלאכת עבודת הקודש מלאכת הדפוס להוציא הספר הקדוש הזה מפעולתיו
תכליתו והמה כוכבים בשמותם על פני הארמה · האחד המיוחד הראש וקצין פרנס ומנהיג הגביר כהר"ר יוסף נר"ו ·
ואחריו יצא אחיו [illegible] בגלמו וברכותו הקצין כהר"ר שלמה נר"ו חותנו של הגאון בן המחבר נר"ו · וחתן האלוף המרומם
המופלג [illegible] ועמודי בני ישיבה דק"ק פוזנא כבוד מהר"ר קאפיל דיין נר"ו והחוט המשולש לא במהרה ינתק רק.
כשנים והולך ברכי וקנים גברא צנועי ומעלי במרות ומעלות האלוף כהר"ר צבי הירש נר"ו · אתה ה' תשלם להם
כפעולתם וצדקתם יעמוד לעד והון ועושר בביתם · ולפניהם יהלוך זכותם בבואם ובצאתם:

[illegible]

[illegible]

TITLE PAGE, FIRST EDITION, SHNEI LUCHOS HABRIS, AMSTERDAM, 1649

The Mitzvah of Kiddush Hashem

*from Shnei Luchos HaBris
by Rabbi Yeshayahu Horowitz*

Blessed are You…
who has sanctified us
with His commandments,
and commanded us to sanctify
His Name in public.

Prayer for Sanctifying God's Name
by the Shlah HaKadosh

You are holy and Your Name is holy, and the holy ones of Israel have always sanctified and hallowed Your Name. They have suffered stoning, burning, beheading, strangulation and every bitter and unbearable form of torture for the sake of Your holy Name and in order to save the Jewish people. Please, O Holy God, if it is Your will that I ever face such a trial, grant me holiness and purity, and let my thoughts and words sanctify Your Name publicly, just as the Ten Holy Martyrs and countless other holy Jews have done. Hashem, my God, You know my innermost thoughts: that I am ready and willing to surrender my flesh and blood to the four types of capital punishment and the worst tortures in the world for the sake of Your unity. For You, Hashem, our God, are the only true Oneness. For the sake of Your holy, true and eternal Torah, and for the sake of Your people Yisroel, a unique nation on earth, a holy and pure nation – answer me, O Hashem, answer me, and let holiness be revealed through me. True and Righteous Judge, our Sages have taught us that whoever wholeheartedly sacrifices his life to sanctify Your Name will not feel the great pain of torture and death. Nevertheless, if I cannot fulfill that criteria, and it does happen, be with me, so that the pain does not cause me to forget You. While suffering, let me rejoice inwardly and grant me the ability to speak and to sanctify You with words of wisdom and understanding, in a way that will be recognized and acknowledged by all. Cleanse me of my sins and transgressions, and set my lot among the martyrs who cling to Your holiness. May the words of my mouth and the thoughts of my heart be acceptable to You, God, my Rock and my Redeemer.

The Mitzvah of Kiddush Hashem
Rabbi Isaiah Horowitz, the "Shlah HaKadosh"

The Commandment

The positive commandment of *Kiddush Hashem* is an expression of faith. It means that a person gives over his life, his soul, and all his possessions to sanctify God's holy Name, as it says: "I will be sanctified among the Children of Israel" (*Vayikra* 22:32). *Kiddush Hashem* occurs when a non-Jew publicly (e.g. before ten other Jews) attempts to force a Jew to transgress his religion and the Jew chooses to die rather than sin (*Sanhedrin* 74b). It applies to all the transgressions of the Torah, and even to the annulment of a Jewish custom, if, through this, the non-Jew seeks to coerce the Jew into denying his religion. Furthermore, in a time of widespread, forced conversions, a person must sacrifice his life even in private (i.e. not before others). The relevant laws are clearly explained in the Talmud [and Halakhic Codes] (*Sanhedrin, Mishneh Torah: Yesodei HaTorah* 5; *Shulchan Aruch, Yoreh Deah*, 157).

By "publicly," I do not mean that ten Jews have to witness the act; for even if it happened privately, and became known only later, it is still considered "among the Children of Israel." Support for this idea can be found in the case of Esther, who was forcibly wed to Achashverus. Even if she was taken to him privately, since the matter became widely known, it was considered as if it happened "among the Children of Israel." [Thus, were it not for the fact that she was a passive participant in the sin, she would have had to sacrifice her life (*Sanhedrin* 74b).]

The Talmud states that "under threat of death, a person may transgress any prohibition of the Torah except for idolatry, incest (and adultery) or murder" (*Sanhedrin* 74a). In these three cases, there is no difference between a time of oppressive decrees or not, or whether the sin is done privately or publicly, or whether the non-Jew's motive is his own enjoyment or to forcibly convert the Jew. Rather, the reason these are singled out lies in the grievousness of the transgressions themselves, and not because God's Name will be desecrated (*Nimukei*

Yosef on *Sanhedrin*). However, the Rambam writes that a person who transgresses any of these three prohibitions does desecrate God's Name, in addition to not having fulfilled the commandment of *Kiddush Hashem*.

The Blessing

It seems to me that if a person is to be killed in a public act of *Kiddush Hashem*, he must make the blessing: "Blessed are You, Hashem, our God, who has sanctified us with His commandments, and commanded us to sanctify His Name in public." This is similar to many other mitzvos over which we recite blessings, as the Tosefta states (*Berachos*, chap. 6): "One who performs a mitzvah should first make a blessing."

On the other hand, there are many positive commandments over which we do not recite a blessing; for instance, "You shall judge justly" (*Devorim* 1:16). This is because, in this case, the plaintiffs might not accept the verdict, or each might forgo his claim against the other, [thereby annulling the mitzvah]. In other cases, we do not make a blessing because the completion of the act depends upon someone else, as in the case of giving charity or *ma'aser oni* to a pauper, or making a convert or widow happy on the Festivals, or selling a non-kosher carcass to a gentile. Since the giver might not be able to complete the act – as in a case where the receiver does not accept the gift – we also do not recite a blessing. Finally, we do not make a blessing over mitzvos that come about as a result of a transgression, such as *chalitza*, which results from transgressing the mitzvah of *yibum*; or the mitzvah of returning a stolen object; or the returning of interest (*Avudraham, Tefilos Shel Chol, sha'ar* 3). Following this logic, there is no reason *not* to make a blessing on *Kiddush Hashem*.

For even if you claim that in the case of *Kiddush Hashem*, the Jew might not end up being killed – either because the prosecutor changes his mind, or because God miraculously saves him, as He did Daniel and his companions – a person would still have to recite the blessing, for at the very moment he hands himself over to death, he sanctifies God's Name [so that whatever happens afterward is irrelevant.]

Initially, it occurred to me that the reason we make no blessing on many of the mitzvos is that the obligation to do so applies only to positive commandments that one must actively seek to fulfill, such as tefillin, circumcision, sukkah, lulav, eating matzah and maror, and so on.

However, a person would not make a blessing over commandments that he is not obligated to actively strive to fulfill. For instance, a person does not have to buy a field in order to fulfill the commandments of *leket, shichechah* and *peyah*. It is only if he already owns a field, that he must fulfill these commandments [doing so without a blessing]. Similarly, a person is not obligated to become a judge, though if he is a judge, he must fulfill the commandment "You shall judge justly." Based on that, one should also not make a blessing on *Kiddush Hashem*, since it may be possible to escape, or to save oneself through bribery.

However, on further consideration, I believe that this reasoning does not apply. After all, we do not recite a blessing over giving charity, even though it is a mitzvah that we should actively pursue and not simply wait for a pauper to approach us. Thus, to explain this exception, we would have to fall back on the Avudraham's principle, that the pauper might not accept the charity, and apply my reasoning only to the other cases; yet that approach seems forced. Furthermore, the Talmud explicitly states that one should actively pursue the mitzvah of *Kiddush Hashem*, as Rabbi Akiva stated (*Berachos* 61b): "My whole life I was distressed over not having the opportunity to fulfill the mitzvah of 'with all your soul' – that is, even if someone takes away your soul." This does not mean that a person must actively put himself in a situation that requires *Kiddush Hashem*; and indeed, that is not the halachah. Nevertheless, in this case there is the element of zeal in mitzvah observance, since his soul longed to be put in a situation where he would be forced to fulfill the mitzvah. Therefore, it is clear that one should make a blessing, since all blessings depend upon sanctification, as it says: "Who has sanctified us...". How, then, could we not make a blessing on the essence of sanctification itself.

I found this explicitly stated by the Kabbalist, Rabbi Menachem Recanati (*Dinei Teshuvah* §70), who writes: "One who is killed for God's honor must make a blessing over the sanctification of His revered and awesome Name, since this is a positive Torah commandment, as it states: 'I will be sanctified among the Children of Israel.'" I was overjoyed that I had, on my own, reached the same conclusion as this great man.

As for the actual wording of the blessing, it seems to me that it should be, "Who has sanctified us with His commandments, and commanded us to sanctify His Name in public (לקדש שמו ברבים)," as opposed to "and commanded us over the sanctification of His Name in public (עַל קִדוּשׁ ה׳ בְּרַבִּים)." Most authorities agree that we say עַל in a blessing when the mitzvah can also be fulfilled through an emissary, but לְ- when the commandment depends upon the person alone, as in the case of sanctifying God's Name.

A Public Sanctification

Finally, we make the blessing over the positive commandment to sanctify God's Name in public, in the presence of other Jews, as it states: "I will be sanctified *among* the Children of Israel." However, no blessing is recited if it does not take place in public, even in the case of forced heresy, murder, incest, or any other transgression (during a period of forced conversion), at which time a person must be ready to die to avoid sinning, and not in sanctification of God's Name.

As for those holy and pure Jews who are tortured in ways more painful than death, to make them confess some act, which would result in great harm to other Jews, no blessing should be made, even if this happens publicly. This is for two reasons. The first is that the commandment to sanctify God's Name only applies when a non-Jew wants to force a Jew to openly transgress the laws of the Torah or Jewish custom. However, even though these people are holy and are on the highest level, they are not being tortured in order to get them to transgress their religion, but only to confess. The second reason no blessing is made is that perhaps they will not be able to withstand the test – how then can they make a blessing? Certainly, such a person will receive great reward; he will be called holy, and will receive honor in the supernal assembly.

The Zohar states (1:124b; 3:195b) that when taking on the yoke of Heaven in *Kerias Shema*, if a person has in mind that he firmly accepts his death for the sake of the holiness of God's Name, then [heaven] considers it as if he actually sacrificed his life., and his act is like the binding of Yitzchak. However, this is only if the person is truly and completely righteous, because any blemish invalidates a sacrifice, [as was the case with the sacrifices offered in the Holy Temple].

I composed a prayer about this, which a person can recite in order to ask God to help him sanctify His Name (see above).

Hanhagos Ha'Adam

Paths to Perfection

These are the things that
you should do and live by.

<small>From the beginning of
The Tzetel Katan</small>

Hanhagos HaAdam
PATHS TO PERFECTION

THESE ARE THE THINGS THAT YOU
SHOULD DO AND LIVE BY:

1 The first thing you should do is study Gemara with Rashi, Tosefos, and other commentaries – based upon your level of understanding. Afterward, continue on to the *halachic* authorities, starting with the *Shulchan Aruch, Orach Chaim*. You should pray to God to help you arrive at the truth; for the sins of your youth can blind you, so that even though you can debate Gemara concepts and instruct others in the law, you will forget it yourself, and not truly observe it. Therefore, you should deeply regret your sins, and spend time alone, before dawn, which is a favorable time to cry repeatedly over the exile of the Shechinah.

───────◦ PRAYERS ◦───────

O God! Please guide me to learn works of *halachah* with great diligence every day, with a comprehending mind and heart, so that I will quickly and properly understand the *halachah* and be able to derive proper conclusions from the holy disputes among the *halachic* masters. May I be blessed with the ability to render *halachic* decisions and thus make peace between them. And as a result, may peace descend and spread throughout the world. And may all Jews be at peace with each other. (*Likutey Tefilos* 1:62)

───────◦ COMMENTARY ◦───────

The Importance of Studying *Halachah*

The evil inclination will never try to convince you to stop studying Torah altogether, for it knows that you will not listen. After all, if you do not study, no one will consider you a scholar. Rather, it convinces you not to study those things that enhance your fear of God, like *mussar* or the *Shulchan Aruch*, which can grant you mastery of the law. Instead, it entices you to spend all your time studying Gemara with all the commentaries. (Baal Shem Tov, *Tzava'as HaRivash* §118)

הנהגות האדם

מהרב המגיד איש אלהי המפורסם
מוהר"ר אלימלך זצ"ל:

אֵלֶּה הַדְּבָרִים אֲשֶׁר יַעֲשֶׂה אוֹתָם הָאָדָם וָחַי בָּהֶם:

א הָרִאשׁוֹן צָרִיךְ הָאָדָם לִלְמוֹד גְּמָרָא וּפֵירוּשׁ רַשִׁ"י וְתוֹסָפוֹת וּמְפָרְשִׁים כָּל אֶחָד לְפִי הַשָּׂגָתוֹ וְהַפּוֹסְקִים אַחֲרֵיהֶם, וּמִתְּחִלָּה יִלְמוֹד שֻׁלְחָן עָרוּךְ אוֹרַח חַיִּים, וְצָרִיךְ לְהִתְפַּלֵּל לְהַשֵּׁם יִתְבָּרַךְ שֶׁיָּבֹא עַל הָאֱמֶת כִּי חֲטֹאת נְעוּרִים שֶׁל הָאָדָם הָרִאשׁוֹן מְסַמְּאִין עֵינָיו שֶׁלֹּא יִרְאֶה אַף שֶׁיָּכוֹל לְפַלְפֵּל וּלְהַגִּיד לַאֲחֵרִים דִּינוֹ אֲבָל הוּא בְּעַצְמוֹ שׁוֹכֵחַ וְלֹא מְקַיְּמָם בֶּאֱמֶת, לָכֵן צָרִיךְ הָאָדָם לְהִתְחָרֵט מְאֹד עַל עֲוֹנוֹתָיו וּלְהִתְבּוֹדֵד עַצְמוֹ קֹדֶם אוֹר הַיּוֹם שֶׁאָז עֵת רָצוֹן לִבְכּוֹת עַל גָּלוּת

⟶ PRAYERS ⟵

O God! I thank you deeply for setting my lot among those who study Torah, and not among those who gather on street corners. May the name of God be blessed and elevated above all blessings and praise! Even if my mouth was filled with song as the sea is full of water, I would not be able to sufficiently praise You for Your overwhelming kindness to me. I am humbled by all Your loving-kindness and by all the truth that You have shown Your servant. May it be Your will, my God and God of my fathers, that just as you blessed us to be among those who study Torah, may You bless us further, our compassionate

---

⟶ COMMENTARY ⟵

Truth Leads to Faith

It is impossible to attain faith except through truth. However, faith only applies to those things that the intellect cannot understand (for if the mind can grasp them, one need not rely on his faith). That being the case, how can one develop true faith, to believe only in that which is proper to believe?

This can only happen by means of truth. That is, by deeply contemplating those very topics that your mind cannot understand, which demand faith alone, you can grasp

You should also spend some time alone during the day. Picture your sins as large as hills and mountains standing before you; for without doing so, you may never remember them. Nor should you do this merely once or twice, but hundreds of times, until God has mercy on you. Pray to Him to lead you on the right path and to teach you His way, so that you do not squander your life. In His great mercy and kindness, God will enlighten you with the light of His holy Torah, so that you can understand it and fulfill it.

―――――⇒○ PRAYERS ○⇐―――――

Father, and grace us, and our children, with wisdom to understand, listen, study and teach, guard and fulfill all the words of Your Torah with love. (*Otzar Tefilos Yisroel*, vol. 3, p. 40).

Prayers for Truth
Master of the World, may we study Your holy Torah a great deal – each and every day – and may we learn many other *seforim* that were written by the holy Sages. Grant me wisdom, understanding and knowledge, until I can understand the true intention of the author of every *sefer* that I study, and not err in grasping his intention, nor interpret it in a strange and inappropriate way, God forbid. (*Tefilos v'Tachanunim*, p. 65)

―――――⇒○ COMMENTARY ○⇐―――――

the truth that these things are worth believing, even though the mind cannot intellectually understand them; such as believing in God, in the holy Torah, and in true Tzaddikim who inspire us to fear God and observe His commandments. Even though, at first, it is impossible to understand these things intellectually (in addition to the fact that all true ideas raise endless questions at first), still, by truly contemplating these things, one arrives at the sense that it is appropriate to believe.

On the other hand, it is forbidden to believe in things that are not based upon the Torah or that do not accord with the understanding of true Tzaddikim. (*Likutey Etzos HaMevu'aros, Emes v'Emunah* 4)

All of your actions and your Torah study should be done sincerely, free of ulterior motives, for even a single drop of ulterior motives can poison your service of God. However, few people are truly free of this. There are many people who practice self-affliction, study Torah and perform good deeds, yet whose actions are invalidated by their hidden, personal agenda, and are thus considered worthless by God. This is like the Gemara's story of the two men who

הַשְׁכִינָה פְּעָמִים הַרְבֵּה עַד אֵין חֵקֶר וְיִבְכֶּה בִּדְמָעוֹת, וְגַם בְּיוֹם לְפְעָמִים יִתְבּוֹדֵד, וְאָז יִרְאֶה בְּעַצְמוֹ שֶׁעָמְדוּ עֲוֹנוֹתָיו נֶגֶד עֵינָיו וְיִזְכּוֹר אֶת חַטֹּאתָיו וַעֲוֹנוֹתָיו וּפְשָׁעָיו כְּהָרִים וּגְבָעוֹת אֲשֶׁר מֵעוֹלָם לֹא זָכַר אוֹתָם אִם עָשָׂה כָּכָה, כָּכָה יַעֲשֶׂה לֹא פַּעַם וְלֹא שְׁתַּיִם וְלֹא מֵאָה פְּעָמִים עַד אֲשֶׁר יְרַחֲמוּ עָלָיו מִן הַשָּׁמַיִם, וְיִתְפַּלֵּל לְהַשֵּׁם יִתְבָּרַךְ שֶׁיַּדְרִיכֵהוּ בְּדֶרֶךְ וְיוֹרֵהוּ דַּרְכּוֹ שֶׁלֹּא יְבַלֶּה יְמֵי חַיָּיו וְאָז הַשֵּׁם יִתְבָּרַךְ בְּרַחֲמָיו וּבְרוֹב חֲסָדָיו יָאִיר עֵינָיו בְּאוֹר תּוֹרָתוֹ הַקְּדוֹשָׁה וְיָבִין וְיַשְׂכִּיל תּוֹכֶן הַדָּבָר לַעֲשׂוֹתוֹ וּלְקַיְּמוֹ:

---→o PRAYERS o←---

Illuminate us with your Torah, so that we may reveal all the levels of interpretation – *peshat, remez, drush* and *sod* – which are bound to our souls. May we arrive at true and original Torah insights, and never err in a matter of *halachah*. May we never declare pure that which is impure, or impure that which is pure; nor rule something to be forbidden, when it is permitted, or permitted, when it is forbidden; nor pronounce guilty one who is innocent, nor innocent one who is guilty. Deliver me from all mistakes, and may I speak only the truth, forever. (*Otzar Tefilos Yisroel*, vol. 3, p. 40)

---→o COMMENTARY o←---

offered Pesach sacrifices (*Nazir* 23a). Both performed the same action; the only difference being their intention – the first did it to fulfill the mitzvah, whereas the other did it to fill his stomach! About this, the verse states: "The ways of God are right; the righteous will walk in them, but transgressors will stumble in them" (*Hoshea* 14:10).

You should pray that all of your actions be only for the sake of God. May He help us serve Him in truth! (*Rachamei HaAv, Emet*)

Admitting the Truth

The drive to always be right prevents a person from admitting the truth. For instance, there are times when a person is unable to acknowledge the validity of another person's position, not because the latter is wrong, but because his own pride and reputation is at stake. Such as person will not admit to the truth even if you explain it to him and try to convince him numerous times. Therefore, if you truly desire the truth, you must rid yourself of the urge to always be right. Then you will be able to see the truth – provided that is what you truly want. (*Likutey Etzos HaMevu'aros, Emes v'Emunah* 33)

PRAYERS

I believe with perfect faith that by toiling in the holy Torah, I will find the hidden light within it – for the sake of Your blessed Name. [O God], illuminate my darkness, so that I can find and follow the path of truth. Behold, I bind my soul to the souls of all the Tannaim and Amoraim, and of all the Tzaddikim, through whom these words of Your Torah were revealed. I bind myself to the soul of the Tzaddik of this generation, whose soul includes the souls of all Yisroel, as well as to the souls of all the true Tzaddikim – both revealed and hidden – who understand the mystery of Torah study, and know how to unite Your holy Names. And I bind myself to the souls of all the Torah scholars who study Your Torah selflessly, and to the souls of all Yisroel, both the great and the small. (*Otzar Tefilos Yisroel*, vol. 3, p. 32)

Private Prayer

Please, God, help me spend time alone in dialogue with You, and may I fulfill the verse: "Arise, cry out in the night, at the beginning of the watches! Pour out your heart like water before the presence of God." Send me holy, heartfelt and inspiring words, full of holy longing and desire for You, until I cry profusely, like a child cries to his father. Help me, when I pray alone and beseech you, to remove all the irrelevant and distracting thoughts of the world from my heart. (*Tefilos v'Tachanunim* p. 77)

COMMENTARY

Regretting Your Sins

Each night, before going to sleep, you should review all your actions of the day, and admit and confess [your mistakes]. The Zohar calls this being a "master of self-accounting." The idea is alluded to in the verse: "The night will be for our watch and the day for work" (*Nechemiah* 4:16). The word "watch," *mishmar*, is related to *mishamer*, which is a type of strainer used to filter wine. Daytime was created for serving God. There is no time then to think about one's low state, and doing so can make a person depressed. In the nighttime, however, when the work is done, a person can sift through and review all of his actions. (*Sur MeRa*, p. 40)

The best time for being alone, meditating, and truly repenting is after midnight. You should rise and beseech God on behalf of your soul, which has fallen far from the Source of Life and become coarse through its involvement in physicality. Speak to God like a servant petitioning his master, or a son pleading of his father. Beg Him for forgiveness, and pray to Him in your own language for whatever you need. Ask God to help you serve Him and to fear Him honestly and sincerely. (*Birchas Chaim*, chap. 10, §10)

⟶○ PRAYERS ○⟵

Loving God, bring me, my children, my children's children and all the Jewish people to speak directly to our Maker, each one of us in our own words, in order to arouse our hearts to heavenly fear. Help us express out thoughts and feelings to You every day in our own native language and appeal for Your compassion. Let us find words that will arouse Your favor and conciliate You. Let us use the strongest pleas and arguments we can, and speak with passion and grace, until we succeed in attaching our hearts to the holy point within us, the "ruling Tzaddik." Let us spend plenty of time each day in these prayers and conversations, and offer many fervent pleas, supplications, confessions and the like, every single day. Let us be extremely persistent with out prayers, and give You no quiet until You show us kindness. We'll call You until You answer us, until Your true love for us is aroused, and we win You over with our prayers and supplications, causing You to shine Your face on us again, show us kindness, and bring us to complete repentance with all our hearts and souls. (*Likutey Tefilos* 1:34)

Hashem, my God and the God of my forefathers, help me always sanctify my speech. Every day, may I speak many holy words of Torah and prayer, making requests of You and praising Your great and holy name. May I study a great deal of Torah, and speak many words of prayer and supplication to You every day. May my mouth never cease uttering words of Torah, prayer, supplications, and songs of praise to Your great and holy Name. May words of Torah and prayer be all

---

Learning Halachah

Every Jew must spend a portion of his day studying the legal codes. This applies under all circumstances. It is a very serious matter, and no one should ever miss his daily session. Even in an emergency, when he has no time, or when a person is traveling, he should still learn at least one paragraph of the *Shulchan Aruch*, even from a different chapter than the one he has reached in his regular daily study routine. Do not let a single day of your life go by without studying something from the *Shulchan Aruch*. Under normal circumstances, when you are not under pressure, go through each of the four sections of the Shulchan Aruch in turn, until you have finished them all. Then go back to the beginning and start again. Follow this practice all your life. It is a great remedy for all the damage caused by sin. The study of the legal codes sifts the good from the bad, and is the ultimate remedy (*Likutey Etzos, Talmud Torah* 62).

———◦ PRAYERS ◦———

that I speak of the entire day. May I confess my sins to You every day, completely and in detail. And may I spend a great deal of time in private prayers to You, until my holy words will help me remember the truth, and return me to You with all my heart. (*Likutey Tefilos* 1:80)

Enlighten Our Eyes with Your Torah

O God! Let me subordinate myself to You in complete truth. Do not let the least hint of pride or arrogance come into my heart or my mind. Cleanse me of motives of trying to impress others and win their

---

2 You should be careful to avoid the following things: Flattery, falsehood, mockery, gossip, jealousy, hatred, competitiveness, anger, arrogance, looking at women or spending too much time talking to them. The latter applies even to one's own wife, [and all the more so, to someone else's wife, as it says in *Pirkei Avos* 1:5]. One should especially avoid spending too much time talking to one's wife during her period of *niddah*..

———◦ PRAYERS ◦———

Prayers to be Saved from Speaking Falsehood

Help me follow the path of truth at all times. Let me never allow a false word to leave my mouth, not even by mistake or unintentionally. Let me always tell the truth. Bind my heart to You, so that I will always be able to direct my mind and my thoughts to the absolute truth, and help me from Heaven to walk the path of truth at all times. Let me not stray from the path of truth in any way, neither to the right nor to the left. "Direct me in Your truth, and teach me that You are the God of my salvation. In You I have hoped all the day. Send Your light

———◦ COMMENTARY ◦———

Avoiding Mockery

Other people can greatly interfere with one's service of God, especially when they are sarcastic. For this greatly prevents a person from finding the truth. There is also a certain sarcasm found even among those who seem religious. This is as harmful as philosophy. This sarcasm is literally the same as philosophical skepticism. It can even be worse, since most Jews recognize the dangers of philosophy and avoid it. They know that it can drag them down into the deepest pit. But Jews are not so heedful of avoiding sarcasm and sophistication when it emanates

PRAYERS

admiration. Let me come to genuine humility, and let Your glory be magnified, sanctified and elevated through me. Help me speak radiant words of Torah, and let the words of the Torah shine for me and help me emerge from my low level. Let the words of the Torah throw light on all the areas of my life where I need to repent, so that I will come to make complete amends for all my sins and transgressions, and for all the disrespect I have shown to Your great glory from my childhood until the present. Grant that I should be able to rectify everything in my lifetime, and help me advance constantly from level to level. (*Likutey Tefilos* 1:11)

ב אֵלֶּה הַדְּבָרִים צָרִיךְ לִיזָּהֵר מֵחֲנוּפָה וּמִשְׁקָרִים וְלֵצָנוּת וְלָשׁוֹן הָרָע וְקִנְאָה וְשִׂנְאָה וְתַחֲרוּת וְכַעַס וְגַאֲוָה וּמִלְהִסְתַּכֵּל בְּנָשִׁים וּמִלְהַרְבּוֹת שִׂיחָה עִם אִשָּׁה אֲפִלּוּ עִם אִשְׁתּוֹ אָמְרוּ וְכוּ' וּבִפְרָט בְּעֵת נִדָּתָהּ צָרִיךְ לְהַרְחָקָה:

PRAYERS

and Your truth: they will guide me and bring me to Your mountain of holiness and to Your sanctuary. Do not take the truth away from my lips in any way, because I have put my hope in Your judgements." (*Likutey Tefilos* 1:9)

Avoiding Improper Speech

In Your great compassion, help me internalize the character of Yaakov, which is the aspect of truth, so that I will always speak words of truth and never lie, accidentally or on purpose, against my will or willingly. Guard me from ever telling a lie, even by mistake. Keep me as far from falsehood as possible. As the verse states: "Distance

COMMENTARY

from people who appear to be religious. This makes it all the more dangerous.

There are people who seem religious and disguise all their sarcasm in the language of truth. People do not avoid them, thinking that they are on the right path. These are the ones who can cause the most harm, frustrating and confusing one who truly wants to serve God.

Happy is the man who walks the true path, avoiding all sophistication. "He who walks in integrity, walks securely" (*Mishlei* 10:9). He will follow the simple and sincere path of our forefathers. (*Sichos Ha-Ran* §81)

———→o PRAYERS o←———

yourself from falsehood." Help me be the embodiment of truth in all things, so that I will walk on the path of truth and speak truth in my heart, without wavering and without turning aside from the core of truthfulness. (*Likutey Tefilos* 1:47)

Please God, save me from malicious slander, worthless pursuits, pride and their offshoots. Hashem, loving God, help me to speak in such a way that everything I say will only be for the sake of Your Name and Your service. Let me never engage in idle talk, but let all my words be words of Torah, service of God and awe of Heaven. In particular, save me and all Your people, the House of Yisroel, from the sin of malicious slander and talebearing, which is serious in the extreme. Let me never say a single bad word about any Jew in the world. "My God, guard my tongue from evil and my lips from speaking slyly." Save me from slander and talebearing, and anything which has even the faintest hint of them, from now on and forever. (*Likutey Tefilos* 1:4)

———→o COMMENTARY o←———

Avoiding Jealousy

Our Sages instituted the following optional prayer (at the end of the *Amidah*): "May I not become jealous of others, and may they not become jealous of me." The question is: Why should I pray over other people's jealousy, more than any other negative trait they may have? The answer lies in the fact that sometimes *our own* actions are the cause of jealousy in others. We must therefore pray not to cause others to stumble [in transgression], since the Torah states: "Do not place a stumbling block before of the blind" (*Vayikra* 19:14).

It is proper for a person and his family not to wear overly fancy clothing, or eat excessively sumptuous meals, or the like, so as not to arouse people's jealousy. A person whom God has blessed with wealth and property should show generosity to both the rich and the poor by always treating them kindly and gently. (*Orchos Tzaddikim, Sha'ar HaKinah*)

Even though jealousy is a reprehensible trait, there are times when it has a positive aspect. For instance, it is good to be jealous of another person's level of piety. Similarly, if you see someone who studies Torah the entire day, you should become jealous and say: "If he can do it, then so can I." You should be jealous of your friends' mitzvos and good traits, and try to copy them. You should even be jealous of the good traits of a sinner, and try to emulate them. (Ibid.)

PRAYERS

Master of the whole universe, have mercy on me for Your sake, and always be with my mouth when I speak. Help me guard the gates of my mouth so that not a hint of slander about any Jew should ever leave my lips. Let me never say anything improper. Save me from every kind of evil talk – slander, talebearing, idle chatter, mockery, flattery and falsehood. Don't let me tell secrets that are not supposed to be revealed. Keep me from using foul language. Don't let me ever speak about Torah and devotion at the wrong place and time. Let me never say anything that is not good, and save me from breathing a word that demeans the holy power of speech, which is the breath of the mouth of the Holy One, blessed be He. (*Likutey Tefilos* 1:38)

COMMENTARY

Damaging One's Livelihood

Anger can make a person lose his money. When a person gets angry, he spoils the blessing of wealth that was due to come to him. He causes a stain upon his good name and, indeed, his very soul. But when a person holds his anger back and behaves patiently even in the most trying of circumstances, he attains wealth, a good name and an unblemished soul. All the other souls yearn to be merged with his soul and he can succeed in drawing many souls closer to God. Through this the glory of God is revealed. (*Likutey Etzos*, *Ka'as* 9)

Against Pride

Do not be proud over the fact that you pray with concentration, or serve God on a level approaching that of our forefathers. For if God weren't helping you, you wouldn't be able to do anything. (*Hanhagos HaTzaddikim m'Rabbi Mendel m'Linsk*, 27)

"Can a man hide in secret places and I – I will not see him?" says the Lord. (Yirmiyahu 23:24)

That is, a person can sit in a secluded place, studying Torah and praying the entire day, yet still be doing it for the sake of his "I". If he thinks to himself, "I am a scholar," "I am a Tzaddik," "I am pious," then God responds: "I will not see him." As Chazal said (*Arachin* 15b): "God and an arrogant person cannot dwell in the same place." (*Ohr Elimelech*, §26)

Is it possible for a person to remain humble when speaking with a sinner – someone he knows to be im-

PRAYERS

Refraining from Anger

Hashem, my God and God of my fathers! Good and loving God, help me! Guard and protect me from all anger, temper and resentment. Even if I do start to become angry at times, have pity on me and keep me from doing anything vicious out of anger. Help me break my anger, and instead show love and kindness. Help me control my impulses and break my temper, and turn anger into love. Let me make a point of acting kindly where I might have wanted to show anger. Don't let me have a strange god inside me, and don't let me worship idols – because if a person becomes angry, it is considered as if he worshipped idols. (*Likutey Tefilos* 1:18)

Master of the Universe: You know how hard it is to break this evil trait of anger and resentment. Once my anger starts to burn, I'm no longer in my right mind. It is so hard to put out the fire of anger and suppress it. Take pity on me for Your Name's sake, and *You* help me! Guard me and protect me at all times. Help me break this trait and totally remove all anger and resentment from within me. Let me never ever become angry or resentful. Let me always be good to everyone, from now on and forever. (*Likutey Tefilos* 1:18)

COMMENTARY

moral, dishonest or treacherous? After all, the person himself is clean of these transgressions.

The answer is yes – if the person realizes that the many small sins that he has carelessly committed throughout his life may add up to far larger sins than those committed by the person standing in front of him.

For instance, the Rambam says that "if a person gets angry, it is as if he worshipped an idol." When a person recalls how many times he's become angry and so "worshipped idols," he will remain humble. (*Sur MeRa*, p. 30)

One should fulfill Chazal's words: "Be humble of spirit before all men" (*Pirkei Avos* 4:4). That is, every individual, according to his spiritual level, should carefully examine himself to see if he is serving God properly in the fierce battle of prayer with *kavanah* (concentration). He should pour out his soul to God with all his might, to the point of exhaustion, and wage war against his body and his animal soul, which impede his devotion.

Similarly, one should make blessings over food with total concentration, and study Torah far beyond his desire or custom to do so. The same applies to the other commandments, especially in monetary affairs, such as giving charity and the like. And it particularly applies to the Torah's verses: "You shall be holy" (*Vayikra* 19:2) and "Sanctify yourselves" (Ibid. 20:7), which means sanctifying oneself even in that which is permissible. (*Sefer HaTanya* chap. 30)

PRAYERS

Guarding Your Eyes

Master of the World, let me completely shut my eyes to this world. May I take control over my eyes and not gaze at the vanities of this world at all. Save me, especially, from staring at things that could arouse in me improper thoughts, God forbid. May I fulfill the verse: "Do not follow after your heart and after your eyes." Rather, may I rule over my eyes, and use them to look only at your holy Torah. May my eyes and heart gaze and long only for God and His holy Torah, and may I not follow after my heart and my eyes. May I not gaze at this world so much as the batting of an eye. But may my eyes look toward You alone. (*Tefilos HaBoker*, p. 65)

O God! Rescue me from blemished gazing. Sanctify my eyes always, so that I will no longer look at anything that impairs my vision, but instead look only at Your Torah, at Your true Tzaddikim, and at everything that sanctifies my eyes, until they will always be truly holy and pure. May I quickly rectify all of the blemishes that I caused with my eyes. Help me in Your compassion, and guard me from the flaw of the sense of sight, Heaven forbid. May the light of my eyes never grow dim. "Even in old age and white hair, do not abandon me." Guard the light of my eyes always, so that I will meditate in Your Torah day and night. Chase sleep away from my eyes, and may I not suffer as a result any damage or sensitivity to my eyes, but may they shine like the sun and moon. (*Likutey Tefilos* 1:51)

Tips for Guarding Your Eyes

I received a tradition from Tzaddikim that if a person happens to see something improper, which may arouse his desire, he should immediately make a vow of some sort. This will save him and weaken the force of his desire. (*Igra d'Pirka*, §104)

I saw in the writings of the Arizal, that if a person unintentionally sees an immodest woman, he should turn away and spit on the ground. This will save him from improper thoughts. It is why Rabbi Akiva spat when he happened across the wife of Tornos Rufus. (*Devash l'Fi, ma'areches* 100:39)

If a person is concerned about walking in the street and seeing something that will awaken in him improper thoughts, he should say the following: "Behold, their valiant ones cry without; the ambassadors of peace weep bitterly" (*Yeshayahu* 33:7). This will save him from the seeing anything indecent. (*Sefer HaMidos, Reiyah* 9)

3 You should constantly be aware of the fact that one day you will die. Do not interrupt your study of Gemara or other *seforim* [to discuss irrelevant things]. This is in order not to transgress Chazal's words: "One who interrupts his Torah study to indulge in idle gossip will be fed glowing coals of juniper, as it is said (*Iyov* 30:4), 'They pluck salt-wort with wormwood; and the roots of juniper are their food'" (*Chagigah* 12b). You should pray to God that all of your studying be *lishmah* – for the sake of God.

───────◦ PRAYERS ◦───────

My Father in Heaven, be my help always. Let my soul rule over my body, and may I purify and sanctify my soul and my body with every type of purity and holiness. In Your great compassion, raise me above the level of mere animal existence, and help me reach the level of a real human being. Raise me from body to soul, from the physical to spiritual, from matter to form, from darkness to light, from forgetfulness to memory. Bless me with the power of memory, so that I always remember all the words of Your Torah and Your service. Help me to remember always that one day I will die, and may I take to heart the reason I came into this world and what will happen to me when I reach my end. May I never forget this my entire life, but remember it each and every day. For the days of our lives are all vanity, like a momentary dream and a passing shadow, like a fading cloud and a passing breeze. For it is impossible to escape death, in any way. (*Otzar Tefilos Yisroel*, vol. 3, p. 220, in the name of *Sefer Kedushah*)

───────◦ COMMENTARY ◦───────

Prayers for One's Children

A father and mother should constantly pray that their children grow up to study Torah; that they become Tzaddikim and virtuous individuals. You should focus on this specifically when you says the blessings over the Torah, and the words "May we, and our children, and our children's children study Torah…." Similarly, you should think about this during the blessing "*Ahavah Rabbah*" (before *Kerias Shema*), and when you say the words "so that we do not toil in vain" (in "*u'Vo l'Tzion*"). (*Shnei Luchos HaBris, sha'ar ha-osiyos* 4)

It is proper for every person to beseech God for his material and financial needs in the prayer "*Elokai, netzur…* " (at the end of the *Shemoneh Esrei*); that he, his children and all his descendents will always study

ג וְיִזְכּוֹר תָּמִיד יוֹם הַמִּיתָה, וּכְשֶׁיִּלְמוֹד גְּמָרָא אוֹ שְׁאָר סְפָרִים לֹא יִפְסוֹק שֶׁלֹּא יַעֲבוֹר עַל דִּבְרֵי חֲכָמֵינוּ זִכְרוֹנָם לִבְרָכָה שֶׁדָּרְשׁוּ עַל "הַקּוֹטְפִים מָלוּחַ עֲלֵי שִׂיחַ", וְיִתְפַּלֵּל לְהַשֵּׁם יִתְבָּרֵךְ שֶׁיִּלְמוֹד תּוֹרָה לִשְׁמָהּ:

———→∘ PRAYERS ∘←———

"I will recall my song even at night. I will speak in my heart as my spirit searches. At night I recall Your name, O God, and keep Your Torah. I recall the works of God; I recall Your wonders from the beginning. I recall the days of old; I consider all of Your deeds. I speak of the work of Your hands. When my spirit is faint, I recall God. And when my spirit recalls, it bows down within me."

I tell myself: "Remember! Don't forget that there is a World to Come. Nothing in this world is permanent. Everything passes by like the blink of an eye, a passing shadow, scattered dust, a drifting cloud, a blowing wind and a fleeting dream. The essence of life and permanence, the essence of a person's dwelling place, exists only in the World to Come. Be good to yourself, and maintain this awareness. Every day, be aware of the World to Come. Do not forget it. In your thoughts, cling to the World to Come. Look at yourself and calm your mind. Consider what you will do when your end comes as swiftly as the blink of an eye. I feel sorry for you, my friend. Wake up from the sleep of your temptations. Have pity on your soul. 'Recall your Creator in the days of your youth.'" (*Likutey Tefilos* 1:54)

———→∘ COMMENTARY ∘←———

Torah, and that all his offspring will be true servants of God; that they will be successful in Torah, be delivered from sin, and all be holy, without blemish. (*Mishnah Berurah* 122:8)

There was a certain Kohen who had a great fear of God, though he hid it and performed all of his good deeds in secret. He had ten children; six boys and four girls. Each and every day, he would bow down to the ground in prayer and beg God for mercy – until his face became soiled from the earth. All of this was in order that his children never stumble in sin or some other despicable action. (*Menoras Zahav, Bereishis* 11, citing *Tanna d'Vei Eliyahu*)

A person should pray each and every day that he, his children, and all his descendents should find God-fearing, Torah-loving and kind-hearted spouses. About these three traits, it is said: "A three-strand rope is not

---o PRAYERS o---

I come to You, Hashem, my God and the God of my fathers, to cast my prayer before You. I raise my eyes to You and ask You to help me constantly maintain my awareness of the World to Come. Cause my thoughts to cling only to the World to Come – in general, and in every detail. Every day when I wake up, as soon as I open my eyes, may I immediately recall the eternal world and not this world, which is vain, empty and without substance–"a passing vanity; all is vanity."

There is no advantage to anyone in all of his efforts in the matters of this world. The only meaningful purpose and goodness is found in constantly trying to reach the World to Come. Help me attain this holy awareness and help me maintain this awareness in every detail, in all of the hints that You send me at every moment, which teach me how to come close to You, so that at every moment I will know where I stand in the world. (Ibid.)

Uninterrupted Torah Study

Enlighten me to see the truth and to reach the truth of the Torah. May I never err in matters of *halachah*, and may my friends never err. May I invest my whole mind and heart into the truth of Torah, and may I never interrupt my studies with unrelated discussions or unnecessary thoughts. May my studies ascend and be pleasing to You. And may You consider them as having been offered with every possible good intention that one can have during the study of the holy Torah. (*Otzar Tefilos Yisroel*, vol. 3, p. 32)

---o COMMENTARY o---

easily broken" (*Koheles* 4:12). Their numerical values hint to their connection, in that *yirat* (יראת, fear of), Torah (תורה), and *gemilus chasadim* (גמילות חסדים, kindness) all have the same numerical value – 611. (*Sefer Chasidim* §156)

Torah Lishmah

There are three aspects to serving God. The first is selfless Torah study (*lishmah*). Chazal, however, also permit us to study Torah *lo lishmah* – with ulterior motives, as they said: "A person should always study Torah, even with ulterior motives (such as for honor and prestige, for the study of Torah even for selfish reasons will eventually bring one to study it selflessly" (*Pesachim* 50b).

Thus, even if you have not yet reached the level of selfless Torah study, you should not give up, for a person can not reach this level easily. It requires great effort in the service of God, and refined character traits. (*Noam Elimelech*, *Bereishis*).

⟶○ PRAYERS ○⟵

God, how can I approach You after all the love and kindness You have shown me? You have given us the Torah of truth and planted within us eternal life. The kindness You have shown us is for all eternity. God, arouse Your love for me. Just as You had mercy on us and lovingly gave us Your holy Torah – that hidden treasure, that daily joy – so too, help me and allow me to constantly immerse myself in Torah study for its own sake. Let me pay no attention whatsoever to the vanities of this world. Let my only desire be for Your Torah. Let me meditate on Your Torah day and night. Let me conduct all my studies in holiness and purity, and let my only motivation be to study Torah for the sake of Your great and holy Name and to cause You delight. Bring me to study, teach, observe, practice and fulfill all the teachings of your Torah with love. Let the light of the holy Torah shine upon me. Let my study and contemplation of the Torah take me from darkness to light, and bring me to repent and come to perfect *teshuvah*. As our Rabbis said: "The radiance of the Torah has the power to bring people back to good." (*Likutey Tefilos* 1:12)

⟶○ COMMENTARY ○⟵

When a person studies Gemara at night, a thread of loving-kindness is drawn down over him so that he can free himself of all his impure motives for studying Torah, such as the desire for recognition, etc. (*Likutey Etzos, Talmud Torah* 7)

The Greatness of Torah Study

Even if a person learns and forgets, it is still very good. In the World to Come he will be reminded of everything he learned, even if he forgot it. Still, it is certainly better if one can remember all the words of the Holy Torah. (*Likutey Etzos, Talmud Torah* 79)

If a person labors in Torah even without understanding what he is studying, it is still very good. All the words rise up to the higher worlds, and God takes joy in them and makes them into "willows of the brook". (Ibid. 50)

The Importance of Diligence

One has to literally steal time from one's business and other activities in order to study Torah. Even someone who is burdened with many obligations and duties cannot be so pressed that it is impossible for him to snatch some period each day to devote to Torah. (Ibid. 61)

4 You should study ethical works every day, in awe and fear, [such as] *Reishis Chochmah*, or *Shnei Luchos HaBris*, or *Chovas HaLevovos*.

━━━━━━━━⇢∘ PRAYERS ∘⇠━━━━━━━━

O God! Have mercy on me, and help me reach the gates of light, wisdom and knowledge that the Tzaddikim opened in their wondrous goodness, by constricting and lowering themselves, and clothing their awesome consciousness in numerous garments, which are the teachings that they revealed to us in their holy and awesome books.

Help me study their books all the days of my life. May I lovingly study, teach, practice and actualize every word of their teachings. (*Likutey Tefilos* 1:69)

━━━━━━━━⇢∘ COMMENTARY ∘⇠━━━━━━━━

Studying in Awe and Fear

I myself saw how the Tzaddikim of our and previous generations devoted their entire lives to studying the written and oral Torah, and to serving God with tremendous self-sacrifice. Their awesome fear of God and His glory was evident in their every movement. Their physical self-denial and whole-hearted search for God made them famous throughout the world. This is the path that every person who searches for God and desires to serve Him should follow. (*Maor VaShemesh, Nitzavim*)

Studying with Humility

God's greatest pleasure is when a person studies *halachah* with great humility. (*Noam Elimelech, Korach*)

The Torah protects and delivers a person. However, this is only when a person is humble, which means not studying Torah for the sake of honor or pride.

Ideally, a good deed should cause the impure forces to fall away. However, if some foreign influence is intermingled with your Torah study, God forbid, then the good deed will also fall away, and will not achieve anything. (*Noam Elimelech, Ki Seitze*)

Studying *Mussar*

Studying *mussar* will grace you with humility, which is the finest of all traits. And since one mitzvah leads to another, you will also come to study and keep the Torah selflessly, which is the very goal of being human. (*Birchas Chaim*, chap. 10, §33)

ד וְיַעֲסוֹק בְּאֵימָה וּבְיִרְאָה בְּאֵיזוֹ סִפְרֵי מוּסָר בְּכָל יוֹם בְּרֵאשִׁית חָכְמָה וּשְׁלֵ"ה וְחוֹבַת הַלְּבָבוֹת:

→o COMMENTARY o←

"Come, my children, listen to me; I will teach you the fear of God" (Tehilim 34:12). A person must make inviolable commitments in his life, for everything depends upon this. And the primary commitment should be to studying Torah, which means, especially, devoting an hour or half an hour each day to *mussar*.

This is like a life-saving medication that must be taken daily – a dose in the morning and a dose at night. If doctors were to claim that a certain medicine benefits a person physically, everyone takes it, even at a cost. Well, my prescription, too, is life-saving in this world; since it keeps a person from running after luxuries and becoming too pampered, and thus preserves his health.

However, its main benefit lies in the eternal life that it bestows. Thus, you should observe it conscientiously. There are many *mussar seforim* available. Afterward, you should study [other areas of] Torah, which can uproot your evil inclination and protect you. You should also make for yourself restrictions. For instance, a person who sinned with women should avoid their company, etc.

The most effective practice is admonishing a friend whom is behaving improperly. "My brother, what you are doing is wrong," you should tell him. "You will fall, and be unable to stand in God's judgment." Of course, once you have warned him, you can humble yourself as well. "Seeing that I've admonished my friend about this, how can I do it myself?" Then you will regret and cease your actions, and return to God, who will heal you. (*Ya'aros Devash*, part 2, *drush* 1)

Learning Mussar

Our Rabbis have told us to learn *mussar* that is drawn from the Torah, for it leads to study Torah amidst feelings of repentance and humility. This type of study annuls the evil inclination; as the Zohar says, that humility annuls the evil inclination. R. Yosef Karo's *maggid* also told him to study *mussar*, and so should every person. In doing so, one discovers its benefits and experiences a spiritual awakening.

True Torah study always has a little bit of *mussar* mixed in with it, in order to become humble and awaken one's fear of God. For this is the goal of the Torah, as it is written: "The beginning of wisdom is the fear of God" (*Tehilim* 111:10), and, as the Sages taught, " One whose fear of sin takes precedence to his wisdom, his wisdom endures (*Pirkei Avos* 3:9). (*Birchas Chaim*, chap. 10, §31)

5 You should occasionally study a little of the Arizal's writings, though it should be done with awe, reverence and the fear of God. The earlier generations had holy souls, and were protected from all types of sins from their youth. Their souls were qualified to study this wisdom. Today, however, our sins have made our bodies foul and dense, and we must purify and cleanse ourselves from all sins and refine our souls. You should realize that if you purify your soul to the point that your evil inclination no longer entices you to foolishness and vanities, as it did once, you will be able to study these teachings [of the Arizal] whenever you desire. If you truly and sincerely sanctify your thoughts, God will open for you the gates of wisdom to the writings of the Arizal. This is not the case, however, if you are still enticed by physical desires for fleeting vanities. Then you will find it very difficult to study this material.

PRAYERS

O God! May You, in Your great and powerful love and compassion, illuminate my eyes in Your Torah, and open my heart so that I can understand well, and very quickly, whatever I learn – to truly grasp the words of Torah. May I learn all the books of Your holy Torah, each day – the Tanach and Gemara, legal authorities and commentators, all the Midrashim, the Zohar and *Tikunim*, all the writings of the Arizal, and all the writings of the true Tzaddikim in our time. May I finish them, and review them from the beginning, many times, all the days of my life. Have mercy upon us for the sake of Your Name. May I study Your holy Torah diligently, for it is our life, and the length of our days, and in it we meditate day and night. May we kill ourselves over the Torah, until it becomes ours permanently. May we break, annul and kill all the evil desires and bad traits in our bodies, so that we can labor at and delve into the Torah in truth. (*Likutey Tefilos* 1:110)

COMMENTARY

The Greatness of the Zohar

To this end, I seek the welfare of my friends and companions, that they should tremble at the word of God and set aside regular times for studying the Zohar... For it contains great *mussar*, and can transform a person into a vessel for the Shechinah. It awakens those who slumber, and removes their heart of stone. It can save a person from the

ה וְלִפְעָמִים יִלְמֹד בְּאֵימָה בִּמְעַט אֵיזֶה כְּתָבִים כְּתָבִים מֵהָאֲרִ"י זֵכֶר צַדִּיק לִבְרָכָה לְחַיֵּי הָעוֹלָם הַבָּא וְכָל זֶה בְּאֵימָה וּבְיִרְאָה וּפַחַד ה', בְּדוֹרוֹת הָרִאשׁוֹנִים הָיוּ נִשְׁמוֹתֵיהֶם נְשָׁמוֹת קְדוֹשׁוֹת וְהָיוּ נִשְׁמָרִים מִנְּעוּרֵיהֶם מִכָּל חֵטְא וְעָוֹן וְהָיוּ נִשְׁמוֹתֵיהֶם רְאוּיִים וּמְסֻגָּלִים לִלְמֹד חָכְמָה זֹאת אֲבָל עַתָּה בַּעֲווֹנוֹתֵינוּ הָרַבִּים שֶׁיֵּשׁ לָנוּ גּוּף עָכוּר וְחֹמֶר עָב צָרִיךְ הָאָדָם לְזַכֵּךְ וּלְכַבֵּס עַצְמוֹ מִכָּל חֵטְא וּלְזַכֵּךְ נִשְׁמָתוֹ וְיָבִין הָאָדָם אִם זִכֵּךְ נִשְׁמָתוֹ כַּאֲשֶׁר אֵין יֵצֶר הָרַע מְסִיתוֹ לִשְׁטוּת וַהֲבָלִים כַּאֲשֶׁר בַּתְּחִלָּה, וְאָז יוּכַל לִלְמֹד בְּכָל פַּעַם הַכְּתָבִים, וְהַשֵּׁם יִתְבָּרַךְ יְזַכֵּהוּ אִם יְזַכֵּךְ מַחֲשַׁבְתּוֹ בִּקְדוּשָׁה בֶּאֱמֶת וּבְתָמִים שֶׁיִּפָּתַח לוֹ שַׁעֲרֵי הַחָכְמָה בְּכִתְבֵי הָאֲרִ"י זַלְלָ"הֵ אֲשֶׁר לֹא כֵן כָּל זְמַן שֶׁמְּלֻבָּשׁ בְּתַאֲווֹת גּוּפָנִיּוֹת בַּהֲבָלִים זְמַן שֶׁהַלִּמּוּד קָשֶׁה לוֹ מְאֹד חַס וְשָׁלוֹם:

⟶○ COMMENTARY ○⟵

bitter waters of secular wisdom. For whoever tastes from the holy Zohar knows that there is no other body of knowledge in existence that is as deep as the mysteries of the Torah; all other areas of knowledge are as nothing in comparison. In your own soul, you will feel Dovid HaMelech's words: "They are more pleasant than gold, and sweeter than honey" (*Sur MeRa*, p. 8)

Studying Zohar and *Kisvei Ari* at Midnight

You should rise at midnight… and devote most of your studying to the Zohar, which has the power to engender deep, spiritual realizations when studied in the wee hours of the night. You should also study the Arizal's writings. Then you will be successful and wise, and go securely on your way.

What more can I say? The Zohar itself offers much practical advice as to how to rise at midnight. For at that time, the Holy One enters *Gan Eden*, to delight with the souls of Tzaddikim. (*Sur MeRa*, p. 42)

Going to the Mikvah

It is impossible to truly experience the awe of God – to pray with fear and trembling – unless you are careful to immerse yourself in a mikvah, when necessary (such as after a seminal emission). If a person learns Torah or prays without first immersing in a mikvah, it is impossible for him to grasp the essence of Torah and mitzvos. If he studies Kabbalistic texts while impure, he may even become a heretic, God forbid…. In-

COMMENTARY

deed, the world was desolate until two great lights appeared – the holy Baal Shem Tov and Rebbe Elimelech of Lizhensk – and opened the gates of the righteous. For they forbid a person to even *think* Torah thoughts, until he has immersed in a mikvah and removed his impurity. The Sages of the Gemara only rescinded *tevilas Ezra* because it was too difficult for most people to observe (*Berachos* 22a). However, if you want to grasp the very essence of Torah and mitzvos, you must be very careful to go to the mikvah for this reason. (*Maor VaShemesh, Emor*)

Grasping the Inner Torah

God implanted three levels of soul in a human being that allow him to grasp the inner secrets of the Torah: his *nefesh, ruach* and *neshamah*. After a person breaks the grip of his animal soul, he receives the intellectual soul (*nefesh hasichlius*). Following this, he receives the *ruach*, and if he is persistent in serving God truthfully, he receives the *neshamah*. Through these three aspects of soul he can grasp the inner dimension of the Torah. (*Noam Elimelech, Vayetze*)

---

6 A person must purify his body and soul by learning Gemara, with Rashi and Tosefos, as written above. Studying the stories in the Gemara (*agadah*) is also very helpful for purifying the soul.

PRAYERS

Purifying the Body and Soul through Torah Study

Behold, I long to study Torah for the sake of God's Name, to fulfill the mitzvah that He gave us – His people, Yisroel – to study His holy Torah, in order that my studies should result in actions and proper traits, and to gain a knowledge of the Torah, in order to learn, guard and observe it.

May it be Your will, my God and God of my fathers, that by means of my study, all the blemishes that I have caused since I have come into this world, whether in this incarnation or another – and all the blemishes in the upper worlds, and in my *nefesh, ruach, neshamah* and higher *neshamah*, and all the blemishes I have caused to Your great Name – will all be repaired. May I merit to learn, to teach, to guard, and to observe Torah. And may I be among those who know Your Name, who dwell in the Palace, and who are privy to Your lofty mysteries. Lead me on the path of truth, and let me not stumble on

⟶∘ COMMENTARY ∘⟵

The written letters of the holy Torah are like the garment and body of the Torah, while the Torah's inner, hidden dimension is like its soul. A Tzaddik, who studies Torah self- lessly, can attain great things; the innermost secrets of the Torah are revealed to him. (*Likutey Shoshanah, "Ger anochi b'aretz"*)

> **Rising at Midnight Opens One's Mind to the Torah's Secrets**
> The Zohar speaks often of the great joy and the spiritual reward that a person receives for rising at midnight. It is an indispensable practice for those who want to gain insight into the mysteries of the Torah, and it opens the door for those who knock in repentance. Therefore, every honest student of Torah and servant of God should attempt to rise at midnight, to be counted among those "who sit in the gardens, the friends hearken to Your voice" (*Shir HaShirim* 8:13), and to receive all the goodness mentioned above. (*Birchas Chaim*, chap. 10, §3, quoting *Sur MeRa*)

ו צָרִיךְ הָאָדָם לְזַכֵּךְ גּוּפוֹ וְנַפְשׁוֹ בְּלִימוּד כַּנִּזְכָּר לְעֵיל בְּלִימוּד הַגְּמָרָא וְתוֹסָפוֹת, גַּם דִּבְרֵי אַגָּדָה שֶׁבַּגְּמָרָא מְסוּגָּלִים מְאוֹד לְזַכֵּךְ נִשְׁמָתוֹ:

⟶∘ PRAYERS ∘⟵

the path of those who err. Open for me the wellsprings and treasuries of wisdom, enlighten my eyes in the light of Your Torah, enlighten me and show me the wonders in Your Torah – the hidden Torah and the revealed. May I become like an overflowing spring and a seamless well, never losing a drop and never forgetting what I learned. Unite my heart in love and fear of Your Name, and purify my heart and my desires so that they should be for Your service. "A pure heart create in me, O God, and a proper spirit renew within me." Let me understand and become wise; let me study, teach, guard, observe and fulfill all the words of your Torah with love. Lead me on the path of Your commandments. Open my eyes, so that they may behold the wonders of Your Torah, and attach my heart to Your commandments. Give me a strong and committed heart in Your Torah and mitzvos, so that I can stand up to the evil inclination. May I fulfill countless mitzvos, in all their general and specific details, including all the deeper intentions upon which they are based. (*Otzar Tefilos Yisroel*, vol. 3, p. 222)

PRAYERS

Our Father in Heaven, let us truly return to You in complete repentance for the wrongs we have done in the past, and may we become strong and committed to serving You from now on. May we merit to attain every good character trait, and constantly study Your Torah and truly serve You with all our strength – with all our heart, with all our soul and with all our might – until the four basic elements of our

COMMENTARY

Torah Study Purifies the Body and Soul

Through studying the holy Torah, a person can attain all spiritual levels. (*Noam Elimelech, Tzav*).

Torah study can bring a person to spiritual attachment to God, as well as awaken Divine compassion. (*Likutey Shoshanah*)

This is the law of the elevation-offering. The elevation-offering shall remain on the fire, above the altar, all night until morning. (Vayikra 6:2)

Torah study can awaken in you a love and fiery enthusiasm for God, for the power of the Torah is equal to all else. "Above the altar" – that is, the Torah's power of atonement is even above that of the altar; for each of the various sacrifices atones for something else, whereas the Torah atones for everything. In this, the Torah is superior to the altar. (*Noam Elimelech, Tzav*)

As long as the Holy Temple stood, the sacrifices would atone for us. Now, due to our many sins, we no longer have the altar. Instead, we gain atonement through the holy Torah, as our Sages said: "What should a person do if he has stumbled in sin and deserves death? If he was accustomed to studying one page [of Torah], let him now study two" (*Vayikra Rabbah* 25:1). Thus we find that the Torah is called "an altar," because it atones for our sins. (*Ibid., Mishpotim*)

In the World to Come, the evil inclination will appear like a mountain. (Sukkah 52a)
A mountain is hard, but iron can split it. (Bava Basra 10a)

The explanation is as follows: Even though the evil inclination is hard to defeat, the holy Torah can cut it away, like iron cuts away a mountain. Not only will you be saved from your evil inclination, you will even be able to subjugate it under the dominion of holiness [so that your evil inclination, too, can assist you in serving God]. (*Noam Elimelech, Shelach*)

―――――◦ PRAYERS ◦―――――

body are all purified and become completely good, without a trace of evil clinging to them. (*Otzar Tefilos Yisroel*, vol. 3, p. 222)

―――――◦ COMMENTARY ◦―――――

Original Thoughts

Anyone who formulates new and original Torah concepts for the sake of Heaven, must have faith in himself. He needs to believe that God takes great joy in his ideas. He should never be dispirited, but should remain diligent in his studies and work to constantly develop new ideas. He should note them down and compile them in books. On account of this all the harsh judgments in the world will be sweetened. (*Likutey Etzos, Talmud Torah* 47)

When you study Torah, you must draw out "judgments of truth" from what you learn. That is, you should try to derive practical directives as to how to live, both for yourself and for those who are under your influence, regardless of whether they are few or many. You will be able to do this if you have faith in the Sages. (*Ibid*, 45).

A Pleasant Fragrance

Avos d'Rebbe Nossan (chap. 29) states: "Someone who knows *halachos* but does not know *midrash* has never tasted the fear of sin." This is because *midrash* contains moral rebuke, which engenders in a person the fear of sin.

From here we learn that simply studying *halachos* is not enough; that one must also study *mussar*. Indeed, you should devote yourself to the study of *mussar* and never abandon it. Developing a sense of humility is the very foundation of our life in this world and the next. A person should recognize his true worth, feel broken-hearted, and thus, avoid sin. Then one's Torah study will ascend as a pleasant fragrance to God. (*Birchas Chaim*, chap. 10, §32)

Therefore, my beloved ones, my brethren and friends, do not commit this great evil [by sitting around idly in synagogue]. Rather, "Give glory unto the Lord your God, before it grows dark." That is, by studying the inner secrets of the Torah – the *agadah* of the *Ein Yaakov* – in groups of ten, on weekday nights, between the *mincha* and *ma'ariv prayers*. For most of the secrets of the Torah are concealed there, and studying it atones for one's sins (as explained in the writings of the Arizal). Furthermore, the revealed aspect of these teachings teaches you the path of God to follow. Studying it will enable you to formulate good advice in your soul, in both religious and secular matters, as is known to all. (*Igeret HaKodesh* 23)

7 You should guard yourself from all sorts of sins and improper thoughts.

PRAYERS

Our Father in Heaven, awaken Your great and abundant mercy and kindness upon us, to cast out and destroy the evil inclination from within us. Rebuke it, until it abandons and leaves us, and no longer entices us to distance ourselves from serving You, God forbid. May no bad thoughts ever arise in our minds, neither when we sleep nor when we are awake – especially, when we are standing in prayer before You, or when we are studying Your Torah, or involved with Your commandments. May our thoughts then be clear and strong, sincere and wholehearted, according to Your beneficent wishes for us. (*From the prayer of Rabbi Elimelech of Lizhensk*)

❦

"O God, You know my folly, and my offenses are not concealed from You." For this reason I come before you, my God and God of my

COMMENTARY

The Importance of Pure Thoughts

Our thoughts are the most important thing. A person must therefore make a slow but steady effort to purify his thoughts, until they become clear; as Chazal have said: "Why are the words of Torah compared to a [woman's] thigh? Just as the thigh is kept private, so the words of Torah are kept private [and not taught in the marketplace]" (*Sukkah* 49b). This alludes to the spiritual impurity and damage caused by improper thoughts, because a person's thoughts are also private. And to repair the damage and remove the impurity, one needs a comparable form of *teshuvah* – that is, studying Torah with pure, selfless thoughts.

Nevertheless, you cannot purify your thoughts all at once, but must do so gradually, a little each day, until God Himself finally comes to your aid. (*Noam Elimelech, Ki Savo*)

❦

Even though physical desires seem pleasant at first, one must remember their ultimate end, for they kill a person in this world and in the World to Come. Chazal said: "A person's sin attaches itself to him and leads him to the Day of Judgment" (*Avodah Zarah* 5a). Then, he won't find the sin so pleasant. In fact, it will become a source of suffering and pain. Even now, it would not feel pleasant, were it not for the evil inclination; a eunuch, for instance, has no desire for marital relations. Why, then, should a person listen to the evil inclination and do its will, which only causes him pain in this world and the next? (*Birchas Chaim*, chap. 4, §36)

ז וְיִשְׁמוֹר עַצְמוֹ מֵעֲבֵירוֹת מֵהִרְהוּרִים רָעִים בְּכָל אוֹפֶן וָאוֹפֶן:

---o PRAYERS o---

fathers, with a broken and downcast heart, bowing, kneeling and prostrating myself before You, with supplications and requests, like a pauper at the door, sighing and broken, asking for a free handout and a generous offering – that you should show me mercy, and in Your great compassion and awesome love, remove me from darkness into the light. Help me, from today on, to constantly sanctify my thoughts, now and forever. (*Likutey Tefilos* 1:5)

I hereby commit myself, from this moment on, to carefully monitor every detail of my actions, thoughts and words, as befits anyone who desires to be sanctified with a supernal sanctification, and so that I should not live a life without restraint, God forbid. May God's right hand of justice support me, and may He instruct me and lead me in His holy way, amidst great spiritual and physical blessing. May I, my whole family, all my friends, and all Yisroel merit long lives of happiness and contentment, lives of genuine goodness, both materially and spiritually, lives illuminated by a light from Above. (*Otzar Tefilos Yisroel*, vol. 3, p. 148)

The Holiness of Thought

Thought is man's highest aspect. It is more elevated than vision, hearing, and in fact everything. With thought it is possible to climb ever higher. This is why you must be so careful about what you think. (*Likutey Etzos, Machshavos* 21)

God's Great Pleasure

The Torah distinguishes between the animals that are pure and those that are impure.

Pure thoughts are like "pure animals" and impure thoughts are like "impure animals." The battle between the different thoughts in a person's mind is a battle between the pure and the impure animals. Heaven allows them to carry on fighting because God has great pleasure when He sees a man struggling hard to defeat these "wild animals." (*Likutey Etzos, Machshavos* 10)

8 Be careful not to hate any Jew, other than those wicked people whom you know clearly cannot be judged favorably. As for those in whom you can find some merit, you must love them like your own soul, with all your might, with your body and soul, in order to fulfill: "Love your fellow like yourself."

———◦ PRAYERS ◦———

On the contrary, may our hearts see only the good in our friends and not their shortcomings. May we speak to each other in a way that is straight and pleasing to You. May there be no hatred between friends, Heaven forbid. Strengthen our ties to You with love, as it is revealed and known to You, that we strive only to please You; for that is our main intention. (*From the prayer of Rabbi Elimelech of Lizhensk*)

May I judge everyone favorably, even those who oppose, belittle and insult me. May I remain silent before them, and not feel any hatred or resentment toward them. May I only judge them favorably, and assume that their intentions are pure, for according to their own thinking, they deem it right to insult me. Especially, since I know that I really deserve all these types of insults and more, due to my many sins and transgressions; all the more so, since I am a member of the holy Jewish people, who are the aspect of the King's crown. How is it that I did not guard myself and keep my deeds from blemishing the King's honor? I deserve all the disgrace in the world! As it is said: "Those who despise Me will be disgraced." How can I complain about and resent those who disgrace me, knowing that I deserve all this and more? (*Tefilos v'Tachanunim*, p. 105)

———◦ COMMENTARY ◦———

Judging Favorably Those Who Oppose You

You should make every effort to search out whatever merit and goodness you can find within the Jewish people. Judge everyone favorably, even those who oppose you and treat you disrespectfully. If you do this, you will never be troubled by opposition and arguments. If you find yourself in the middle of a dispute, it is very good if you can remain silent and pay no attention to the abuse that people throw at you. When you can hear negative things said against you without responding, you have attained true repentance. It is the remedy for all past sins. Someone who achieves this can truly be said to be wise. He will receive a share in the glory of God and a goodly portion in the World to Come. (*Likutey Etzos, Machlokes* 2, 3)

ח וְיִשְׁמוֹר עַצְמוֹ מִלְּשֵׂנוֹא שׁוּם אָדָם מִיִּשְׂרָאֵל כִּי אִם הָרְשָׁעִים שֶׁנּוֹדָעִים לוֹ בְּבֵירוּר שֶׁאִי אֶפְשָׁר לְדוּנָם לְכַף זְכוּת, וְכָל שֶׁאֶפְשָׁר לְדוּנָם לִזְכוּת מְחוּיָב לֶאֱהוֹב כְּנַפְשׁוֹ בְּכָל מְאוֹדוֹ בְּגוּפוֹ וּבְנַפְשׁוֹ לְקַיֵּים וְאָהַבְתָּ לְרֵעֲךָ כָּמוֹךָ:

→ PRAYERS ←

Father in Heaven, who sits on high, what can I say before You? Speaking negatively is so deeply ingrained in me that I know absolutely no way to avoid it in the future. I have therefore come before You, my God and God of my fathers, to beg You to help me and guide me along the straight path so that through Your mercy, I'll be able to keep myself from stumbling and speaking evil. Don't let me say anything that is not in accordance with Your will. Let me always be good to all. Don't let me ever look for people's faults. On the contrary, let me always make a determined effort to find merit and goodness in every single member of Your holy Jewish People, even the lowliest and least respectable, even my opponents and those who persecute me. Help me judge all of them positively at all times, and grant me wisdom and understanding so that I'll know how to keep searching until I'll always be able to find good points and merit in them. (*Likutey Tefilos* 1:35)

Help us come close to the true Tzaddikim, who in their wisdom constantly seek the good points within each and every Jew, even Jewish sinners. The Tzaddikim gather up all their good points and bring them to the side of merit, and build from them wondrous and awesome structures of holiness through which they raise up before You such delights as have not ascended since the beginning of time. And by gathering this good, they merit creating holy songs and melodies. (*Likutey Tefilos* 1:90)

→ COMMENTARY ←

Rather than look for the shortcomings in another person, reflect upon your own. (*Madanei HaMelech* 142)

There are many holy books in existence today, and many more are destined to be printed in the future. The world needs all of them, and it is wrong to cast aspersions on any of them. It is forbidden to reject or mock any book that is based upon our holy Torah. One who does so will be subject to the judgment of boiling excrement, and he will never succeed in gaining any practical guidance from the Torah he studies. (*Likutey Etzos, Machlokes* 19)

→o COMMENTARY o←

The Tzaddik Sees Only the Good

And Moshe heard the people weeping with their families… and Moshe considered it evil. And Moshe said to God: "Why have You treated Your servant so badly? Why have I not found favor in Your eyes, that You place the burden of this entire people upon me?" (Bamidbar 11:10-11)

When a Tzaddik sees that the Jewish people have fallen to a low state, he becomes despondent and is unable to pray for them. This is why Moshe said: "Why have You treated Your servant so badly" – that is, why have You raised me to this level on which I can see the bad in the Jewish people, leaving me unable to pray for them?

"Why have I not found favor in Your eyes, that You place the burden of this entire people upon me?" That is, it would have been better had you placed their burden upon me, so that I could provide for all their needs, and not have to see them in this lowly state. I prefer to see only their good points, so that I can pray for them

9 **Be very careful not to say anything before you pray in the morning – not even a single word – since this will ruin your concentration in prayer.**

→o PRAYERS o←

Rebuke the evil inclination, so that it abandons us and leaves us, and does not seduce us to distance ourselves from serving You, God forbid. May no bad thoughts ever arise in our minds, neither when we sleep nor when we are awake – especially, when we are standing in prayer before You, or when we are studying Your Torah, or involved with Your commandments. May our thoughts then be clear and strong, sincere and wholehearted, according to Your best wishes for us. (*From the prayer of Rabbi Elimelech of Lizhensk*)

→o COMMENTARY o←

Not to Speak Before Prayers

After rising from bed [in the morning], do not become involved in any activity, or speak even a single word. Rather, you should relieve yourself and wash up, and then attach your thoughts to God, who is One and Unique. Think about how the King of kings is the Master, Source and Root of all the worlds. Say to yourself: "How great are Your works, O God!" Contemplate the greatness of His works in creating the earth and everything it contains, and all the amazing wisdom that this involved. [Contemplate, too,] the great sea and everything in it. Think how He

COMMENTARY

and draw upon them many blessings. (*Noam Elimelech, Beha'alosecha*)

The Baal Shem Tov said that before Heaven issues a harsh decree against a person, they first ask him if he agrees, and only then do they issue it. How does this happen? A person sees or hears of someone else doing something similar to what he himself has done. When he passes judgement on that other person, he is actually sealing his own fate. We find that this happened to Dovid HaMelech, when Nossan HaNavi came to him and told him the story of the guest and the lamb (*Shmuel 2* 12:1). Dovid became liable for the very punishment he decreed on the other. Whenever you hear a story about someone else, be very careful not to pass judgment, as it is very dangerous; for in the matter of telling over stories, there are lofty things. (*Kitzur Likutey Moharan*, 113)

ט וְיִשְׁמוֹר אֶת עַצְמוֹ מִלְּדַבֵּר שׁוּם דִּבּוּר קוֹדֶם הַתְּפִלָּה אֲפִילוּ דָּבָר אֶחָד כִּי זֶה מְבַטֵל כַּוָּנַת הַתְּפִלָּה:

COMMENTARY

is the Creator of the mountains, the wind and fire, the celestial spheres and myriad hosts of angels, without end. He is the First Cause, and there is none else.

Then you will be filled with an awe of God, and love of God will also fill your heart, as well as a desire to cleave to Him. (*Shnei Luchos HaBris, sha'ar ha'osiyos* 1, *emes v'emunah* 13)

You should realize that the forces of evil attack precisely the trait of brotherly love, creating schisms between friends, between Tzaddikim, and between those who serve God. On the other hand, the gentiles live in tranquility, with the forces of evil creating union and peace among them – something that has never been before.

Thus, a person who is blessed with wisdom and understanding should make every effort to increase love, brotherliness, peace and friendship among Jews, and to repair this trait of controversy.

Believe me, my words are no more than a drop in the ocean of what there is to say. I remember in my youth, when the light of the disciples of the Baal Shem Tov began to shine, how I longed to attach myself to them, for I beheld the endless love and unity between them, which was like the brotherly love among the disciples of the Arizal, as it states in *Sha'ar HaGilgulim*. (*Sur MeRa*, p. 59)

10 Be careful to relieve yourself before praying or eating, as well as any other time you feel the need. You should never delay, and so transgress the prohibition: "Do not defile yourself" (*Vayikra* 11:43).

→o COMMENTARY o←

There is another point that I will mention, concerning those pious individuals whose desire to pray with a clean body leads them to pray after the appointed time. This is a ruse of the evil inclination. A person needs only to follow the guidelines of the *Shulchan Aruch*, which means checking himself before prayer. If he does not need to relieve himself, then there is no reason for concern – not unless he cannot hold himself in for the time it takes to walk a *parsa* (about two and a half miles), as the *Shulchan Aruch* states. However, the evil inclination has a way of deceiving a person with pious stringencies, since it is written in the spiritual handbooks that extraneous thoughts arise in the mind because one has not properly relieved himself. However, this stringency is only for people on a high spiritual level. Can you imagine the average Jew missing the time of prayer and *Kerias Shema* because of this? God forbid to even mention the idea. (*Sur MeRa*, p. 27)

There are many people who spend a great deal time in the lavatory, at-

11 Be careful to keep your shirt and pants free of any dirt, feces or semen, God forbid.

→o PRAYERS o←

Loving God, help me and be with me, and from now on, protect my clothes from ever getting stained. You alone know the great blemish caused to the Shechinah in the upper worlds when a person fails to guard his clothes from stains and dirt. His own clothes judge him for failing to protect them from stains. But because of my many sins, I find it very hard to guard my clothes against stains. I find it impossible to keep my mind on them at all times, especially when I am studying Torah or praying or going about my various other activities. My clothes get dirty without my noticing. It's my sins and jumbled thinking that are the cause of all this. As a result, I find it impossible to protect my clothes properly and keep them clean and free of stains and dirt.

I've come to pray to You about all this, O God and God of my fathers. Loving God, who bestows goodness on the guilty: "With wondrous miracles You answer us in righteousness, God of our salvation, You, the confidence of all the ends of the earth and the far

י וְיִזָּהֵר לְנַקּוֹת אֶת עַצְמוֹ קוֹדֶם הַתְּפִלָּה וְקוֹדֶם סְעוּדָה, גַּם בְּכָל פַּעַם שֶׁצָּרִיךְ לִנְקָבָיו שֶׁלֹּא לְהַשְׁהוֹת וְיַעֲבוֹר עַל בַּל תְּשַׁקְּצוּ:

COMMENTARY

tempting to totally cleanse their bodies before praying in the morning. Rabbi Nachman spoke out strongly and ridiculed this practice.

He said that the main thing to remember is that the Torah was not given to ministering angels (*Berachos* 25b). It is not necessary to go beyond the requirement of the law, and the codes state that it is only forbidden to worship when one actually feels the need to relieve himself.

The Talmudic dictum is: "One who finds it necessary to move his bowels should not worship" (ibid. 23a). Still, there are many laws in chapter 92 of the *Shulchan Aruch*, especially in an emergency or when one has no other choice. The *Magen Avraham* follows the opinion of the *Rif* that one may worship even if he feels a need, as long as he can contain himself long enough to walk a *parsa*. From all this we see that there is no need to be overly strict in this respect…. The best thing is to worship as soon as you wake up in the morning. If you can easily attend to your needs, then do so, but if not, pray immediately. Even if you have a slight feeling in your bowels, it can be ignored. (*Sichos HaRan* 30)

יא וְיִזָּהֵר שֶׁיִּהְיֶה בְּגָדָיו הַכְּתֹנֶת וּמִכְנָסַיִם מְנוּקִּים מִלְּכְלוּךְ וְצוֹאָה וְשִׁכְבַת זֶרַע חַס וְשָׁלוֹם:

PRAYERS

distant seas." Do awesome wonders for Your Name's sake, and help me remedy all this very quickly in my lifetime. From now on, let me guard the Covenant perfectly. Help me awaken and elevate my mind and attain holy wisdom and awareness so as to cleanse myself of the damage to the blood in my three hundred and sixty-five arteries and veins, corresponding to the three hundred and sixty-five prohibitions of the Torah. Help me make amends for all the stains on my clothes caused by my past neglect. Forgive me for all the damage caused, and from now on, help me and guard me from stumbling or sinning in any way. Let me take good care of my clothes in the future, and treat them with respect and keep them clean. Don't let my clothes ever have any stains or dirt on them at all. Protect both me and my clothes at all times. Let my body, my soul and my clothes and garments be clean, pure and holy at all times, from now on and forever. (*Likutey Tefilos* 1:29)

———o COMMENTARY o———

Clean Clothing

The rectification of speech, which corresponds to *Malchus peh* (the Kingship of the mouth), is the aspect of white clothing (*Koheles* 9:8). A person has to take great care of his clothing and not disrespect them; that is, he must care for them properly, so that they do not become spotted and dirty. For clothing is the aspect of *Malchus* – Kingship – and a person who disrespects them is rebelling against the Kingship. Then "the law of the land is the law" – *dina d'malchusa dina* – the negative judgments are aroused against him. Furthermore, the greater a person is, the more he has to care for his clothing, for the more they are exacting with him. A Torah scholar who has a spot on his clothing deserves death, God forbid. (*Kitzur Likutey Moharan* 29:3)

A person's clothing reflects his spiritual efforts. By fulfilling Torah and mitzvos, in general, one merits white

———o o———

12 Do not cast excessive fear in your home, and do not be too exacting. If you are upset with someone or over something, immediately remember the sins that you committed in your youth. Say to yourself: "It is only because of my own sins that I am annoyed by this." Apply this to all other things, as well. Remember your sins, which will humble you and break the force of your evil inclination.

———o PRAYERS o———

Master of the World, You are good and do good to all. Teach me the ways of Your goodness so that I will be able to emulate Your holy traits by being good to all people always. May I completely break the traits of anger and irritability until my heart does not contain the slightest trace of anger. And whenever my evil inclination entices me to grow angry, may I know and believe with complete faith that at this moment Heaven wishes to pour great wealth onto me and that the evil inclination desires to ruin that influx of wealth and turn it into anger, in order to rip apart my soul. With this awareness, may I strengthen myself to eradicate that anger and transform it into compassion. And in this way, may I attain great wealth of holiness, which is the root of souls. May the power of evil have no power to damage the flow of wealth by means of anger. (*Likutey Tefilos* 1:68-69)

---→ COMMENTARY ←---

clothing, which is the aspect of "the garment of the Rabbis." This is the garment in which the soul is clothed in the World to Come.

Conversely, sins cause our clothing to become soiled, and give off a bad smell; for smell is specifically drawn from the clothing. On the other hand, when we perform mitzvos, our clothing emits a good smell, as the verse says: "The fragrance of your garments is like the fragrance of Lebanon" (Shir HaShirim 4:11).

The mitzvah of *tzitzis* rectifies our clothing. Through this, we draw down a thread of loving-kindness from Above. This transforms our sins into merits so that they exude a good smell, which is the aspect of "Myrrh, aloes and cassia are all your garments" (Tehilim 45:9). On this, Chazal say: "Do not read the word as 'your garments' (*bigdosecha*), but as 'your traitors' (*b'gidosecha*), for all of your traitors give off a good smell." (Otzar HaYirah, Begadim 7)

יב לֹא יַטִּיל אֵימָה יְתֵרָה בְּתוֹךְ בֵּיתוֹ וְלֹא יַקְפִּיד שׁוּם הַקְפָּדָה בְּתוֹךְ בֵּיתוֹ, וְאִם יִהְיֶה לוֹ שׁוּם הַקְפָּדָה עַל שׁוּם אָדָם אוֹ עַל דָּבָר אֶחָד יִזְכּוֹר מִיָּד חַטֹּאת נְעוּרָיו וְיֹאמַר בְּלִבּוֹ: אֵין זֶה כִּי אִם עֲוֹנוֹתַי הֱבִיאוּנִי לִידֵי הַקְפָּדָה זוֹ, וְכֵן בְּכָל דָּבָר יִזְכּוֹר מִיָּד חַטֹּאתָיו, וְעַל יְדֵי זֶה יוּכְנַע וְיֻשְׁבַּר כֹּחַ הַיֵּצֶר הָרַע:

---→ PRAYERS ←---

Hashem, my God and God of my fathers! Good and loving God: Help me! Guard and protect me from all anger, temper and resentment. Even if I do start to become angry at times, have pity on me and keep me from doing anything vicious out of anger. Help me break my anger, and instead show love and kindness. Help me control my impulses and break my temper, and turn anger into love. Let me make a point of acting kindly where I might have wanted to show anger. Don't let me have a strange god inside me, and don't let me worship idols – because this injunction applies to someone who becomes angry: he is considered as if he worshipped idols. (Likutey Tefilos 1:18)

---→ COMMENTARY ←---

The True Nature of Life

All the hardships and misfortunes that a person faces in life can distance him from serving God. A person must be strong and brave to deal

COMMENTARY

with all that happens in life. He must always be prepared for hardships, even before they happen. "If they don't come today, they will come tomorrow," he should tell himself. If he can do this, he will not be disturbed or forget to serve God when misfortune strikes. He will be ready and prepared to accept them. This is the approach of a righteous person, who knows that this world is a den of hardships, and is thus neither troubled nor dismayed when they occur.

On the other hand, a person who trusts too much in this world, who believes that his life will forever remain untroubled, will be panic-stricken when the opposite of what he expects actually occurs. He will lose both his composure and his ability to serve God. A wise person must be constantly on guard, not to rely on the goodness of the world, but to realize that misfortune will eventually strike. Then he will be successful and persevere in his service of God. (*Sefer HaYashar* of Rabbeinu Tam, *ha-sha'ar ha-shishi*)

There is no one in the world who does not suffer in one way or another. People experience all kinds of hardships and difficulties. It may be problems connected with making a living, health problems, or domestic ills related to one's wife and children or other household members. Nobody can escape a certain amount of suffering and hardship, because "man was born to struggle" (*Iyov* 5:7), and it is written: "for his days are vex-

---

13 Pray to God to help you completely repent, so that you do not die without having done *teshuvah*. Consider yourself united with all the other *baalei teshuvah*, so that God will help you repent completely. Pray for the forgiveness of your own sins, together with the sins of all the Jewish people.

PRAYERS

Woe is me, God! Woe is me, my Master and King! What will I do on the day of judgment? What will I do when I come to the eternal world, to the day that is entirely Sabbath and tranquility? A person can only enter and be absorbed into that reality if he has adorned himself with holiness and removed his mind entirely from the sights of this world and has instead clung only to the true and eternal goal. What will I do? My sins have so affected me that "I have sunken into the deep mud, and there is nowhere to stand. I have entered into the depths of the water, and the current has swept over me." My Father, my Master, "My King and my God, I pray to You." I throw myself before You in prayer. Act for Your own sake in Your great compassion and bring me back to You in complete repentance. Grant me merit

COMMENTARY

ation and pain" (Koheles 2:23). The only way to escape is to seek refuge in God and His Torah. It takes great patience to bear what one has to go through in life.... Even the lowest of the low can still take refuge in God, because God is to be found in all places. As soon as a person takes refuge in God, no matter what the experience, it will turn out for the good, and the good will be truly enduring (*Likutey Etzos, Savlanut* 11).

Accepting Suffering in Silence

A person should contemplate his sins and willfully accept the path of purification, chastisement and suffering. If he asks: "Which is the best form of suffering in the world, which does not interfere with my service of God?" – the answer is, the suffering a person feels when other people insult and belittle him. This does not make him physically weak or sick; no one denies him food or clothing, nor is his life or the lives of his family endangered. For that reason, he should welcome it. "Why should I fast and afflict myself, becoming too weak to serve God?" he should say. "It's better to be afflicted by the insults of others."

Then, whenever people insult him, he will actually be happy and look forward to them doing so. (*Tomer Devorah*; *Shnei Luchos HaBris, sha'ar ha-osiyos* §70)

יג וְיִתְפַּלֵּל לְהַשֵּׁם יִתְבָּרַךְ שֶׁיַּעַזְרֵהוּ לַעֲשׂוֹת תְּשׁוּבָה שְׁלֵימָה וְשֶׁלֹּא יָמוּת בְּלֹא תְּשׁוּבָה וְיִכְלוֹל אֶת עַצְמוֹ בְּתוֹךְ שְׁאָר בַּעֲלֵי תְּשׁוּבָה שֶׁיַּעֲזְרוּ שֶׁיַּעֲשֶׂה תְּשׁוּבָה שְׁלֵימָה וְיִתְפַּלֵּל עַל מְחִילַת עֲוֹנוֹתָיו בִּכְלַל מְחִילַת עֲוֹנוֹת בֵּית יִשְׂרָאֵל:

PRAYERS

from this moment on. Help me, save me, be with me always. Guide me to seal my eyes, heart, mind and thoughts from the sight of this lowly world. May I never look at the vanities, desires and troubles of this world. The entire world is not worth the blink of an eye: "for it is all vanity and an evil spirit–and what advantage does a person have of all his toil," of all his desires and vanities? (*Likutey Tefilos* 1:65)

You who are filled with compassion, rescue me from insult and disgrace. When I die, may no harmful and destructive entities have the power to approach me and follow my coffin. While I am still alive, may I rectify everything that I have damaged, so that You will then forgive all [of my sins] and I will not be judged after my death. I am aware

→o PRAYERS o←

that I do not deserve such favor. But I trust in Your compassion. I rely upon Your kindness. I hope for Your forgiveness and look forward to Your salvation – all in the power and merit of the true Tzaddikim, those of our generation and those who dwell in the dust. You desire the restitution of the wicked person. It has been taking me a long time to return [to You, and] in the meantime every day I bring about

→o COMMENTARY o←

The Essence of *Teshuvah*

The Torah's commandment to repent simply entails acknowledging one's sin. That is, to resolve in one's heart, with perfect sincerity, never to revert to folly again, not to rebel against God's rule, nor ever again violate the King's command, God forbid, whether a positive commandment or a prohibition. This is the basic meaning of *teshuvah* – to return to God with all one's heart and soul, to serve Him, and to keep all His commandments. As it is written: "Let the wicked abandon his way, and the sinner his thoughts, and return to God, who will have compassion on him" (*Yeshayahu* 55:7).

However, all this refers to atonement and forgiveness of the sin; for when a person has fully repented, he is pardoned completely for having violated the King's command. However, in order to be acceptable to God, to be as beloved to Him as before the sin, so that the Creator delights in his service, a person, in the past, would have had to bring a sacrificial offering. Today, when we no longer have sacrifices to appease God, fasting replaces the offering. (*Likutey Amarim, Igeres HaTeshuvah* 1, 2)

Teshuvah in our Time

Here is advice as to how to return to God. It is not good to reveal your faults to others, as Dovid HaMelech said: "Happy is the man whose transgression is forgiven, whose sin is concealed" (*Tehilim* 32:1). On the other hand, just because you do not express them verbally, you should also not bury them in your heart, which might lead you to forget them. The proper approach is to pour out your heart to God when you are alone, at home or outside, confessing all of your sins and begging God to open for you the gates of *teshuvah* and teach you His pleasant ways. So too, when you lie on your bed at night, thoughts like these should flow to God from the depths of your heart. If you do this for many hours and days, even when you are out involved in your business, you can rest assured that God will open for you the gates of *teshuvah*. (*Ohel Elimelech*, §64)

The first thing to do, before going to sleep, is to review all your actions and activities of the day, to see if, perhaps, they include a trace of sin or transgression. This is a great obligation, as the Zohar states (*Zohar Chadash, Noach* 21b): "A person must examine what he did each day. If he needs to repent over it, he should do

PRAYERS

more damage and [commit more] sins. Nevertheless, every day I still anticipate my redemption. May I, my children, my grandchildren and all of Your nation, the house of Yisroel, quickly awaken from our sleep, arise from our descent, live after our deaths and return to You in truth with all of our hearts, to be in accordance with Your good will, from now and forever. Amen, *Selah*! (*Likutey Tefilos* 1:85)

COMMENTARY

so before going to sleep." That is, he must make a commitment to correct the problem immediately, the very next day, however possible.

The essential rule is that whatever you can fix immediately, do so. If you remember that you spoke wrongly to a friend – for instance, if you spoke harshly to him and hurt his feelings, or embarrassed him publicly – you should cry and regret what you did, and make a commitment to appease him the following day. Then, do it the first thing in the morning. It goes without saying that if you sinned against someone greater than you, you should regret it immediately and beg God not to record it in His book of liabilities. You should take upon yourself to fix it immediately, the very next day. On the other hand, if someone spoke badly about you, you should forgive him. You should say: "May God forgive anyone who offended me." (*Yesod Yosef*, chap. 61)

Teshuvah Brings Parnasah

You shall surely tithe (עַשֵּׂר תְּעַשֵּׂר) all the seed crop that the field gives forth, year by year. (Devorim 14:22)

Tithe in order to become rich (עַשֵּׂר בִּשְׁבִיל שֶׁתִּתְעַשֵּׁר). (Ta'anis 9a)

A man once came to the Tzaddik Rabbi Pinchas of Koretz with the following complaint. "I have been giving a tenth of my income to charity my entire life, yet I have not yet become rich."

Rabbi Pinchas answered him: "Let me answer you with a story. There is a wagon driver living in my neighborhood who owns several strong, well-groomed horses, which do all his work for him. One day, after feeding them well and hitching them to his wagon, they refused to move. He even struck them with his whip, but still they wouldn't budge. A passerby saw what was happening and suggested that he stop hitting them. 'Don't you see why they aren't moving? You've locked the brakes on your wagon. How do you expect them to pull it?'

"The same thing applies to you, my friend," Rabbi Pinchas continued. "It's true that you are tithing your income. However, if you've locked the brakes of Divine beneficence through your misdeeds, then all the tithing in the world won't start the wheels of blessing turning." (*Imrei Pinchas*, p. 103)

14 You should speak gently with others. And if they praise you, you should quickly leave. You should regret what happened, and say to yourself: "Why are they praising me for things that don't apply to me? They don't know how low I really am, or all my foolishness and transgressions. How can I even face my Creator, who at all times knows and sees what I do. Even so, He has mercy on me, despite what I do."

⟶∘ PRAYERS ∘⟵

Hashem our God and God of our fathers: May it be Your will to completely remove all pride from me. Don't let even the slightest hint of pride or arrogance enter my heart. Bring me to genuinely understand my own lowliness, and let me nullify myself to the point where I will look upon myself as being even less significant than I really am. (*Likutey Tefilos* 1:14)

⟶∘ COMMENTARY ∘⟵

Speaking Softly

Be careful to always speak gently to your family and friends, whether concerning the fulfillment of the commandments, or in mundane matters. Regarding a Jewish slave, the verse states: "It shall be good for him with you" (*Devorim* 15:16), which means that you must provide him with the same type of food that you eat, and the same type of mattress. Thus, Chazal said: "Whoever acquires for himself a slave, acquires for himself a master." If this applies to a slave whom one purchases, how much more does it apply to your wife and children, whom you must cherish and never treat badly.

As for other people, your relationship to them depends upon their level. If you have a friend who is on a lower level than you in his deeds, or is of lesser lineage or intelligence, you should nonetheless honor and esteem him as though he were your equal. And if he is on the same level as you, you should regard him as being even higher. And if he is greater than you, you should recognize that difference between you, and show him the honor that he deserves – certainly more than the honor he shows you! Likewise, if you possess a certain virtue and your friend possesses another, you should hold his good trait in higher esteem than you do your own and honor him for it! Don't let your evil inclination trick you into feeling superior to your friend. Even if your friend does not honor you as much as you deserve, you should still honor him when you are together. (*Igeres Ohr HaShem* by the Mabit)

יד וְיִהְיוּ דְבָרָיו בְּנַחַת עִם בְּנֵי אָדָם, וְאִם מְשַׁבְּחִין אוֹתוֹ יֵלֵךְ בִּזְרִיזוּת וְיִצְטַעֵר אֶת עַצְמוֹ וְיֹאמַר: מַה זֶּה מְשַׁבְּחִין אוֹתִי וְאֵין בִּי, אִלּוּ הָיוּ מַכִּירִין בִּשְׁפְלוּתִי וּשְׁטוּתִי וּמַעֲלָלַי וּמַעֲשַׂי הָרָעִים וְאֵיךְ אֶשָּׂא פָנַי לִפְנֵי הַבּוֹרֵא יִתְבָּרַךְ שְׁמוֹ שֶׁהוּא יוֹדֵעַ וְרוֹאֶה מַעֲשַׂי בְּכָל עֵת וְרֶגַע אַף עַל פִּי כֵן הוּא מְרַחֵם עָלַי בְּכָל דְּבָרַי:

→○ PRAYERS ○←

God, majestic and awesome King of Glory! You created the entire universe for Your glory, as it is written: "All who are called in My Name, I created, formed and made them for My glory." Loving God, Let Your majesty be increased, enhanced and heightened through me. Help me to be able to nullify myself completely, and not seek the least honor for myself. Let me think nothing of my own importance, and pay no attention whatsoever to receiving honor for myself. Let all my efforts be only to magnify the glory of God. Let all my involvements and everything I do, think and want, be only for the sake of Your great glory, blessed God. (*Likutey Tefilos* 1:11)

→○ COMMENTARY ○←

Tricks of the Evil Inclination

The evil inclination can deceive you at times, by telling you that your worship of God will only be complete when you hide your good deeds from others. "Present yourself as being the very opposite of what is in your heart," it tells you. "Pray quickly, study Torah privately, so that no one but God knows. Don't display a single good trait. Rather, make your every act of worship appear burdensome, otherwise, you will get a good name and lose your [eternal] reward. Don't exhibit even a trace of the fear of God; rather, act like everyone else, and imitate their ways. Take part in their meals, their pleasures, and their entertainments."

You should realize, though, that this is a trap, and that by doing so – even for the sake of a mitzvah – you lose infinitely more than you gain. It's like running away from a small fire straight into a huge one. The correct approach is to pray slowly and with concentration, to do that which is good and avoid that which is bad, and to perform good deeds both openly and in private. If people honor you and praise you, it won't affect you, since you never intended that in the first place. Rather, if you would have acted the same way in private as you did in public, then you know that your deeds are perfect. (*Orchos Tzaddikim, sha'ar haga'avah*)

15 Imagine that someone is constantly standing next to you and watching your actions, so that if he saw you doing something wrong, you would crawl into a mouse hole out of shame. How much more does this apply since the Holy One constantly stands over you and watches your deeds at every moment, so that it is impossible to hide from Him, as the verse says: "Can a man hide in secret places so that I cannot see him?" (*Yirmiyahu* 23:24), as stated in the *Shulchan Aruch* (*Orach Chaim* 1:3).

---⟶○ PRAYERS ○⟵---

Hashem our God and God of our fathers, Master of all works, Lord of all souls: shine on me from Your holy dwelling-place. Inspire me with fear and dread of You, and help me attain holy shame. Clothe me with awe and cloak me in shame before Your great and holy Name. Let me always feel truly ashamed before You, so that I will never deviate right or left from Your will. Let Your fear be upon my face so that I will never sin: that is the meaning of being ashamed before God.

---⟶○ COMMENTARY ○⟵---

The Disciples of Rabbi Elimelech

How can I convey their greatness! There was no end to it! They would constantly reveal their shortcomings, and publicly embarrass themselves. If they had an improper thought, or spoke some empty, mundane words, or even walked a few steps without holiness, they would proclaim it at once, in order to embarrass themselves. Then, they would immediately repent, as though they had committed the gravest sin of the Torah, God forbid. They always saw their own faults, yet viewed other people favorably.

---

16 You should be happy if God causes you to meet someone who disparages you over your shameful deeds. Furthermore, you should consider every person as being better than you.

---⟶○ PRAYERS ○⟵---

Please, God, help me not to be arrogant – neither over things that I have accomplished, nor over things that I really have not. And at those times that I start to become angry, or face tribulation, help me to stay silent and accept what is happening with great love and humility. If people praise me, let me not become conceited. And

טו יְדַמֶּה בְּעֵינָיו כְּאִלּוּ אָדָם עוֹמֵד לְנֶגְדּוֹ תָּמִיד וְלֹא יֶרֶף מִמֶּנּוּ הַשְׁגָּחָתוֹ בְּמַעֲשָׂיו תָּמִיד וְאִלּוּ הָיָה רוֹאֶה בּוֹ דָּבָר מְכֹעָר הָיָה מִתְבַּיֵּשׁ וְנִמְאָס בְּעֵינָיו וְהָיָה מַטְמִין אֶת עַצְמוֹ בְּאַמְתַּחַת עָכְבָּר מִגֹּדֶל הַבּוּשָׁה, עַל אַחַת כַּמָּה וְכַמָּה יִתְבָּרֵךְ שְׁמוֹ עוֹמֵד עָלָיו וְרוֹאֶה בְּמַעֲשָׂיו בְּכָל עֵת וָרֶגַע בִּלְתִּי אֶפְשָׁר לְהַטְמִין עַצְמוֹ מִמֶּנּוּ כְּמוֹ שֶׁכָּתוּב אִם יִסָּתֵר כְּמוֹ שֶׁאָמְרוּ בְּאוֹרַח חַיִּים:

———→o PRAYERS o←———

Master of the Universe! Loving God! Have mercy on me! Help me feel the proper shame before You in this world, and let me never do anything contrary to Your will – and certainly nothing that is sinful in even the slightest way – so that I will not be ashamed or confounded in the World to Come. Let the fear and shame I feel before You be as real and intense as the fear and shame I feel before human beings, who are mere flesh and blood. (*Likutey Tefilos* 1:22)

———→o COMMENTARY o←———

Each one was humble, and considered his friend to be greater than he. They learned from each other how to serve God and keep the holy Torah, and they were never proud about a single good trait they had. They were constantly repenting their entire lives, and they did not take a single step without heartfelt thoughts of *teshuvah*. They had a rebuker in their hearts, who constantly chastised them harshly, though always with an inner love. (*Igeres HaKodesh m'R Zechariah Mendel*)

———————

טז אִם יְגַנֶּה אוֹתוֹ שׁוּם אָדָם יִשְׂמַח מְאֹד שֶׁהַקְּרָה ה' לְפָנָיו אִישׁ כָּזֶה שֶׁמִּתְגַּנֶּה בְּמַעֲשָׂיו הַמְכֹעָרִים, וְכָל אָדָם יִהְיֶה בְּעֵינוֹ טוֹב מִמֶּנּוּ:

———→o PRAYERS o←———

may I accept both the praises and the insults of others equally. May I consider my good deeds as nothing, though may You consider them as great. Support me and grant me the ability to know Your greatness and Your mitzvos, and to do good to other people, so that I do not talk badly about them, but speak only in their favor. May my spirit be precious and my soul exalted in matters pertaining to the World to Come. (*Otzar Tefilos Yisroel*, vol. 3, p. 171)

―――○ PRAYERS ○―――

God, may I work hard to never be overly strict about anything, neither in my home, nor with others. May I accept everything that happens to me with joy, and with the perfect faith that it is all from You – for it is not the serpent that kills, but sin that kills. And it is a great kindness that You repay us for our sins in this world and so safeguard our place in the Eternal World. May I make every effort to always be happy, and in the merit of this faith and joy, help me, O God, to repent for all my sins, and to then taste from the Tree of Life; that is, the pleasantness of the holy Torah and its commandments. May I rejoice over Your words, like one who has found a great treasure. (*Otzar Tefilos Yisroel*, vol. 1, p. 162)

―――○ COMMENTARY ○―――

Appreciating Disgrace

The suffering that atones for a person's sins is indeed hard to bear, especially when it entails the death of one's children, or one's own death, God forbid. Furthermore, if a person punishes himself over his sins, it may distance him from Torah study and prayer. How much better for a person to receive bearable afflictions – suffering that does not prevent him from studying and praying, but which atones for his sins, with love.

For this reason, you should be happy when others belittle or insult you, for you know that God loves you, and is sending you easily bearable afflictions to purify you of your sins. As for the person who insulted you, he will have to bear the consequences of his own action.

It is good to pray to God to help you learn humility, in order for you to rejoice in these types of afflictions. Then, God will delight in you and forgive you for all the sins you committed until now, in anger and arrogance, since your request is that you no longer become angry or answer back to someone that insults you. (*Reishis Chochmah, sha'ar ha'anavah*, chap. 3)

Accepting Suffering with Love

You should accept with love all the troubles and suffering that happen to you. Considering what you have done, God is still dealing with you with great compassion. You should know that according to your deeds, you deserve much worse. (*Likutey Etzos, Savlanut* 6)

When things don't go your way and you feel depressed or angry about what has happened, you should realize that these feelings are a result of your pride; for you imagine that you really deserve many great things. However, if you were honest about your level, you would accept these signs of rejection with love. Indeed, arrogance has a myriad similar ways of expressing itself. May God show His people the straight path. A wise person will hear these words and benefit from them. (*Sur MeRa*, p. 34)

PRAYERS

"Happy is the man whom You discipline, O God, and from Your Torah You teach him. To grant him peace from days of evil, while a pit is dug for the wicked." Master of the World, full of compassion, who is good and does good to all. Save me and help me accept everything with love, even when You occasionally send me, with Your love, some affliction that appears like evil, God forbid. May I truly accept it all with great love. Open my heart with great holiness, so that I may know and understand the truth, that considering who I am and what I have done against You, whatever You do to me is an expression of Your great compassion and tremendous loving-kindness, and is of infinite value. For it is impossible to tell the world the great compassion, love and kindness that You have shown me, and that You continue to show me, and that You will show me in the future, at every moment. What can I say? How can I relate it? "How can I repay God for all the goodness that He has bestowed upon me?" (*Likutey Tefilos* 1:121)

COMMENTARY

Anger and a Lack of Faith

Chazal said: "When a person becomes angry, it is as though he worships idols." This is because at the moment of anger, he loses his faith in God. For had he believed that the situation was from God, he would not have become angry at all. Even though the person who cursed him, or hit him, or damaged his property has free will, and so will be held accountable for his evil deed – both in the courts of man and in the court of Heaven – still, in regards to the one who was hurt, it was a decree from on high, for God has many messengers [to carry out His will]. (*Sefer HaTanya, Igeres HaKodesh* 25)

If a person takes to heart that everything that happens to him is from God, who oversees life's smallest detail – as Chazal say: "A person does not hit his finger below unless it is decreed Above" – he would never be angry over God's actions. As it says: "Entrust your actions to God, and He will establish your plans" (*Mishlei* 16:3). (*Reishis Chochmah, sha'ar anavah*, chap. 3)

What You See in Another, You Can Find in Yourself

I heard in the name of the Baal Shem Tov that when a person sees something impure in his fellow, he should imagine that he is looking at himself in a mirror. For this is the purpose of life, to recognize one's own low stature – that there is no one in the world lower than he. (*Sur MeRa*, p. 56)

17 Distance yourself from anything that does not serve the purpose of keeping your body healthy to serve the Holy One, be it food, drink, or any other desires or pleasures.

---⟶o PRAYERS o⟵---

Removing Worldly Pleasures

Draw me after You and I will run. Fix me, so that I can abandon the cravings of this world, and so that the delights of this world will not confuse me. Keep me from desiring worldly pleasures, and in particular, the desire to eat and drink, so that I do not become a glutton. May I not eat to fill my desire, but rather, like a Tzaddik, who eats to satisfy his soul, and with proper intentions. Remove from me all other bad traits and desires, and let me instead have good and refined qualities, so that I find grace in Your eyes and in the eyes of people. (*Otzar Tefilos Yisroel*, vol. 3, p. 137)

May I lead a good life in the future. Grant me wisdom, understanding, good counsel, strength and power so that I will be able to save my soul from destruction and keep myself well away from all bad traits

---⟶o COMMENTARY o⟵---

Avoiding Overeating

A person who eats excessively is like an animal. To be human is to eat only what is necessary. Excessive eating brings on diphtheria. Another cause of fever is consuming food that is unfit for human consumption. (*Likutey Etzos, Achilah* 13)

Every Action for the Sake of Heaven

Whatever pleasure you get from this world, your intention should not be to take that pleasure for yourself, but to use it for serving the Creator, blessed be He. As it is written: "In all your ways, know Him" (*Mishlei* 3:6). And as our Sages have said: All your actions should be for the sake of heaven. Even when you eat or drink, or when you sleep, you should think you are doing this to be fit and strong to serve Him. Likewise, when you go to work, your thoughts should be on making money in order to support yourself and your family, in order to be healthy to serve God. The bottom line is, a person must consider well his path, and weigh his every action on the scales of his intellect. When he sees that a certain action can bring him to serving the Creator, he should do it, and if not, then not. A person who acts this way is serving his Creator constantly. (*Rambam, Mishnah Torah, Hilchos Dei'os* 3)

יז יַרְחִיק אֶת עַצְמוֹ מִכָּל דָּבָר שֶׁאֵין בּוֹ צוֹרֶךְ לְתַכְלִית בְּרִיאַת גּוּפוֹ לַעֲבוֹדַת הַשֵּׁם יִתְבָּרַךְ הֵן בַּאֲכִילָה וּשְׁתִיָּה הֵן בְּכָל תַּאֲוֹת וְהֲנָאוֹת:

———→o PRAYERS o←———

and desires. Help me eradicate them completely. Let my body be pure and cleansed of all lusts and evil, and help me attain the holiness and purity that befit a Jew. (*Likutey Tefilos* 1:10)

Grant me the trait of contentment, so that I derive only the minimum benefit from this world, and not use the things of this world beyond what is absolutely necessary, and even then, to do so in holiness and purity, for the sake of Your Name and Your remembrance alone. (*Otzar Tefilos Yisroel*, vol. 3, p. 221)

Help me, in Your great mercy, to become holy and pure, to sanctify myself even in permissible things. Let me continually ascend in holiness, until I reach true holiness and sanctification; until I can bring about the supernal unification and the lower unification. (*Likutey Tefilos* 1:11)

———→o COMMENTARY o←———

> *Eliyahu came near to all the people and said, "How long will you waver between the two opinions (shtei se'ifim)?"* (Melachim 1 18:21)

I heard from Rabbi Zushia that *shtei sifim* alludes to two *se'ifim* (chapters) in the *Shulchan Aruch*: chapter 1:1, which states: "I have set God before me always," and chapter 131:2, which states: "In all your ways, know Him." In other words, Eliyahu was saying to the people: How long will you fail to keep these two *se'ifim*, which are the very essence of the Torah? (*Sur MeRa*, p. 28)

One Who Breaks His Lower Nature Receives Supernal Holiness

Even regarding things that are fully permissible, the more you sacrifice your base impulses with the intention of subduing your evil inclination – even if only briefly – the more the glory and holiness of the Holy One ascends Above. For example, when you want to eat but postpone your meal for an hour or less, using that time instead to study Torah; or, if you refrain from speaking about, or even thinking about, mundane matters that you have a desire to discuss – this holy act causes a supernal holiness to flow down upon you, to greatly help you serve God. This is aside from the fact that you are fulfilling the positive commandment

───○ COMMENTARY ○───

"You shall sanctify yourselves" (*Vayikra* 11:44), which means, sanctifying yourself in that which is permitted to you. (*Sefer HaTanya*, chap. 27).

The Value of Being Frugal

The main loss of a person's days stems from his desire for money and the burden of earning a living. We see this empirically, and about this the verse says: "He amasses wealth unjustly; in the middle of his days, they will leave him" (*Yirmiyahu* 17:11). Because of his pursuit of wealth, he does not live out all his days, because he has lost them. This is as the *mussar seforim* say: "A person worries about the money that he loses, but does not worry about the days that he loses." (*Otzar HaYirah, mamon*, §35)

The true purpose of life is not as it appears to our eyes, with nearly everyone chasing after money, and hurrying through the world's busi-

───────

18 It is very important to avoid alcoholic beverages. Drinking is an evil sickness that seriously degrades a person, as the Talmud says: "Do not drink, so that you do not sin" (*Berachos* 29b).

───○ PRAYERS ○───

O God, keep me from ever becoming drunk. Protect me from intoxicating wine and from the fervor and dance that come from the Side of Evil. May I never experience any excitement of the evil inclination for any lust at all. Instead, may I only drink the wine "that gives joy to God and man." Whenever I need to drink wine or alcohol – on Shabbos and the Festivals, or over a cup of blessing – may I drink a very small amount, just enough to expand my mind in holiness, so

───○ COMMENTARY ○───

In the synagogue of Rabbi Elimelech of Lizhensk, it was forbidden to drink any intoxicating beverages on the last days of Sukkos, until the end of the dancing on Simchas Torah. This was to prevent any foreign influence from becoming mixed with the holy rejoicing. (*Heichal HaBerachah, Shemini*)

[The spirit of] Moshe is enclothed within each and every Jew, in every single limb, reminding that limb to perform the mitzvah connected to it; for the 248 mitzvos parallel the 248 limbs in the human body. Therefore, Moshe is referred to as *mechokek*

———→∘ COMMENTARY ∘←———

ness centers and shopping malls in pursuit of wealth and luxuries. There are two negative consequences of this: The first is that these people separate themselves from Torah and from serving God; the second is that when they go out to work, they forget the Creator of the world. Then, they become no better than the rest of the world, who are preoccupied with acquiring money and goods from morning to night, who desire new and better things before they have even enjoyed what they already have – fancy clothing, beautiful homes and every worldly indulgence, while denying themselves nothing.

If we act as they do, then how are the Chosen People different from the other nations? It follows, that there is no greater evil than this, in that they have completely erased the Holy One from their hearts, when they go out to work from morning till night. For when you ask them, "Where is your God?" they are unable to answer. (*Ohr HaMeir, Chukos*)

יח וְעִיקָר שֶׁיִּשְׁמוֹר אֶת עַצְמוֹ מִמַּשְׁקֶה הַמְשַׁכֵּר כִּי זֶה חוֹלִי רַע וּמֵבִיא אֶת הָאָדָם לִשְׁפָלוּת גָּדוֹל כְּמַאֲמַר הַתַּנָּא לֹא תִרְוֵי וְלֹא תֶחֱטָא:

———→∘ PRAYERS ∘←———

that I will attain the joy of the mitzvah, a true joy that leads to a holy fervor in my heart and sets it aflame with great sanctity for the sake of Your Name, so that I will truly serve you, just as You desire. Protect me from overindulging in drink. Prevent me from ever becoming intoxicated. Instead, give me the strength to arouse the spiritual root of "wine that gives joy," of wine that "causes the heart of man to rejoice." (*Likutey Tefilos* 1:41)

———→∘ COMMENTARY ∘←———

(law-giver) (*Devorim* 33:21), which has the numerical value of 248 (רמ"ח – מחקק), equal to the number of limbs in the body. But when one gets drunk, he forgets the commandments, as it is written: "Lest you drink and forget the *mechokek*" (*Mishlei* 31:5); for drinking to the point of inebriation causes one to forget the 248 mitzvos given by Moshe. (*Likutey Moharan* 2:26)

Rabbi Mordechai of Chernobyl wrote that a person should not drink any intoxicating beverages, other than at *kiddush* on Shabbos and Yom Tov. (*Hadracha*)

19 Be careful to never utter God's Name in vain.

→o PRAYERS o←

Every Morning, Say the Following before Reciting the Blessings Over the Torah

Behold, I intend with every detail of my actions, words, and thoughts, from this moment until tomorrow at this time, to unite the Holy One with His Shechinah, in the name of all Yisroel, in order to put myself, all the Jewish people, and the entire world, on the scale of merit.

Furthermore, may it be that whenever I mention the Holy Name Y-H-V-H, from this moment until tomorrow at this time, that I intend it to signify God's eternal Being – He is, was and will always be – and in the manner in which it is read, as the Name A-D-N-Y, meaning that He is the Master of All. And when I mention the Name Elokim, my

→o COMMENTARY o←

Whenever you mention God's Name, you should feel fear and your entire body should tremble. Furthermore, it is not only forbidden to mention God's Holy Name in vain (Y-H-V-H), it is forbidden to utter in vain any of the unique Names ascribed to Him; that is, all those Names that are forbidden to erase, in any language. (*Chayei Adam, Klal* 5)

After making sure that your body, your clothing and the place you located are all clean, prepare yourself to say the blessings. Be very careful to recite them with awe and proper intention. You should never recite any blessing in vain; for instance, by making a blessing where one is not required; or, by causing a blessing to be made unnecessarily, such as in a case where a single inclusive blessing would generally suffice, but you cause an additional blessing to be required. An example of this is the person who speaks between laying the arm tefillin and the head tefillin, which results in him having to make a separate blessing on the head tefillin. A person who makes a blessing in vain has transgressed the rabbinic aspect of the prohibition "You shall not take the Name of your God in vain." (Ibid.)

The Chida cites the Rokeach, who states that the one hundred blessings a person must recite each day protect him from the one hundred curses (mentioned in *Vayikra* 28:61

יט וְיִשְׁמוֹר מִלְהַזְכִּיר שֵׁם לְבַטָּלָה:

---o PRAYERS o---

intention is that He is powerful and omnipotent, the Lord of all forces, the Cause of all causes, who reigns in all the worlds. (*Tefilah l'Dovid*, Rabbi Avraham of Butshatsh)

Praying with Concentration

Master of the World! May it be Your will that I concentrate on every word that I say; especially when I mention Your Holy Names. And deliver me from every stumbling block and sin. (*Otzar Tefilos Yisroel*, vol. 1, p. 166)

and *Devorim* 28). Of course, this is only when a person makes the blessing slowly, fully enunciating the letters, with the simple meaning of the words in mind.

In truth, praying slowly has the power to extend one's life, as the Sages said: "Whoever draws out his prayers, has his days and years drawn out" (*Berachos* 54b). He will be successful in his work and all his dealings, and in raising his children and marrying them off. The main thing is what the Midrash states: "The Holy One says, 'No one ever loses out by listening to Me.'" Certainly, if you draw out your prayers a little bit, you won't lose out, but will only benefit physically and spiritually. You will not have to spend time in a doctor's office or in a hospital, God forbid.

May God protect us together with the souls of all Yisroel. (*Hakdama Ben Yisachar*)

The life and vitality of all the Divine Names is God Himself. Yet God Himself has no name, for His essence is concealed. All the Names that we call Him relate only to His actions, and not to His essence, which is beyond all thought. Thus, when we mention any of God's Names in prayer, our mind must be on God Himself; for He lies behind all the Names, yet works through them, and it is to Him alone that we direct our words of praise. To focus on the Name alone would be like relating to a body without a soul. (*Likutey Halachos, Birchas HaShachar* 3:34)

20 Be careful not to speak or think a single holy word in an unclean place. For the evil inclination works especially hard to cause a person to speak about holy things in unclean places.

⟶o COMMENTARY o⟵

You should be mindful of your Creator no matter where you are: In a clean place, think about Torah. In a place where people are immodest, think about the mitzvah of modesty. And in the bathroom, think about all the excrement that your body produces. How then could you possibly be haughty? (*Hanhagos Rabbi Zechariah Mendel mi'Yaroslav*, §199. See *Piskei Teshuvos* 85:3)

21 Do not discuss even ethical teachings (*mussar*) in the holy synagogue, so that you are not drawn into talking about irrelevant things.

⟶o COMMENTARY o⟵

The reason why the Holocaust never reached the Sephardic lands is because the Jews there preserved the honor of the synagogues and study-halls by never engaging in idle conversation in them. This merit protected them. We are obliged to make this known, in order to stop the terrible plague that has spread in our generation on account of people speaking [unnecessarily] in synagogues and study-halls. (*Notrei Omen*, in the name of the *Imrei Emes*)

Woe to the person who speaks about mundane matters in a synagogue. Woe to him for fostering division in the upper worlds. Woe to him for diminishing faith. Woe to him, for he has no portion in the God of Yisroel. He acts as if he has no God; as if He were not there, and that he has no portion in Him, and does not fear Him. And he shows disrespect for the supernal rectifications that are accomplished through prayer. (*Zohar* 2:131b)

כ וְיִשְׁמוֹר עַצְמוֹ מִלְּדַבֵּר וּמִלַּחְשׁוֹב שׁוּם דָּבָר קְדוּשָׁה בְּמָקוֹם מְטוּנָף:

———→o COMMENTARY o←———

The great and holy Rabbi Yitzchak Yaakov Weiss (1902–1989) would rebuke people for wasting their precious time gossiping about news and politics while immersing in the mikvah before prayer. He writes in *Minchas Yitzchak* (4:61): I saw how the [pure] thoughts of my Rabbis and the Tzaddikim whom I followed were reflected in their actions. When they disrobed, immersed in the mikvah, and then got dressed, they did so with fear and love of God, without saying a word, unless it was absolutely necessary. (*Piskei Teshuvos* 85:1, note 6)

כא וְיִשְׁמוֹר עַצְמוֹ לְדַבֵּר בְּבֵית הַכְּנֶסֶת הַקָּדוֹשׁ אַף דִּבְרֵי מוּסָר שֶׁלֹּא יוּמְשַׁךְ מִתּוֹךְ כֵּן לְדָבָר בָּטֵל:

———→o COMMENTARY o←———

"God will fight for you; and you shall remain silent." (Shemos 14:14)

The Midrash says that God fights against the archangels [of the nations] who raise accusations against the Jewish people. He dismisses their arguments, by stating that the Jews are nevertheless better than the other nations of the world. However, when Satan accuses the Jewish people of talking in synagogues and study-halls – unlike the nations of the world, who sit quietly [during prayer] – God, so to speak, has nothing to reply. This is implied in the verse above: "God will fight for you." That is, He will fight for you against the nations of the world. However, this is only when "you shall remain silent" during prayer. But if you speak during prayer, the Holy One will not fight against them. (In the name of Reb Yeivi).

Every synagogue and study-hall in this world has a corresponding synagogue and study-hall in the world Above. Therefore, you must be careful not to speak about anything unrelated to Torah and prayer in them. To do so is akin to speaking with a king and suddenly turning away from him, saying: "My lord, the king, I cannot speak with you, because I prefer to talk about things that interest *me*." This drives away the Divine Presence from the world. (*Avodas Yisroel, Avos* 5:7)

TITLE PAGE, FIRST EDITION, NO'AM ELIMELECH, 1787, LEMBERG

Stories & Teachings

Telling stories of Tzaddikim
is a very great thing, for through
them, the heart is greatly inspired
and aroused for God, with a
powerful yearning.

Likutey Moharan 1:248

Rabbi Nachman of Breslov said, " I myself was greatly motivated to serve God through stories of Tzaddikim. "Many great Tzadikim used to visit the home of my holy parents. We lived in Medziboz, and this was also the home of the Baal Shem Tov. Many would come and visit the Baal Shem Tov's grave, and they would mostly stay at my father's house. It was from them that I heard many stories of Tzadikim, and this moved me toward God." It was through this that the Rebbe attained the great things that he did. (*Sichos HaRan* 138)

Rabbi Yechezkel of Shinov was once traveling with his chasidim in an open carriage. It was a very windy day, and although he desired to smoke a cigarette, the wind blew out all the matches that his chasidim lit for him. He then told them the following story: One very hot Friday afternoon, in the home of R. Mendel of Riminov, after the Shabbos candles were already lit, a strong wind started blowing through the open window and threatened to extinguish the flames. R. Mendel walked to the window and said: "Master of the World, don't we need these candles for the holy Shabbos?" Immediately, the wind stopped blowing into the house, and continued blowing only outside.

When R. Yechezkel finished telling this story, he asked his chasidim to try lighting his cigarette again. This time, they did so with a single match.

Afterward, he told his chasidim: "Don't think that that was a miracle, for a person can accomplish amazing things by telling stories about Tzaddikim that are relevant. Stories told about Tzaddikim have great power to deliver a person. Indeed, we've seen many Tzaddikim who were able to save people from their troubles by telling stories related to their circumstances. This brought great deliverance into the world. (*Zechus Avos* p. 39)

Stories & Teachings
TZETEL KATAN

1 **Whenever you are not studying Torah ... you should have in mind the mitzvah "I shall be sanctified among the Bnei Yisroel."**

During the dark days of the Holocaust, the great Chasidic Rebbe, Rabbi Chaim Halberstam of Sanz (1793–1876), appeared in a dream to his son, Rabbi Yeshaya of Tshkhoiv, and told him: "You should know that the souls of the Jews who are being killed in sanctification of God's Name rise to the highest Heavenly Chamber. Even if you were to live hundreds of years, studying Torah and serving God the way I did my whole life, you would still not reach their level." (*Oros v'Nesivos* p. 442)

---

2 **When reciting the first verse of *Kerias Shema*, or the first blessing of the *Shemoneh Esrei*, you should have in mind all that we wrote above.**

One Shabbos afternoon, Rabbi Chaim Vital entered the study of his holy teacher, the Arizal, and found the latter napping on a bench. He noticed that the Arizal's lips were moving in his sleep, and so leaned over to see if he could hear what his master was saying. Suddenly, the Arizal woke up and discovered Rabbi Chaim leaning over him.

"What are you doing?" the Ari asked.

"I saw my master's lips moving in his sleep and wanted to hear what he was saying."

"I was learning the mysteries of Torah in the Supernal Academy," the Arizal replied. "Whenever I sleep, my soul ascends on high, where I'm allowed to choose which yeshivah I wish to study in. Sometimes it is the yeshivah of Rabbi Shimon bar Yochai, sometimes the yeshivah of Rabbi Yehudah HaNasi, and sometimes the yeshivah of Rabbi Yochanan ben Zakkai or Rabbi Eliezer HaGadol. There, they transmit to me the deepest secrets of the Torah."

Another time, the Arizal said to one of his students: "Last night my soul learned such deep Torah secrets in the Supernal Academy that it would take me forty years to record them all."

Although no one in our generation can attain this level of enlightenment, a person should still try to sanctify himself as much as possible; for God desires holiness and purity, combined with fear and humility. (*Yesod Yosef*, chap. 61)

3 You should likewise keep these thoughts in mind whenever you eat...

A person's thoughts and opinions are a result of the particular food he eats, and the manner in which he consumes them. This is because one's food eventually becomes one's blood, which is the seat of the soul, which constitutes a person's thoughts and opinions... Thus, when the food is kosher and a person eats it mindfully – following the dictate: "In all your ways know Him" (*Mishlei* 3:7) – his thoughts and opinions will be straight and correct. However, if the food is lacking in some way, or even worse, if it is prohibited, for some reason, then his blood will also be impure. And since the blood is the soul, his opinions will become warped. Therefore, a person must always be careful about what and how he eats. (*Rambam*, Letters, quoted in *Menoras Zahav, Vayera*)

During the period when Rabbi Yosef Kibo served as Chief Rabbi of Salonika, Greece, a simple, local man became famous for being visited by a *maggid*, a personal spiritual guide, who would reveal to him amazing secrets. The Rabbis of the city investigated the matter, and were amazed to find that it was true: he was privy to secret knowledge, such as he had never known before.

When word of this reached Rabbi Yosef, he replied: "Tell me how this man eats and drinks." The Rabbis sent back the message: "We've observed that he eats and drinks a lot."

"In that case," Rabbi Yosef answered, "you needn't look further for an answer. His knowledge comes from the Side of Impurity. For holiness does not rest upon a glutton. Therefore, I order everyone to stop speaking with him."

The people stopped visiting the man, and it was eventually revealed that his knowledge did indeed derive from the evil forces of the "Other Side."

When a person seeks to repent, it is important that he limit the amount of food which he consumes. (*Menoras Zahav*, in the name of the *Chida, Vayera*)

Chazal say: "*Kiddush* can only be recited in the setting of a meal" (*Pesachim* 101a). Meaning to say: A person attains *kedushah*, holiness, primarily at the time that he eats. (*Noam HaChasidim, Achilah*)

Rabbi Tzvi of Ziditchov once said: "When I was young, I prayed to be able to accomplish the same spiritual rectifications through eating that I was able to accomplish through prayer. Today, thank God, I ask for the reverse. (Ibid.)

4 Accustom yourself to say: "Behold, I perform this action for the sake of the union of the Holy One and His Shechinah.

You should think the following, whenever you study Torah: "Behold, I make myself into a vessel for the Shechinah." Do this even a thousand times a day. My teacher, Rabbi Elimelech of Lizhensk, said that this purifies one's body very much, and that when a person becomes habitual in this, his mind becomes pure and clean, and he will be able to pray with holy thoughts. (*Darchei Tzedek*, §26)

5 When a bad character trait begins to stir in you… you should immediately say, with all of your might: "HaCana'ani, HaChiti, HaEmori, HaPrizi, HaChivi, v'HaYivusi v'HaGirgoshi."

Transforming Vices to Virtues

It is known that the Tzaddik Rabbi Zushia of Anipoli was an extremely stubborn child, so much so that if his mother refused to do his bidding, or give him something he wanted, he would refuse to eat for days. Once, Rabbi Zushia overheard some chasidim discussing the idea that every bad character trait actually has a root in holiness; the only problem being that the side of evil has latched onto it. Precisely with that trait, they concluded, a person can best exalt God and come wondrously close to Him. When young Zushia heard this, he considered his own behavior. "Why must I hurt my mother so much and cause others great pain through my stubbornness?" he thought. "It would be much better if I could use this trait to serve God and conquer my own evil inclination." And he did! According to Rabbi Nachman, Rabbi

Zushia served God with the fiery passion of a beginner for twenty-one years. (*Leket Amorim* by Rabbi Yaakov Meir Shechter, p.50)

The first thing to point out to you, my precious son, concerns the great sin of idleness, which is the root of all major offenses. For idleness is the beginning of all transgression, and the great tree upon which many sins grow. Woe to us that it has become so commonplace! On account of idleness, the Land of Yisroel was lost and the gates of teshuvah are locked; for this sin leads to many serious transgressions. A person's heart becomes closed, and he imagines that he is already righteous, as Chazal have said: "One sin leads to another." A person should rectify his actions while he is still young and strong, before he grows old. (*Divrei Emes*, chap. 2)

It is known that in addition to leading to numerous sins, idleness is, in itself, a great sin. For every hour that a person wastes is an irrevocable loss; a moment in time that will never return. A person must take pity on his precious time and on his life in this world; for he can bring merit to his soul with Torah study and good deeds – each person according to his level. Even those Jews who lack knowledge and have not merited the crown of Torah can acquire life in the World to Come, if they are careful with their time and do not trifle it away. This is easy to do, for one can always find books written in one's own language – such as mussar or *halachah* – to study when he is not working. This brings a person great merit. (*Divrei Emes*, chap. 2)

Each man has two wives: the one whom the Creator commanded him to marry, in order to bear his children; and the other, the holy soul that God gave him, whose only desire is to serve the Creator and to ascend to the Source from which it was hewn. This second wife is called "a woman of valor," and [of her it is said,] "A good woman is a gift to her husband," for the soul can bring a person to an infinitely high level. A person who truly chooses to serve God will find no obstacles in his worship – even from his real wife; for, she will help him, as well. (*Noam Elimelech, Vayishlach*)

6 **Do not let impure thoughts dwell in your mind.**

We have seen the holiness and purity of numerous Jewish homes become destroyed due to the accursed radio that people bring into their houses. With the voices of disbelievers spouting heresy and of wanton men and women singing love songs, the radio has spiritually damaged our sons and daughters and led them astray, God save us! It has had a bad influence on adults as well. (From a pronouncement of the Badatz of Yerushalayim, 1955)

Computers are meant for adults to use for their livelihood. Children should never be allowed to play games on them, just as a soldier would never allow children to play with his gun. (*Kuntress "Tzofiyah,"* in the name of the *Pnei Menachem* of *Gur*)

A new danger has recently arisen, which is infinitely worse than those of the past – the Internet. Many people connect to the Internet in their homes as a means of earning a livelihood, even though it's known that the Internet entices a person to view the most shameful and forbidden things. Found in new computers, the Internet can bring every type of impurity into the home. Fathers and mothers have come and cried to us in anguish. And so we say, "Enough of this plague!" (*Kuntress "Tzofiyah,"* quoting Rabbi Shmuel *HaLevi* Wosner)

Rabbis from every group have signed a petition against the viewing of films, be they live, animation, or nature documentaries, including DVDs. It is forbidden for schools, yeshivos or seminaries to show videos. May God, in His compassion, heal the breach in His people and remove this abomination from Israel. (*Kuntress "Tzofiyah"*)

Whoever is not careful concerning [the conduct of] his wife, his children and the members of his household, warning them and constantly scrutinizing their ways so that he knows that they are completely without sin or transgression, is himself a sinner. (Rambam, *Mishneh Torah, Hilchos Sotah* 4:19)

7 **If a person accidentally sees something indecent ... he should immediately recite the verse: "Do not follow after your heart."**

In the town of the Baal Shem Tov, there was a famous, blind musician whose sweet melodies aroused feelings of genuine joy and repentance in all who heard them. When this musician's time came to leave the world, he suddenly revealed to his family and friends standing around his bed that actually he had never been blind at all! Rather, when he was young, he decided to refrain from looking at women or forbidden things. In reality, his "blind" eyes were clear and bright.

During the same period, there lived a wealthy man known as "Yosseleh the Miser." Despite his great riches, he never gave as much as a penny to the poor. Fortunately, there was another rich man in his city who generously supplied all the needs of the community. As time passed, this rich man grew in fame for his generosity, while Yosseleh the Miser became ever more despised.

The day finally arrived for Yosseleh to leave this world. Yet no one grieved his death, for he passed away with a tight fist and a closed heart. But the following day, when all the poor of the city came to the other rich man's home, they were shocked and disappointed by what he told them. "I'm sorry," he said. "I have nothing to give you. It was never my own money in the first place. All that charity came from the hidden Tzaddik, Yosseleh the Miser, who passed away yesterday. He provided me with the funds that I distributed to you, because he did not want to receive any honor for his generosity. He sought only to fulfill the mitzvah of charity perfectly, without any ulterior motives." After relating this, the man broke down in tears. The poor people cried as well – on account of the hidden Tzaddik whom they had scorned and abused for so many years.

After the Baal Shem Tov told these two stories, he turned to his chasidim and asked: "Which of the two was higher – the 'blind' musician or the 'stingy' millionaire?"

Seeing that his students did not know what to answer, the Baal Shem Tov said: "Is it hard to decide? Well, in the supernal worlds, they are unable to decide, as well." (*Mavir Levavos*, p. 314)

The Tanna, R. Masiya ben Charush, spent all his days in the study hall, toiling at Torah. His face shone like an angel, for he had never once gazed at a woman. However, this made Satan jealous of him, and he decided to try to make him sin.

"How important do you consider R. Masiya ben Charush?" Satan asked God.

"He is a complete Tzaddik," God replied.

"Let me try to make him sin," Satan requested.

"You will fail," came the reply.

"Still, allow me to try."

"Go!" said God.

Satan appeared before R. Masiya in the form of the most beautiful woman in the world. However, as soon as R. Masiya saw him, he turned his face away. Satan moved into his field of vision, and R. Masiya turned away again. Wherever Satan went, R. Masiya looked away.

"I'm worried that my desires will overcome me and cause me to sin," R. Masiya said to himself. He ordered his attendant to bring him fire and nails, with which he blinded himself in both eyes. When Satan saw this, he vanished in shock.

At that moment, God called to the angel Raphael, "Go and heal R. Masiya ben Charush." Raphael flew down and stood before R. Masiya.

"Who are you?" R. Masiya asked.

"I am the angel Raphael," he replied. "God has sent me to heal you."

"Leave me alone," R. Masiya replied. "Whatever happened, happened."

Raphael returned to God, and related R. Masiya's words.

God replied, "Go and tell him that I promise that his desires will never threaten him again." Only when R. Masiya heard this promise, did he allowed himself to be healed.

From here, the Sages deduced that a person who does not look at women -- especially another man's wife -- will be free from the attacks of the evil inclination. (*Yalkut Shimoni, Vayechi*, 161)

8 Train yourself not to speak to anyone, save out of great necessity.

Once, the Chofetz Chaim and fellow Torah scholar journeyed together to fulfill a mitzvah. Along the way, they stayed overnight in the house of a certain Jew, who treated them to dinner. During the meal, the man's wife asked her two distinguished guests if they were enjoying the food. "The food is excellent," responded the Chofetz Chaim. "I agree," responded the other Torah scholar, "though perhaps it could use a little more salt. However, in general, it is indeed excellent."

The woman thanked them for their comments and left the room. Immediately, the Chofetz Chaim let out a loud sigh: "Oy! My whole life I have been careful never to speak or hear *lashon hora*, and now I've had to listen to it! I'm sorry I made this trip with you. I'm sure our traveling together cannot have been a mitzvah."

Shocked by the Chofetz Chaim's reaction, the other Rabbi became distraught. "Rabbi Yisroel Meir," he said, "what did I say that was so bad? What in my words was *lashon hora*?"

The Chofetz Chaim replied: "Wasn't it *lashon hora* when you told the woman that the food needed salt? Keep in mind that the woman of the house didn't prepare the food herself. She had her maid, probably a poor widow, cook it for her. As soon as she heard your comment, the woman went straight to the kitchen to criticize the maid for not putting salt in the food. As you can imagine, the maid defended herself, insisting that she had.

"Then, of course, the woman raised her voice and declared, 'We have two great Rabbis eating at our table who say that the food lacks salt. How dare you claim otherwise? You are a liar!' 'I'm sure that I added salt,' the maid insisted. To which the woman replied: 'Then you're saying that the Rabbis are liars! You're fired! I don't want you to cook for me anymore!'"

The Chofetz Chaim's companion listened to this story in amazement. "How does he know all this?" he thought to himself. "Why is he building castles in the air based upon two or three spoken words?"

"Rabbi Yisroel Meir," the Rabbi said, "surely you are exaggerating."

"Am I?" responded the Chofetz Chaim. "Then come with me to the kitchen to see what is happening."

They rose from the table and went into the kitchen, where they found both women distraught and in tears, each one having accused the other, just as the Chofetz Chaim had predicted.

When the Torah scholar saw what had happened, he did everything possible to correct the situation. He even offered money to help the widow keep her position. Eventually, peace was restored between the two women. (*Sama d'Chaya*, chap. 6, in the name of *Shaal Avicha VaYagedcha*)

Never Shame Anyone

The Tzaddik, Rabbi Dovid of Lelov, once set out on a trip to visit his Rebbe, Rabbi Elimelech of Lizhensk. Since he was still a young Torah scholar and lacked the funds to hire a carriage, Rabbi Dovid had to travel by foot. Along the road, a rich Chasid from Warsaw passed him in a carriage. Rabbi Dovid called out to him and asked where he was headed. "To the Tzaddik of Lizhensk, Rabbi Elimelech!" came the reply. The young Torah scholar asked if he could get a ride, to which the Chasid agreed.

Unfortunately, the rich Chasid was far from being a refined individual. Not recognizing Rabbi Dovid, he assumed that he was just a vagabond, and mocked and belittled him the entire trip. Rabbi Dovid, for his part, kept silent, and bid his benefactor farewell when they finally reached their destination.

Once in Lizhensk, the rich Chasid went straight in to see Rabbi Elimelech, whereas Rabbi Dovid took time to prepare himself before entering the Tzaddik's chambers. When he was finally admitted, Rabbi Dovid and Rabbi Elimelech spoke at length. On leaving Rabbi Elimelech's room nearly two hours later, the young Torah scholar chanced upon the rich Chasid waiting outside. "I need to stay a little longer in Lizhensk," Rabbi Dovid told him. "Please don't wait for me to return home." Then he added: "And if on your way home you hear someone crying for help, follow the voice. You will know what to do."

Now, having seen how long Rabbi Dovid had spent with Rabbi Elimelech, the rich Chasid realized that he was no ordinary tramp. He regretted having spoken with him so rudely, and understood that he should take the young man's words very seriously.

Halfway on his journey home, while passing through a forest, the rich Chasid heard someone crying out in Polish. Remembering what Rabbi Dovid had said, he turned his carriage in the direction of the voice, on a path that took him deep into the forest. There, he found a

Polish nobleman, his carriage and horses sunk deep in the mud. The Chasid quickly attached a strong rope to both carriages and then ordered his horses to pull. After a few minutes, the nobleman's horses and carriage were extracted from the mud.

Apparently, the nobleman had been stranded there for a long time. Seeing that he was cold and dirty, the Chasid gave him a warm coat and some food, and sat with him until he had regained his strength.

"Where are you from?" the Chasid asked.

"From Warsaw," the nobleman replied.

"I am also from Warsaw," said the Chasid. "You can travel back with me and even rest in my home until you have fully recuperated."

Back at home, the Chasid helped the nobleman remove his wet and muddy clothing. He provided him with a good meal, and made a warm bed for him. In the morning, the nobleman was feeling better and took his leave, with a deep feeling of gratitude.

Several days later, the Chasid was summoned to the home of the nobleman. "How can I repay you for all your kindness?" the nobleman asked him. "If you hadn't saved me, I might have died from exposure."

"I don't need any reward," the Chasid replied. "It's enough for me that I saved you from death."

"At the very least, I will take your name and address," said the nobleman, "so that I will always remember that you saved me." And so the grateful noblemen wrote down the Chasid's information in his notebook.

Years passed and the wheel of fortune turned. In time, the Chasid lost his entire business and was forced to sell his home and pawn all his beautiful clothing and furniture. He was left with nothing, and had no choice but to go begging from door to door, and from town to town. For ten years he suffered such abject poverty that he all but forgot that he had ever been rich. After a decade of wandering, the Chasid one day found himself back in Warsaw. The shame he felt over having to beg in his hometown was greater than any he had previously suffered.

One day, the Chasid came upon a nobleman sitting in a gilded carriage. He approached the carriage, respectfully removed his hat, and stretched out his hand for a donation. The nobleman, who was the governor of Warsaw, looked the Chasid square in the face and said, "Come here, Jew!"

The Chasid grew frightened. Thinking that he had perhaps overstepped his bounds, he turned and ran from the area. However, the governor immediately ordered his men to pursue the Chasid and bring him back. On returning, the Chasid stood trembling before the man, expecting the worst, but the governor spoke to him kindly.

"Don't be afraid," he said. "I'm not going to hurt you. I just want to ask you your name." The Chasid told him.

"That's what I thought," exclaimed the governor. "Don't you recognize me? I am the man you saved in the forest ten years ago. What has happened to you since then? How did you end up in such a terrible condition?"

The Chasid recounted for the governor all the misfortunes that had befallen him over the last decade. Without hesitating, the governor took out his wallet and handed him two thousand rubles. The Chasid opened a business and soon became very successful. In no time at all, he returned to his former standing.

By this time, the Tzaddik, Rabbi Elimelech of Lizhensk, had already passed away, and his disciple, the Seer of Lublin, had taken his place. Rabbi Dovid of Lelov had also become famous as one of the leading Rabbis of the generation.

The Chasid decided to visit the Tzaddik of Lelov and tell him all that had happened. When he entered the Tzaddik's chamber, the Chasid did not recognize the young scholar whom he had shamed so many years before. Rabbi Dovid, however, recognized the Chasid immediately, and asked to hear all that had befallen him over the past ten years.

When the Chasid had finished his story, Rabbi Dovid identified himself as that young man who had journeyed with him to Lizhensk so many years ago. The Chasid was shocked. "You should know, my friend," Rabbi Dovid continued, "at the very moment you mocked and belittled me, a death sentence was decreed upon you in heaven. I was aware of this, as was Rabbi Elimelech, and for the two hours we sat alone in his study, we sought a way to annul the decree. Finally, we were able to change it from death to poverty – for the Sages teach that a pauper is considered like a dead man. However, since you did me a favor by giving me a ride, I tried to do you a favor in return, and was able to reduce your sentence of poverty to just ten years." (*Sipurei Chasidim, Shemos*)

Don't Publicize Your Good Deeds

On the ground floor of the home of Rabbi Shlomo Luria (the "Maharshal," 1510–1573), there was a small vegetable store run by a man named Avraham. He was a humble man, who rarely spoke with others and seemed, to all appearances, fairly illiterate. He slept in the back of the shop.

Late one night, the Maharshal awoke and heard Rabbi Avraham studying a passage of Gemara downstairs. He was amazed at how well the latter understood the difficult passage and was able to explain it to himself. Over the next few days, the Maharshal paid close attention to his neighbor, and soon reached the conclusion that he was not a simple person at all, but a genuine *Talmid Chocham*, with a deep and comprehensive understanding of the Talmud. He summoned Rabbi Avraham to his study, in order to test his knowledge of various subjects. Rabbi Avraham, for his part, declined to answer. "I'm an ignoramus! I don't know how to learn!" he insisted. However, Rabbi Luria ordered him to admit the truth. Having no choice, Rabbi Avraham began a complex explanation of the various topics that the Maharshal had raised. When he finished, he begged the Maharshal not to reveal his secret. The Maharshal promised that for the time being he would tell no one, but would not agree to keep the secret indefinitely. And so, when the time came for the Maharshal to leave this world, he revealed Rabbi Avraham's great knowledge to the Jews of the city and instructed them to appoint the hidden *Talmid Chocham* as their next Chief Rabbi. The people approached Rabbi Avraham and offered him the position, but he would not hear of it. Finally, after repeated requests, he agreed.

This story is a great lesson in the tremendous value of selfless Torah study, free of the desire for fame or recognition. God never withholds His goodness from those who walk sincerely in this path. (*Shem HaGedolim, maareches* 1:76)

Avoiding Trivial Discussion

A person who speaks about empty things loses all his desire for Torah and mitzvos, due to the impurity of the words. He will fall from his level of spirituality, and draw upon himself a powerful form of impurity. Furthermore, he mixes together the holy and the mundane. (Rabbi Eliyahu of Vilna, *Vechay Bohem*, p. 207)

How powerful the evil inclination is! People sit around, with nothing to talk about but the weather – if it's too hot or too cold, too wet or too dry. Their evil inclinations stir them up, and make them too embarrassed to sit silently. So, they go from topic to topic, looking for something to discuss, with everyone feeling the need to say something, so that the others shouldn't wonder why he is quiet. This is actually quite foolish, since he could always excuse himself by saying that he simply has nothing to add.

A God-fearing person has no place among those who hang out on street corners, or among scoffers who sit together and speak of idle matters. Nor should he sit alone in his house serving God. Rather, he should go to the Sages and become wise. If it occasionally happens that he must sit among such people, for social reasons and the like, he should keep silent. In truth, this too, is far from desirable, for a person should not even hear such empty talk, since the ears are easily affected. However, if he cannot avoid the situation, he should choose the lesser of two evils. He should be deeply concerned about being there, and find some pretext to slip away from them as soon and as amicably as possible. (*Pele Yoetz, Dibur*)

A person who is careful with his words can attain *ruach hakodesh* – Divine inspiration. (*Vechay Bohem*, p. 40, citing *Reishis Chochmah*)

9 Immediately upon waking, you should accustom yourself to say: "I give thanks to You, living and eternal King…."

One wintry day, the Chasam Sofer accompanied his Rebbe, Rav Nossan Adler, on a trip. The roads were covered with snow, and along the way, their carriage slipped into a ditch and became stuck. The wagon driver was unable to extricate it on his own, so he set off for the nearest town to look for help.

A short while later, the driver returned with two strong bulls. Tying them to the carriage, alongside the horses, he began pulling the carriage from the ditch.

Instantly, Rabbi Nossan Adler jumped from the carriage and then began dancing and singing in the snow. The Chasam Sofer looked on in amazement. Noticing his disciple's bewilderment, Rabbi Nossan Adler explained his actions:

"Do you see what the driver has done? He's tied the bulls to the wagon while the horses are still attached. The Torah prohibits this! It is the transgression of *kelayim*. I jumped out so as not to participate in the sin. And since refraining from the *kelayim* of animals is a rare mitzvah, this is the first time in my life I've had the opportunity to observe it. How could I not dance for joy? (*Elef Sippurim*)

The Power of Tzitzis

A young yeshivah student once became sick with a life-threatening disease. The poor boy suffered terribly, and had to undergo chemotherapy at a local hospital. On one occasion, the nurse informed him that for his next treatment – a particularly difficult procedure – he would be required to wear sterilized garments, which the hospital would provide.

The young man agreed. However, knowing that the hospital would not supply him with a *tallis katan*, he brought along his own, which he had cleaned, pressed and sterilized as much as possible. But when the nurse saw him wearing the *tallis katan* over his hospital garments, she ordered him to remove it, and refused to administer the treatment as long as he was wearing the *tzitzis*.

The young man tried to talk the nurse out of her demand. His *tzitzis* were almost part of his body, he explained. There was no way he could give them up. But his words fell on deaf ears. The nurse refused to administer treatment as long as he wore the *tallis katan*. Yet the boy was equally adamant, and so ended up sitting at the entrance to the ward, unable to receive treatment and unwilling to part from the mitzvah. His family, who were waiting outside, had no idea of the battle that was going on within.

Three hours later one of the senior doctors arrived at the chemotherapy ward to examine the patients. When he saw the young man sitting by himself, he asked him what he was doing there. The young man explained the situation, after which the doctor entered the ward to speak with the nurse. A few moments later he returned, with an expression of shock and concern.

The boy asked the doctor what was wrong, but he replied only that the boy should first go in and receive his treatment; afterward, he would explain what happened. "I've told the nurse that there is no problem with you wearing your *tzitzis*," the doctor added.

When the young man finished the treatment, the doctor came to his bedside. "I am not an observant Jew," he explained in tears. "However, today, I saw with my own eyes how God protects those who keep the mitzvos. When I entered the ward to speak with the nurse, I looked over the treatment that you were supposed to receive. I was shocked to discover that you had been assigned the wrong procedure! This was an accident, of course, but if you hadn't insisted on wearing your *tzitzis*, the treatment would already be over. I have no doubt that had you received it, you would not be here with us now! Your obstinacy saved your life!" (*Mesoviv HaShulchan*, §445)

Washing One's Hands in the Morning

After the passing of Rabbi Elimelech of Lizhensk in 1787, one of his chasidim, Rabbi Gavriel Tatzhak, decided to seek a new Rebbe. Together with another Chasid, they decided to travel to the home of Rabbi Elimelech's brother, the famous Tzaddik, Rabbi Zushia of Anipoli. "Let us observe his actions and behavior. Perhaps we can accept him as our spiritual guide."

After a long and exhausting day on the road, the two chasidim stopped at a wayfarer's inn and rented a room. Upon retiring, however, they realized that they did not have any water for *netilas yadayim* the following morning. They turned to the innkeeper and offered to pay him for some cups of water with which to wash their hands. However, the innkeeper declined. There was no extra water available in the inn, and the hour was too late and the weather too inclement to go out to fetch some more.

"What more can we do at this point?" asked Rabbi Gavriel. "I'm tired and need to sleep. God doesn't hold a person accountable for things that are beyond his control." His traveling companion, however, was not so easily dissuaded, and refused to go to sleep without having water beside his bed. After Rabbi Gavriel fell asleep, his companion sought out the innkeeper again, and purchased from him a pint of beer, which he used to wash his hands in the morning.

The next day they continued on to Anipoli, to the Tzaddik's house. They had barely crossed the threshold, when Rabbi Zushia called out to Rabbi Gavriel: "Do you realize that all the spiritual impurity that my holy brother Rabbi Elimelech was able to remove from you returned this morning when you set out without washing your hands?!"

Hearing these words, Rabbi Gavriel felt like crying. A moment later, however, he was overjoyed. "Thank You God for bringing me to the right address!" he exclaimed. "I have indeed found another holy Tzaddik who knows the secrets of creation, just as my Rebbe, Rebbe Elimelech, did." (*Ohel Elimelech*, §337)

---

10 Be very diligent in your set program of Torah study....

Rabbi Avraham HaLevi, author of *Tikunei Shabbos*, lived in Tzefas at the time of the Arizal. Every night, at midnight, he would rise and walk through the Jewish quarter of the city, crying out in a lamenting tone: "My fellow Jews! Don't you know that the Shechinah is in exile due to our sins. The Holy Temple is destroyed! The Jewish people are suffering in this bitter exile, and pious men and women are being slaughtered in the cruelest ways – while you lie on your beds feeling safe and sound! Get up and cry out to God, the gracious and compassionate King. Perhaps He will hear your prayers and have mercy on the remnant of His people."

No one could sleep after hearing Rabbi Avraham's distressed cry. The entire community would awake and rush to the synagogue, where they would recite *tikun chatzos* and then study Torah together – Tanach, Mishnayos, Gemara, Kabbalah and the Zohar, each person studying material appropriate for him. At a certain point, they would stop studying and recite various prayers and hymns until the morning. In this way, the people of Tzefas would arouse God's mercy for all the Jewish people.

The Arizal was very impressed with Rabbi Avraham's activities, and praised him greatly. He said that Rabbi Avraham's soul was a reincarnation of the soul of Yirmiyahu HaNavi. One day, the Arizal summoned Rabbi Avraham to his home. "You must know that your days are numbered," he told him. "Your time to leave this world is soon approaching. However, if you perform one act of spiritual rectification that I will teach you, you will live another twenty-two years. Here is what you must do. Travel to Yerushalayim, to the Kosel HaMaaravi, and pour out your prayers to God there. You will then merit seeing the Shechinah.

Rabbi Avraham returned home and locked himself in his study for three days and nights, doing nothing but praying, studying Torah, and performing acts of penitence.

Afterward, he traveled to Yerushalayim and made his way to the Kosel, where he poured out his heart to God amidst tearful prayers. Suddenly, the image of a woman, dressed in black, appeared on the Kosel. In great fear, he fell upon his face and began crying: "Oy that I've seen this! Woe to my soul!"

He cried bitterly for a long while and began pulling the hairs from his head, until he fainted. In a dream, he saw the Shechinah approaching him, this time adorned in beautiful garments. "Do not worry, my son, Avraham. There is hope. The children will yet return to their borders, for I will bring them back from their captivity and show them compassion."

Rabbi Avraham awoke from his faint and made his way back to Tzefas. Upon entering the Arizal's chambers, the master Kabbalists declared: "I see that you beheld the face of the Shechinah. Be assured that you will now live another twenty-two years." And that is exactly what happened. (*Ohr Tzaddikim, amud ha-avodah*, chap. 17)

Not to Budge from One's Studies

The holy Klausenberger Rebbe once said: "When the *sefer Nodah b'Yehudah* was first published, someone gave a copy to my holy forefather, author of the *Baruch Taam*. It was late afternoon, around the time of the *Minchah* prayer. My great-great-grandfather took the *sefer* into his private study and sat there, totally absorbed in it for a full twenty-four hours. His family and disciples were afraid to disturb him. When he finally emerged the next day, my great-great-grandfather asked his chasidim, "Have you prayed *Minchah* yet?" (*Hi Sichosi*, p. 662)

The Light in the Torah

The power of the Torah is strong enough to free one from one's sins. No matter how trapped a person might be, if he simply makes it his business to set a regular time for Torah study every day without fail, he will be able to emerge from the hold of his evil past through the great strength of the Holy Torah. (*Likutey Etzos, Talmud Torah* 77)

Midnight

The exile has already lasted so long. God is only waiting for the moment to return to us and rebuild the Holy Temple. It could happen at any time. Our task is to see that from our side, we do nothing to obstruct the rebuilding of the Temple. On the contrary, we must make every effort to hasten it. This is why we should be so careful to get up each night at midnight and mourn for the destruction of the Holy Temple. Perhaps in a previous incarnation we ourselves were responsible for something which brought about its destruction. Even if not, it could still be that our sins in our present lifetime are holding up the rebuilding of the Temple, which is as bad as if we had actually destroyed it. This is the reason why we must weep and mourn every night at midnight. When we do so, it is as if we were actually making a tremendous effort to rebuild the Holy Temple. Then we will be able to draw closer to truth, to the true Tzaddikim and to those who are genuinely God-fearing. For they are the embodiment of truth, in its beauty, splendor and pleasantness. Through drawing closer to them your eyes will be opened and you will be able to see how far your own development has advanced and in which areas you need to work in order to return to God and to know and acknowledge His great and holy Name. (*Likutey Etzos, Chatzos*, §4)

Teshuvah before Torah study

There is no better time than the wee hours after midnight, when you can sit alone quietly and repent of your misdeeds. You should speak to God with words of love and supplication, and ask Him to forgive you for your past misdeeds. You should also beseech Him over the future – that you be entirely bound to the wisdom of the Torah and its pleasant commandments, and never experience any misfortune, G-d forbid, that you should be attached to the Creator the entire day, with a constant fear of G-d, and that you be should delivered from foreign thoughts. (*Birchas Chaim*, chap. 10, §7)

---

11 Accustom yourself to praying with all your might...

Every day, following the afternoon *Minchah* prayer, Rabbi Elimelech would sit and speak personally with his disciples. Afterward, he would enter his private room for the evening *Maariv* prayer. Rabbi Naftali Zvi of Ropshitz, who was then one of Rabbi Elimelech's students, longed to see how his Rebbe prayed. One day, he snuck into Rabbi Elimelech's private room and hid under the bed. Soon, Rabbi Elimelech came in and closed the door. He picked up his *gartel* and began to wrap it around his waist. With the first wrap of the prayer belt, Rabbi Naftali suddenly felt a powerful, spiritual light filling the room. With the second wrap, the light became so intense that Rabbi Naftali couldn't bear it any longer and let out a yell. Rabbi Elimelech immediately stopped and called out to his disciple: "Naftali, are you here? You're lucky that you didn't wait until I wrapped my *gartel* a third time, because the light would have been too strong for you, and you would have died! Now, please leave the room." (*Darchei Noam*, chap. 4)

Praying in a Loud Voice

Rabbi Shimshon bar Eliezer, author of the famous work *Baruch She'Omar*, was a contemporary of the 13th century sage, the Maharam of Rotenburg. When he was a child of eight, Rabbi Shimshon was orphaned of both his parents. He used to say the *Baruch She'Omar* prayer each morning in synagogue with such a sweet voice that he gained the nickname "*Baruch She'Omar*," and so chose this for the title of his book. (*HaChidah, mareches seforim* 2:107)

Not Interrupting Prayer

Once, the Chozeh of Lublin entered the study of his Rebbe, Rabbi Elimelech of Lizhensk, and found him sitting and sighing in anguish. Distressed by what he saw, the Chozeh asked his Rebbe what happened.

"How can I not be upset after having committed such a sin today?"

The Chozeh couldn't imagine what sin his Rebbe had committed, and so he asked him.

"This morning, during *Shacharis*, I interrupted the prayers by speaking about something unrelated. I had already started saying *Hodu*, when a distraught woman came to me and told me that her daughter was struggling in childbirth. I asked the woman for her daughter's name so that I could pray for her. That was my sin!"

"But, Rebbe," replied the Chozeh, "you did it to save her life, which takes priority over everything. And also, according to the *nusach Sefard* prayerbook, it is permitted to speak in the middle of *Hodu*, since it precedes *Baruch She'Omar*."

"Even so, it was a sin," replied Rabbi Elimelech, "since that does not apply to *nusach Ashkenaz*. And, in any case, why did this have to happen after I started praying. It's still a sin!" Rabbi Elimelech continued sighing and refused to be comforted. Finally, he exclaimed, "I only hope that God will accept my repentance."

Whenever the Chozeh of Lublin would relate this story, he would conclude. "From here, we learn how great a person's fear of sin should be, and how pained he should feel over even a hint of a transgression. But also, this story teaches that if one does stumble in any way, he should repent and return to God." (*Ohel Elimelech*, §294)

Sealing a Blessing with Amen

Rabbi Chaim of Volozhin was careful never to recite a blessing unless there was someone present to answer Amen. Once, while studying late at night, he became extremely thirsty. He reached out for a bottle of water and a cup on a nearby table, but then suddenly stopped himself. He was alone in his study, and all the members of his household had already gone to sleep. With no one to answer Amen to his blessing, he decided that he would wait until someone appeared.

Time passed and Rabbi Chaim's thirst grew stronger. Still, he did not interrupt his Torah study. Suddenly, he heard a faint knocking on the door. Rabbi Chaim opened it and found one of his disciples standing there. "Rebbe," the young man said, "I'm not able to sleep. My mind keeps turning over a difficult question in the Gemara." Rabbi Chaim invited the young man in and, with great *kavanah*, made a blessing on the water, to which the student answered Amen. He then answered the student's question.

The next day, Rabbi Chaim found the student and thanked him for coming to his home in the middle of the night.

"But Rebbe," the student replied with surprise, "I didn't come to your home!"

Apparently, Rabbi Chaim's late-night visitor had been an angel disguised as his student. In the merit of Rabbi Chaim's unbending commitment to making blessings in the most perfect way – which included the "Amen" – Heaven sent him an angel to enable him to quench his thirst while studying.

We say in the Rosh Hashanah prayers: "He stands alone, and who can answer him? His soul desires and He does; Awesome and Holy" (based on *Iyov* 23:13).

Rabbi Shmelke of Nikolsburg's commentary on this verse beautifully fits the story of Rabbi Chaim: "He stands alone" – when a person is alone, "and who can answer him" – with no one to answer Amen to his blessing. "His soul desires" – he longs to praise God, "and He does; Awesome and Holy" – and so the Awesome and Holy One creates an angel for him, to answer Amen. (*Shaal Avicha VaYagedcha*, vol. 1, p. 87)

---

13 Tell your spiritual mentor all your improper thoughts.

The *Tzetel Katan* advises a person to relate all his improper thoughts to his teacher. However, this does not mean that he should enter into a detailed discussion about the thought itself, for it is forbidden to talk about such things. (This is aside from the problem mentioned in many *seforim*, that one should not enter into a debate with the thought itself.) Rather, it means that you should tell your teacher, in a general way, that you are suffering from certain thoughts, which are interfering with your service of God. Furthermore, you should tell only your teacher; that is, someone on a higher spiritual level than you, and not a friend on your own level. (Rabbi Yitzchak Moshe Erlanger, *Kuntress Chasidus* 13, p. 89)

A person must possess holy boldness, as it is written: "Be bold as a leopard" (*Pirkei Avos* 5:20). One must be bold even in relation to one's Rabbi, in order to speak to him about everything, without shame. The reason one person is closer [to a Rabbi than another] is only because he is bolder, and so speaks to him more.

Furthermore, these two things are interdependent. The fact that a person is bold enough to speak to his Rabbi is because he serves God a great deal. And inversely, by speaking with his Rabbi, he becomes inspired to serve God even more. Thus, one depends on the other. (*Likutey Moharan* 1:271)

15 **When sitting down to a meal, before washing your hands, recite the *Tefilas HaShov*.**

The Shlah writes that a person should attach his heart to God when he eats, more than at any other time of the day (*Sha'ar HaOsiyos, Kedushas HaAchilah*). It's known that many Tzaddikim considered eating a greater act of worship than prayer. The Baal Shem Tov had a disciple who would go to the mikvah before eating, though not before praying.

The fact that eating is on a higher level than praying was so obvious to Tzaddikim that R. Tzvi Hirsh of Riminov once asked: "Why did Chazal decree that a person should first pray in the morning, and then eat?" (*Berachos* 10b). Since eating is higher than praying, he should eat first! The answer is that "we ascend in holiness, and do not descend" (*Berachos* 28a). Thus, a person should pray first, and then eat. (*Sichos b'Avodas Hashem*, p. 111)

Eating in Holiness

Performing the following practices during meals has the power to greatly sanctify a person and turn his eating into an offering to God:

- Immediately after eating the first piece of bread, you should recite *Tehilim* 23: "God is my shepherd; I shall not lack." This not only fulfills the requirement to speak Torah at the table, but also reminds you of God's beneficence. What's more, it causes you to pause at the beginning of your meal, when you are the hungriest, and thus prevents you from indulging in desire. This is a powerful form of self-sacrifice.

- You should eat in a mannerly fashion, like a member of royalty, as the *Sefer HaChinuch* (*mitzvah* 16) teaches. It is not fitting for a member of royalty to eat voraciously, since the way one eats affects one's personality. Rather, the more dignified a person is while eating, the more he benefits his soul, and his entire personality is elevated. The *Sefer HaChinuch* writes: "A person is influenced by his actions, which constantly pull his whole mind and heart, for good or for bad... for one's heart is drawn after his actions." Make sure that you eat slowly, consciously. Do not eat or drink while standing. Don't gaze at your friend's plate, and don't talk too loud while eating. All the more, you should not speak in a way that is prohibited, such as mockery, or gossip, and the like. All these things help a person sanctify himself while eating, so that his food becomes like an offering on the altar. (*Sichos b'Avodas Hashem*, p. 111)

16 A person should strive to fix his personality traits...

In his deep desire to perfect his soul and make it shine with the light of Torah and mitzvos, Rabbi Mordechai Bennet hardly allowed himself to sleep. Often, he would stay up the entire night studying Torah. And when he would sleep, he would rise from his bed with the swiftness of the leopard at two in the morning, and with the strength of the lion begin to serve God. He kept to this practice his entire life, using the nighttime hours to study the works of Rabbeinu Yitzchok Alfasi (the Rif), or Rambam's Mishneh Torah from beginning to end. (*Hi Sichasi*, p. 89)

Making Torah Study Habitual

I knew that people would whisper behind my back, saying, "Is Shaul also one of the prophets?" (*Shmuel* 1 10:11). Why, he's been a Leipzigian merchant for more than fifteen years. When did he have the time to study? Doesn't the Torah say: "It is not across the sea" – that is, you won't find knowledge of Torah among people involved in business. Though you should know, my brother, that I traveled great distances not in order to become wealthy, but only to support my family.

You should also know, my brother, that Torah study is an expression of the soul and its manifestations. Chazal say: "If a woman does not plan on marrying, and she waits ten years without a husband, she will no longer be able to bear children. However, if she plans on marrying, even though she waits many years for a husband, her soul remains fertile, and when she weds, she will give birth." It is the same for a Jew. If he abandons the Torah, she in turn distances herself from him, and his soul will lose its fertility. However, if he never meant to abandon her, but is simply unable to study and cling to her due to extenuating circumstances, then the Torah sits like a grass widow, separated from her husband, but waiting for him to return, for he has not intentionally estranged himself from her. Then, the power of the Torah remains in his soul.

I can say this much about myself: Even though I was a merchant and traveled afar, what I studied stayed with me; for even while I was on the road, I kept my mind on the Torah, and when I sat in my shop, my thoughts were upon her. And also when I engaged in business, many times my mind was on her, thinking about various commentaries or attempting to resolve some difficulty. (Introduction to *Chochmas Adam*)

The Siyum of Rabbi Zelig Reuven Bengis

Rabbi Zelig Reuven Bengis was the Chief Rabbi of Yerushalayim's Eidah Charedis in the mid-twentieth century. A tremendous *Talmid Chocham*, he finished *Shas* one hundred and one times during his lifetime. And since he was accustomed to review every page four times when studying it, he actually finished the entire Talmud over four hundred times.

On one occasion, Rabbi Zelig Reuven invited all his family and friends to a lavish *siyum* celebrating his conclusion of yet another cycle of the Talmud. The guests were curious as to why this time merited a greater celebration than usual. "This is not the first time you've finished *Shas*," they said to him, "yet you've never before invited us to such a sumptuous meal. Why is this time different?"

"This time is indeed special," he replied. "For today I am celebrating the completion of the Talmud that I studied in my spare time, for instance, while waiting on a line or traveling in a car. In each case, I took the opportunity to study a little more Gemara, picking up from where I left off. Thus, I'm even happier than usual, because I was able to save all those wasted moments and weave them together into a complete *Shas*!" (*Hi Sichosi*, p. 171)

Stories & Teachings
HANHAGOS HA'ADAM

1 The first thing you should do is study Gemara...

Studying *Gemara* with Rashi and Tosafos is no less an obligation than putting on tefillin. (*Birchei Yosef, Yoreh Deah* 246:4)

Studying *masechta Berachos* is a great thing. Studying *masechta Shabbos* is a glorious thing. Studying *Kesuvos* is like studying the entire Talmud – *Chulin, Avodah Zarah, Nidah* – for it encompasses them all! (Ibid. 6)

Studying the legal codes (that is, both the *Shulchan Aruch* and the advice found in the teachings of true Tzaddikim, which together strengthen one's faith and observance of the mitzvos) has the power to eradicate all strife and contention at its root. It eliminates the divisiveness in the lower worlds, including the turmoil which the evil inclination stirs up in the heart. This turmoil manifests as all the doubts and questions about faith which rise persistently in a person's heart and separate him from God, to the point that he finds it impossible to pray as he should. The main reason people find it hard to pray with the proper devotion is that their faith is less than perfect. If a person knew and believed with all his heart that the entire world is full of God's glory, and that God stands over him while he is praying and listens to his every word, he would certainly pray with tremendous fervor and be sure to concentrate on every word he was saying. It is only because people are not entirely firm in their faith that they are not as enthusiastic as they should be about their prayers. This is due to the turmoil stirred up in the heart by the evil inclination. The remedy is to study the legal codes, which puts this turmoil to rest and brings peace. (This is because a legal decision represents the resolution of all the arguments on the subject between the Sages.) By striking at the roots of strife, the heart is no longer divided, and one can serve God with all one's heart – with both inclinations. The gates of wisdom will be opened to him and he will know how to reply to the atheist within his heart. He will then be worthy of praying with all his heart (*Likutey Etzos, Talmud Torah* 48).

Rabbi Nachman of Breslov said: "In the morning, from the time the congregation begins to assemble and prepare themselves to pray until they actually begin praying, I have already studied four pages of *Shulchan Aruch*." (*Sichos HaRan*, §76)

Praying for Guidance

Rabbi Menachem Mendel of Riminov was extremely poor as a young man, but he was very diligent in his studies, which he devoted mainly to studying the Rif (by Rabbeinu Yitzchok Alfasi). Each night he would rise and cry and afflict himself, praying to attain fear of God, until he became a great Torah scholar. Ultimately, Rabbeinu Alfasi himself appeared to him and told him to travel to Rabbi Elimelech of Lizhensk, who would show him the proper way to serve God. And so he did. (*Madanai Melech*, §111)

Rabbi Elimelech of Bizna owned five volumes of the Talmud that had belonged to his grandfather, Rabbi Elimelech of Lizhensk. He once gave a volume to Rabbi Yechezkel Halberstam of Shinov, who was very moved by the gift. The Shinover Rav related how his father, Rabbi Chaim Halberstam of Sanz, had told him that when Rabbi Elimelech studied *Gemara*, he would cry so much to God, to help him understand, that his tears would wet the pages. Then, the *Tanna* or *Amora* whose words he was studying would appear before him. According to the Shinover Rav, the tear stains on those *Gemara* pages were still visible in his day. (Ibid. §76, related by Rabbi Moshe Halberstam of Yerushalayim)

2 **You should be careful to avoid the following things: Flattery, falsehood, mockery, gossip...**

There was once a devout and pious scholar who studied Torah and fulfilled mitzvos his entire life. However, towards the end of his life, he spoke slanderously about a certain sinner. In that single moment, all of his merits were taken from him and transferred to the sinner, while all of the sinner's sins were given to him. When the Torah scholar died, an angel came and read to him a list of all the sins that he had committed during his life. "It's a lie!" the scholar cried out. "I never even thought about committing such sins. I've been sitting and studying Torah my entire life!" But the angel refused to listen to him and immediately transported the scholar to Gehennom, where he was punished for all the sins with which he had been charged. Lacking an explanation, the scholar assumed that the angel had made a terrible mistake, and that he was the victim of a grievous miscarriage of justice.

Not long afterward, the sinner also died. Expecting the worst, he was astonished to encounter the good angels coming out to meet him and escort him to heaven. "This is the man who studied Torah day and night!" they announced. Once in heaven, they bestowed upon him all sorts of spiritual delights. The man was absolutely bewildered, for he couldn't imagine what he had done to receive such a reward. He knew that he had never studied Torah, and so, like the pious scholar, assumed that a mistake had been made on high. However, the sinner kept silent, since he was delighted with the treatment he was receiving.

Now, when Shabbos came, the scholar and the sinner happened to meet, for on Shabbos even the wicked are granted a reprieve from Gehennom. Each one told the other what had happened to him. When the scholar heard how the angels had praised the sinner for studying certain *seforim* which he himself had studied, he began to suspect that there had been a mix-up. Each had been given the other one's reward.

Suddenly, the Torah scholar understood. "Now I realize that God is just in all of His ways. For I learned from the holy books that if one person slanders another, the slanderer's merits are all transferred to the person he spoke badly about, and the other person's sins are given to him. I remember now that I once spoke very badly about you. Therefore, you have all of my mitzvos, while I have all of your sins."

This is the meaning of the verse: "God's judgments are true; they are righteous together" (*Tehilim* 19:10); that is, when the scholar and the sinner meet *together*, people are able to understand that God's judgments are true.

This is only a parable, meant to teach us a lesson. (*Erech Apayim*, 1:36, note 27)

The Angel of Unholy Words

The Zohar writes of a certain agent of the *Sitra Achra* (the Side of Evil) that waits for and collects every improper word that a person speaks by lying, gossiping, slandering, mocking others, and so on. Later, when a person speaks holy words, such as in prayer or Torah study, this agent comes with all its evil forces to seize and defile those holy words. As a result, the person receives no spiritual benefit from them, for the forces of evil usurp the sustenance in the holy words for themselves. Woe to that person in this world and the next! All because he spoke too much! For speaking too much inevitably leads to saying something improper, which empowers the *Sitra Achra*. Therefore, it's better for a person to accustom himself to talk about things pertaining to the fear of God or moral improvement, as well as to converse in *lashon hakodesh*, which is a pure language that enriches the soul. (*Kav HaYashar*, chap. 3)

Avoiding Anger

It is written in the holy Zohar (*Pikudei*): The first chamber in Gehennom is called "Empty of Everything." Whoever enters there is pushed down and prevented from getting up. A chief angel comes with its legion of helpers who punish sinners. They take all the bad words that this person spat out in anger, and all the objects that he threw in anger, and present them as an offering to the *Sitra Achra*. "Here is this sinners offerings!" they announce. "Woe to him for worshipping a false god!"

Fortunate is the man who is careful in all that he does, who does not descend into the deep pit from which he cannot rise. (*Erech Apayim*, 1:5)

There was a certain man who loved and respected his father greatly. Before his father passed away, he called to his son and said to him: "You have honored me greatly during my life. Please do so after I die by showing me the following honor. A time will come when you will have to restrain your anger. On that day, hold yourself back and say nothing."

After his father passed away, the man had occasion to travel to a distant land, not knowing that his wife, who remained behind, was pregnant. The man was in that country for a long time, and returned home only many years later. The night he returned, he quietly entered his house and headed for the bedroom, planning to surprise his wife.

However, before he could try the bedroom door, he was stopped by sounds coming from inside. First he heard the voice of a young man talking with his wife and then the sound of a kiss. The man instantly became enraged and drew his knife, with the intention of killing both his wife and her love. But at that very moment, he recalled the promise he had made to his father. He returned the knife to its sheath, and listened further.

A moment later, he heard the young man say: "Mother, it's been so many years since father has been gone. If he knew that he had a son, I'm sure he would have returned by now."

Hearing this, the man cried out: "Open the door for me, my beloved! Thank God I controlled myself, and blessed is my father for warning me. Otherwise, I would have murdered both you and my son." The three of them were extremely happy, and made a large banquet for the entire town.

Had this man not restrained his anger, he would have murdered his wife and son. Indeed, how many people have died needlessly as a result of anger, hatred and conflict? How many times have fine, upstanding people killed others out of anger? This has even happened to teachers of small children, who in anger strike their pupils and kill them! Anger is a terrible stumbling-block, and the cause of untold, irreparable harm. (Ibid. 1:7, citing *Sefer Chasidim* 655)

⁘

Our Sages have warned us not to hurt our wives' feelings (*Bava Metziah* 59b), for women cry easily and God brings swift retribution for our acts. Rabbi Moshe Cordovero writes that most people who are cruel to their wives live short lives. We should not make excessive demands upon them, "for it is enough that they raise our children, and save us from sin." (Ibid. 1:17)

The Fruit of Anger

The following frightening, true story happened to the Jewish community of Salonika, Greece, in the sixteenth century.

A certain wicked Jew had an argument with Rabbi Yosef ben Lev (author of *She'eilos u'Teshuvos Mahari ben Lev*) over a legal decision that the latter's *beis din* had issued against him. The man became so angry that he slapped Rabbi Yosef in the face, publically disgracing him. However, because the man was rich and powerful, no one said anything. Rabbi Yosef tore his clothing in distress and cried out loudly: "May Heaven avenge this!"

That night, a fire swept through the town. Heavy winds stoked the flames, which burned for six hours straight. Trying to escape, people were dragging their possessions from their homes into the fields, yet the fire caught up with them and consumed them. Nearly two hundred people lost their lives, some five thousand Jewish homes burned down, and many synagogues, study halls and *seforim* were destroyed. Salonika had never seen a fire like it. In the days that followed, a plague swept through the town, killing numerous Jews each day. The numbers kept growing until one day 314 Jews lost their lives – the numerical value of God's Name *Sha-dai*. After that, the plague began to subside, until it finally stopped. (Ibid. 1:22)

Advice for Dealing with Anger

- Don't be quick to express your anger. Let it sit overnight. Hold yourself back and do not talk at all when you are angry. (*Sefer Chasidim*, §83)
- Pray to God to help you for the sake of His Name. Concentrate on God's Name א-ה-י-ה spelled out with the letter *hey*, as follows: אלף הה יוד הה. This Name has a numerical value of 151, which is the same as the word *ka'as* (כעס, anger), when the number 1 is added for the word itself. (*Sur MeRa*, p. 30)
- Look at the corners of your *tzitzis*, since the word *kanaf* (כנף, corner) has the same numerical value as the word *ka'as* – 150. In addition, the verse says: "You shall see them and remember... and not follow after your heart." (Ibid.)
- If you feel yourself getting angry, immerse yourself in a mikvah, since the numerical value of "mikvah" is 151. (Ibid.)
- One who is prone to anger should vow to donate a certain amount of money to charity each time he gets angry. This will prevent him from being influenced by his negative inclination. (*The disciples of R. Moshe Cordovero*)

Guarding Your Eyes

The gaon and Tzaddik, Rabbi Zev Dov Tzhechik, became very sick one *chol hamo'ed* Pesach and urgently required a special medicine.

Unfortunately, all the local pharmacies had already closed for the night. One of his students heard about the situation, and immediately called Rabbi Tzhechik and offered to pick up the medicine in downtown Yerushalayim, where a late-night pharmacy on Rechov Yaffo was still open.

To the student's great surprise, Rabbi Tzhechik declined his offer. At first, he thought that the Rabbi did want to trouble him, and so assured him that it was no trouble at all. Yet Rabbi Tzhechik was still reluctant.

"Is the Rebbe worried that the medicine contains a trace of *chumetz*?" the student asked. "No," replied Rabbi Tzhechik. "This is a matter of life and death, so there is no concern over *chumetz*." Unable to fathom what was troubling Rabbi Tzhechik, the student pressed him for an explanation.

"I'm ready to go right now. Why does the Rebbe hesitate?"

"I'll tell you the truth," Rabbi Tzhechik answered. "The pharmacy is in the center of town, and you would have to take a bus to get there. It's almost impossible for a person to properly guard his eyes on public transportation. I can't allow you to put yourself in such a situation on my account. However, since this is a matter of life and death, and you sincerely want to go, I will allow it on condition that you promise me that you will guard your eyes and not look at anything forbidden."

The student promised and left for the pharmacy. He returned a little while later with the medicine. As soon as he walked in the door, Rabbi Tzhechik asked him: "Did you fulfill my condition?" The young man assured him that he had. Only then did Rabbi Tzhechik relax, and take the much needed medicine. (*Toras Zev, Zevachim, Hakdamah*, p. 16)

---

3 You should constantly be aware of the fact that one day you will die. Do not interrupt your study of Gemara or other seforim...

A single hour in one's youth is equal to a whole year in one's middle age. (From a letter by Rabbi Moshe Teitelbaum, author of Yismach Moshe)

A certain merchant was once traveling through the town of Altona, Hamburg, and stopped at the house of Rabbi Yaakov Emden to ask advice on some important financial matter. Although he had traveled from afar and urgently needed the great sage's counsel, the attendant refused to let him. Rabbi Emden was studying Torah and would not receive visitors. The merchant, however, was unwilling to wait, and barged into the Rabbi's private study without permission. He found Rabbi Emden sitting at a large, round table, deeply engrossed in the many *seforim* open before him. The merchant stood right in front him, so that the elderly sage would be forced to notice. Yet, Rabbi Emden did not even look up. He merely lifted his white beard with his hand several times, and showed it to the merchant.

Seeing that this puzzled the merchant, the assistant explained: Rabbi Emden is telling you that he is already old and so needs to increase his Torah study. Thus, he never interrupts his studies to speak with people. (*Hi Sichasi*, p. 833)

The Final Guarantee

There is a tradition among Torah scholars and pious individuals that Rabbi Elimelech of Lizhensk guaranteed he would help anyone who prayed at his grave, just as he had helped whoever came to him when he was alive. Furthermore, that person would not leave this world without having repented.

The number of people praying at Rabbi Elimelech's gravesite each year on his *yartzheit* continues to grow. Even Kohanim, who are unable to approach the grave themselves, send emissaries in their stead. (*Ohel Elimelech*, §261)

People asked Rabbi Elazar, the son of Rabbi Elimelech of Lizhensk, if his father left an ethical will after his passing. Rabbi Elazar replied: "If you want to read my father's will, look into his work *Noam Elimelech*. Although he delivered its teachings twenty-two years before his death, I know for a fact that he looked upon each day of his life as if it were his last." (*Ohel Elimelech*, §170)

Studying Gemara

The Oral Torah is known as *Gemara* (גמרא), which is an acronym for the names: Gavriel, Michael, Raphael, Uriel. This teaches that when a person studies the *Gemara*, he is surrounded by angels: "On his right is Michael, on his left, Gavriel, in front of him, Uriel, and behind him, Raphael. And above his head is *Shechinat El* – the Divine Presence." (*Sefer HaChaim*, part 1, chap. 2, p. 6)

When a person sits down to study Torah, he should realize that the Tzaddik in Gan Eden, whose teachings he is about to study, will be listening to his voice. Therefore, he must bind himself to that *Tanna* or Tzaddik who originally said that teaching, so that their two souls might join together in a "kiss." This not only brings great joy to the *Tanna*, but also enables the learner to return to God and regain all the days of his life that were spent in darkness.

However, this can only happen when the person studies Torah for its own sake. That is, with the express intention of fulfilling God's commandment to study Torah, which is equal to all the other commandments, and with the aim of fulfilling the Torah that he learns. But when someone studies because he wants to be considered learned, or to attain some other personal benefit, he is worse than the carcass of a dead animal, and will certainly not be able to attach himself to the spirit of the *Tanna*. This person will never see the truth. Instead, he will become an enemy of the true Tzaddik and cause the Shechinah to be exiled, because the Oral Torah is in exile on the lips of this so-called Torah scholar. (*Likutey Etzos, Talmud Torah* 13)

You should pour out your soul with the following words, in order to strengthen your commitment to Torah study:

"Now that you have thrown Torah to the ground and removed from yourself its light, what will protect you from suffering? What will annul harsh decrees and protect you from the fire of Gehennom? What will save you from the burning flame of Judgment Day. What will go before you and declare your merits when you leave this world… and what will protect you when you lie in the grave?" (*Vechay Bohem*, p. 234, citing *Chosen Yehoshua*)

4 You should study ethical works every day.

And so my dear and precious friends, you should make every effort to set aside frequent times for studying *mussar*. This applies to both men and women. You should constantly be teaching *mussar* to your children and grandchildren, when you sit together at the Shabbos and holiday table. Tell them stories about our forefathers and leaders, as well as engaging tales from the Talmud and Midrash. These can help a person acquire good character traits, love of Torah, fear of God, and upright behavior. (*Hanhagos Rabbi Shmuel Tefilinsky, Hadrachah* 6)

Kav HaYashar

Rabbi Elimelech studied the work *Kav HaYashar* one hundred and two times. This number is hinted at in the book's title (*Kav,* , ק״ב 102), and is also the number of its chapters. It is known that before Rabbi Elimelech passed away, he promised that anyone who studies his work, the *Noam Elimelech*, will be blessed with livelihood, and that whoever studies it on Shabbos will receive an additional soul. (*Madanai Melech*, 20 and 157)

---

5 You should occasionally study a little of the Arizal's writings...

Studying the Zohar can make you enthusiastic for all your holy studies. The very language of the Zohar is precious and can inspire you to serve God. (*Likutey Etzos, Talmud Torah* 70)

The forces of evil (*Sitra Achra*) hold no sway over a person who can recite a page of Zohar by heart. He is a mighty warrior, who holds a powerful shield against the enemy. (*Imrei Pinchas*, p. 57)

---

6 A person must purify his body and soul by learning Gemara...

It's said in the name of Rabbi Shlomo of Karlin that the word *Gemara* is from the Aramaic *gumra*, "a glowing coal." This is because the great holiness of the *Gemara* can burn up all the forces of *kelipos* that separate us from God, including all the temptations and lures of the evil inclination. All of them are incinerated and annulled. (*Sichos b'Avodas Hashem*, p. 92)

Studying two pages of *Gemara* with the Rosh (the commentary of Rabbeinu Asher) has more spiritual benefits than fasting. (Rabbi Elimelech of Lizhensk, *Ohel Elimelech*, §104, quoting *Nesiv Mitzvosecha*)

Chazal said that Torah can only be acquired by "making signs" (i.e. *simanim*, mnemonic devices). It is also possible to interpret their words as alluding to incense, *simanei haketores*. In other words, Torah study is pleasing to God only when it is offered with a variety of pleasant scents – such as holiness, purity, abstinence, heedfulness, and enthusiasm. This is the meaning of the verse: "Now, write this song for yourselves, and teach it to the Children of Israel. *Simah b'pihem* – Place it in their mouth" (*Devorim* 31:19). That is, Torah study ascends like *simanei haketores* (incense) to God when a person avoids any type of malicious speech. It brings delight to God, redeems the Shechinah from exile, and hastens our final redemption. (*Noam Elimelech, Misphotim*)

Torah Study Brings a Person to a High Level of Holiness

[On many occasions, Rabbi Yosef Karo was visited by a *maggid*, a personal, spiritual guide. Of one such visit he related:] As I was reading mishnayos, the voice of my beloved knocked in my mouth and the lyre played by itself. "God is with you wherever you go," it said. "He will make you successful in all that you have done, and in all that you will do. You must only cleave to Me – to the fear of Me, to My Torah and My mishnayos, constantly. Do not do as you have done tonight. For although you sanctified yourself in the way you ate and drank, you slept like a sluggard – for 'the door revolves on its hinges, and a sluggard on his bed' (*Mishlei* 27:14). You did not follow your good habit of rising to study mishnayos. You yourself see that no one has attained such a high level in many generations, save for a few unique individuals. Therefore, my son, heed my voice and do that which I command you: occupy yourself with My Torah, day and night. Forget all worldly matters, other than my Torah, the fear of Me, and My mishnayos."

Afterward, I was reciting mishnayos, and the voice of my beloved knocked in my mouth and said: "Know that the Holy One and the entire Heavenly Academy send you greetings. You should mortify yourself, as I told you, in order for you to see Eliyahu, face to face, while in a waking state. He will greet you and become your teacher and master, and teach you all the mysteries of the Torah....

"Therefore, meditate on My Torah. Even when you eat, you should think about My mishnayos, so that your meals be considered like sacrifices and offerings to the Holy One....

"You will be elevated and uplifted, for I will make you great and exalted. I will make you a leader of My people, Israel, and your yeshivah will become greater than even that of My chosen one, Yitzchak

Abuhav. Your children will be members of the Sanhedrin in the Chamber of Hewn Stone, and you will see them teaching the laws of *kemitzah*. Your son will be a Rabbi, a leader, and a great sage in *Gemara* and Kabbalah....

"Therefore, my son, toil at my Torah unceasingly, and devote all your thoughts to My service... I will provide for all your needs and see to your affairs. You need only to cling to Me and to My mishnayos, and not let your thoughts be distracted from them for even an instant. Then you will be elevated." (*Hi Sichosi*, quoting the *Maggid Mesharim*)

Becoming an Angel

Rabbi Mordechai of Chernobyl taught: "A person must draw upon himself fear of God when studying Torah, because the four *amos* of *halachah* are like the Holy of Holies, where the Shechinah dwelt." (*Sha'ar Hitkashrus*, drush 3)

The verse in *Vayikra* (16:17) states: "No person shall be in the Sanctuary from the time that [Aharon] enters to make atonement until he comes out." On this, Rabbi Abahu asked: "Is no one allowed to be in the Sanctuary? What about the Kohen Gadol himself? Wasn't he a person?" The answer is that when the Kohen Gadol entered the Sanctuary, the Divine Spirit would rest upon him, and his face would burn like flame. He was no longer human, but an angel, as the verse says: "For a priest's lips shall guard knowledge, and they should seek the Torah from his mouth; for he is an angel of the God of hosts" (*Malachi* 2:7).

We can add to his thought as follows: Why is studying Torah similar to entering the Holy of Holies? The Talmud teaches that we should show greater honor to a *mamzer* who is a Torah scholar than to a Kohen Gadol who is an ignoramus, as the verse says: "She is more precious than pearls (*peninim*)" (*Mishlei* 3:15). That is, Torah study is more precious than the High Priest, who entered the innermost sanctuary (*liphnai u'liphnim*). This teaches us that a Torah scholar is like the Kohen Gadol.

Now, if the face of the Kohen Gadol who entered the Holy of Holies burned like fire, a Torah scholar, who is even greater than the High Priest, certainly transcends the level of a human being and attains an aspect of divinity when he clings to the Torah, which is the "Name of God."

The Chazon Ish similarly writes in his letters (*Igeres HaChazon Ish* 15 and 33): "When a person studies Torah in depth, he becomes like an angel. A spirit from on high rests upon him, and raises him to the level of *ruach hakodesh*." (*Yair Nesivos*, p. 15)

7 You should guard yourself from all sorts of sins and improper thoughts.

A person's thoughts are totally under his control, to turn in whatever direction he wants. Even if your thoughts run wild at times, and fly to areas you ought to keep away from, you can still direct them, by force, back to the true path. Thought is just like a horse which turns aside from the road and tries to go in the wrong direction. The rider controls the horse with the bridle and forces it to go in the right direction. In the same way, as soon as you see your thoughts pulling in the wrong direction, take them in hand and bring them back to the right direction. (*Likutey Etzos, Machshavos* 16)

All Suffering Comes from a Blemish in Holiness

All the troubles and problems that a person faces in life – whether in terms of livelihood, or health – derive, for the most part, from a blemish of the Covenant, baseless hatred, and *lashon hora*. Furthermore, each of these things delays the final redemption. (*Birchas Chaim*, chap. 4, §33)

Studying the Laws of Shabbos Rectifies the Covenant

Studying the laws of Shabbos can repair a blemish in holiness. This is because the rectification of such a blemish depends primarily upon Torah study, especially in-depth Torah study. This is because the in-depth study of *halachah* demands the mind's full engagement. This is even truer if one can develop new insights into the material while studying. (*Hakdamah, Eglei Tal*)

Don't wait to sanctify yourself

You should strive to sanctify and purify yourself as much as you can in your life. This is the foundation of the entire Torah and the service of God, as the Zohar and many other holy books state. Even if you have neglected this for years, you should start to purify yourself as soon as you become aware of it – as best you can. These actions will also rectify your past (see *Yoma* 86b, and *Reishis Chochmah, sha'ar hakedushah*). Everything depends on the depth of your *teshuvah* and the degree to which you sanctify yourself from this point onward. For God knows the innermost thoughts of all His creatures. (*Birchas Chaim*, chap. 4, §12)

---

8 Be careful not to hate any Jew...

Once, while Rabbi Zushia was in the house of his teacher, Rabbi Dov Ber, the Maggid of Mezritch, a man came to seek advice on some personal matters. Rabbi Zushia looked at the man and, with his Divine Inspiration, could tell that he was an unrepentant sinner. At once, Rabbi Zushia became enraged. How dare this man speak to the holy Maggid without having even a thought of repentance! After the man left, however, Rabbi Zushia apologized to the Maggid for his outburst in his teacher's presence. The Maggid gave him a blessing: "From now on, you will only see the good in others, and never the bad." And so it was. From that day on, Rabbi Zushia only saw the good in other Jews. (*Divrei Elimelech, Noach*)

A Story of Rabbi Uri of Strelisk

The Tzaddik Rabbi Uri of Strelisk was a disciple of Rabbi Elimelech of Lizhensk. He once saw a man waiting to talk with Rabbi Elimelech, who, he could tell, had committed numerous sins. Saying nothing at first, Rabbi Uri waited for the man to leave Rabbi Elimelech's study. Then, he berated him severely: "Aren't you ashamed of yourself? How could you enter the Rebbe's presence so covered in filth!" However, before he could say another word, Rabbi Elimelech opened the chamber door and announced: "Lemberger Chasid! Leave my house immediately!" (He meant Rabbi Uri, as Strelisk was near the city of Lemberg.)

Immediately reacting to his Rebbe's command, Rabbi Uri jumped out of the nearest window, since he was not sure if he was allowed to stay in the room even long enough to reach the door. Once outside, however, he did not know where to go. He was so broken-hearted that he could not even return to his lodgings, for he thought that he might be unworthy to enter the home of a Jew. Finally, he found an empty barn, where he sat alone for a few hours, until Rabbi Elimelech summoned him back.

"Rabbi Uri," Rabbi Elimelech said, "I saw in that man exactly what you saw. In fact, I even saw the sins he committed in previous lifetimes. Nonetheless, it is forbidden to shame a fellow Jew!" From that moment on, Rabbi Uri was unable to see the bad in any Jew, even a person who committed a sin right in front of him. (*Darchei Noam*, p. 507)

Erev Shabbos is like Erev Yom Kippur

I heard in the name of Rabbi Elimelech of Lizhensk that the eve of Shabbos is similar to the eve of Yom Kippur. (*Ohr LaShamayim, Behar*)

It's said that in the home of Rabbi Elimelech, even the servants felt the holiness of Friday afternoon. Once, Rabbi Elimelech's son, Rabbi Elazar, took Rabbi S. Deutsch into his father's kitchen, where the maids were preparing the Shabbos meals, and showed him how they were all asking forgiveness from one another for any wrongs that they may have committed – just like on the eve of Yom Kippur. They wanted to remove any bad feelings from among them, so that they could experience the holiness of the coming Shabbos. (*Ohr Elimelech*, §165)

---

9 Be very careful not to say anything before you pray in the morning...

A Chasid of Rabbi Chaim Hagar of Kosov (author of the *Toras Chaim*) once complained to his Rebbe about the many foreign thoughts that ran through his mind during prayer, which distracted him from praying with concentration. Rabbi Chaim asked about the man's day: What time did he wake up in the morning? How did he prepare himself for prayer? From the man's answers, it was obvious that he didn't prepare himself at all.

Rabbi Chaim said to him: "If a person rises at five in the morning, spends several hours studying and preparing himself for prayer, and still experiences foreign thoughts, then he needs my advice as to how to remove them. However, if a person wakes up at eight or nine in the morning and starts his day by discussing all sorts of trivial matters, then the distracting thoughts that come to him during prayer aren't foreign at all. They are his thoughts alone!" (*Mesoviv HaShulchan*, §444)

Rabbi Avraham, the father of the Tzaddik Rabbi Pinchas of Koretz, was careful never to talk before praying in the morning. One morning, on his way to *shul*, a non-Jew stopped him in the street and wanted to sell him a gold nugget that he had found. Since the man did not know if it was real gold, or merely copper, he was willing to sell it for a very low price. Rabbi Avraham did not want to speak, and so he gestured to the man to meet him after prayers, in order to then buy the nugget. However, the gentile did not want to wait, and sold the gold to a different Jew, who became very wealthy, as a result.

That night, Rabbi Avraham's father, Rabbi Pinchas, the preacher of Shklov, appeared to him in a dream. "Heaven was very impressed by your refusal to purchase the gold this morning, in keeping with your custom of not speaking before prayer. Thus, they have decided to reward you with a son whose light will shine through the world like gold."

Not long afterward, Rabbi Avraham had a son named Pinchas, who became the famous Rabbi Pinchas of Koretz, whose Torah and holiness illuminated the entire Jewish world. (*Likutey Imrei Pinchas*, p. 110)

Speaking Less

The Arizal once told Rabbi Chaim Vital that the soul of a certain Tzaddik would soon attach itself to his own soul in an act of "impregnation (*ibur*)," and that this additional soul would help him reach new levels of Divine awareness. This, he explained, was primarily in the merit of Rabbi Chaim's humility and fear of God, which were reflected in the fact that he never spoke about unnecessary things.

This is similar to the story of a certain pious man who passed away, and appeared to his wife in a dream. She saw that the hair of his head and beard shone like a torch. "What did you do to deserve this great light?" she asked him. He replied: "Even though I was pious my whole life, it was not enough to grant me this. However, because I refrained from speaking about things unrelated to Torah or the fear of God, God has rewarded me in this way."

The Holy One Himself protects a person who refrains from speaking about mundane things, and whose sole desire is to cling to the fear of God. This story is proof that God watches over all those who lead pious lives, and keeps them from sinning, as the verse states: "No wrong shall befall the righteous" (*Mishlei* 12:21). (*Kav HaYashar*, chap. 12)

10 Be careful to relieve yourself before praying or eating.

You should also not spend too much time in the lavatory in general, which can cause serious health problems. This is especially true in lavatories where one must squat, since remaining in such a position too long can result in hemorrhoids. Therefore, you should avoid spending too much time there. In general, in these matters you should not seek unnecessarily harsh disciplines, which can lead to depression. What might have been written earlier was not said for our generation. Rabbi Nachman himself had made this error in his youth, doing many unusual things to achieve bodily purity. He went so far that he endangered his health and even his life, may the Merciful One spare us. But finally he realized that it was foolishness and a waste of precious time.

It is actually impossible to ever purify the body completely of all waste matter. Even a person who fasts from Shabbos to Shabbos must still move his bowels, even at the end of the week. He may have gone several days without food, but something still remains in the body.

Rabbi Nachman said that it was very important for him to speak about this, stressing that people should not waste time in such foolishness. Even if one must spend time in the lavatory, it is better to leave and return rather than to remain for a long time at once. (*Sichos HaRan* 30)

11 Be careful to keep your shirt and pants free of any dirt...

A God-fearing person should make every effort to dress respectfully. This is especially true for a Tzaddik. For then, people will respect him, and desire to serve God, whereas, if he dresses slovenly, no one will respect him at all.

Even God Himself dons "garments" when He wants the world to recognize Him and become aware of His existence. For instance, all the signs and miracles that He performed in Egypt were a type of "garment" that He wore, so that people could recognize His greatness and draw close to him, as He desires. This is the meaning of the verses: "May your garments at all times be white" (*Koheles* 9:8), and "I will rejoice in God; my soul shall exult in my Lord, for He has attired me with garments of salvation..." (*Yeshayahu* 61:10). (*Otzar HaYirah*, *begadim*, part 2)

12 Do not cast excessive fear in your home...

A certain wealthy man once insulted a Torah scholar who lived in the same town as Rabbi Chaim ben Atar. Rabbi Chaim heard about the incident, and suggested to the scholar that he forgive the man and make up with him.

"I already forgave him," the scholar replied. "It says in the Zohar that the sins of Israel weigh down the wings of the Shechinah. If I didn't forgive him, his actions would have been considered a sin, which would cause pain to the Shechinah, God forbid. Thus, I forgave him immediately."

Rabbi Chaim was delighted by his answer. (*Erech Apayim*, 1:25, in the name of the Chida)

⌘

Once, the wife of Rabbi Yomtov Lipman of Kapulia was publicly insulted by her neighbor, a simple, lower-class woman. The community leaders felt that the woman deserved to be punished for insulting the wife of their Rabbi. However, Polish law forbade Jewish communal leaders from carrying out any penalties without the consent of the local Rabbi. Approaching Rabbi Lipman was out of the question, since they knew that he never punished anyone for showing disrespect to community leaders. In addition, he would never interrupt his studies for matters unrelated to Torah or mitzvos. Instead, they decided to approach his wife, hoping that she would agree to relate the incident of the neighbor to her husband, who would then consent to their plan.

Late that Friday night, when Rabbi Lipman returned home to recite the Midnight Prayer, his wife was up, waiting for him. She related all that had happened – how she had been insulted by the neighbor and the community leaders' reaction. To her surprise, Rabbi Lipman's response was the very opposite of what she expected.

"This all happened several days ago," he said, "and yet you still bear a grudge toward her! It's forbidden to go to sleep if you are angry with any other person. This is why we say before bed: 'I have forgiven anyone who has vexed me' (*Megillah* 28a). I forbid you to go to sleep tonight until you ask her forgiveness for not forgiving her sooner!"

Despite the late hour, Rabbi Lipman's wife immediately fulfilled her husband's wishes and ran to the neighbor's home. The family was already asleep, and she had to knock loudly on the door to wake them up. At first, they were frightened when they heard her voice. But when they understood that she had not come for revenge, but to ask forgiveness, they were astonished. Each women fell upon the other's shoulder and cried: "Forgive me for what I said!" "No, you forgive me!" The following day, the entire city heard of the incident, and Rabbi Lipman was held in higher esteem than ever. (*Erech Apayim, ibid.*)

The Humility of Rabbi Elimelech

Rabbi Elimelech of Lizhensk used to say: "It's my fault that the entire world comes crying to me over their needs. My own sins have tilted the scales of the world to the side of debt and loss. Thus, people come crying to me: "Elimelech, give us *parnasah*! Elimelech, give us children! It's your fault that we lack all these things!" (*Ohel Elimelech*, §54)

The holy Rabbi Elimelech once said to himself: "Here I am, sixty years old, and I still haven't fulfilled a single mitzvah."

His disciple, the Seer of Lublin, once said about himself: "I haven't yet started serving God, and I am full of sins. Nor is there any relief for my predicament. At least when I am dead and buried, I won't be sinning any more." (*Ohr HaNer*, by Rabbi Yechezkel of Kozhmir)

Rabbi Shneur Zalman of Liadi, the *Baal HaTanya*, once met a Lithuanian Torah scholar who asked him the following question: "I have a copy of the *Noam Elimelech* in my home, lying beneath a bench. I heard that the author was a student of the Maggid of Mezritch, as were you. What can you tell me about him?"

Rabbi Shneur Zalman replied: "Let me tell you about his great humility. If you put the author himself beneath your bench, he wouldn't say a thing." (*Ohel Elimelech*, §29)

13 Pray to God to help you completely repent...

It's said that Rabbi Elimelech of Lizhensk repented so thoroughly that he even regretted the pain he caused his mother while she was carrying him in her stomach. He was also so deeply distressed by the possibility that he had inadvertently struck his mother while she was nursing him, that he put his hand in fire, in an act of repentance. (*Ohel Elimelech*, §224, in the name of the *Maor VaShemesh*)

Avoiding Fasting and Self-Affliction

In our generation, when we are no longer strong enough to afflict ourselves, we should not observe any fasts beyond those instituted by the Sages. Today, it is impossible to perfect ourselves through fasting – unless a person is sure that he is strong enough to bear the fasts, or unless he has committed grave sins and has been instructed by the Tzaddikim of the generation to fast in repentance. A wise person will do as he understands best. (Rabbi Elimelech of Lizhensk, *Ohel Elimelech*, §64)

The Black Dog

There was a rich and pious man by the name of Rabbi Avraham Ibn Puah who lived in Tzefas at the time of the Arizal. He was a very generous person, and his doors were always open to the poor. Rabbi Avraham's wife used to do some business with a neighbor of theirs.

One day, without warning, the neighbor contracted a terrible disease. His skin became putrid and slowly started peeling off. He spent a fortune on doctors, but could find no cure. His pain was so intense that people could hear him screaming many houses away. Finally, he died, amidst great suffering.

A short time after this neighbor's death, a large black dog began circling Rabbi Avraham Ibn Puah's house, apparently looking for a way in. The dog appeared dangerous, and the entire family was frightened of it. Each morning, when Rabbi Avraham would leave his house for prayers, the dog would be waiting by the front door, and Rabbi Avraham had to chase it away with a stick so that it wouldn't come in. Then he would lock the door behind him.

One day, on his way out, Rabbi Avraham forgot to lock the door. The dog immediately pushed its way into the house and ran straight into the bedroom where Rabbi Avraham's wife lay sleeping. It attacked her viciously, and bit her over her entire body. Then the dog turned and ran out of the house.

Rabbi Avraham went to the Arizal, seeking an explanation for this event. The Arizal told him: "Your wife was unfaithful to you. She committed adultery with your neighbor, who passed away, and his soul has come back in that dog. And since she was the one who seduced him, he attacked her in revenge."

When Rabbi Avraham questioned his wife and made her swear to tell the truth, she admitted her crime.

May God save us from such punishment, and may we always follow the commandments of the Torah. Amen! (*Kav HaYashar*, chap. 34)

There was an elderly man in Rabbi Elimelech's town who had been a sinner for most of his life. Now, in his old age, he wanted to do *teshuvah*. However, the years had left him physically weak, and little of his youthful desires remained, so that he barely ate and slept. However, he was convinced that his meager appetite resulted from his desire for repentance, and that the reason he woke up so early was because he wanted to rise and serve God before dawn. He was totally unaware of the fact that it was a result of his age and feebleness. Rabbi Elimelech commented: "This man is forgiving himself for his own sins, and will ultimately die without doing real *teshuvah*." (*Ohel Elimelech*, §142)

14 You should speak gently with others.

You should act humbly and generously in all your business dealings, and be modest and pleasant in all your interactions with the world. This is mainly expressed when you act humbly towards people of a lower status than you, such as household staff, family members, or the poor whom you support; in other words, those who you derive no benefits from, nor are afraid of.

A person who deals humbly with widows and converts and shoulders their burdens, and who does not respond when insulted, possesses genuine humility. (*Orchos Tzaddikim, sha'ar anavah*)

Rabbi Pinchas of Koretz used to quote the "Epistle of the Ramban," about the importance of always speaking gently with people. The Epistle was very precious in his eyes. He had a small book with the Epistle printed inside it, which he would take with him to daily prayers, and many times, he would read it before praying. He would speak of the Ramban's promise that on the same day which a person reads the

Epistle, Heaven will answer all of his requests, as the Epistle itself states, at the end.

Nonetheless, Rabbi Pinchas also taught that sometimes, a person has to instill a little fear into his household, if they do not heed his words. He may even have to speak strongly and sharply to them. However, even so, one must be careful not to harbor any anger in one's heart. (*Imrei Pinchas, Darchei Avodas Hashem*)

Honor Reduces One's Merits

Do not be happy when people show you honor for your good deeds in this world, for it will reduce your reward in the World to Come to the same degree. (*Sefer Chasidim*, §84)

---

16 You should be happy if God causes you to meet someone who disparages you…

When a person shows kindness to the poor, yet is rewarded with insults and curses, his reward is especially great. Similarly, if a person is digraced for fulfilling a mitzvah, he should be very happy!

The Talmud (*Yerushalmi Pe'ah*, chap. 8) tells the story of Rabbi Elazar, who was head of his town's charity fund. He once asked his family: "What charitable deeds did you do today?"

They replied: "A group of poor people came to our home today. We fed them, and then they praised you."

"That doesn't lead to good reward," Rabbi Elazar replied.

On another occasion, he asked them again: "What charitable deeds did you do today?"

"A group of poor people came. We fed them, but they cursed you!"

Rabbi Elazar was pleased: "Now *that* will lead to good reward," he said. (*Erech Apayim*, p. 157)

Accepting Suffering with Love

Commenting on the verse: "Let him offer his cheek to the one who strikes him, and let him be filled with disgrace" (*Eichah* 3:30), the work *Kol Bochim* cites Rabbi Moshe Cordovero, who said that the most effective *teshuvah* in the world for scouring away sins is to bear insults and disgrace in silence. This is greater than all the self-affliction and fasting in the world. For whereas fasting or self-affliction weakens a person and prevents him from studying Torah, which is itself a sin, quietly bearing insults and disgrace enables a person to eat, drink and work, yet still have his sins atoned.

Imagine someone asked you the following questions: "Would you like to experience financial loss or have your home collapse?" Your answer would be a resounding: "No!" If they asked you: "Are you willing that your children should die?" You would reply: "God forbid! May God protect them!" If they asked you: "Do you agree to have God strike you with leprosy or sickness?" You would immediately answer: "God save us!" Likewise, if they suggested death, or Gehennom, or an evil reincarnation, you would reply: "God forbid!" to all of them. Yet, if you reject all these things, how will you atone for all the sins and transgressions that you committed from the day you were born until now, not to mention all the blemishes that you caused on high, according to the root of your soul? There isn't a single day on which the evil inclination does not pursue you!

However, God Himself gives us the following advice: "Let him offer his cheek to the one who strikes him, and let him be filled with disgrace." [The words "let him be filled with disgrace" also suggest that a person should not starve himself with fasting. That is, even if he is filled with food, he can find atonement if he is filled with disgrace.] There is no good reason *not* to repent this way. Were God to ask you: "Why didn't you repent, fast, and afflict your body," you could always claim that you lacked the strength; for God does not make excessive demands of His creatures. However, if He asks you: "Why did you get angry and cast off your fear of God," what answer will you give Him? (*Ibid.* p. 159)

Suffering Brings One Closer to God

The reason people have to endure opposition and even persecution is that this very experience brings them closer to God. The more persecution and hardship they suffer, the more they must turn to Him for relief, because there is no other solution. This is how persecution and suffering bring us closer to God. (*Likutey Etzos, Savlanut* 10)

Everything is from God

You should never think that anything is accidental, the result of one particular cause or another. Rather, you should know that everything is directed by God. About a person who thinks that things happen accidentally, the Torah says: "If You treat My [acts] as accidental... I will again increase the punishment for your sins sevenfold" (*Vayikra* 26:21). I have a tradition that when a person experiences any gloom or suffering, God forbid, he should recite the verse: "See my affliction and my toil, and forgive all my sins" (*Tehilim* 25:18). This will help him remember that what is happening comes from God, in response to his sins, and motivate him to repent. For there are many sins that a person commits that are not fully atoned for through repentance or Yom Kippur. Their verdict is suspended, until they are cleansed by suffering. And so God sends a person easily bearable suffering, to atone for his sins, as Chazal said: "What is considered divinely ordained suffering? If a person puts his hand into his pocket to take out a nickel, and he takes out a dime." However, this principle applies only to a person who realizes that his each and every movement is under God's total control and direction. (*Igra d'Pirka* §134)

---

17 Distance yourself from anything that does not serve the purpose of keeping your body healthy to serve the Holy One...

The entire purpose of this world is to reach the ultimate goal of the World to Come. Whether or not you have money, do not worry about it. For you will surely waste away your days, regardless of whether you actually make any money or not. This world is completely deceptive. It constantly makes people think they are gaining, but in the end it is all an illusion, as everybody knows very well at heart. Even if you do become rich, eventually you will be taken away from your money. It is a basic rule that man and money cannot remain together. Either the money is taken from the man or the man is taken from the money. In all of human history there has never been a case where a person stayed with his money. (*Likutey Etzos, Mamon v'Parnasah* 52)

[The Egyptians] afflicted them with their burdens, and they built store cities for Pharaoh – Pisom and Ramses.... And they embittered their lives with hard labor, with mortar and with bricks, and with all kinds of work in the fields.... (Shemos 1:11, 14)

By giving charity generously to people who truly deserve it, you rectify your money, making it all holy, with the ability to reveal the greatness of the Creator. Then, the power of the imagination is subdued and you can ascend to the Holy Intellect, which is the aspect of the "great riches" that the Children of Israel took with them when they left Egypt.

This is because Egypt is the spiritual root of all the desires and mental confusions that overwhelm the Holy Intellect, with the greatest harm being caused by avarice. This is the meaning of the verse: "They embittered their lives with hard labor" – alluding to the hard work and bitterness that most people subject themselves to while trying to make money. "With mortar and bricks" (*ibid.*) – that is, people built large homes for themselves, like "Pisom and Ramses," which only embitters their lives further. And also: "with all kinds of work in the field" – that is, people are constantly on the move, traveling far from home [in search of work], and suffering greatly from their bitter, self-imposed slavery.

Yet, this is all the product of the imagination [that makes a person seek wealth and power], which is the aspect of the "Egyptian exile" in each person and in every age. (*Otzar HaYirah, mamon, §39*)

A person should always feel contented with what he has. He should take no more from the world than is absolutely essential. He should not live in luxury, like so many people do today, because of our many sins. People who lack this sense of contentment are referred to in the saying that "the belly of the wicked shall want" (*Mishlei* 13:25), because they are always in need of something. A man should be content with what God has given him, and even out of this minimum, he should still contribute a portion to charity. This brings about great unification in the worlds above, and the world is blessed with abundance. (*Likutey Etzos, Mamon v'Parnasah 27*)

18 It is very important to avoid alcoholic beverages.

One should not drink more than just a bit of wine or a different intoxicating beverage – and even then, it should only be on Shabbos, holidays, or at a *seudas mitzvah*. You should drink in order to raise your spirits and open your mind, so that you can better appreciate the sweetness of the holy Torah, of Israel, and of Shabbos, which is drawn down upon us through the power of the true Tzaddikim. In all cases, a person should be careful to drink just the right amount, so that it is in the aspect of "wine that brings rejoicing," which leads to holy joy and a greater sense of attachment to God, Torah, and Tzaddikim – each person according to his level.

On the other hand, there are people who make a habit of drinking wine during the week, which brings them to contemptuousness, controversy and opposition to the true Tzaddikim. Even people who are somewhat upright – who go only slightly astray after drinking, and do not fall prey to outright mockery – can still reach the point where they pervert the truth and speak negatively about the truly God-fearing, whom they think have strayed from the true path, God forbid. All these misconceptions result from too much wine. (*Otzar HaYirah, Achilah*, §157)

19 Be careful to never utter God's Name in vain.

The following true story is presented here in the hope that it will inspire people to be careful about not taking God's Name in vain:

When a certain Torah scholar passed away, his soul appeared before the Heavenly Court. "Make way for this righteous man who has died," the angels proclaimed. The Court welcomed him with great honor, handed him a Sefer Torah, and asked: "Did you fulfill what is written here?" "Yes," he replied. Then they handed him the four volumes of the Codes of Law. "Did you fulfill the Oral Torah?" they asked him. Again, he answered affirmatively. "Who will testify to this?" the Court asked, and all the accompanying angels rose to his defense.

However, when they asked him: "Were you careful never to mention God's Name in vain?" he fell silent. They repeated their question, but again he said nothing. "Is there anyone who can testify about this?" the Court asked. Suddenly, thousands of black-clad angels appeared. "I was created on such and such a day, when this scholar uttered God's Name without concentrating on his prayers," several of the angels announced. The other angels similarly bore witness against him, each one with a different tale to tell.

Following this, all the members of the Heavenly Court rent their garments in distress. "You putrid drop!" they said to him. "How were you not scared to do this?" They concluded that he would have to be punished, either in Gehennom, or by being reincarnated. Rather than having to return to this world, the Torah scholar chose Gehennom.

How, then, can a person not take great care to utter God's Name with the utmost fear and concentration? (*Chayei Adam, klal 5*)

---

20 **Be careful not to speak or think a single holy word in an unclean place.**

You should be very careful not to think about Torah in an unclean place. There were great Sages of the *Gemara* who prided themselves in not having entertained thoughts of Torah in dirty alleyways. For it is the evil inclination which leads a person to think about spiritual concepts in such places, in order for the Side of Evil to derive sustenance from the realm of holiness, God forbid. This is the very opposite of what happens when a person prays. Then, the evil inclination fills his mind with all the vanities of this world, in order to distract him from holiness. Therefore, a person should be very careful about this.

When you relieve yourself, think about how you are nothing more than dust while alive, and food for worms after your death. Think of yourself as nothing, and cast away your pride and [material] desires, as the author of *Reshis Chochmah* writes: "The word *basar* (flesh) is an acronym for *bushah, sirchon, rimah* – shame, stench, and maggots. A person's body is malodorous while he is alive, and food for maggots after he dies. He will be ashamed when he stands in judgment in the World to Come.

A pious man once admonished a king who bragged about his great wealth and physical indulgences. As they were walking past a garbage heap, the pious man remarked: "Here are all your pleasures and physical delights. They all stink! Animals don't partake of human pleasures, and so their waste does not smell like this." The king took the man's words to heart and abandoned his pride. For God arranges all these things in order to humble a person's heart. (*Mizmor L'Asaf*, p. 9)

---

21 **Do not discuss even ethical teachings in the holy synagogue…**

Rabbi Dovid Shlomo Eibshutz, author of *Arvei Nachal*, moved to Eretz Yisroel toward the end of his life. Even though he had been a leading Rabbi in Europe, he left behind all the honor and prestige and found his place in a small synagogue in Tzefas, among the poor and simple folk. He didn't tell anyone who he was, and made a living teaching local students.

In the same synagogue, sitting up front, along the *mizrach* wall, was a man who received support from his children abroad. One day, he arrived at the synagogue depressed. He had run out of funds, and had not heard from his children for quite some time. Suddenly, in the middle of the prayers, a messenger arrived with money for the man. The messenger handed him the money and they began discussing the reason for the delay.

When Rabbi Dovid Shlomo saw this, he got up from his seat in the back, walked straight to the front of the synagogue, took the man by the arm and walked him out to the lobby. "You can speak *here*," he said to him, and returned to his place.

The man was furious and decided to teach Rabbi Dovid Shlomo a lesson after the prayers. However, by the time the services had ended, the man had undergone a change of heart. He now felt that Rabbi Dovid Shlomo had actually been correct – it was improper to speak about his business affairs during prayer. The man walked over to Rabbi Dovid Shlomo with a sum of money and handed it to him as a donation. But Rabbi Dovid Shlomo refused to take it. "I don't need your money," he insisted. "I make my living teaching students." So, instead, the rich man bought a bottle of expensive liquor and together they made a toast. (*Toldos HaArvei Nachal*)

Two stories from the Holocaust:
In the winter of 1944, I was standing with my companions near the train station in the town of Rachov. A woman whom we did not know approached us and said: "Jews, do you know why you are suffering so much? It is because you discuss mundane matters in the middle of your prayers, and review your business affairs in the synagogue." A moment later, the woman was gone. None of us knew who she was, where she came from, or where she went.

I, Yehudah Noyzetz, of Rechov Breslov 19, Bnei Brak, signed on the truth of this story on *motzo'ai Shabbos, Vayeshev*, 24 Kislev 5735. The Rabbi of Debretzin also verified this account.

A certain Jew from Antwerp related the following story: There was a congregation in Germany whose members showed great respect for the holiness of their synagogue. No one ever spoke a single mundane word there. If a stranger who was visiting the synagogue spoke during prayer, the attendant would show him a card on which was written: "In this synagogue, we do not talk during prayer." If the man continued to talk, the attendant would usher him out. This synagogue was not destroyed during the Holocaust. The Nazis were powerless over it. All the *seforim* and holy items remained in their places, undamaged. (*Kavod Beis Hashem*)

THE GRAVE OF RABBI ELIMELECH, IN LIZHENSK, POLAND

Be Strong and Don't Give Up

The main thing is to continually strive toward holiness, even if reaching it seems incredibly difficult. A person should push himself relentless, until God shows him compassion.

Noam Elimelech, Noach

Be Strong and Don't Give Up!

IN THE FOLLOWING PAGES, we consider different strategies for winning the fierce battle against the evil inclination – especially as they apply to our generation. Included, as well, are several practical pieces of advice, which each person can apply in his life.

There are seven main categories:
1. Constant joy in serving God.
2. Performing the commandments joyfully, as the verse says: "Taste and see that God is good" (*Tehilim* 34:9).
3. Taking pride in serving God, as the verse says: "His heart became proud in the way of God" (*Divrei HaYomim* 2, 17:6).
4. Thanking and praising God for each success, whether big or small, spiritual or material.
5. Remaining strong and committed to your spiritual level, even if you fall, by picking yourself up and starting anew each time.
6. Being as careful about minor mitzvos and sins as about major ones.
7. Devoting each and every moment of the day to Torah study and serving God, always keeping in mind the verse: "Today, if you will heed His voice" (*Tehilim* 95:7).

Let us now examine each principle in depth:

1. Constant Joy in Serving God

We all know in our hearts that there is nothing more important than serving God through Torah, mitzvos and good deeds, for these alone will accompany us when we eventually leave this world. How much, then, should we thank God for allowing us to fulfill His commandments – even for simply letting us *look* Jewish, such as by wearing a kippah, having a beard and *peyos*, or dressing modestly. God takes pride in even the smallest "Jewish" gesture, for instance, when a Jew simply ruffles his *peyos*.

Rabbi Simchah Zisel, the *Saba* of Kelm, used to say that it is worthwhile for God to have created the entire universe and all the spiritual worlds, and to have maintained them for six thousand years, all for the sake of a single time a Jew declares: "Blessed is He and blessed is His Name!" Furthermore, a single "Amen" recited by a Jew is a thousand times more valuable than that. And saying "*Amen, yehei shemei rabbah...*" is a thousand times greater still. And a single word of Torah which a person learns is a thousand times greater than even that! If so, we can't even imagine the tremendous pride God takes in us when we fulfill His mitzvos and study His Torah. We should be dancing from joy just thinking about this! We should recite the blessings "Who has not made me a gentile" and "Who has chosen us from among the nations" with immense joy.

Imagine that a great king, or a Chasidic Rebbe, or a Rosh Yeshivah asked us for a favor. We would *run* to do it. Afterward, we would boast about how we merited fulfilling the request of that great man. How much more should we rejoice over the fact that the King of the Universe asks each and every Jew to do something for Him. And even if we failed many times and couldn't fulfill His will precisely, we still should be extremely happy, and thank God for the single time that we were successful!

However, the evil inclination dons a mask of piety, in order to make us constantly depressed over commandments that we did not perform with proper intentions, or in the most perfect way. Instead of letting us rejoice over our accomplishments, the evil inclination demoralizes us over small things done improperly. It tells us that we have not truly fulfilled the commandments. Yet, the real source of this problem is our own ego, which needs to be uprooted entirely. Simply put, a person must keep trying, without heeding these claims. This is especially true since a person never really knows his actual spiritual level and how he served God until he finally leaves this world. Only then can he truly see what he has accomplished.

⁂

A person should sing and rejoice, even several times a day, by saying the words "Blessed is our God, who has created us for His glory, and has separated us from those who err and given us the Torah of truth." Likewise, when reciting the words of the *Aleinu* prayer: "It is incumbent upon us to praise the Lord of all… who has not made us like the nations of the world" – one should be extremely happy, like someone who was rescued from near death and appointed to be king. (*Pele Yoetz, simchah*)

You should know that God derives glory from even the most insignificant Jew, even from sinners. Every single one – so long as the name Yisroel still applies to him – gives God a particular glory which no one else can give. It follows that no one should ever despair of getting closer to God. Even if he has caused great damage, God forbid, God's love for him has not ceased. This person can still return to God. Primarily, it is the men of truth who are able to detect the goodness and the glory which are to be found in even the worst of men, and to draw up everything to God. (*Meshivas Nefesh* §4)

Another way to fight the forces of evil is to bring yourself to joy and delight on account of the vital spark that burns within you, your "good point." Think of the true preciousness of being of the seed of Yisroel, of having drawn close to men of truth who can lead you and guide you along the path of truth. This gives you the hope of gaining enduring good. Through this joy, you can break the forces of evil and spiritual obstacles that lurk at every level. (Ibid. §8)

True happiness is when a person's heart rejoices over his opportunity to serve God, to whom none compare. (*Mesilas Yesharim*, chap. 19)

It is written: "For in joy they will go out" (*Yeshayahu* 55:12). That is, when a person is joyful, he can escape from all his problems and misfortune. (*Degel Machaneh Ephraim, likutim*)

Happiness is the key to making a living. If you are always happy, God will help you in all types of situations. But if not, who knows what your end will be. (*Toras Avos*, pp. 169, 172)

2. Performing the Commandments Joyfully

It is very important to be content and happy from the simple fact of performing a mitzvah, without any expectation of a reward. Thus, Chazal have said: "The reward of a mitzvah is a mitzvah" (*Pirkei Avos*

4:2). Meaning to say that the joy we find in fulfilling a mitzvah is itself a mitzvah (*Rabbeinu Bachaya, Naso*). Even if you do not fulfill the mitzvah as well as you had hoped to, you should not have any complaints against God. Rather, you should thank Him for the great merit you have to serve and please Him. Rabbi Nachman explains in *Likutey Moharan* (1:5) that Tzaddikim do not expect reward for the mitzvos that they do, even in the World to Come. For them, the entire World to Come can be found in the performance of the mitzvah itself. Thus he explains: "The reward of a mitzvah is a mitzvah." For the only reward that a Tzaddik wants from the mitzvah is the mitzvah itself. This is also how he interprets the verse: "You are to pay him his wages on that day, and not let the sun set with him waiting for it" (*Devorim* 24:15). That is, one should receive reward from his mitzvos themselves, while he is still alive, and not wait until his "sun sets" – until he leaves this world, to then receive his reward in the next world.

We can explain this in a different way. Imagine that you have a close connection with a great Rosh Yeshivah or Chasidic Rebbe – so close, in fact, that they agree to have their photo taken together with you. After the photo is taken, you wait anxiously for it to be developed, and then, frame it and proudly display it in your home. If that is true for a Rosh Yeshivah or Chasidic Rebbe, how much more should it apply when we learn God's Torah. It states in many *seforim*, that when we study the words of a particular Tzaddik or *Talmid Chocham*, there is a union of our two souls, which join together in a single breath. And when we learn God's Torah, our soul's unite with the Shechinah itself, for God and the Torah are one. When we study Torah, it is as if God stands before us, and inscribes all that we are studying in a special book. As it states in *Pirkei Avos* (2:1): "All your deeds are written in a book." The Zohar is filled with statements describing the great delight that God takes in our Torah study Torah and fufillment of the mitzvos.

Rejoicing in the fulfillment of the mitzvos and the love of God who commanded them is a great service. Whoever refrains from this rejoicing is worthy of retribution, as the verse states: "...because you did not serve the L-rd your God with happiness and a glad heart" (*Devorim* 28:47). (Rambam, *Mishneh Torah, Lulav* 8:15)

The foundation upon which everything depends is this: when you perform a mitzvah, do not consider it a burden that you are in a hurry to dispose of. Rather, you should think of the mitzvah as priceless, and a source of endless joy. You should do it with all your heart and soul, and with great longing, as though you were making a profit of hundreds of thousands of dollars. (*Hakdamah, Sha'ar HaMitzvos*)

Every single mitzvah that you have the chance to do is a gift from God. And the happier you are with it, the greater is your reward. The Arizal revealed to his disciples that everything that he grasped – the gates of wisdom that were opened for him, and Divine Inspiration that he received – all came in reward for performing the mitzvos with immeasurable joy. (*Sefer Chareidim, Hakdamah l'Mitzvos*)

A person whose soul tastes even a drop of the sweetness of the Torah and the performance of mitzvos with love knows that there is no end to the pleasantness of this sweetness. As the verse says: "Its ways are pleasant" (*Mishlei* 3:17), and "Taste and see that God is good." (*Be'er Mayim Chaim, Shemini*)

If a person could grasp even just a small percent of the sweetness and pleasantness of the outermost edge of the supernal light, he would disdain even the chance to become the greatest king in this world, [for it is nothing] in comparison to fulfilling a single mitzvah. (*Ohr HaChaim, Vayikra* 26:14)

It's possible for a person to momentarily become like an angel in this world, and to bask in the light of holiness. Then, all the pleasures of this world are like nothing in comparison to the sheer delight of clinging to one's Creator. (R. Avraham Yeshaya Karelitz, *Emunah u'Betachon*, 1:19)

The more a person studies Torah and serves God, the greater he desires more. The opposite is true when a person lacks these things in his life. Then he doesn't desire them at all. As Chazal commented on the verse: "If you have heard, you will hear (אם שמוע תשמע)" (*Shemos* 15:26) – if you have heard the old, you will hear the new; but if not, then not. (*Arvei Nachal, Likutim* §1)

Chazal tell us that "there is no reward for mitzvos in this world" (*Kidushin* 39b). Meaning to say, the reward of a mitzvah – which is the joy felt in observing the mitzvah itself – cannot be experienced by someone who is sunk "in this world"; that is, trapped in its mundane concerns. A person must shake off his attachment to this world in order to understand and feel in the depths of his heart the taste and the joy of the mitzvah. (*Kisvei Rabbi Moshe Midner*)

A person should rejoice in the opportunity to perform mitzvos, such as building and sitting in a sukkah, praying with concentration, studying Torah enthusiastically or resolving a challenging problem in learning. There were many great Jewish leaders who were unable to contain their great joy and attachment to the mitzvos, the Torah and the Holy One. The Kuzari states that just as there is a path of worship that entails the fear and awe of God, so there is one that revolves around the love of God, which brings a person joy. He writes: "The general rule is that the feeling of submissiveness that you experience on a fast day does not bring you as close to God as the joy you feel on Shabbos and holidays – when that joy is intentional and wholehearted. [That is, when you fulfill the mitzvah with joy, as though you were invited to eat at the table of the King of kings.] You should be grateful, inwardly and outwardly. And if that joy leads you to sing and dance, that is also considered a form of devotion, since it derives from your attachment to God." (*Otzar Nechmad-Kuzari*, 2:50)

3. Taking Pride in Serving God

There is a type of pride that is permitted and even appropriate. We can explain this by way of a parable: A king sent his son to a distant land, where he had to dress like a commoner, so that no one would recognize him. The king, however, was concerned that after having to act like a peasant for a long time, his son might actually forget that he was a prince, and fall into drink and other lowly activities. Therefore, the king commanded his son to remind himself each day that he was a prince, so that he would always remember to act in ways befitting his royal descent.

So, too, our souls are hewn from a holy and exalted place, though they have fallen and become lost in this lowly world. We must always remember that we are children of the great and awesome King, and it is wrong for us to act like commoners. It is good to feel proud of this and dress oneself accordingly; to declare that we are the children of the King of kings, blessed be He. It is below us to behave like the other nations of the world; rather, we should comport ourselves with dignity, in accordance with our pedigree.

This type of pride is permitted, and is pleasing to God; for a person constantly remembers his own honor and value and acts properly, according to his exalted worth.

I have said many times that if a person could keep in mind the greatness of the Jewish people, which is loftier than the ministering angels, he would never become involved in the vacuity of this world, or follow his base desires. He would be ashamed of himself, and say: "All of God's angels are beloved and pure, yet I am greater than an angel! How can I act so despicably?" (*Ya'aros Devash*, part 1, *derash* 15)

The holy Rabbi Shlomo of Karlin said: "The greatest deception of the evil inclination is that it makes us forget that we are children of the King." (*Shema Shlomo, Re'eh*)

I heard from my Master, the Baal Shem Tov, that being too humble can actually impede a person from serving God, for the person will not believe that his prayers and his Torah study can engender a flow of blessing to all the worlds, and that even the angels are nourished from his Torah study and prayers. For were he to believe this, he would serve God with great joy and awe. He would recite every letter, word and intonation of prayer with the greatest care and intention.

A person should also keep in mind Dovid HaMelech's words: "If you lie between the *sifosa'im*" ("border" or "lips"). That is, that God waits upon a person's lips, to kiss them when he says words of Torah and prayer with fear and love. If a person were only aware of this – that the great and awesome King actually cares about what a lowly person says – he would be filled with awe and trembling. He should realize that he is like "a ladder standing upon the earth, with its head reaching heaven," and that his every word, gesture and activity makes its mark above. Then he would certainly be careful that all of his actions be for the sake of Heaven.

This is not the case if a person thinks of himself as low and blemished and unable to rectify what is above and below; that he does not realize that all of his deeds are inscribed on high. For then, he will act carelessly, without considering the repercussions of his deeds. But such an attitude is mistaken; for through his good deeds a person can cling to God. (*Toldos Yaakov Yosef, Ekev*)

※

Even though humility is a very important trait in God's eyes – more than any other, as Chazal say: "Humility is greater than everything" (*Avodah Zarah* 20b) – and, conversely, arrogance is the worst of all traits (*Sotah* 5a), still, in the realm of holiness, pride is at times very admirable. Thus, it says of Yehoshaphat: "His heart became proud in the way of God" (*Divrei HaYomim* 2, 17:6). For if a person thinks that he and his mitzvos are worthless, he won't be careful to do them in the best possible way, and his heart will not be in them. Why should he observe them carefully, since they aren't important in any case? At times, he won't do them at all, since they seem so worthless to him.

But if a person realizes that his mitzvos give God great pleasure and satisfaction, and each of his mitzvos and prayers rises above and sits like a crown on the head of the Lord of Hosts, and that all the upper worlds receive blessing, light, compassion and life from his mitzvos, he will be inspired with great fervor, as he runs after each and every mitzvah. He will fulfill them with unceasing devotion, like a roaring lion! He will seek out opportunities to perform God's commandments, and fulfill them with his whole heart and soul, with all his limbs, and with all his strength. And he will be careful to do them in the best and most beautiful way. (*Be'er Mayim Chaim, Ki Sisa*)

※

A person who wants to devote himself to Torah study and prayer must be strong, and not listen to the words of the evil inclination, which seeks to trap him and cool off his passion, by showing just how low he is: "Who are you to devote yourself to the holy work [of serving God]?" it tells him. "You, who are so full of sin and transgression!"

However, when a person comes to serve God, he must cast off all his lowliness and feelings of unworthiness, as it is written: "Do not pass over a mitzvah" – "*ein mavirim al hamitzvos*" (*Pesachim* 64b). That is, one doesn't mention sins – *aveiros* – at a time that he is fulfilling the mitzvos. Instead, he should fulfill the mitzvah with great desire, and repair what he may have damaged another time – but not while he is serving God. This is also the meaning of "fulfilling a positive commandment pushes off a negative one (עֲשֵׂה דּוֹחֶה לֹא תַעֲשֶׂה)." (*Tiferes Shlomo, Va'eschanan*)

4. Thanking and Praising God for Each Success

It's well known that when the supernal angels mention the word "Holy," they are consumed by the fire of their great fear of God. Afterward, they are recreated, only to again be consumed when they mention the word "Holy" a second time. This happens three times. Yet, we, the Jewish people, say the words "Holy, holy, holy!" – kadosh, kadosh, kadosh – several times a day. We should praise God's great Name and rejoice over this! (*Beis Aharon l'Pesach*, p. 95a)

When a person faces serious difficulties in life, when he feels far from God, and also suffers physically, spiritually or financially, or even when some calamity befalls him, God forbid, he must never become completely disoriented, God forbid. Rather, at all times, and especially during misfortune itself, he should think deeply about the great loving-kindness that God has shown him until then.

It is therefore fitting that every Jew, no matter who he is – since he is still a member of the Jewish people, and he still dons tallis and tefillin each day, and recites the *Shema* twice a day – should offer praise and thanks to God each and every day, for His great kindness in making him a member of the Jewish people, the receivers of the Torah. This is even more true when he thinks about all the amazing goodness that God has bestowed upon him personally, from the moment he was born until the present. One should accustom oneself to thanking and praising God for all His generosity, as our Rabbis have said, a person should thank God for the past, and pray for the future.

For if we do not thank God for the past, our hearts may close due to all of our suffering, making it very difficult to call out to Him. This is especially true today, in the midst of exile, when each new day is worse than the day before it. It's hard to make a living, and the evil inclination throws itself full force against each and every individual. Controversy, accusations, jealousy, and hatred are on the rise. As much as a person wants to escape from all this and find some means of serving God, they don't allow him, and attack him only more, God forbid. The great number of obstacles prevent a person from even opening his mouth and speaking to God. Therefore, you should follow this path, for through it you will feel secure in your heart that even now, God has not removed his love and goodness from you. (*Likutey Halachos, Kelaei Behemah 4*)

In the future, all that will remain is praise and thanks to God, because all the suffering in the world will be annulled and everything will be good. People will engage only in praising and thanking Him.

However, you must also draw the holiness of the World to Come into this world, which is similar to drawing the holiness of Shabbos into the days of the week. Because Shabbos is an aspect of the World to Come, which is entirely good, while the weekdays are the aspect of this world, which is filled with suffering and tribulations, as it is written: "A person is born to toil" (*Iyov* 5:7), and "All their days are filled with vexation and pain" (*Koheles* 2:23). However, God desires the world's continued existence, and in His great kindness, goodness and deliverance, He constantly sweetens and annuls the suffering and troubles of this world. You should consider this carefully, and thank and acknowledge God for all the goodness that He bestows upon us. This is the aspect of drawing the holiness and joy of Shabbos into the six weekdays; that is, the holiness and joy of the World to Come, "the day that is entirely Shabbos," when the essence of thanks and praise will be drawn into this world even during difficult times. Even in such times, we will look only at the goodness that God has done for us until then. Furthermore, one can certainly find some benefit in the trouble itself, provided he looks carefully for it, as Rabbi Nachman taught in *Likutey Moharan* 1:195. (*Likutey Halachos, Kelaei Behemah 4*)

5. Remaining Strong and Committed to Your Spiritual Level

If a person falls from his level, he should know that it is from the hand of Heaven. The whole purpose of the rejection is that he should be drawn closer. The reason for the fall is to awaken this individual so that he steps up his efforts to come closer to God. The proper thing to do is to begin afresh, as if you were just starting to serve God. Start now as if you had never begun before at all. This is one of the greatest principles in serving God. Every day, literally, make a completely new start. (*Meshivas Nefesh* §25)

Every moment of the day, the evil inclination attempts to overpower us. It fans the desires, even if we refuse to pay attention to it and look determinedly in the other direction. Still, it comes back and bites us again, a third time, a fourth and more. We must stay firm and obstinate. We must be absolutely determined that under no circumstances will we turn our attention toward the evil inclination. In the end, it will be lifted from us and it will totally disappear. The same is true of the irrelevant thoughts which persist in coming to confuse us when we are trying to pray. The same thought comes to mind over and over again. What we need is firmness. Pay no attention to the thought whatsoever. (Ibid. §38)

Every moment of the day, we are wracked by confusion, desires, corrupt and bizarre thoughts, and worse troubles. They trouble us in all ways, never more than when we are trying to pray. To withstand it all, you must be slow to anger. This is really an aspect of faith. You must have perfect faith in God, in Tzaddikim and in the truly righteous individuals. Serve God with determination. And let nothing throw you or upset you or make you lose your temper. It is the Evil One who wants to weaken you and insinuate his way into your mind, to persuade you that there is no hope. Pay no attention! Steel yourself in your resolve. Despair is totally out of the question. You may have fallen countless times. Perhaps you gave up hope long ago. But you can still strengthen yourself *now* and begin completely afresh. Don't fall for the "old-age mentality" of the forces of the Other Side.

Every fall in the world comes from this "old-age mentality." A person thinks that he has already grown old in his sins. He feels that they have become such a habit that they are second nature now, and there is no way that he can escape from them. It's not true. Every day, every hour, and every moment, man has the strength to renew and revive himself and become a totally new creation. God makes new creations every day. *No one moment is like any other.*

Strengthen yourself and make a completely new beginning. Even on the very same day, you may have to start again several times. Forget completely about what happened in the past. Keep your thoughts directed to God. Begin anew from *now*. This is the meaning of being "slow to anger." You need to have endless patience to endure all the confusions and the obstacles, to let nothing distract you or make you lose your temper. Whatever happens to you, with all your might, make

God your strength. For God is filled with love at every moment. The fount of his kindness is never exhausted. (Ibid. §6)

⁂

Most people have a profoundly mistaken concept of the very nature of their own existence. They do not understand that the soul which they have been given is drawn from the holiest source. They find it unthinkable that they themselves might ever really return to God and lead a life that is truly righteous and honest. You can hear this regularly as soon as people start talking about a particular individual who is noteworthy for his piety. For a moment, there is a stirring in their own hearts, and they too yearn to return to God. That is the nature of the People of Israel: to be filled with yearning to return and come closer to God. No sooner do these people feel this stirring than they immediately stop short. "Well, of course I can hardly compare myself to such a person. He was born that way. It is part of his make-up." As if to say that all that the Tzaddikim have achieved came only from the innate holiness of their souls inherited from earlier generations.

The fact of the matter is that all the achievements of all the Tzaddikim came about only through hard work and effort in God's service over a period of years and years. It was only through determination, steadfastness, prayers and entreaties that they were granted their spiritual heights. Every single person can achieve the same. The choice is in your hands! You are free! "The crown of a good name is above the others" (*Pirkei Avos* 4:17). (Ibid. §10)

⁂

It is written in *Sefer Chasidim* (§93), on the verse "...two or three times to a man" (*Iyov* 33:29), that if a person guards himself from sinning and subdues his lower desires three times, God will protect him from then on.

This teaches us just how much we have to try and strengthen ourselves: one time, after another, after another. And even if we don't successfully defeat our inclination, or defeat it merely once in a hundred times, we should not give up, but should still long and hope for God. Indeed, we have to thank God for that one time that we were victorious!

We can add to this a thought based on Chazal's statement: "Only a little bit separates *chometz* from matzah." This is the "little bit" that God asks of a person – to act a little holier, to take on another stringency, to recite one more passage of prayer with concentration, or to study a little more Torah, for every little thing counts.

We can also say that the evil inclination grabs a person and declares: "Now I've got you! You can't escape from me anymore." This is like the letter *ches*, in the word *chometz*, which is closed all along the sides (חמץ). However, as soon as person makes even a small effort to return to God, the *ches* becomes a *hey*, as in the word matzah (מצה), and a little space opens up above, through which he can flee. Thus, the Gemara says (*Menachos* 29a) that this world is like a letter *hey*, for while it is possible to sin and fall out the bottom, one can always repent, and escape through the little hole at the top. Even if a person fell to the lowest place, he should take heart, for he can still go out from there and return to the world of holiness.

A similar story is told about the Vilna Gaon. Once, when the Gaon was on the road, he stopped in a small hotel where a heretical Jew also happened to be staying. The latter opened a bottle of whisky and started to drink it in the Gaon's presence. "You should make a blessing," the Gaon told him, but the man only laughed. "What does a blessing help, when I don't observe anything!" "That may be true," answered the Gaon, "however in the World to Come you will receive reward for even that blessing, or punishment for not reciting it. This is because a person receives reward for the smallest mitzvah and punishment for the smallest sin." The man heeded the Gaon's words and made a blessing. This started him on a long journey which eventually led him back to God.

That being said, a person should think about the great delight that the Holy One takes each time he displays an act of commitment. It is impossible to grasp the great reward that awaits a person for this single time alone – even if he has to suffer painful retribution for all the times that he succumbed to his evil inclination. A person must have tremendous patience, until the time comes that he can finally free himself from his base desires. The fact that he wants to leave it all behind immediately is only due to his latent pride, which itself must be uprooted. For if a person was aware of his low stature, he would willingly wait and bear countless trials, until he finally escapes his lowly situation, with God's help.

The Chofetz Chaim taught a parable about this. A young girl was selling apples in the marketplace. Some hooligans overturned her cart, and the apples rolled everywhere. People started grabbing the apples and running away. The girl stood there crying, until someone told her: "Why are you standing here? You should grab some too! That way, you won't be left without anything."

We, too, should follow that person's advice and grab whatever Torah and mitzvos we can, as Shlomo HaMelech said: "Wage war with strategies" (*Mishlei* 24:6). This is our whole task in this world: To do whatever we can, and leave the rest to God.

When a person wishes to begin serving God – and this applies to everybody, even a person on the lowest level, who is literally "sunk in the earth" – he must make constant effort to advance and rise from level to level. However, every time a person is about to move from one level to the next, he has to encounter the full force of the *kelipos*, the evil forces, time after time. These are all his desires and fantasies and wild thoughts, the distractions and obstacles which rise against a person at every moment and try to prevent him from entering the gates of sanctity.

This often produces great confusion in the minds of honest people who have truly worked hard on themselves. Suddenly, they find all their old desires, confusions and obstacles rising up against them. They imagine that they must have fallen from their level because before this, they seemed to have escaped all these desires and confusions. Really, though, they were laying dormant. Now that they have reappeared, these people think that they must have fallen down. But this is no fall. What is happening is that the time has come for the person to advance to the next level. This is why all the desires, confusions and obstacles – all the "crookedness in the heart" – are stirred up against them with fresh force.

Each time this happens, you must fortify yourself and refuse to lose heart. Strengthen yourself against these forces and break them anew. (*Meshivas Nefesh* 1:6)

---

6. Being as Careful with Minor Mitzvos and Sins as Major Ones

Deep inside, the Jewish people are completely good and virtuous; however, "the wicked circle all around" (*Tehilim* 12:9). That is, the evil inclination waits to trap a Jew in its snare, which entails the transgression of some small, Rabbinic prohibition. However, "one sin leads to another," until the person utlimately becomes separate from the Jewish people entirely, and descends to hell.

There is a story about this connected to the Baal Shem Tov. The Baal Shem Tov once rectified a soul that had been cast off and forced to go through numerous reincarnations for hundreds of years. Initially, the person involved had been careless about washing his hands upon rising in the morning. But this led him, step by step, into the net of the evil inclination, until he died without repentance.

A person must therefore be careful with even the small things that he does, in order to prevent the forces of evil from attaching themselves to him. (*Tiferes Shlomo, Balak*)

As for those Jews who were forced to convert (to Islam), let them follow my suggestion. They should set their sights on fulfilling whatever commandments that they can. Even if they already transgressed many commandments, or desecrated the Shabbos, nonetheless they should now avoid moving things that are forbidden to move (on Shabbos). They should *not* say: "I've already committed far greater transgressions than this." Rather, let them be careful with whatever they can.

A person should know that the basic principle of our religion is that Yeravom ben Nevat, and those like him, will be called to account [for their deeds]: not just for erecting [golden] calves for idolatry, but also for having annulled the commandment of *eruvei tavshilin*. God requites a person for both his major transgressions and his minor ones, and He repays him for his every deed. A person should know that he will be held accountable for his every transgression and rewarded for his every mitzvah. The matter is not like people think. (*Rambam, Mamar al Kiddush Hashem*)

7. Devoting Each and Every Moment to Torah Study and Serving God

"Today! if you heed His voice" (Tehilim 95:7).

This is an important principle in serving God: One should focus on today only. Concerning your livelihood and personal needs, you should not worry from one day to the next, as is explained in the holy books; and with regard to your serving God, you should not consider anything beyond this day and this moment. For when a person wants to begin serving God, it seems to be a heavy burden that is impossible to bear. However, when a person considers that he has only one day [to deal with], it will not feel heavy at all.

A person should also not procrastinate from one day to the next, saying: "I'll start tomorrow. Tomorrow I'll pray more attentively, with the right level of enthusiasm." For a person's world consists only of the present day and moment – tomorrow is a different world entirely. "Today! if you heed His voice." Specifically "Today!" Understand this. (*Likutey Moharan* 1:272)

> "Whoever speculates about four things, it would have been better had he never been born: What is above, what is below, what is before and what is after." (Chagigah 2:1)

That is, if a person thinks about what was and what will be, and as a result, misses *what is*, it would have been better had he not been created. For the entire creation exists only in the present. (Rabbi Yaakov Meir Shechter, *Leket Amarim*, p. 43)

A person has to completely erase from his mind everything that happened to him in the past. He must imagine that each day – indeed, each hour – he is born again and renewed. As it says: "Today, I have given birth to you" (*Tehilim* 2:7), and, as it is written: "Today, if you heed His voice" (*ibid.* 95:7). A person must constantly think that he was born and entered the world today, and now wants to begin to recognize and acknowledge his Creator. Even if he has tried a million times to start again and to come close to God, but never succeeded and fell in the worst way each time, he should forget it, and not think about it at all. Because this moment of his life never existed before, and who knows what you can achieve today, in this very moment. (*Likutey Halachos, Bassar b'Chalav*)

"You are to pay him his wages on that day, and not let the sun set..." (*Devorim* 24:15). A person's soul is like a day laborer, because it is the cause of all the body's movements and vitality. One who treads the path of holiness, and subjugates his body to his soul, turns his soul into a king. It reigns over the body and is free. This is the aspect of: "All Jews are the children of kings." However, when the body does not totally yield to the soul, the soul becomes like an indentured servant, who works for the body.

A person must have pity on his soul, and at the very least, should not steal from it or exploit it. He must pay it its due; that is, to at least provide it with several mitzvos and good deeds each day, in addition to Torah study and prayer – according to one's daily obligation.

Ideally, a person should deal only with his soul's needs. However, if he is not on that level, and the soul is like a day laborer inside him, he must be careful to fulfill the mitzvah "You are to pay him his wages each day."

Nor should you delay paying him his daily wages, as some people say: "Today, I can't pray. Today, I can't study Torah. Today, I can't serve God," pushing off their obligations until the future. Thus, the verse warns us: "You are to pay him his wages each day before the sun sets...."

The main thing is to carefully fulfill one's obligations each day, as it says: "Today! if you heed His voice." For there is no day that does not have some good in it. (Ibid. *Pikadon* 5)

In truth, for an intelligent person, time does not exist at all. The past is gone, the future hasn't yet arrived, and the present is like the blink of an eye. It turns out that the time a person has is only that fleeting moment that he exists in now. (Ibid. *Matanah* 5)

Glossary

Agadah – The narrative portions of the Talmud.
Amen, Yehei Shemei Rabbah – The congregation's response in the *kaddish* prayer: "May His great Name be blessed…"
Amidah – The silent, standing prayer at the heart of the three daily prayer services.
Amorah (Amoraim) – The Sages of third to fifth century Israel and Babylonia, who to elucidated and clarified the Mishnah, and whose statements are recorded in the Talmud.
Ashuris – The Hebrew script used in writing *sifrei Torah*, tefilin and mezuzos.
Av, Sag, Mah, Ban – The numberical value of God's holy Name, when spelled out fully in different ways. These correspond to the four primary spiritual worlds.
Avodah – Service, or worship. *Avodas Hashem* is the service of God through Torah study, prayer, and mitzvos, as well as any other action performed in a true spirit of worship.
Ayin Hora – The evil eye.
Beis HaMikdash – The Holy Temple in Jerusalem (may it soon be rebuilt).
Beis Din – A court of Jewish law.
Beis HaKneses – A synagogue.
Chazal – An acronym for Chochomeinu, *zichronom livracha*; Our Sages, of blessed memory.
Chok l'Yisroel – A collection of Torah teachings arranged according to the days of the year.
Chol HaMo'ed – The intermediary days of Sukkos or Pesach.
Chometz – Leavened wheat products.
Eruvei Tavshilin – A Rabbinic practice that allows one to cook from Yom Tov to Shabbos.
Gan Eden – The Garden of Eden.
Gartel – A cloth belt or sash worn by chasidim during prayer.
Gematria – The numerical equivalent of a Hebrew word.
Halachah – Jewish law.
Terumah – The priestly tithes of produce.
Ma'aser – Tithes given to the Levi'im.
Bechoros – The firstborn animal that is offered in the Temple and given to the kohanim.

Kavanah – Concentrated intention.
Kedushas HaBris – The holiness of the covenant (sexual purity).
Kelayim – The forbidden mixing of various plants or animals.
Kelipah (Kelipos) – Impure
Kemitzah – The taking of a handful of fine flour, as an offer in the Temple.
Kerias Shema – The statement of God's unity, recited twice daily.
Kiddush – A ceremony, made over wine, sanctifying the Shabbos or Yom Tov.
Kinos – Lamentations, recited on Tisha b'Av.
Lashon HaKodesh – The Holy Tongue (classic Hebrew).
Lashon Hora – Gossip and slander.
Lishmah – A selfless deed, such as *limud Torah lishmah* – studying Torah selflessly.
Ma'ariv – The evening prayer.
Masechta – A tractate of the Mishnah or Gemara.
Midos – Personality traits.
Midrash – The anecdotal teachings of the Oral Torah.
Minchah – The afternoon prayer.
Mishnah – Brief, halachic statements that comprise the earliest transcription of the Torah Torah. Compiled by Rabbi Yehudah HaNasi in the second century, C.E.
Mussar – Ethical teachings.
Nefesh – The lowest level of the soul, which enlivens the body and is found in both humans and animals.
Neshamah – The higher level of the soul, which rests in the intellect.
Netilas Yadayim – Ritual washing of the hands upon waking.
Niddah – Menstrual impurity.
Nusach Sefard – The version of prayers used by chasidim.
Parnasah – One's livelihood.
Peshat, Remez, Drush, Sod – The four levels of Torah exposition: literal, symbolic, homiletic and mystical.
Peyos – Side curls.
Poskim – Rabbis who excel in Jewish law.
Ruach – The level of the soul that is manifest through one's emotions.
Ruach HaKodesh – The holy spirit; a level of Divine revelation.
Sefer (Seforim) – Torah books.
Sefiros – Spiritual channels bringing Divine influence into the world.

Seudas Mitzvah – A festive meal, held on Shabbos, holidays, or other important occasions, such as a *brit milah*, wedding, etc.
Shas – An acronym for *shisha sedarim*, the Six Orders of Mishnah and Talmud
Shechinah – The Divine Presence within creation.
Shemoneh Esrei – Literally, "Eighteen Blessings." Another term for the *amidah*.
Shemurah Matzah – Matzos that have been carefully guarded from the time of harvest.
Shlit"a – An acronym for *"Sheyichiyeh Lirot Yamim Tovim Arukim,"* "May he live a good long life."
Shulchan Aruch – The Code of Jewish Law, written by Rabbi Yosef Karo.
Siddur (Siddurim) – The prayerbook.
Sitra Achra – The "Other Side"; the force of evil in creation.
Siyum – The conclusion of a significant
Ta'avah - Desire
Talmid Chocham – A Torah scholar.
Tanna – A sage of first and second century Israel, whose opinions are recorded in the Mishnah.
Teshuvah – Repentance.
Tikun – Spiritual repair and rectification.
Tikun Chatzos – The midnight prayer recited over the destruction of the Holy Temple.
Tikunim – Sections of the Kabbalistic work, the Tikunei Zohar.
Tzaddikim – Righteous, holy people. Also, leaders of the Chasidic movement.
Tzitzis – Fringes on the edges of a four-cornered garment.
Zerizus – Alacrity and quickness.

Bibliography

- *Arvei Nachal* – R. Dovid Shlomo Eibenschutz (1755–1813) Russian-born Rabbi, Kabbalist and author.
- *Avnei Zikaron* – R. Yaakov Yitzchak Horowitz, the Seer of Lublin (1745–1815); the chief disciple of R. Elimelech of Lizhensk.
- *Avodas Penim* – R. Aharon Yosef Luria (1894–1969); a Slonimer chasid of Tzefat.
- *Avodas Yisroel* – R. Yisroel Hopstien, the Maggid of Kozhnitz (1737–1814); a disciple of the Maggid of Mezritch.
- *Az Tis'chazek* – R. Moshe Yehudah Shwartz (Monsey, NY).
- *Be'er Mayim Chaim* – R. Chaim Tyrer (1740–1817); a disciple of R. Yechiel Michel of Zlotchov.
- *Beis Tefilah* – R. Eliezer Papo (1785–1828); Rabbi of Silistra, Bulgaria, author of the Pele Yoetz.
- *Bikurei Aviv* – R. Yaakov Aryeh Guterman (1792–1874); a disciple of R. Simcha Bunim of Pashischa and R. Yitzchak of Vorki.
- *Birchas Chaim* – R. Chaim Yeshaya HaKohen Halbersberg (1848–1910); chasidic Rabbi in Poland. Author of *Misgeret HaShulchan*.
- *Birchei Yosef* – R. Chaim Yosef Dovid Azulai, the "Chida" (1724–1806); 18th century, Jerusalem Kabbalist.
- *Bnei Yisaschar* – R. Tzvi Elimelech Spira of Dinov (c. 1783 – 1841), a disciple of the Seer of Lublin.
- *Chayei Adam* and *Chochmas Adam* – R. Avraham Danzig (1748–1820).
- *Chovas HaLevovos* – Rabbeinu Bachya ben Yosef ibn Paquda (c. 1050–1120).
- *Darchei Noam* – Commentary on *Noam Elimelech* (Machon Nachlas Yehoshua, 2007)
- *Darchei Tzedek* – R. Zechariah Mendel of Yaroslav (18th century); a close disciple of R. Elimelech of Lizhensk.
- *Degel Machaneh Ephraim* – R. Moshe Chaim Ephraim of Sudilkov (1748–1800); grandson of the Baal Shem Tov
- *Derech Pikudecha* – R. Tzvi Elimelech Spira of Dinov (1783–1841); a disciple of the Seer of Lublin.
- *Devash l'Fi* – R. Chaim Yosef Dovid Azulai (see above).
- *Divrei Elimelech* – R. Elimelech Shapira of Grodzhisk (1824–1892); chasidic Rebbe, and great-grandson of R. Elimelech of Lizhensk.

- *Divrei Emes* – R. Alexander Moshe Lapidus (1819–1906).
- *Eglei Tal* – R. Avraham Borenstein (1838–1910); a close disciple and son-in-law of R. Menachem Mendel of Kotzk. Author of the responsa *Avnei Nezer*.
- *Elef Ksav* – R. Yitzchak Weiss (1873–1942).
- *Emunah u'Betachon* – R. Avraham Yeshaya Karelitz (1878–1953); the "Chazon Ish."
- *Erech Apayim* – R. Avraham Yellin (d. 1935).
- *Hadracha shel R. Shmuel Tefilinsky* and *Hanhagos R. Shmuel Tefilinsky* – R. Shmuel Tefilinsky (1888–1945).
- *Hakdama Ben Yisachar* – R. Eliyahu Weinberg.
- *Hanhagos HaTzaddikim m'R. Mendel m'Linsk* – Rabbi Menachem Mendel Rubin of Linsk (c. 1740–1803); father of the chasidic Rebbe, R. Naftali Zvi Horowitz of Ropshitz.
- *Hanhagos R. Shmuel Valtzis* – A disciple of R. Raphael of Bershad (who was himself a disciple of R. Pinchas of Koretz).
- *Hanhagot R. Zechariah Mendel m'Yaroslav* and *Igeres HaKodesh m'R. Zechariah Mendel* – R. Zechariah Mendel of Yaraslav (see above).
- *Hanhogos HaTzaddikim* – R. Chaim Shlomo Rottenberg. (Published, Jerusalem, 1997); author of *Shevacho shel Tzaddik*.
- *Heichal HaBerachah* – R. Yitzchak Eisik Yehuda Yechiel Safrin of Komarno (1806–1874); Kabbalist and chasidic Rebbe. Nephew of R. Tzvi Hirsh of Zidichov.
- *Hi Sichosi* – anonymous author. Published in Bnei Brak, 1999.
- *Hischazkus b'Tefilah l'Hashem* – R. Moshe Meir Yadler. Published in Jerusalem, 1997.
- *Histapchus HaNefesh* – R. Alter Teplicker (d. 1919); third generation Breslover chasid. Published works collected from the writings of R. Nachman and R. Nossan.
- *Igeres Ohr HaShem* – R. Moshe of Terani, the "Mabit" (1500–1580).
- *Igeret HaKodesh* – R. Shneur Zalman of Liadi, the Alter Rebbe of Lubavitch (1745–1812); a disciple of the Maggid of Mezritch. The first Chabad Rebbe.
- *Igeres HaChazon Ish* – R. Avraham Yeshayahu Karelitz (1878–1953).
- *Igra d'Pirka* – R. Tzvi Elimelech Spira of Dinov (see above).
- *Imrei Emes* – R. Avraham Mordechai Alter of Gur (1866–1948); the third Gerrer Rebbe.

- *Imrei Kodesh* – R. Uri, the "Seraph" of Strelisk (1757–1826); a disciple of R. Elimelech of Lizhensk and R. Shlomo of Karlin.
- *Imrei Pinchas*– R. Pinchas of Koretz (1728–1790); a disciple of the Baal Shem Tov.
- *Kav HaYashar* – R. Tzvi Hirsh Kaidenover (d. 1711).
- *Kavod Beis Hashem* – R. Avraham Meir Krois.
- *Kisvei R. Moshe Midner* – R. Moshe Midner (c. 1859–1929); grandson of R. Avraham Weinberg (the first Slonimer Rebbe).
- *Kitzur Likutey Moharan* – R. Nossan of Breslov (1780–1844); chief disciple of R. Nachman of Breslov.
- *Kumi Roni* – R. Yeshayahu Zelig Margolios (1889–1971); Belzer chasid, Kabbalist and author in Jerusalem.
- *Kuzari* – R. Yehudah HaLevi (c. 1075–1141).
- *Leket Amorim* – R. Yaakov Meir Shechter (b. 1932); one of the current leaders of Breslover chasidism in Jerusalem.
- *Likutei Shoshanim* – R. Chaim Yeshaya Halbersberg (see above).
- *Likutey Etzos* – R. Nossan Sternhartz of Breslov, based upon *Likutey Moharan*.
- *Likutey Etzos HaMevu'aros* – R. Shimshon Barsky (d. 1934); leading Breslover chasid in Uman, Ukraine.
- *Likutey Moharan* – R. Nachman of Breslov (1772–1810).
- *Likutey Shoshanah* – R. Elimelech of Lizhensk (1717–1787).
- *Likutey Tefilos* – R. Nossan of Breslov.
- *Ma'or VaShemesh* – R. Kalonymous Kalman Epstein HaLevi (1754–1823); youngest disciple of R. Elimelech of Lizhensk.
- *Madanei HaMelech* – R. Yitzchok Weingarten; commentary on the *Tzetel Katan* (pub. 1980).
- *Maggid Mesharim* – R. Yosef Karo (1488–1575); author of the *Shulchan Aruch*.
- *Mavir Levavos* – R. Amram Horowitz (d. 2009); Breslover chasid, Jerusalem.
- *Menoras Zahav* – Collected teachings of R. Zushia of Anipoli (1718–1800); brother of R. Elimelech of Lizhensk, and a disciple of the Maggid of Mezritch.
- *Meshivas Nefesh* – R. Alter Tepliker (see above): collected from the writings of R. Nachman and R. Nossan.

- *Midrash Pinchas* – R. Pinchas of Koretz (see above)
- *Minchas Yitzchak* – R. Yitzchak Yaakov Weiss (1901–1989); head of the Beit Din (Badatz), Jerusalem.
- *Mishnah Berurah*, R. Yisroel Meir Kagan (1838–1933); the "Chofetz Chaim."
- *Mishneh Torah*, R. Moshe ben Maimon, the Rambam (c. 1135–1204).
- *Mishpot Tzedek* al *Tehilim* – R. Moshe of Zalshin (d. 1831); disciple of the Seer of Lublin and the Maggid of Kozhnitz. Author of *Tikunei Shabbat*.
- *Mizmor L'Asaf* – R. Sasson Shandoch (d. 1830): Kabbalist and author, Baghdad.
- *Nesiv Mitzvosecha* – R. Yitzchak Eisik Yehuda Yechiel Safrin of Komarno (see above).
- *No'am Elimelech* – R. Elimelech of Lizhensk.
- *Notrei Omen* – R. Avraham Kessler. Published, Bnei Brak, 2001.
- *Ohel Elimelech* – R. Avraham Chaim Simcha Michelson (published in Premishlan, 1910)
- *Ohev Yisroel* – R. Avraham Yehoshua Heshel, the Apter Rav (1748–1825); Polish chasidic Rebbe. Disciple of R. Elimelech of Lizhensk and R. Yechiel Michal of Zlotichov.
- *Ohr Elimelech* – R. Elimelech of Lizhensk.
- *Ohr HaChaim* – R. Chaim ben Atar (1696–1743).
- *Ohr HaMeir* – R. Zev Wolf of Zhitomir (1740–1798); a disciple of the Maggid of Mezritch.
- *Ohr HaNer* – R. Yechezkel of Kozhmir (1771–1855); a disciple of R. Shmuel of Karov, and other Polish chasidic Rebbes.
- *Ohr LaShamayim* – Rabbi Meir HaLevi Rottenberg of Stubnitz (1760–1831); disciple of R. Avraham Yehoshua Heshel of Apt and the Seer of Lublin.
- *Ohr Tzaddikim* – R. Meir Poppers (1624–1662); 17th century Kabbalist.
- *Orchos Tzaddikim* – Anonymous. Written in Germany, 15th century.
- *Oros v'Nesivos* – R. Avraham Eliezer Waldman; Rabbi in Manchester, England.
- *Otzar HaYirah* – R. Nachman of Tcherin (d. 1894); based on the works of R. Nachman and R. Nossan of Breslov.

- *Otzar Nechmad* – R. Yisroel ben Moshe of Zamoshtash (1700–1772); commentary on the Kuzari.
- *Otzar Yisrael* – R. Yisroel Rosenzweig (1913–1990).
- *Pele Yoetz* – R. Eliezer Papo (1785–1828); Rabbi of Selestria, Bulgaria.
- *Piskei Teshuvos* – R. Simcha Rabinowitz.
- *Pnei Menachem* – R. Pinchas Menachem Alter (1926–1996); the sixth Gerrer Rebbe.
- *Pri Tzaddik* – R. Tzadok HaKohen of Lublin (1823–1900); disciple of R. Mordechai Yosef Leiner of Izhbitz.
- *Rachamei HaAv* – R. Yaakov Katina (d. 1890); disciple of R. Yehuda Tzvi of Rozla, R. Chaim of Sanz, and R. Asher of Ropshitz.
- *Reishis Chochmah* – R. Eliyahu de Vidas (1518–1592); student of R. Moshe Cordovero (the Ramak) and R. Yitzchak Luria (the Arizal).
- *Sama d'Chaya* – R. Elazar ben Aryeh Leib Löw of Piltz (1758–1837); head of the Beis Din of Santav, author of *Shemen Rokeach*.
- *Sefer Chasidim* – R. Yehudah HaChasid (1150–1217).
- *Sefer HaChaim* – R. Chaim ben Betzalel (1530–1588); brother of the Maharal of Prague.
- *Sefer HaMidos* – R. Nachman of Breslov.
- *Sefer HaYashar* – R. Yaakov ben Meir, "Rabbeinu Tam" (1100–1171); grandson of Rashi.
- *Sefer Kedushah* – R. Shmuel Hominer (1913–1977); author and member of the Old Yishuv, Jerusalem.
- *Sha'ar Hitkashrus* – R. Yisroel Dov of Vildnick (1789–1850); a student of R. Mordechai of Chernobyl. Known as the "Tzaddik of Vildnick."
- *Sha'arei Teshuvah* – Rabbeinu Yonah of Gerondi (d. 1263).
- *Sha'arei Tzion* – R. Nossan Nota Hanover (1620–1683); author and Kabbalist.
- *Shaal Avicha VaYagedcha* – R. Shalom Mordechai Shwadron (1912–1997); famous Jerusalem *darshan*.
- *Shem HaGedolim* – R. Chaim Yosef Dovid Azulai (see above).
- *Shevet HaLevi* – R. Shmuel Wosner (b. 1913); leading halachic authority in Bnei Brak.
- *Shnei Luchos HaBris* – R. Yeshayahu Horowitz, the "Shlah HaKodesh" (c. 1565–1630).

- *Shomer Emunim* – R. Aharon Roth (1894–1947); the first Toldos Aharon Rebbe.
- *Shomer Yisroel* – R. Chaim Yosef Dovid Azulai (see above).
- *Shulchan Aruch* – R. Yosef Karo.
- *Sichos b'Avodas Hashem* – R. Yaakov Yitzchak Elazar Meizlish; contemporary teacher of chasidism, Jerusalem.
- *Sichos HaRan* – R. Nossan of Breslov.
- *Sur MeRa* – R. Tzvi Hirsh of Zidichov (1763–1831); chasidic Rebbe and Kabbalist. A disciple of R. Moshe Leib of Sassov, R. Menachem Mendel of Rimanov, the Maggid of Koznitz and Seer of Lublin.
- *Tefilah l'Dovid* – R. Dovid Amar (d. 1986).
- *Tefilos HaBoker* – R. Ephraim Weinberg (c. 1800–1883); second generation Breslover chasid, son of R. Naftali Weinberg, one of R. Nachman's close disciples.
- *Tefilos v'Tachanunim* – R. Nachman of Tcherin (see above).
- *Tiferes Shlomo* – R. Shlomo HaKohen Rabinowitz of Radomsk (1801–1866); a disciple of R. Meir of Apt.
- *Toldos Yaakov Yosef* - R. Yaakov Yosef Katz of Polnoye (1695–1782); a leading disciple of the Baal Shem Tov.
- *Tomer Devorah* – R. Moshe Cordovero (1522–1570); one of the greatest Kabbalists of Tzefat, in the 17th century.
- *Toras Avos* – A collection of writings by the Rebbes of Slonim (pub. Jerusalem: 1979).
- *Toras Chaim* – R. Chaim Hagar of Kosov (1795– 1854).
- *Toras Zev* – R. Zev Dov Tzhechik (1922–1980).
- *Tzava'as HaRivash* – R. Yisroel ben Eliezer, the "Baal Shem Tov" (1698–1760).
- *Tzidkas HaTzaddik* – R. Tzaddok HaKohen of Lublin (see above).
- *Tziporen Shamir* – R. Chaim Yosef Dovid Azulai.
- *Ya'aros Devash* – R. Yonatan Eybeschütz (1690–1764).
- *Yair Nesivos* – R. Nachman Rothstein, Rosh Yeshivah Nezer HaTorah, Jerusalem.
- *Yesod HaTeshuvah* – Rabbeinu Yonah (see above).
- *Yesod Yosef* – R. Yosef Yoska of Dubno (d. 1800); a disciple of the Maggid of Mezritch.

- *Yismach Moshe* – R. Moshe Teitelbaum (1759–1841); chasidic Rebbe in Ujhely, Hungary. Disciple of the Seer of Lublin.
- *Yisroel Kedoshim* – R. Tzadok HaKohen of Lublin.
- *Zohar* – R. Shimon bar Yochai; a first century Tanna.

Other Tzaddikim mentioned in this book

- R. Avraham of Butshatsh (1771–1840) – author of *Eshel Avraham*. A student of R. Levi Yitzchok of Berditchov, and R. Moshe Leib of Sasov.
- R. Chaim Halberstam of Sanz (1793–1876) – author of *Divrei Chaim*. A disciple of R. Naftali Zvi of Ropshitz.
- R. Chaim of Volozhin (1749–1821) – author of *Nefesh HaChaim*. A disciple of the Gaon of Vilna.
- R. Chaim Shaul Dweck HaKohen (1857–1933) – head of the Kabbalistic yeshiva Rechovot HaNahar, Jerusalem.
- R. Chaim Vital (1543–1620) – chief disciple of the Arizal, and author of the *Shemonah Shearim*.
- R. Dov Ber, the Maggid of Mezeritch (1710–1772) - chief disciple of the Baal Shem Tov.
- R. Dovid Biderman of Lelov (1746–1814) – the first Lelover Rebbe. A disciple of the Seer of Lublin.
- R. Alexander Ziskind (1738–1794) – author of *Yesod v'Shoresh HaAvodah*.
- R. Eliyahu ben Shlomo Zalman Kremer (1720–1797) – the Gaon of Vilna.
- R. Mordechai Twersky of Chernobyl (1798–1837) – the Maggid of Chernobyl. Son of Rabbi Menachem Nachum Twersky.
- R. Moshe Halberstam (1932–2006) – prominent member of the Edah Charedis Rabbinical court of Jerusalem.
- R. Naftali Tzvi Berlin (1816–1893) – head of the Volozhin Yeshivah, author of *HaEmek Davar*.
- R. Shlomo Luria (1510–1573) – the "Maharshal," author of *Yam Shel Shlomo*.
- R. Shlomo of Karlin (1738–1792) – disciple of R. Aharon HaGadol of Karlin.

- R. Simcha Bunim of Pashischa (1765–1827) – disciple of Rabbi Yaakov Yitzchok Rabinowitz, the "Yehudi HaKodosh."
- R. Yaakov Emden (1697–1776) – author of *Sha'agas Aryeh* and many other works; a leading Rabbi in Germany.
- R. Yeivi (1738–1791) – an acronym for R. Yaakov Yosef of Ostrag. A disciple of the Maggid of Mezritch.
- R. Yechezkel Halberstam (1813–1898) – the Shinover Rav, eldest son of the *Divrei Chaim* of Sanz.
- R. Yisachar Dov Ber (1764–1842) – the *Sabba Kaddisha* of Radoshitz. A disciple of the Seer of Lublin and of the Yehudi HaKodesh of Pashischa.
- R. Yissacher Dov of Belz (1851–1926) – the third Belzer Rebbe.
- R. Yitzchak Abuhav (early 15th cent.) – author of *Menoras HaMe'or*.
- R. Yitzchak Moshe Erlanger – present-day teacher of Kabbalah at Sha'ar HaShamayim Yeshivah, Jerusalem.
- R. Yosef ben Lev (1505–1580) – a leading sage of Salonika, Greece.
- R. Zelig Reuven Bengis (1864–1953) – author of *Leflagos Reuven*.
- R. Shlomo Yitzchaki (1040–1105) – Rashi.

GRAVESTONE OF R. ELIMELECH OF LIZHENSK

Hebrew Prayers

For the Tzetel Katan,
Hanhagos Ha'Adam
and more

להזהר מלהזכיר שם לבטלה

רִבּוֹנוֹ שֶׁל עוֹלָם, יְהִי רָצוֹן מִלְּפָנֶיךָ שֶׁתְּזַכֵּנִי לְכַוֵּן דַּעְתִּי בְּכָל הַדִּבּוּרִים שֶׁאוֹמַר לְפָנֶיךָ, וּבִפְרָט בְּהַזְכָּרַת שְׁמוֹתֶיךָ הַקְּדוֹשִׁים, וְהַצִּילֵנוּ מִכָּל מִכְשׁוֹל וְעָווֹן. (מדרש פנחס - אוצר תפלות ישראל א, עמ' קס"ו)

הנהגות האדם יח

להזהר ממשקה המשכר

וְתַצִּילֵנִי מִשִּׁכְרוּת תָּמִיד, וְתִשְׁמְרֵנִי וְתַצִּילֵנִי בְּרַחֲמֶיךָ מִיַּיִן הַמְשַׁכֵּר וּמֵהִתְלַהֲבוּת הַלֵּב וְרִקּוּדִין הַנִּמְשָׁכִין מֵהַסִּטְרָא אַחֲרָא חַס וְשָׁלוֹם וְלֹא יִהְיֶה לִי שׁוּם הִתְלַהֲבוּת הַיֵּצֶר לָשׂוּם תַּאֲוָה כְּלָל וּתְזַכֵּנִי לְיַיִן "הַמְשַׂמֵּחַ אֱלֹהִים וַאֲנָשִׁים" וּבְכָל עֵת שֶׁיִּהְיֶה הַהֶכְרֵחַ לִשְׁתּוֹת יַיִן וְשֵׁכָר בְּשַׁבָּתוֹת וְיָמִים טוֹבִים וּבְכוֹס שֶׁל בְּרָכָה, תְּזַכֵּנִי שֶׁתְּהֵא שְׁתִיָּתִי בְּצִמְצוּם גָּדוֹל רַק כְּדֵי לְהַרְחִיב דַּעְתִּי בִּקְדֻשָּׁה גְּדוֹלָה, וְלָבוֹא לְשִׂמְחָה שֶׁל מִצְוָה, לְשִׂמְחָה אֲמִתִּית דִּקְדֻשָּׁה עַל יְדֵי זֶה, לְהִתְלַהֲבוּת הַלֵּב דִּקְדֻשָּׁה, שֶׁיִּתְלַהֵב לִבִּי בִּקְדֻשָּׁה גְּדוֹלָה לְשִׁמְךָ וְלַעֲבוֹדָתְךָ בֶּאֱמֶת כִּרְצוֹנְךָ הַטּוֹב וְתִשְׁמְרֵנִי וְתַצִּילֵנִי בְּרַחֲמֶיךָ מִשְּׁתִיָּה מְרֻבָּה וְלֹא אָבוֹא לִידֵי שִׁכְרוּת לְעוֹלָם: (ל"ת מ"א)

הנהגות האדם יט

בכל יום בבוקר קודם ברכת התורה יאמר זאת

הֲרֵינִי מְכַוֵּן מֵעַתָּה עַל כָּל פְּרָט וּפְרָט מִמַּעֲשַׂי וְדִבּוּרַי וּמַחְשְׁבוֹתַי שֶׁל כָּל הַיּוֹם עַד לְמָחָר בָּעֵת הַזֹּאת לְשֵׁם יִחוּד קֻדְשָׁא בְּרִיךְ הוּא וּשְׁכִינְתֵּהּ בְּשֵׁם כָּל יִשְׂרָאֵל לְהַכְרִיעַ אֶת עַצְמִי וְאֶת כָּל עַם בְּנֵי יִשְׂרָאֵל וְאֶת כָּל הָעוֹלָם לְכַף זְכוּת:

וַהֲרֵינִי מְכַוֵּן מֵעַתָּה עַד לְמָחָר בָּעֵת הַזֹּאת בְּכָל פַּעַם שֶׁאַזְכִּיר שֵׁם הוי"ה הַקָּדוֹשׁ שֶׁהוּא בִּכְתִיבָתוֹ הָיָה הֹוֶה וְיִהְיֶה וּבִקְרִיאָתוֹ א-ד-נ-י שֶׁהוּא אָדוֹן הַכֹּל. וּכְשֶׁאַזְכִּיר שֵׁם א-ל-ק-י-ם יִהְיֶה כַּוָּנָתִי שֶׁהוּא תַּקִּיף וּבַעַל הַיְּכֹלֶת וּבַעַל הַכֹּחוֹת כֻּלָּם עִילַּת כָּל הָעִילּוֹת וְסִיבַּת כָּל הַסִּיבּוֹת וְשַׁלִּיט בְּכָל הָעוֹלָמוֹת: (תפילה לדוד מהרד"ק מבוטשאטש זי"ע)

הנהגות האדם יז

להרחיק את עצמו מכל דבר שאין בו תועלת

מָשְׁכֵנִי אַחֲרֶיךָ נָּרוּצָה, וּתְתַקְּנֵנוּ שֶׁאוּכַל לַעֲזֹב אֶת תַּאֲוֹות עוֹלָם הַזֶּה, וְלֹא יְבַלְבְּלוּ הֲנָאוֹת הָעוֹלָם אֶת מַחְשְׁבוֹתַי, וְלֹא אֶתְאַוֶּה לְתַעֲנוּגֵי הָעוֹלָם, וּבִפְרָט שֶׁלֹּא אֶהְיֶה לְהוּט אַחַר תַּאֲוֹות אֲכִילָה וּשְׁתִיָּה, וְלֹא אֶהְיֶה גַּרְגְּרָן וּבַלְעָן, וְלֹא תִהְיֶה אֲכִילָתִי לְמַלֵּאת תַּאֲוָתִי, כִּי אִם כְּצַדִּיק שֶׁאוֹכֵל לְשֹׂבַע נַפְשׁוֹ וּשְׁאָר כַּוָּנוֹת טוֹבוֹת. גַּם שְׁאָר מִדּוֹת וְתַאֲוֹות רָעוֹת הַרְחֵק מִמֶּנִּי, וְיִהְיוּ לִי מִדּוֹת טוֹבוֹת יָפוֹת וּכְשֵׁרוֹת, שֶׁאֶמְצָא בָּהֶם חֵן וְשֵׂכֶל טוֹב בְּעֵינֵי אֱלֹהִים וְאָדָם.

(יצחק ירנן - אוצר תפלות ישראל ג, עמ' קל"ז)

~

וּתְזַכֵּנִי מֵעַתָּה וְתִתֵּן לִי חָכְמָה וָשֵׂכֶל וְעֵצוֹת דִּקְדֻשָּׁה וְכֹחַ וּגְבוּרָה מֵאִתְּךָ, בְּאֹפֶן שֶׁאֶזְכֶּה לְמַלֵּט נַפְשִׁי מִנִּי שַׁחַת, לִמְשֹׁךְ אֶת עַצְמִי וּלְהַרְחִיק אֶת עַצְמִי מִכָּל הַתַּאֲוֹות וּמִכָּל הַמִּדּוֹת רָעוֹת עַד שֶׁאֶזְכֶּה לְגָרֵשׁ וּלְבַטֵּל מִמֶּנִּי כָּל מִינֵי תַּאֲוֹות וּמִדּוֹת רָעוֹת, עַד שֶׁיִּהְיֶה גּוּפִי זַךְ וְצַח וְנָקִי מִכָּל מִינֵי תַּאֲוֹות וּמִכָּל מִינֵי מִדּוֹת רָעוֹת, וְאֶזְכֶּה לִהְיוֹת קָדוֹשׁ וְטָהוֹר בֶּאֱמֶת כָּרָאוּי לְאִישׁ יִשְׂרְאֵלִי: (ל"ת י')

~

וְזַכֵּנִי לְמִדַּת הַהִסְתַּפְּקוּת, שֶׁאֶזְכֶּה לִהְיוֹת מִסְתַּפֵּק בִּמְעַט מֵהָעוֹלָם הַזֶּה, וְלֹא אֶשְׁתַּמֵּשׁ בְּעִסְקֵי הָעוֹלָם הַזֶּה כִּי אִם מַה שֶּׁמֻּכְרָח לְבַד, בִּקְדֻשָּׁה וְטָהֳרָה, לְשִׁמְךָ וּלְזִכְרְךָ לְבַד: (ספר קדושה - אוצר תפלות ישראל ג, עמ' רכ"א)

~

וְתַעַזְרֵנִי בְּרַחֲמֶיךָ הָרַבִּים, שֶׁאֶזְכֶּה לִקְדֻשָּׁה וְטָהֳרָה, שֶׁאֶזְכֶּה לְקַדֵּשׁ עַצְמִי בַּמֻּתָּר לִי, וְאֶזְכֶּה בְּכָל פַּעַם לְהוֹסִיף קְדֻשָּׁה עַל קְדֻשָּׁה, עַד שֶׁאֶזְכֶּה לִקְדֻשָּׁה וּפְרִישׁוּת בֶּאֱמֶת, עַד שֶׁאֶזְכֶּה שֶׁיִּתְיַחֵד עַל יְדֵי יִחוּדָא עִלָּאָה וְיִחוּדָא תַּתָּאָה: (ל"ת י"א)

וְיִגְדְּלוּ לְפָנֶיךָ, וְכָל תְּנוּעוֹתַי שְׁקוּלוֹת עַל דֶּרֶךְ הַשַּׁחוּת וּכְנִיעָה. וְתֵן לִי עֵזֶר וָאֹמֶץ לָדַעַת גְּדֻלָּתְךָ וּמִצְוֹתֶיךָ, וְלַעֲשׂוֹת הַטּוֹב לִבְנֵי אָדָם, וְשֶׁלֹּא אֲסַפֵּר בִּגְנוּתָם אֶלָּא לִזְכוּת. וְיִהְיֶה יְקַר רוּחַ וְגָבַהּ נֶפֶשׁ בְּעִנְיְנֵי עוֹלָם הַבָּא. (מרגליות טובות - אוצר תפלות ישראל ג, עמ' קע"א)

§

וְאִתְאַמֵּץ שֶׁלֹּא לְהַקְפִּיד עַל שׁוּם דָּבָר, הֵן בְּבֵיתִי, הֵן לִבְנֵי אָדָם אֲחֵרִים, וְלִסְבֹּל הַכֹּל בְּשִׂמְחָה בֶּאֱמוּנָה שְׁלֵמָה שֶׁהַכֹּל הוּא הַשְׁגָּחָה, וְלֹא הַנָּחָשׁ מֵמִית כִּי אִם הַחֵטְא, וְטוֹבָה גְּדוֹלָה לְהִשְׁתַּדֵּל מֵעֲוֹנוֹתַי בָּעוֹלָם הַזֶּה שָׁמוּר לָעוֹלָם הַנִּצְחִי. וְאִתְאַמֵּץ בְּכָל כֹּחִי לִהְיוֹת שָׁרוּי תָּמִיד בְּשִׂמְחָה, וּבִזְכוּת הָאֱמוּנָה וְהַשִּׂמְחָה יַעַזְרֵנִי הַשֵּׁם יִתְבָּרַךְ לָשׁוּב עַל עֲוֹנוֹתַי, וְאַחַר כָּךְ לִזְכּוֹת לִטְעוֹם מֵעֵץ הַחַיִּים, מִנַּעַם הַתּוֹרָה הַקְּדוֹשָׁה וּמִנֹּעַם מִצְוֹתֶיהָ, לִהְיוֹת שָׂשׂ עַל אִמְרָתְךָ כְּמוֹצֵא שָׁלָל רָב.
(שאול בחיר ה' - אוצר תפלות ישראל א, עמ' קס"ב)

§

"אַשְׁרֵי הַגֶּבֶר אֲשֶׁר תְּיַסְּרֶנּוּ יָהּ וּמִתּוֹרָתְךָ תְלַמְּדֶנּוּ, לְהַשְׁקִיט לוֹ מִימֵי רָע עַד יִכָּרֶה לָרָשָׁע שָׁחַת כִּי לֹא יִטֹּשׁ יְהֹוָה עַמּוֹ וְנַחֲלָתוֹ לֹא יַעֲזֹב", רִבּוֹנוֹ שֶׁל עוֹלָם מָלֵא רַחֲמִים טוֹב וּמֵטִיב לַכֹּל עָזְרֵנִי וְהוֹשִׁיעֵנִי שֶׁאֶזְכֶּה לְקַבֵּל הַכֹּל בְּאַהֲבָה, וַאֲפִלּוּ כְּשֶׁאַתָּה שׁוֹלֵחַ עָלַי בְּרַחֲמֶיךָ לִפְעָמִים אֵיזֶה יִסּוּרִין הַנִּדְמִים לְרָעוֹת חַס וְשָׁלוֹם, אֶזְכֶּה לְקַבֵּל הַכֹּל בְּאַהֲבָה גְּדוֹלָה בֶּאֱמֶת, וְתִפְתַּח אֶת לִבִּי בִּקְדֻשָּׁה גְּדוֹלָה שֶׁאֶזְכֶּה לֵידַע וּלְהָבִין בֶּאֱמֶת אֲשֶׁר כְּמוֹנִי כְּמוֹ שֶׁאֲנִי הוּא, כְּמוֹ שֶׁעָשִׂיתִי נֶגְדְּךָ, כָּל מַה שֶּׁאַתָּה עוֹשֶׂה עִמִּי, הַכֹּל רַחֲמִים רַבִּים וַחֲסָדִים גְּדוֹלִים בְּלִי שִׁעוּר וָעֵרֶךְ עַד אֵין סוֹף וְאֵין תַּכְלִית, כִּי אִי אֶפְשָׁר לְבָאֵר וּלְסַפֵּר לְעוֹלָם עֹצֶם רִבּוּי הָרַחֲמָנוּת וְהַחֲסָדִים וְהַטּוֹבוֹת אֲשֶׁר עָשִׂיתָ עִמִּי וַאֲשֶׁר אַתָּה עוֹשֶׂה עִמִּי, וַאֲשֶׁר אַתָּה עָתִיד לַעֲשׂוֹת עִמִּי בְּכָל עֵת וָרֶגַע, מָה אוֹמַר, מָה אֲדַבֵּר, "מָה אָשִׁיב לַיהֹוָה כָּל תַּגְמוּלוֹהִי עָלָי":
(ל"ת קכ"א)

יִרְאָתְךָ וְאֵימָתֶךָ. וְנִזְכֶּה לְמִדַּת הַבּוּשָׁה הַקְּדוֹשָׁה וְתַלְבִּישׁ אוֹתָנוּ בִּלְבוּשׁ הַיִּרְאָה וּבְמַעֲטֵה הַבּוּשָׁה מִשִּׁמְךָ הַגָּדוֹל וְהַקָּדוֹשׁ וְנִתְבַּיֵּשׁ מִמְּךָ תָּמִיד בֶּאֱמֶת, לְבִלְתִּי לָסוּר מֵרְצוֹנְךָ הַטּוֹב יָמִין וּשְׂמֹאל, וְתִהְיֶה יִרְאָתְךָ עַל פָּנֵי לְבִלְתִּי אֶחֱטָא, זוֹ הַבּוּשָׁה: (ל״ת כ״ב)

☙

רִבּוֹנוֹ שֶׁל עוֹלָם, חוּסָה עָלַי בְּרַחֲמֶיךָ וֶהֱיֵה בְּעֶזְרִי, שֶׁיִּהְיֶה לִי בּוּשָׁה גְּדוֹלָה בָּעוֹלָם הַזֶּה מִפָּנֶיךָ, שֶׁלֹּא לַעֲשׂוֹת שׁוּם דָּבָר נֶגֶד רְצוֹנְךָ, חַס וְשָׁלוֹם, מִכָּל שֶׁכֵּן וְכָל שֶׁכֵּן שֶׁלֹּא לַעֲשׂוֹת, חַס וְשָׁלוֹם, שׁוּם נְדְנוּד עֲבֵרָה, חָלִילָה, וְלֹא אֵבוֹשׁ וְלֹא אִכָּלֵם לָעוֹלָם הַבָּא, וְזַכֵּנִי שֶׁיִּהְיֶה מוֹרָא שָׁמַיִם עָלַי כְּמוֹרָא בָּשָׂר וָדָם, שֶׁיִּהְיֶה לִי יִרְאָה וּבוּשָׁה מִפָּנֶיךָ כְּמוֹ מִפְּנֵי בָּשָׂר וָדָם מַמָּשׁ: (ל״ת כ״ב)

☙

וְנִזְכֶּה לְהִסְתַּכֵּל עַל עַצְמֵנוּ הֵיטֵב בְּכָל עֵת עַל מַה בָּאנוּ לְהַאי עָלְמָא, וּלְהִסְתַּכֵּל בְּכָל הַמִּדּוֹת לְזַכְּכָם וּלְטַהֲרָם וּלְקַדְּשָׁם תַּכְלִית הַשְּׁלֵמוּת, וּלְהִסְתַּכֵּל בִּגְדֻלַּת הַבּוֹרֵא יִתְבָּרַךְ וּבְנִפְלְאוֹתָיו הַנּוֹרָאִים, אֲשֶׁר הוּא עוֹשֶׂה חֲדָשׁוֹת וְנִפְלָאוֹת בְּכָל עֵת וָעֵת. (ספר קדושה - אוצר תפלות ישראל ג, עמ' רכ״ב)

הנהגות האדם טז

ישמח במה שמגנים אותו

וְעָזְרֵנוּ שֶׁלֹּא אֶהְיֶה גַּס רוּחַ, לֹא בַּמֶּה שֶׁיֵּשׁ בִּי וְלֹא בַּמֶּה שֶׁאֵין בִּי. וּבְעֵת כַּעֲסִי אוֹ בְּעֵת בִּיאַת יִסּוּרִין, סַיְּעֵנִי שֶׁאֲכַבֵּשׁ נַפְשִׁי וַאֲקַבְּלֵם בְּאַהֲבָה וּבִכְנִיעָה גְּדוֹלָה. וְאִם מְשַׁבְּחִים לִי לֹא אֶתְגָּאֶה, וְיִשְׁתַּוֶּה לְפָנַי שֶׁבַח וּגְנוּת בְּנֵי אָדָם. וְהַעֲלֵה עַל לִבִּי, שֶׁיִּקְטְנוּ מַעֲשַׂי לְפָנַי

בֶּאֱמֶת וּבְלֵב שָׁלֵם לִהְיוֹת כִּרְצוֹנְךָ הַטּוֹב בֶּאֱמֶת אֲנִי וְזַרְעִי וְזֶרַע זַרְעִי וְכָל זֶרַע עַמְּךָ בֵּית יִשְׂרָאֵל מֵעַתָּה וְעַד עוֹלָם, אָמֵן סֶלָה. (ל"ת פ"ה)

הנהגות האדם יד

דיבור בנחת ולהכיד שפלות

יְהִי רָצוֹן מִלְּפָנֶיךָ יְהֹוָה אֱלֹהַי וֵאלֹהֵי אֲבוֹתַי, שֶׁתְּרַחֵם עָלַי בְּרַחֲמֶיךָ הָרַבִּים וּתְבַטֵּל מֵעָלַי מִדַּת הַגַּאֲוָה בְּבִטּוּל גָּמוּר, שֶׁלֹּא יְהֵא בְּלִבִּי שׁוּם צַד גֵּאוּת וְגַבְהוּת בָּעוֹלָם כְּלָל, וְאֶזְכֶּה לֵידַע שִׁפְלוּתִי בֶּאֱמֶת לַאֲמִתּוֹ, וְאֶזְכֶּה לְבַטֵּל עַצְמִי לְגַמְרֵי עַד שֶׁאֶהְיֶה קָטָן בְּעֵינַי יוֹתֵר מִמַּדְרֵגָתִי הַשְּׁפֵלָה מְאֹד: (ל"ת י"ד)

אָנָּא הַשֵּׁם הַנִּכְבָּד וְהַנּוֹרָא, מֶלֶךְ הַכָּבוֹד, אֲשֶׁר בָּרָאתָ כָּל הָעוֹלָם כֻּלּוֹ בִּשְׁבִיל כְּבוֹדְךָ יִתְבָּרַךְ, כְּמוֹ שֶׁכָּתוּב: "כֹּל הַנִּקְרָא בִשְׁמִי וְלִכְבוֹדִי בְּרָאתִיו יְצַרְתִּיו אַף עֲשִׂיתִיו", וּבְכֵן תַּעַזְרֵנִי בְּרַחֲמֶיךָ הָרַבִּים, שֶׁאֶזְכֶּה שֶׁיִּתְגַּדֵּל וְיִשְׁתַּבַּח וְיִתְעַלֶּה כְּבוֹדְךָ עַל יָדִי, וְתִהְיֶה בְּעֶזְרִי שֶׁאוּכַל לְבַטֵּל עַצְמִי לְגַמְרֵי וּלְמַעֵט בִּכְבוֹדִי, שֶׁיִּהְיֶה כְּבוֹדִי לְאַיִן וָאֶפֶס, וְלֹא אַשְׁגִּיחַ עַל כְּבוֹד עַצְמִי כְּלָל, רַק לְהַרְבּוֹת כְּבוֹד הַמָּקוֹם, וְיִהְיוּ כָּל עֲסָקַי וַעֲשִׂיּוֹתַי וּמַחְשְׁבוֹתַי וּרְצוֹנִי כֻּלָּם רַק בִּשְׁבִיל כְּבוֹדְךָ הַגָּדוֹל יִתְבָּרַךְ: (ל"ת י"א)

הנהגות האדם טו

בושה מהשי"ת

יְהִי רָצוֹן מִלְּפָנֶיךָ יְהֹוָה אֱלֹהֵינוּ וֵאלֹהֵי אֲבוֹתֵינוּ, רִבּוֹן כָּל הַמַּעֲשִׂים אֲדוֹן כָּל הַנְּשָׁמוֹת שֶׁתַּשְׁפִּיעַ עָלֵינוּ מִמְּעוֹן קָדְשָׁתֶךָ, וְתַמְשִׁיךְ עָלֵינוּ

שָׁלֵמָה לְפָנֶיךָ בֶּאֱמֶת, זַכֵּנִי מֵעַתָּה, עָזְרֵנִי מֵעַתָּה, הוֹשִׁיעֵנִי מֵעַתָּה, וֶהֱיֵה עִמִּי תָּמִיד, וְעָזְרֵנִי וְזַכֵּנִי לִסְגֹּר וּלְהָעֵצִים וְלִסְתֹּם עֵינַי וְלִבִּי וְדַעְתִּי וּמַחֲשַׁבְתִּי מֵחֵיזוּ דְּהַאי עָלְמָא שְׁפָלָה לְגַמְרֵי, וְלֹא אֶסְתַּכֵּל עַל הַבְלֵי עוֹלָם הַזֶּה וְתַאֲוֹתָיו וּטְרָדוֹתָיו כְּלָל, כִּי כָּל הָעוֹלָם הַזֶּה אֵינוֹ עוֹלֶה כְּהֶרֶף עַיִן, כִּי הַכֹּל הֶבֶל וּרְעוּת רוּחַ "וּמַה יִּתְרוֹן לָאָדָם מִכָּל עֲמָלוֹ" וּמִכָּל תַּאֲוֹתָיו וַהֲבָלָיו: (ל"ת ס"ה)

~

מָלֵא רַחֲמִים חוּס וְרַחֵם עָלַי וְהַצִּילֵנִי מֵחֲרָפוֹת וּבִזְיוֹנוֹת, שֶׁלֹּא יִהְיֶה כֹּחַ לְשׁוּם מַזִּיק וּמַשְׁחִית לְהִתְקָרֵב אֵלַי בְּעֵת מִיתָתִי וְלֹא יֵלְכוּ אַחַר מִטָּתִי חַס וְשָׁלוֹם, רַק בְּרַחֲמֶיךָ הָרַבִּים תְּגָרְשֵׁם מִפָּנַי וּתְבַטְּלֵם בְּבִטּוּל גָּמוּר מֵעַתָּה וְעַד עוֹלָם וְתָחוּס עָלַי בְּחֶמְלָתְךָ הַגְּדוֹלָה וּבַחֲנִינוֹתֶיךָ הָעֲצוּמִים, שֶׁאֶזְכֶּה לְתַקֵּן אֶת חַיַּי אֶת כָּל אֲשֶׁר שִׁחַתִּי, וְתָחוּס וְתִמְחֹל וְתִסְלַח לִי עַל הַכֹּל בַּחַיִּים חַיּוּתִי, בְּאֹפֶן שֶׁלֹּא יִהְיֶה עָלַי שׁוּם דִּין וּמִשְׁפָּט אַחַר כָּךְ אִם אָמְנָם יָדַעְתִּי בֶּאֱמֶת כִּי אֲנִי רָחוֹק מִישׁוּעָה כָּזֹאת, כִּי בַּמֶּה יִזְכֶּה נַעַר כָּמוֹנִי לָזֶה, אַךְ עַל רַחֲמֶיךָ הָרַבִּים אֲנִי בּוֹטֵחַ, וְעַל חַסְדְּךָ אֲנִי נִשְׁעָן וְלִסְלִיחוֹתֶיךָ אֲנִי מְקַוֶּה, וְלִישׁוּעָתְךָ אֲנִי מְצַפֶּה, בְּכֹחַ וּזְכוּת הַצַּדִּיקִים אֲמִתִּיִּים שֶׁבְּדוֹרֵנוּ, וּבִזְכוּת כָּל הַצַּדִּיקִים אֲמִתִּיִּים שׁוֹכְנֵי עָפָר עֲלֵיהֶם אָנוּ נִשְׁעָנִים, בָּהֶם תָּמַכְתִּי יְתֵדוֹתַי לִשְׁאֹל כָּל אֵלֶּה מִלְּפָנֶיךָ, עַל כֵּן עֲדַיִן אֲנִי עוֹמֵד וּמְצַפֶּה וּמְקַוֶּה וּמְיַחֵל לִישׁוּעָתְךָ הַגְּדוֹלָה, שֶׁאֶזְכֶּה מְהֵרָה לְכָל מַה שֶּׁבִּקַּשְׁתִּי מִלְּפָנֶיךָ, כִּי אַתָּה צוֹפֶה לָרָשָׁע וְחָפֵץ בְּהַצְדִּיקוֹ. וְאִם אֲנִי מִתְמַהְמֵהַּ הַרְבֵּה לָשׁוּב, וְעוֹד הוֹסַפְתִּי קִלְקוּלִים וַעֲוֹנוֹת הַרְבֵּה גְּדוֹלִים וַעֲצוּמִים בְּכָל יוֹם, אַף-עַל-פִּי-כֵן עֲדַיִן אֲנִי מְחַכֶּה בְּכָל יוֹם שֶׁיָּבֹא גְּאֻלָּתִי וּפְדוּת נַפְשִׁי, שֶׁאֶזְכֶּה מְהֵרָה לְהִתְעוֹרֵר מִשְּׁנָתִי וְלָקוּם מִנְּפִילָתִי וְלַעֲמֹד מִיְּרִידָתִי וְלִחְיוֹת מִמִּיתָתִי וְלָשׁוּב אֵלֶיךָ

שׂוּם כֹּחַ לְהַבַּעַל דָּבָר לְקַלְקֵל הַשְׁפָּעַת הָעֲשִׁירוּת חַס וְשָׁלוֹם עַל יְדֵי הַכַּעַס וְהַחֵמָה חַס וְשָׁלוֹם: (ל"ת ס"ח ס"ט)

וּבְכֵן יְהִי רָצוֹן מִלְּפָנֶיךָ יְהוָה אֱלֹהֵינוּ וֵאלֹהֵי אֲבוֹתֵינוּ, מָלֵא טוֹב מָלֵא רַחֲמִים, מָלֵא רָצוֹן, שֶׁתִּהְיֶה בְּעֶזְרִי, וְתִשְׁמְרֵנִי וְתַצִּילֵנִי מִן הַכַּעַס וּמִן הָרֹגֶז וּמִכָּל מִינֵי קְפֵדוֹת וְתָגֵן עָלַי בְּרַחֲמֶיךָ וְתִשְׁמְרֵנִי תָּמִיד וַאֲפִלּוּ בְּשָׁעָה שֶׁיָּבוֹא חַס וְשָׁלוֹם, לִידֵי אֵיזֶה כַּעַס, תַּחְמֹל עָלַי בְּרַחֲמֶיךָ וְתִשְׁמְרֵנִי וְתַצִּילֵנִי שֶׁלֹּא אֶפְעַל בְּכַעֲסִי שׁוּם אַכְזָרִיּוּת כְּלָל רַק אֶזְכֶּה לְשַׁבֵּר וּלְהָפֵר הַכַּעַס בְּרַחֲמָנוּת, וְאֶזְכֶּה לְהִתְגַּבֵּר עַל יִצְרִי לְשַׁבֵּר הַכַּעַס וְלַהֲפֹךְ הַכַּעַס לְרַחֲמָנוּת, לְרַחֵם דַּיְקָא בְּרַחֲמָנוּת גְּדוֹלָה בְּמָקוֹם שֶׁהָיִיתִי רוֹצֶה לִכְעֹס, חַס וְשָׁלוֹם וְלֹא יִהְיֶה בִּי אֵל זָר וְלֹא אֶשְׁתַּחֲוֶה לְאֵל נֵכָר, שֶׁזֶּה נֶאֱמַר עַל הַכּוֹעֵס, שֶׁנֶּחֱשָׁב כְּאִלּוּ עוֹבֵד עֲבוֹדָה זָרָה: (ל"ת י"ח)

הנהגות האדם יג

לזכות לעשות תשובה שלימה

אֲהָהּ יְהוָה, אֲהָהּ אֲדוֹנֵנוּ מַלְכֵּנוּ, מַה נַּעֲשֶׂה לְיוֹם פְּקֻדָּה מַה נַּעֲשֶׂה לְעוֹלָם הַנִּצְחִי, מַה נַּעֲשֶׂה לְיוֹם שֶׁכֻּלּוֹ שַׁבָּת וּמְנוּחָה, אֲשֶׁר אִי אֶפְשָׁר לְהִכָּנֵס וּלְהִכָּלֵל שָׁם כִּי אִם מִי שֶׁמְּקַשֵּׁט עַצְמוֹ בָּעוֹלָם הַזֶּה וּמַפְשִׁיט דַּעְתּוֹ לְגַמְרֵי מֵחִיזוּ דְּהַאי עָלְמָא וּמְדַבֵּק אֶת עַצְמוֹ רַק בְּהַתַּכְלִית הָאֲמִתִּי וְהַנִּצְחִי, וּמֶה נַּעֲשֶׂה וַחֲטָאֵינוּ עָשׂוּ לָנוּ מַה שֶּׁעָשׂוּ, עַד אֲשֶׁר "טָבַעְתִּי בִּיוֵן מְצוּלָה וְאֵין מָעֳמָד, בָּאתִי בְמַעֲמַקֵּי מַיִם וְשִׁבֹּלֶת שְׁטָפָתְנִי" אָבִי אָבִי אָבִי, אֲדֹנִי אֲדֹנִי אֲדֹנִי, "מַלְכִּי וֵאלֹהַי אֵלֶיךָ אֶתְפַּלָּל", אֵלֶיךָ אֶשְׁתַּטַּח, אֵלֶיךָ אֶתְנַפֵּל וְאֶתְחַנַּן, עֲשֵׂה לְמַעַנְךָ לְבַד, עֲשֵׂה מַה שֶּׁתּוּכַל בְּרַחֲמֶיךָ הָרַבִּים וְהַחֲזִירֵנִי בִּתְשׁוּבָה

קַצְוֵי אֶרֶץ וְיָם רְחוֹקִים" נוֹרָאוֹת הַפְלֵא לְמַעַן שְׁמֶךָ, וְעָזְרֵנִי וְהוֹשִׁיעֵנִי שֶׁאֶזְכֶּה לְתַקֵּן בְּחַיַּי כָּל זֶה חִישׁ קַל מְהֵרָה, שֶׁאֶזְכֶּה מֵעַתָּה לְתַקֵּן תִּקּוּן הַבְּרִית בִּשְׁלֵמוּת וְאֶזְכֶּה לְהָדִים וּלְעוֹרֵר אֶת הַדַּעַת דִּקְדֻשָּׁה, וּלְהַמְשִׁיךְ לְבַנּוּנִית דִּקְדֻשָּׁה מֵהַדַּעַת הַקָּדוֹשׁ, לְתַקֵּן פְּגַם כָּל הַדָּמִים שֶׁל כָּל הַשַּׁ"ס גִּידִין, שֶׁהֵם כְּנֶגֶד שַׁ"ס לָאוִין שֶׁבַּתּוֹרָה, וּתְזַכֵּנִי לְתַקֵּן פְּגַם כָּל הַכְּתָמִים שֶׁל הַבְּגָדִים שֶׁלֹּא שָׁמַרְתִּי אוֹתָם עַד הֵנָּה וְתִמְחֹל וְתִסְלַח לִי עַל כָּל הַפְּגָמִים הָאֵלֶּה וְתַעַזְרֵנִי מֵעַתָּה וְתִשְׁמְרֵנִי וְתַצִּילֵנִי מִכָּל חֵטְא וְעָוֹן וּמִכְשׁוֹל וְתַעַזְרֵנִי מֵעַתָּה לִשְׁמֹר אֶת הַבְּגָדִים וְהַלְּבוּשִׁים שֶׁלִּי לְכַבְּדָן וּלְהַחֲזִיקָן בִּנְקִיּוּת וּתְזַכֵּנִי שֶׁלֹּא יִמָּצֵא עַל כָּל בְּגָדַי וּלְבוּשַׁי שׁוּם כֶּתֶם וְשׁוּם לִכְלוּךְ וְרֶבֶב כְּלָל וְתָגֵן בַּעֲדִי, וְתִשְׁמְרֵנִי אוֹתִי וְאֶת בְּגָדַי תָּמִיד וְיִהְיוּ גּוּפִי וְנַפְשִׁי וּבְגָדַי וּלְבוּשַׁי כֻּלָּם נְקִיִּים וּטְהוֹרִים וּקְדוֹשִׁים תָּמִיד מֵעַתָּה וְעַד עוֹלָם: (ל"ת כ"ט)

⁓⁓⁓◦⁓⁓⁓

הנהגות האדם יב

לא להטיל אימה יתירה

רִבּוֹנוֹ שֶׁל עוֹלָם, טוֹב וּמֵטִיב לַכֹּל חוּס וַחֲמֹל עָלַי, וְלַמְּדֵנִי דַּרְכֵי טוּבְךָ בְּאֹפֶן שֶׁאֶזְכֶּה לֶאֱחֹז בְּמִדּוֹתֶיךָ הַקְּדוֹשִׁים, לִהְיוֹת טוֹב לַכֹּל תָּמִיד, וּלְשַׁבֵּר מִדַּת הַכַּעַס וְהַחֶרוֹן אַף וְהַקְפֵּדוּת לְגַמְרֵי, שֶׁלֹּא יִהְיֶה בְּלִבִּי שׁוּם צַד כַּעַס כְּלָל וּבְכָל עֵת שֶׁיִּרְצֶה הַיֵּצֶר לְהָסִית אוֹתִי לִכְעֹס חַס וְשָׁלוֹם אֶזְכֶּה לָדַעַת וּלְהַאֲמִין בֶּאֱמוּנָה שְׁלֵמָה, שֶׁבְּשָׁעָה זוֹ רוֹצִים לְהַשְׁפִּיעַ לִי עֲשִׁירוּת גָּדוֹל, וְהַיֵּצֶר הָרָע רוֹצֶה לְקַלְקֵל חַס וְשָׁלוֹם זֹאת הַהַשְׁפָּעָה שֶׁל הָעֲשִׁירוּת, וְלַעֲשׂוֹת מִמֶּנָּה כַּעַס, וְלִטְרֹף אֶת נַפְשִׁי חַס וְשָׁלוֹם עַל יְדֵי זֶה, וְעַל יְדֵי זֶה אֶזְכֶּה לְהִתְחַזֵּק וּלְהִתְגַּבֵּר לְשַׁבֵּר וּלְבַטֵּל הַכַּעַס לְגַמְרֵי, וְלַהֲפֹךְ הַכַּעַס לְרַחֲמָנוּת, וְאֶזְכֶּה עַל יְדֵי זֶה לַעֲשִׁירוּת גָּדוֹל דִּקְדֻשָּׁה, שֶׁהוּא שֹׁרֶשׁ הַנְּפָשׁוֹת וְלֹא יִהְיֶה

הנהגות האדם ט

להזהר מלדבר לפני התפילה

וְתִגְעַר בּוֹ שֶׁיֵּסוּד וְיֵלֵךְ מֵאִתָּנוּ, וְאַל יָסִית אוֹתָנוּ לְהַדִּיחֵנוּ מֵעֲבוֹדָתְךָ חָלִילָה. וְאַל יַעֲלֶה בְּלִבֵּנוּ שׁוּם מַחֲשָׁבָה רָעָה חָלִילָה הֵן בְּהָקִיץ הֵן בַּחֲלוֹם. בִּפְרָט בְּעֵת שֶׁאֲנַחְנוּ עוֹמְדִים בִּתְפִלָּה לְפָנֶיךָ, אוֹ בְּשָׁעָה שֶׁאֲנַחְנוּ לוֹמְדִים תּוֹרָתְךָ. וּבְשָׁעָה שֶׁאֲנַחְנוּ עוֹסְקִים בְּמִצְוֹתֶיךָ, תְּהֵא מַחֲשְׁבוֹתֵינוּ זַכָּה צְלוּלָה וּבְרוּרָה וַחֲזָקָה, בֶּאֱמֶת וּבְלֵבָב שָׁלֵם כִּרְצוֹנְךָ הַטּוֹב עִמָּנוּ. (מתפלת הרה״ק ר״א זצוק״ל)

הנהגות האדם יא

להזהר שבגדיו יהיו נקיים

וְתַעַזְרֵנִי וְתוֹשִׁיעֵנִי וְתִהְיֶה עִמִּי תָּמִיד וְתִשְׁמֹר אֶת לְבוּשַׁי וּבִגְדֵי שֶׁלֹּא יָבֹא עֲלֵיהֶם שׁוּם לִכְלוּךְ וְשׁוּם כֶּתֶם וְשׁוּם רְבָב כִּי אַתָּה לְבַד יָדַעְתָּ גֹּדֶל הַפְּגָם הַנּוֹגֵעַ בַּשְּׁכִינָה בְּעַצְמָהּ וּבְעוֹלָמוֹת עֶלְיוֹנִים, עַל יְדֵי פְּגָם הַבְּגָדִים כְּשֶׁאֵין שׁוֹמְרִים אוֹתָם מִכְּתָמִים וְלִכְלוּכִים וְהַבְּגָדִים בְּעַצְמָן דָּנִין אֶת הָאָדָם עַל זֶה, כְּשֶׁאֵין שׁוֹמְרִים אוֹתָם מִכְּתָמִים וּבַעֲווֹנוֹתַי הָרַבִּים, קָשֶׁה וְכָבֵד עָלַי דָּבָר הַזֶּה, לִשְׁמֹר אֶת הַבְּגָדִים מִכְּתָמִים כִּי אִי אֶפְשָׁר שֶׁלֹּא אַסִּיחַ דַּעְתִּי מֵהֶם וּבִפְרָט בִּשְׁעַת עֵסֶק הַתּוֹרָה וְהַתְּפִלָּה וּשְׁאָר עֲסָקִים וְאָז בָּאִים חַס וְשָׁלוֹם עֲלֵיהֶם כְּתָמִים בְּהֶסַּח הַדַּעַת וְכָל זֶה גָּרַמְתִּי עַל יְדֵי עֲוֹנוֹתַי הַמְרֻבִּים, וּמַחְשְׁבוֹתַי הַמְבֻלְבָּלוֹת מְאֹד, אֲשֶׁר עַל יְדֵי זֶה אֵינִי זוֹכֶה לִשְׁמֹר אֶת הַבְּגָדִים וּלְהַחֲזִיקָן בִּנְקִיּוּת, וּלְהַצִּילָן מִכְּתָמִים וְלִכְלוּכִים, הֵן עַל כָּל אֵלֶּה בָּאתִי לְפָרֵשׁ שִׂיחָתִי לְפָנֶיךָ יְהֹוָה אֱלֹהַי וֵאלֹהֵי אֲבוֹתַי, מָלֵא רַחֲמִים, גּוֹמֵל לְחַיָּבִים טוֹבוֹת "נוֹרָאוֹת בְּצֶדֶק תַּעֲנֵנוּ אֱלֹהֵי יִשְׁעֵנוּ מִבְטָח כָּל

בְּלִבִּי עֲלֵיהֶם מֵאַחַר שֶׁאֲנִי רָאוּי לְכָל זֶה וְיוֹתֵר עוֹד מִזֶּה. (תפילות ותחנונים עמ' ק"ה)

אָבִינוּ שֶׁבַּשָּׁמַיִם, מַה נֹּאמַר לְפָנֶיךָ יוֹשֵׁב מָרוֹם וּמַה נְּסַפֵּר לְפָנֶיךָ שׁוֹכֵן שְׁחָקִים, כִּי מֵרֹב רְגִילוּתֵנוּ בְּדִבּוּרִים פְּגוּמִים, אֵין אָנוּ יוֹדְעִים שׁוּם דֶּרֶךְ אֵיךְ לְהַרְחִיק עַצְמֵנוּ מֵהֶם מֵעַתָּה, עַל כֵּן בָּאתִי לְפָנֶיךָ יְהֹוָה אֱלֹהַי וֵאלֹהֵי אֲבוֹתַי, שֶׁתַּעַזְרֵנִי בְּרַחֲמֶיךָ וְתַדְרִיכֵנִי וְתוֹרֵנִי דֶּרֶךְ יְשָׁרָה, בְּאֹפֶן שֶׁאֶזְכֶּה לִשְׁמֹר עַצְמִי בְּרַחֲמֶיךָ שֶׁלֹּא אֶכָּשֵׁל בְּשׁוּם דִּבּוּר שֶׁאֵינוֹ טוֹב וְלֹא אוֹמַר דָּבָר שֶׁלֹּא כִּרְצוֹנֶךָ וּתְזַכֵּנִי לִהְיוֹת טוֹב לַכֹּל תָּמִיד, וְלֹא אֶחְקֹר לְעוֹלָם אַחַר חוֹבוֹת בְּנֵי אָדָם חַס וְשָׁלוֹם, רַק אַדְּרַבָּא אֶזְכֶּה לְהִשְׁתַּדֵּל תָּמִיד בְּכָל כֹּחַ וָעֹז וּגְבוּרָה לִמְצֹא תָּמִיד זְכוּת וָטוֹב בְּכָל אֶחָד וְאֶחָד מִבְּנֵי יִשְׂרָאֵל עַמְּךָ הַקָּדוֹשׁ, אֲפִלּוּ בְּהַפְּחוּתִים שֶׁבַּפְּחוּתִים, וַאֲפִלּוּ בְּהַקַּל שֶׁבַּקַּלִים, אֲפִלּוּ בַּחוֹלְקִים וְהָרוֹדְפִים אוֹתִי, כֻּלָּם אֶזְכֶּה בְּרַחֲמֶיךָ לְדוּנָם לְכַף זְכוּת תָּמִיד, וְתִתֵּן לִי שֵׂכֶל וָדַעַת מֵאִתְּךָ, אֵיךְ לְחַפֵּשׂ וְלִמְצֹא בָּהֶם זְכוּת וּנְקֻדּוֹת טוֹבוֹת תָּמִיד: (ל"ת ל"ה)

וּתְזַכֵּנוּ לְהִתְקָרֵב לְהַצַּדִּיקִים הָאֲמִתִּיִּים הָאֵלּוּ, הָעוֹסְקִים בָּזֶה תָּמִיד, לְחַפֵּשׂ וּלְבַקֵּשׁ וְלִמְצֹא נְקֻדּוֹת טוֹבוֹת בְּכָל אֶחָד וְאֶחָד מִיִּשְׂרָאֵל, אֲפִלּוּ בְּפוֹשְׁעֵי יִשְׂרָאֵל, בְּכֻלָּם מְחַפְּשִׂים וּמוֹצְאִים בְּחָכְמָתָם נְקֻדּוֹת טוֹבוֹת, וּמְלַקְּטִים וּמְקַבְּצִים אוֹתָם "אַחַת לְאַחַת לִמְצֹא חֶשְׁבּוֹן" וּמַכְנִיסִים גַּם אוֹתָם בְּכַף זְכוּת, וּבוֹנִים מֵהֶם בִּנְיָנִים דְּקָדֻשָּׁה נִפְלָאִים וְנוֹרָאִים וּמַעֲלִים לְפָנֶיךָ שַׁעֲשׁוּעִים גְּדוֹלִים שֶׁלֹּא עָלוּ לְפָנֶיךָ מִימוֹת עוֹלָם, וְזוֹכִין לַעֲשׂוֹת זְמִירוֹת וְנִגּוּנִים קְדוֹשִׁים עַל יְדֵי קִבּוּץ הַטּוֹב הַזֶּה מִמְּקוֹמוֹת הָאֵלֶּה: (ל"ת צ')

חַס וְשָׁלוֹם הֶפְקֵר. וְהַשֵּׁם יִתְבָּרַךְ יִתְמְכֵנִי בִּימִין צִדְקוֹ, וְיוֹרֵנִי וְיַדְרִיכֵנִי בְּדַרְכּוֹ דֶּרֶךְ הַקֹּדֶשׁ, מִתּוֹךְ כָּל טוּב רוּחָנִי וְגוּפָנִי. וְנִזְכֶּה אֲנִי וְכָל בְּנֵי בֵיתִי, וְכָל חֲבֵרַי וְכָל בֵּית יִשְׂרָאֵל, לַאֲרִיכוּת יָמִים וְשָׁנִים טוֹבִים, שְׂמֵחִים וּמְאֻשָּׁרִים, בַּחֲסָדִים טוֹבִים, חֲסָדִים נִגְלִים, בְּעִנְיְנֵי גּוּף נֶפֶשׁ רוּחַ וּנְשָׁמָה, וּמְאִירִים בָּאוֹר שֶׁל מַעְלָה. אָמֵן. (אוצר תפלות ישראל ג, עמ' קמ"ח)

הנהגות האדם ח

לדון לכף זכות

אַדְּרַבָּה, תֵּן בְּלִבֵּנוּ שֶׁנִּרְאֶה כָּל אֶחָד מַעֲלַת חֲבֵרֵינוּ וְלֹא חֶסְרוֹנָם, וְשֶׁנְּדַבֵּר כָּל אֶחָד אֶת חֲבֵרוֹ בַּדֶּרֶךְ הַיָּשָׁר וְהָרָצוּי לְפָנֶיךָ, וְאַל יַעֲלֶה שׁוּם שִׂנְאָה מֵאֶחָד עַל חֲבֵרוֹ חָלִילָה: וּתְחַזֵּק הִתְקַשְּׁרוּתֵנוּ בְּאַהֲבָה אֵלֶיךָ, כַּאֲשֶׁר גָּלוּי וְיָדוּעַ לְפָנֶיךָ. שֶׁיְּהֵא הַכֹּל נַחַת רוּחַ אֵלֶיךָ, וְזֶה עִקַּר כַּוָּנָתֵנוּ. (מתפלת הרה"ק ר"א זצוק"ל)

וְאֶזְכֶּה לָדוּן אֶת הַכֹּל לְכַף זְכוּת, וַאֲפִלּוּ אוֹתָן הַקָּמִים עָלַי וּמְבַזִּין וּמְחָרְפִין אוֹתִי אֶזְכֶּה לָדוּן וְלִשְׁתֹּק לָהֶם, וַאֲפִלּוּ בְּלִבִּי לֹא יִהְיֶה לִי שׁוּם שִׂנְאָה וְקִפֵּדָא וְתַרְעוֹמוֹת עֲלֵיהֶם, רַק אֶזְכֶּה לְדוּנָם לְכַף זְכוּת שֶׁכָּל כַּוָּנָתָם לְשֵׁם שָׁמַיִם, כִּי לְפִי דַעְתָּם וּסְבָרָתָם נִדְמָה לָהֶם שֶׁרָאוּי לִבְזוֹת אוֹתִי. בִּפְרָט כִּי בֶּאֱמֶת יָדַעְתִּי כִּי כָּל מִינֵי בִּזְיוֹנוֹת שֶׁבָּעוֹלָם אֵינָם מַסְפִּיקִים לִי לְפִי גֹדֶל פְּשָׁעַי וַעֲוֹנוֹתַי הַמְרֻבִּים. בִּפְרָט כִּי גַם אֲנִי מִזֶּרַע יִשְׂרָאֵל הַקְּדוֹשִׁים שֶׁהֵם בְּחִינַת כִּתְרָא דְמַלְכָּא, וְאֵיךְ לֹא נִזְהַרְתִּי בְּנַפְשִׁי שֶׁלֹּא לִפְגֹם עַל יְדֵי מַעֲשַׂי בִּכְבוֹד הַמֶּלֶךְ חַס וְשָׁלוֹם, וּבְוַדַּאי רָאוּי אֲנִי לְכָל מִינֵי בִּזְיוֹנוֹת שֶׁבָּעוֹלָם, כְּמוֹ שֶׁנֶּאֱמַר "וּבוֹזַי יֵקָלּוּ". וְאֵיךְ אֶפְשָׁר לִי לְהִתְרָעֵם עַל הַמְבַזִּים אוֹתִי וְלִהְיוֹת

טוֹבוֹת, וְלַעֲסֹק תָּמִיד בְּתוֹרָתְךָ וּבַעֲבוֹדָתְךָ בֶּאֱמֶת בְּכָל כֹּחֵנוּ, בְּכָל לְבָבֵנוּ וּבְכָל נַפְשֵׁנוּ וּבְכָל מְאֹדֵנוּ, עַד שֶׁנִּזְכֶּה שֶׁכָּל הָאַרְבַּע יְסוֹדוֹת שֶׁבְּגוּפֵנוּ יִזְדַּכְּכוּ בֶּאֱמֶת, וְיִהְיוּ כֻלָּם טוֹב בְּלִי שׁוּם אֲחִיזַת רַע. (אוצר תפלות ישראל ג, עמ' רכ"ב)

הנהגות האדם ז

שמירה מעבירות והרהורים

אָבִינוּ שֶׁבַּשָּׁמַיִם: תְּעוֹרֵר נָא עָלֵינוּ רַחֲמֶיךָ וַחֲסָדֶיךָ הַגְּדוֹלִים וְהַמְרֻבִּים לְגָרֵשׁ וּלְבַעֵר אֶת יִצְרֵנוּ הָרַע מִקִּרְבֵּנוּ, וְתִגְעַר בּוֹ שֶׁיָּסוּר וְיֵלֵךְ מֵאִתָּנוּ, וְאַל יָסִית אוֹתָנוּ לְהַדִּיחֵנוּ מֵעֲבוֹדָתְךָ חָלִילָה. וְאַל יַעֲלֶה בְלִבֵּנוּ שׁוּם מַחֲשָׁבָה רָעָה חָלִילָה הֵן בְּהָקִיץ הֵן בַּחֲלוֹם. בִּפְרָט בְּעֵת שֶׁאֲנַחְנוּ עוֹמְדִים בִּתְפִלָּה לְפָנֶיךָ, אוֹ בְּשָׁעָה שֶׁאֲנַחְנוּ לוֹמְדִים תּוֹרָתְךָ. וּבְשָׁעָה שֶׁאֲנַחְנוּ עוֹסְקִים בְּמִצְוֹתֶיךָ, תְּהֵא מַחְשְׁבוֹתֵינוּ זַכָּה צְלוּלָה וּבְרוּרָה וַחֲזָקָה, בֶּאֱמֶת וּבְלֵבָב שָׁלֵם כִּרְצוֹנְךָ הַטּוֹב עִמָּנוּ. (מתפלת הרה"ק ר"א זצוק"ל)

"יְהֹוָה אֱלֹהִים אַתָּה יָדַעְתָּ לְאִוַּלְתִּי, וְאַשְׁמוֹתַי מִמְּךָ לֹא נִכְחָדוּ", הֵן עַל כָּל אֵלֶּה בָּאתִי לְפָנֶיךָ יְהֹוָה אֱלֹהַי וֵאלֹהֵי אֲבוֹתַי בְּלֵב נִשְׁבָּר וְנִדְכֶּה, בִּקְידָה וּבִכְרִיעָה וּבְהִשְׁתַּחֲוָיָה, בִּתְחִנָּה וּבְבַקָּשָׁה, כְּעָנִי בַּפֶּתַח נֶאֱנָח וְנִדְכֶּה, שׁוֹאֵל וּמְבַקֵּשׁ מַתְּנַת חִנָּם וְנִדְבַת חֶסֶד, שֶׁתְּחָנֵּנִי בְּרַחֲמֶיךָ הָעֲצוּמִים וַחֲסָדֶיךָ הַנִּפְלָאִים, וְתוֹצִיאֵנִי מֵאֲפֵלָה לְאוֹרָה, וְתַעֲזוֹר לִי מֵהַיּוֹם לְקַדֵּשׁ אֶת מַחְשַׁבְתִּי תָּמִיד מֵעַתָּה וְעַד עוֹלָם: (ל"ת ה')

וְהִנְנִי מְקַבֵּל עָלַי מֵעַתָּה, לְהַשְׁגִּיחַ עַל כָּל פְּרָטִיּוּת מַעֲשַׂי מַחְשְׁבוֹתַי וְדִבּוּרַי, כְּפִי שֶׁרָאוּי לְאִישׁ שֶׁנִּתְקַדֵּשׁ בִּקְדֻשָּׁה עֶלְיוֹנָה, וְלֹא שֶׁאֶהְיֶה

הנהגות האדם ו

זיכוך גופו ונפשו על ידי לימוד התורה

הִנְנִי רוֹצֶה לִלְמֹד בְּתוֹרָתוֹ לִשְׁמוֹ יִתְבָּרַךְ, לְקַיֵּם מִצְוָתוֹ יִתְבָּרַךְ אוֹתָנוּ, יִשְׂרָאֵל עַמּוֹ, לַהֲגוֹת בְּתוֹרָתוֹ הַקְּדוֹשָׁה, וּכְדֵי שֶׁיְּבִיאֵנִי תַּלְמוּד זֶה לִידֵי מַעֲשֶׂה וְלִידֵי מִדּוֹת יְשָׁרוֹת, וְלִידֵי יְדִיעוֹת הַתּוֹרָה, עַל מְנָת לִלְמֹד, לְשַׁמֵּר וְלַעֲשׂוֹת. וִיהִי רָצוֹן מִלְּפָנֶיךָ ה' אֱלֹהַי וֵאלֹהֵי אֲבוֹתַי, שֶׁבַּתַּלְמוּד הַזֶּה שֶׁאֶלְמַד יְתֻקְּנוּ כָּל הַפְּגִימוֹת שֶׁעָשִׂיתִי מֵעוֹדִי, בֵּין בְּגִלְגּוּל זֶה, בֵּין בְּגִלְגּוּלִים הַקּוֹדְמִים, בָּעוֹלָמוֹת עֶלְיוֹנִים, וּבְנַפְשִׁי וְרוּחִי וְנִשְׁמָתִי וּנְשָׁמָה לְנִשְׁמָתִי. וּתְמַלֵּא כָּל הַשֵּׁמוֹת שֶׁפָּגַמְתִּי בְּשִׁמְךָ הַגָּדוֹל. וּתְזַכֵּנִי לִלְמֹד וּלְלַמֵּד לִשְׁמֹר וְלַעֲשׂוֹת, וְלִהְיוֹת מִיּוֹדְעֵי שְׁמֶךָ וּמִבְּנֵי הֵיכָלָא דְּמַלְכָּא וּמִבְּנֵי עֲלִיָּה, וְהַדְרִיכֵנִי בִּנְתִיב הָאֱמֶת, שֶׁלֹּא אֶכָּשֵׁל בְּדַרְכֵי הַטּוֹעִים, וּפְתַח לִי מַעְיְנוֹת וְאוֹצְרוֹת הַחָכְמָה, וְהָאֵר עֵינַי בִּמְאוֹר תּוֹרָתֶךָ, לַמְּדֵנִי, חַכְּמֵנִי וְהַרְאֵנִי נִפְלָאוֹת בְּתוֹרָתֶךָ, בַּנִּגְלֶה וּבַנִּסְתָּר, וְאֶהְיֶה כְּמַעְיָן הַמִּתְגַּבֵּר וּכְבוֹר סִיד שֶׁאֵינוֹ מְאַבֵּד טִפָּה, שֶׁלֹּא אֶשְׁכַּח מִכָּל מַה שֶּׁאֶלְמַד. וְיַחֵד לְבָבִי לְאַהֲבָה וּלְיִרְאָה אֶת שְׁמֶךָ, וְטַהֵר רַעְיוֹנַי וְלִבִּי לַעֲבוֹדָתֶךָ, לֵב טָהוֹר בְּרָא לִי אֱלֹהִים וְרוּחַ נָכוֹן חַדֵּשׁ בְּקִרְבִּי, וְתֵן בְּלִבִּי לְהָבִין וּלְהַשְׂכִּיל לִלְמֹד וּלְלַמֵּד, לִשְׁמֹר וְלַעֲשׂוֹת וּלְקַיֵּם אֶת כָּל דִּבְרֵי תַלְמוּד תּוֹרָתֶךָ בְּאַהֲבָה. וְהַדְרִיכֵנִי בִּנְתִיב מִצְוֹתֶיךָ. גַּל עֵינַי וְאַבִּיטָה נִפְלָאוֹת מִתּוֹרָתֶךָ. וְדַבֵּק לִבִּי בְּמִצְוֹתֶיךָ, וְתֵן לִי לֵב חָזָק וְאַמִּיץ בְּתוֹרָתְךָ וּבְמִצְוֹתֶיךָ, לַעֲמֹד כְּנֶגֶד יֵצֶר הָרַע שֶׁאוֹר שֶׁבָּעִסָּה, וּתְזַכֵּנִי לַעֲשׂוֹת חֲבִילוֹת חֲבִילוֹת שֶׁל מִצְוֹת, בְּשָׁרְשֵׁיהֶם וּכְלָלֵיהֶם וּפְרָטֵיהֶם וְדִקְדּוּקֵיהֶם וְכַוָּנוֹתֵיהֶם:

(אוצר תפלות ישראל ג, עמ' נ"א)

※

אָבִינוּ שֶׁבַּשָּׁמַיִם, זַכֵּנוּ לָשׁוּב בִּתְשׁוּבָה שְׁלֵמָה בֶּאֱמֶת עַל הֶעָבָר, וּלְהִתְחַזֵּק מֵעַתָּה בֶּאֱמֶת בְּכֹל עֹז וְתַעֲצוּמוֹת, וְלִזְכּוֹת לְכָל הַמִּדּוֹת

הנהגות האדם ד

ללמוד באימה ויראה

וְרַחֵם עָלֵינוּ וְזַכֵּנוּ שֶׁנִּזְכֶּה לִמְצֹא וּלְהַשִּׂיג שַׁעֲרֵי הַחָכְמָה וְהַמַּדָּע שֶׁפָּתְחוּ הַצַּדִּיקִים בָּעוֹלָם, עַל יְדֵי טוּבָם הַגָּדוֹל, שֶׁצִּמְצְמוּ אֶת עַצְמָן וְהוֹרִידוּ אֶת עַצְמָן, וְהִלְבִּישׁוּ שִׂכְלָם הַנּוֹרָא בְּכַמָּה לְבוּשִׁים וְצִמְצוּמִים, עַד אֲשֶׁר פָּתְחוּ לָנוּ שַׁעֲרֵי אוֹרָה שַׁעֲרֵי הַחָכְמָה וְהַמַּדָּע עַל יְדֵי תוֹרָתָם וְשִׂיחָתָם שֶׁגִּלּוּ לָנוּ בְּסִפְרֵיהֶם הַקְּדוֹשִׁים וְהַנּוֹרָאִים מְאֹד, זַכֵּנוּ שֶׁנִּזְכֶּה לַעֲסֹק בָּהֶם כָּל יְמֵי חַיֵּינוּ בְּאֹפֶן שֶׁנִּזְכֶּה לְקַיְּמָם בֶּאֱמֶת וְנִזְכֶּה לִלְמֹד וּלְלַמֵּד לִשְׁמֹר וְלַעֲשׂוֹת וּלְקַיֵּם אֶת כָּל דִּבְרֵי תוֹרָתָם בְּאַהֲבָה: (ל"ת ס"ט)

הנהגות האדם ה

לימוד כתבי האר"י זצ"ל

וְאַתָּה בְּרַחֲמֶיךָ הָרַבִּים וַחֲסָדֶיךָ הָעֲצוּמִים תָּאִיר עֵינֵינוּ בְּתוֹרָתֶךָ, וְתִפְתַּח לִבֵּנוּ שֶׁנִּזְכֶּה לְהָבִין הֵיטֵב בִּמְהִירוּת גָּדוֹל בְּכָל מָקוֹם שֶׁנִּלְמֹד שָׁם וּלְהַשִּׂיג דִּבְרֵי הַתּוֹרָה בֶּאֱמֶת, וְנִזְכֶּה לִלְמֹד כָּל סִפְרֵי תוֹרָתְךָ הַקְּדוֹשָׁה בְּכָל יוֹם, תָּנָ"ךְ וְשַׁ"ס וּפוֹסְקִים וּמְפָרְשֵׁיהֶם, וְכָל סִפְרֵי הַמִּדְרָשִׁים, וְסִפְרֵי הַזֹּהַר הַקָּדוֹשׁ וְתִקּוּנִים, וְכָל כִּתְבֵי הָאֲרִ"י זִכְרוֹנוֹ לִבְרָכָה, וְכָל סִפְרֵי הַצַּדִּיקִים הָאֲמִתִּיִּים שֶׁבְּיָמֵינוּ, וְנִזְכֶּה לְגָמְרָם וְלַחֲזֹר וּלְהַתְחִילָם כַּמָּה וְכַמָּה פְּעָמִים כָּל יְמֵי חַיֵּינוּ, רַחֵם עָלֵינוּ לְמַעַן שְׁמֶךָ, וְזַכֵּנוּ לְהַתְמִיד בְּתוֹרָתְךָ הַקְּדוֹשָׁה בְּהַתְמָדָה גְדוֹלָה, כִּי הֵם חַיֵּינוּ וְאֹרֶךְ יָמֵינוּ וּבָהֶם נֶהְגֶּה יוֹמָם וָלַיְלָה וְנִזְכֶּה לְהָמִית עַצְמֵנוּ עַל הַתּוֹרָה עַד שֶׁתִּתְקַיֵּם בְּיָדֵינוּ, וְנִזְכֶּה לְשַׁבֵּר וּלְבַטֵּל וּלְהָמִית כָּל הַתַּאֲווֹת רָעוֹת וְכָל הַמִּדּוֹת רָעוֹת שֶׁבְּגוּפֵנוּ, עַל יְדֵי עֵסֶק וְעִיּוּן הַתּוֹרָה בֶּאֱמֶת: (ל"ת ק"י)

לא להפסיק באמצע הלימוד

הָאֵר עֵינַי לִרְאוֹת הָאֱמֶת וּלְכַוֵּן לַאֲמִתָּהּ שֶׁל תּוֹרָה, וְלֹא אֶכָּשֵׁל בִּדְבַר הֲלָכָה וְאַל יִכָּשְׁלוּ חֲבֵרַי בִּדְבַר הֲלָכָה, וְאֶזְכֶּה לְהַעֲמִיק מֹחִי וְלִבִּי בַּאֲמִתִּיּוּת הַתּוֹרָה, וְשֶׁלֹּא לְהַפְסִיק בָּהּ בְּשׁוּם דִּבּוּר זָר וּמַחֲשָׁבָה בְּטֵלָה. וְיַעֲלֶה לִמּוּדִי לְפָנֶיךָ לְנַחַת רוּחַ, וְיֵחָשֵׁב לְפָנֶיךָ כְּאִלּוּ כִּוַּנְתִּי בְּכָל הַכַּוָּנוֹת שֶׁאֶפְשָׁר לְכַוֵּן בִּשְׁעַת לִמּוּד הַתּוֹרָה הַקְּדוֹשָׁה. (אוצר תפלות ישראל ג, עמ' ל"ב)

בַּמֶּה נְקַדֵּם יְהֹוָה, כְּעַל כֹּל אֲשֶׁר גְּמָלָנוּ בְּרַחֲמָיו וְרֹב חֲסָדָיו, אֲשֶׁר נָתַן לָנוּ תּוֹרַת אֱמֶת וְחַיֵּי עוֹלָם נָטַע בְּתוֹכֵנוּ, וְעַתָּה יְהֹוָה אֱלֹהֵינוּ אֲשֶׁר חֲסָדֶיךָ מֵעוֹלָם וְעַד עוֹלָם עָלֵינוּ, יֶהֱמוּ מֵעֶיךָ עָלֵינוּ, וּכְשֵׁם שֶׁחָמַלְתָּ עָלֵינוּ, וְנָתַתָּ לָנוּ בְּרַחֲמֶיךָ הָרַבִּים תּוֹרָתְךָ הַקְּדוֹשָׁה, חֶמְדָּה גְנוּזָה, שַׁעֲשׁוּעַ יוֹם יוֹם, כֵּן תְּזַכֵּנוּ בְּרַחֲמֶיךָ הָרַבִּים, וּתְחָנֵּנוּ בַּחֲסָדֶיךָ הַגְּדוֹלִים, וְתִהְיֶה בְּעֶזְרֵנוּ שֶׁנִּזְכֶּה כֻּלָּנוּ לִלְמֹד וְלַעֲסֹק בְּתוֹרָתְךָ הַקְּדוֹשָׁה לִשְׁמָהּ תָּמִיד, וְנַהֲפֹךְ פָּנֵינוּ מֵהַבְלֵי הָעוֹלָם הַזֶּה לְגַמְרֵי, כִּי אִם בְּתוֹרַת יְהֹוָה תִּהְיֶה חֶפְצֵנוּ, וּבְתוֹרָתְךָ נֶהְגֶּה יוֹמָם וָלַיְלָה וְכָל לִמּוּדֵנוּ יִהְיֶה בִּקְדֻשָּׁה וּבְטָהֳרָה, וְכָל כַּוָּנָתֵנוּ תִּהְיֶה רַק בִּשְׁבִיל שִׁמְךָ הַגָּדוֹל וְהַקָּדוֹשׁ בֶּאֱמֶת, לַעֲשׂוֹת נַחַת רוּחַ לְפָנֶיךָ בְּלִמּוּדֵנוּ, וְנִזְכֶּה לִלְמֹד וּלְלַמֵּד לִשְׁמֹר וְלַעֲשׂוֹת וּלְקַיֵּם אֶת כָּל דִּבְרֵי תוֹרָתְךָ בְּאַהֲבָה, וְתַעְזְרֵנוּ שֶׁיָּאִיר לָנוּ אוֹר הַתּוֹרָה הַקְּדוֹשָׁה שֶׁנִּזְכֶּה לִלְמוֹד וְלַהֲגוֹת בָּהּ, לְהוֹצִיאֵנוּ מֵאֲפֵלָה לְאוֹרָה, לְהַחֲזִירֵנוּ בִּתְשׁוּבָה שְׁלֵמָה לְפָנֶיךָ, כְּמוֹ שֶׁאָמְרוּ רַבּוֹתֵינוּ, זִכְרוֹנָם לִבְרָכָה: 'הַמָּאוֹר שֶׁבָּהּ מַחֲזִיר לְמוּטָב': (ל"ת י"ב)

[רִבּוֹנוֹ שֶׁל עוֹלָם] "אֶזְכְּרָה נְגִינָתִי בַּלָּיְלָה עִם לְבָבִי אָשִׂיחָה וַיְחַפֵּשׂ רוּחִי, זָכַרְתִּי בַלַּיְלָה שִׁמְךָ יְהֹוָה וָאֶשְׁמְרָה תּוֹרָתֶךָ, אֶזְכֹּר מַעַלְלֵי יָהּ כִּי אֶזְכְּרָה מִקֶּדֶם פִּלְאֶךָ, זָכַרְתִּי יָמִים מִקֶּדֶם הָגִיתִי בְכָל פָּעֳלֶךָ בְּמַעֲשֵׂה יָדֶיךָ אֲשׂוֹחֵחַ בְּהִתְעַטֵּף עָלַי נַפְשִׁי, אֶת יְהֹוָה זָכוֹר תִּזְכֹּר וְתָשׁוֹחַ עָלַי נַפְשִׁי" וְאָעַן וְאֹמַר לְנַפְשִׁי, זְכוֹר אַל תִּשְׁכַּח שֶׁיֵּשׁ עָלְמָא דְאָתֵי, וְאֵין שׁוּם קְבִיעוּת בָּזֶה הָעוֹלָם כִּי הָעוֹלָם הַזֶּה עוֹבֵר כְּהֶרֶף עַיִן, כְּצֵל עוֹבֵר, וּכְאָבָק פּוֹרֵחַ, וּכְעָנָן כָּלָה, וּכְרוּחַ נוֹשֶׁבֶת, וְכַחֲלוֹם יָעוּף, וְעִקַּר הַחַיִּים וְעִקַּר הַקְּבִיעוּת דִּירָה שֶׁל הָאָדָם הוּא רַק בְּעָלְמָא דְאָתֵי, חוּסָה עָלֶיךָ וּשְׁמֹר אֶת הַזִּכָּרוֹן הֵיטֵב, שֶׁתִּזְכּוֹר תָּמִיד בְּכָל יוֹם בְּעָלְמָא דְאָתֵי וְלֹא תִּשְׁכַּח, וְהַדְבֵּק מַחֲשַׁבְתְּךָ בְּעָלְמָא דְאָתֵי וְאַל יָזוּז זִכְרוֹן עָלְמָא דְאָתֵי מֵרַעְיוֹנֶךָ הִסְתַּכֵּל עַל עַצְמְךָ הֵיטֵב, וְיֵשֵׁב דַּעְתְּךָ בֶּאֱמֶת לַאֲמִתּוֹ, וּזְכֹר וְתֵן לְלִבְּךָ מַה תַּעֲשֶׂה בְּאַחֲרִיתֶךָ בְּעֵת יָבֹא קִצְּךָ כְּהֶרֶף עַיִן, צַר לִי עָלֶיךָ אָחִי, הָקִיצָה אָחִי מִשְּׁנַת פְּתִיּוּתֶךָ וַחֲמֹל עַל נַפְשְׁךָ "וּזְכֹר אֶת בּוֹרְאֶךָ בִּימֵי בְּחוּרוֹתֶיךָ": (ל"ת נ"ד)

וּבְכֵן בָּאתִי לְפָנֶיךָ יְהֹוָה אֱלֹהַי וֵאלֹהֵי אֲבוֹתַי, לְהַפִּיל תְּחִנָּתִי לִפְנֵי רַחֲמֶיךָ הָאֲמִתִּיִּים, וְלָשֵׂאת עֵינַי לַחֲסָדֶיךָ הָעֲצוּמִים, שֶׁתְּזַכֵּנִי לִשְׁמֹר אֶת הַזִּכָּרוֹן הַזֶּה הֵיטֵב שֶׁאֶזְכֹּר תָּמִיד בְּעָלְמָא דְאָתֵי וּלְאִדַּבְּקָא מַחֲשַׁבְתִּי רַק בְּעָלְמָא דְאָתֵי בִּכְלָל וּבִפְרָט, וּבְכָל יוֹם וָיוֹם בַּהֲקִיצִי מִשְּׁנָתִי תֵּכֶף וּמִיָּד כְּשֶׁאֶפְתַּח אֶת עֵינַי אֶזְכֶּה לִזְכֹּר מִיָּד בָּעוֹלָם הַבָּא, שֶׁהוּא עוֹלָם הָעוֹמֵד וְהַקַּיָּם לָעַד וּלְנֶצַח נְצָחִים, וְהָעוֹלָם הַזֶּה הוּא הֶבֶל וָרִיק הֲבֵל הֲבָלִים אֵין בּוֹ מַמָּשׁ, "הֲבֵל נָדָף הֲבֵל הֲבָלִים הַכֹּל הָבֶל" וְאֵין שׁוּם יִתְרוֹן לָאָדָם בְּכָל עֲמָלוֹ שֶׁיַּעֲמֹל בְּעִסְקֵי הָעוֹלָם הַזֶּה, וְאֵין שׁוּם תַּכְלִית וָטוֹב בָּעוֹלָם כִּי אִם לִרְדּוֹף תָּמִיד לְהַשִּׂיג הָעוֹלָם הַבָּא, וּתְזַכֵּנִי שֶׁאֶזְכֹּר זֹאת הֵיטֵב בְּכֹחַ הַזִּכָּרוֹן דִּקְדֻשָּׁה וְאַחַר כָּךְ אֶזְכֶּה לְקַיֵּם זֹאת בִּפְרָטִיּוּת: (ל"ת נ"ד)

אֲפָלוּ כְּהֶרֶף עַיִן, רַק עֵינַי יִהְיוּ צוֹפִיּוֹת וּמְיַחֲלוֹת אֵלֶיךָ לְבַד. (תפילות הבוקר עמ' ס"ה)

וְתַצִּילֵנִי מִפְּגַם הָרְאוּת, וּתְקַדֵּשׁ אֶת עֵינַי תָּמִיד וְלֹא אֶסְתַּכֵּל עוֹד בְּשׁוּם דָּבָר הַפּוֹגֵם אֶת הָרְאוּת, רַק אֶזְכֶּה לְהִסְתַּכֵּל בְּעֵינַי בְּתוֹרָתֶךָ, וּלְהִסְתַּכֵּל עַל צַדִּיקֶיךָ הָאֲמִתִּיִּים וְעַל כָּל הַדְּבָרִים הַמְקַדְּשִׁין אֶת הָעֵינַיִם, עַד שֶׁיִּהְיוּ עֵינַי קְדוֹשִׁים וּטְהוֹרִים תָּמִיד בֶּאֱמֶת לַאֲמִתּוֹ, וְאֶזְכֶּה לְתַקֵּן מְהֵרָה אֶת כָּל הַפְּגָמִים שֶׁפָּגַמְתִּי בְּעֵינַי, וְתַעַזְרֵנִי בְּרַחֲמֶיךָ וְתִשְׁמְרֵנִי מִקִּלְקוּל חוּשׁ הָרְאוּת חַס וְשָׁלוֹם, וְלֹא יִכְהֶה מְאוֹר עֵינַי לְעוֹלָם "וְגַם עַד זִקְנָה וְשֵׂיבָה אַל תַּעַזְבֵנִי" וְתִשְׁמֹר אֶת אוֹר עֵינַי תָּמִיד, לְמַעַן אֶזְכֶּה לַהֲגוֹת בְּתוֹרָתְךָ יוֹמָם וָלַיְלָה, וּלְנַדֵּד שֵׁנָה מֵעֵינַי וְלֹא יַגִּיעַ לִי עַל יְדֵי זֶה שׁוּם הֶזֵּק וּמִחוּשׁ לְעֵינַי, וְיִהְיוּ עֵינַי מְאִירוֹת כַּשֶּׁמֶשׁ וְכַיָּרֵחַ: (ל"ת נ"א)

הנהגות האדם ג

לזכור תמיד יום המיתה

אָבִי שֶׁבַּשָּׁמַיִם, הֱיֵה בְּעֶזְרִי תָּמִיד, שֶׁתִּתְגַּבֵּר נַפְשִׁי עַל הַגּוּף, וְאֶטַּהֵר וַאֲקַדֵּשׁ אֶת נַפְשִׁי וְגוּפִי בְּכָל מִינֵי טָהֳרוֹת וּקְדֻשּׁוֹת. וּבְרַחֲמֶיךָ הָרַבִּים תּוֹצִיאֵנִי וְתַעֲלֵנִי מִבְּחִינַת בְּהֵמָה לִבְחִינַת אָדָם, מִגּוּף לְנֶפֶשׁ, מֵחֹמֶר לְצוּרָה, מֵחֹשֶׁךְ לְאוֹר, מִשִּׁכְחָה לְזִכָּרוֹן. וְתַשְׁפִּיעַ עָלַי כֹּחַ הַזִּכָּרוֹן, לִזְכֹּר תָּמִיד אֶת כָּל דִּבְרֵי תוֹרָתְךָ וַעֲבוֹדָתֶךָ. וְזַכֵּנִי לִזְכֹּר תָּמִיד הֵיטֵב אֶת אַחֲרִיתִי וְסוֹפִי, וְלָשׂוּם לִבִּי הֵיטֵב עַל מַה אָתִינָא לְהַאי עַלְמָא, וּמַה יִּהְיֶה בְּסוֹפִי וְאַחֲרִיתִי כַּאֲשֶׁר יָבוֹא קִצִּי. וְלֹא אֶשְׁכַּח זֹאת כָּל יְמֵי חַיָּי. וְאֶזְכֶּה לִזְכֹּר זֹאת הֵיטֵב בְּכָל יוֹם וָיוֹם, כִּי כָּל יָמֵינוּ וּשְׁנוֹתֵינוּ הֵם הֶבֶל, כַּחֲלוֹם יָעוּף וּכְצֵל עוֹבֵר, כֶּעָנָן כָּלָה וּכְרוּחַ נוֹשָׁבֶת, וְאִי אֶפְשָׁר לְהִמָּלֵט מִן הַמִּיתָה בְּשׁוּם אֹפֶן. (ספר קדושה - אוצר תפלות ישראל, ג עמ' ד"כ)

בְּשָׁעָה שֶׁיָּבוֹא חַס וְשָׁלוֹם, לִידֵי אֵיזֶה כַּעַס, תַּחְמֹל עָלַי בְּרַחֲמֶיךָ וְתִשְׁמְרֵנִי וְתַצִּילֵנִי שֶׁלֹּא אֶפְעַל בְּכַעֲסִי שׁוּם אַכְזְרִיּוּת כְּלָל רַק אֶזְכֶּה לְשַׁבֵּר וּלְהָפֵר הַכַּעַס בְּרַחֲמָנוּת, וְאֶזְכֶּה לְהִתְגַּבֵּר עַל יִצְרִי לְשַׁבֵּר הַכַּעַס וְלַהֲפֹךְ הַכַּעַס לְרַחֲמָנוּת, לְרַחֵם דַּיְקָא בְּרַחֲמָנוּת גְּדוֹלָה בְּמָקוֹם שֶׁהָיִיתִי רוֹצֶה לִכְעֹס, חַס וְשָׁלוֹם וְלֹא יִהְיֶה בִּי אֵל זָר וְלֹא אֶשְׁתַּחֲוֶה לְאֵל נֵכָר, שֶׁזֶּה נֶאֱמַר עַל הַכּוֹעֵס, שֶׁנֶּחְשָׁב כְּאִלּוּ עוֹבֵד עֲבוֹדָה זָרָה: (ל"ת י"ח)

רִבּוֹנוֹ שֶׁל עוֹלָם, אַתָּה יָדַעְתָּ כַּמָּה קָשֶׁה לָנוּ לְשַׁבֵּר וּלְבַטֵּל מִדָּה רָעָה זוֹ שֶׁל כַּעַס וְקַפְּדָנוּת כִּי כְּשֶׁמַּתְחִיל הַכַּעַס לִבְעֹר בָּנוּ, חַס וְשָׁלוֹם, כִּמְעַט אֵין אָנוּ בְּדַעְתֵּנוּ, וְקָשֶׁה עָלֵינוּ לְכַבּוֹת אֵשׁ הַכַּעַס וּלְכָבְשׁוֹ, עַל כֵּן רַחֵם עָלֵינוּ לְמַעַן שְׁמֶךָ, וֶהֱיֵה בְּעֶזְרֵנוּ וְשָׁמְרֵנוּ וְהַצִּילֵנוּ תָּמִיד בְּרַחֲמֶיךָ וַחֲסָדֶיךָ הַגְּדוֹלִים, וְעָזְרֵנוּ לְשַׁבֵּר וּלְבַטֵּל מִדַּת הַכַּעַס וְקַפְּדָנוּת מֵעָלֵינוּ וּמֵעַל גְּבוּלֵנוּ, וְלֹא נִכְעֹס לְעוֹלָם, וְלֹא אֶהְיֶה שׁוּם קַפְּדָן כְּלָל, רַק אֶזְכֶּה לִהְיוֹת טוֹב לַכֹּל תָּמִיד מֵעַתָּה וְעַד עוֹלָם: (ל"ת י"ח)

הִסְתַּכְּלוּת אֲסוּרוֹת

רִבּוֹנוֹ שֶׁל עוֹלָם, זַכֵּנִי לִסְתֹּם עֵינַי מֵחֵיזוּ דְּהַאי עָלְמָא לְגַמְרֵי, וְאֶזְכֶּה שֶׁיִּהְיֶה לִי מֶמְשָׁלָה עַל עֵינַי שֶׁלֹּא אֶסְתַּכֵּל עַל הַבְלֵי עוֹלָם הַזֶּה כְּלָל, וּבִפְרָט תַּצִּילֵנִי שֶׁלֹּא אֶסְתַּכֵּל בְּעֵינַי, חַס וְשָׁלוֹם, עַל הַדְּבָרִים שֶׁיְּכוֹלִים לָבוֹא לִידֵי הִרְהוּרִים, וַאֲקַיֵּם מִקְרָא שֶׁכָּתוּב: "וְלֹא תָתוּרוּ אַחֲרֵי לְבַבְכֶם וְאַחֲרֵי עֵינֵיכֶם", רַק יִהְיֶה לִי מֶמְשָׁלָה עַל הָעֵינַיִם שֶׁלִּי, וְאַבִּיט וְאֶסְתַּכֵּל בְּעֵינַי רַק בְּתוֹרָתְךָ הַקְּדוֹשָׁה, וַאֲצַפֶּה וַאֲיַחֵל בְּעֵינַי וּבְלִבִּי רַק לְהַשֵּׁם יִתְבָּרַךְ וּלְהַתּוֹרָה הַקְּדוֹשָׁה, וְלֹא אָתוּר אַחֲרֵי לִבִּי וְאַחֲרֵי עֵינַי, רַק אֶזְכֶּה שֶׁלֹּא יִהְיֶה לִי שׁוּם הִסְתַּכְּלוּת בְּזֶה הָעוֹלָם

לשון הרע

[אָנָּא] ה' תְּזַכֵּנוּ בְּרַחֲמֶיךָ הָרַבִּים לְהִנָּצֵל מִלָּשׁוֹן הָרָע וּדְבָרִים בְּטֵלִים וְגַאֲוָה וְתוֹלְדוֹתֵיהֶם, וְתַעַזְרֵנוּ בְּרַחֲמֶיךָ יְהֹוָה אֱלֹהֵינוּ שֶׁיִּהְיֶה כָּל דִּבּוּרֵנוּ לִשְׁמְךָ וְלַעֲבוֹדָתֶךָ, וְלֹא נְדַבֵּר דְּבָרִים בְּטֵלִים לְעוֹלָם, רַק כָּל דִּבּוּרֵנוּ יִהְיֶה בַּתּוֹרָה וַעֲבוֹדָה וְיִרְאַת שָׁמַיִם, וּבִפְרָט מֵחֵטְא וְעָוֹן הַגָּדוֹל מְאֹד שֶׁהוּא עֲוֹן לָשׁוֹן הָרָע וּרְכִילוּת שֶׁהוּא חָמוּר בְּיוֹתֵר, תַּצִּיל אוֹתִי וְכָל עַמְּךָ בֵּית יִשְׂרָאֵל, שֶׁלֹּא יֵצֵא מִפִּי לְעוֹלָם שׁוּם דִּבּוּר רַע עַל שׁוּם יִשְׂרָאֵל שֶׁבָּעוֹלָם, אֱלֹהַי, נְצֹר לְשׁוֹנִי מֵרָע וּשְׂפָתַי מִדַּבֵּר מִרְמָה, וְתַצִּילֵנִי מִלָּשׁוֹן הָרָע וּמֵאֲבַק לָשׁוֹן הָרָע וּמֵרְכִילוּת וּמֵאֲבַק רְכִילוּת מֵעַתָּה וְעַד עוֹלָם: (ל"ת ד')

מָרָא דְעָלְמָא כֹּלָּא, רַחֵם עֲלַי לְמַעֲנָךְ, וֶהֱיֵה עִם פִּי תָּמִיד בְּעֵת דִּבּוּרִי, וְזַכֵּנִי שֶׁאֶשְׁמֹר פִּתְחֵי פִי, שֶׁלֹּא יֵצֵא מִפִּי שׁוּם דִּבּוּר לָשׁוֹן הָרָע וַאֲבַק לָשׁוֹן הָרָע עַל שׁוּם יִשְׂרָאֵל שֶׁבָּעוֹלָם, וְלֹא דִּבּוּר שֶׁאֵינוֹ הָגוּן, וְתַצִּילֵנִי מִכָּל מִינֵי דִּבּוּרִים רָעִים, מִלָּשׁוֹן הָרָע וּמֵרְכִילוּת וּמִדְּבָרִים בְּטֵלִים וּמְלִיצָנוּת וּמַחֲנִיפוּת וּמְשַׁקָּרִים, וּמִלְגַלּוֹת סוֹד שֶׁאֵין צְרִיכִים לְגַלּוֹת, וּמִנִּבּוּל פֶּה, וּמִלְגַלּוֹת וְלוֹמַר דִּבְרֵי תוֹרָה וְיִרְאַת שָׁמַיִם בְּמָקוֹם וּבִזְמַן שֶׁאֵין רָאוּי לְאָמְרָם וּלְגַלּוֹתָם וּמִכָּל מִינֵי דִּבּוּרִים שֶׁאֵינָם טוֹבִים, וּמִכָּל מִינֵי הֶבֶל פֶּה הַפּוֹגְמִין אֶת הַדִּבּוּר הַקָּדוֹשׁ שֶׁהוּא רוּחַ פִּיו שֶׁל הַקָּדוֹשׁ בָּרוּךְ הוּא: (ל"ת ל"ח)

כעס

יְהִי רָצוֹן מִלְּפָנֶיךָ יְהֹוָה אֱלֹהֵינוּ וֵאלֹהֵי אֲבוֹתֵינוּ, מָלֵא טוֹב מָלֵא רַחֲמִים, מָלֵא רָצוֹן, שֶׁתִּהְיֶה בְּעֶזְרִי, וְתִשְׁמְרֵנִי וְתַצִּילֵנִי מִן הַכַּעַס וּמִן הָרֹגֶז וּמִכָּל מִינֵי קְפֵדוֹת וְתָגֵן עָלַי בְּרַחֲמֶיךָ, וְתִשְׁמְרֵנִי תָּמִיד וַאֲפִלּוּ

הנהגות האדם ב
להזהר מהדברים המרחיקים ומפסידים
שקר

וְתַעַזְרֵנִי בְּרַחֲמֶיךָ הָרַבִּים לֵילֵךְ בְּדֶרֶךְ אֱמֶת תָּמִיד, וְאֶזְכֶּה שֶׁלֹּא יֵצֵא דְּבַר שֶׁקֶר מִפִּי לְעוֹלָם, וְתִשְׁמְרֵנִי בְּרַחֲמֶיךָ הָרַבִּים שֶׁלֹּא יֵצֵא שׁוּם שֶׁקֶר מִפִּי אֲפִלּוּ בְּטָעוּת שֶׁלֹּא בְּכַוָּנָה, רַק כָּל דִּבּוּרַי יִהְיוּ דִבּוּרֵי אֱמֶת תָּמִיד וּתְיַחֵד אֶת לְבָבִי אֵלֶיךָ, שֶׁאֶזְכֶּה תָּמִיד לְהַטּוֹת דַּעְתִּי וּמַחְשַׁבְתִּי אֶל הָאֱמֶת לַאֲמִתּוֹ וְאַתָּה תְּסַיְּעֵנִי מִן הַשָּׁמַיִם לֵילֵךְ בִּנְתִיב הָאֱמֶת תָּמִיד, וְלֹא אֶטֶּה מִדֶּרֶךְ הָאֱמֶת יָמִין וּשְׂמֹאל "הַדְרִיכֵנִי בַאֲמִתֶּךָ וְלַמְּדֵנִי כִּי אַתָּה אֱלֹהֵי יִשְׁעִי אוֹתְךָ קִוִּיתִי כָּל הַיּוֹם, שְׁלַח אוֹרְךָ וַאֲמִתְּךָ הֵמָּה יַנְחוּנִי, יְבִיאוּנִי אֶל הַר קָדְשְׁךָ וְאֶל מִשְׁכְּנוֹתֶיךָ, וְאַל תַּצֵּל מִפִּי דְבַר אֱמֶת עַד מְאֹד, כִּי לְמִשְׁפָּטֶיךָ יִחָלְתִּי": (ל״ת ט׳)

~

וּבְכֵן תַּעַזְרֵנִי וּתְזַכֵּנִי בְּרַחֲמֶיךָ הָרַבִּים, שֶׁאֶזְכֶּה לִהְיוֹת נִכְלָל בְּמִדָּתוֹ שֶׁל יַעֲקֹב אָבִינוּ עָלָיו הַשָּׁלוֹם, שֶׁמִּדָּתוֹ אֱמֶת וְאֶזְכֶּה לְדַבֵּר דִּבְרֵי אֱמֶת תָּמִיד, וְלֹא יֵצֵא שׁוּם דְּבַר שֶׁקֶר מִפִּי לְעוֹלָם, בֵּין בְּשׁוֹגֵג בֵּין בְּמֵזִיד בֵּין בְּאֹנֶס בֵּין בְּרָצוֹן, וְתִשְׁמְרֵנִי וְתַצִּילֵנִי שֶׁלֹּא אֶהְיֶה נִכְשָׁל בְּשׁוּם דְּבַר שֶׁקֶר אֲפִלּוּ בְּטָעוּת וְאֶזְכֶּה לְהַרְחִיק עַצְמִי מִדִּבְרֵי שֶׁקֶר בְּתַכְלִית הָרִחוּק, כְּמוֹ שֶׁכָּתוּב: "מִדְּבַר שֶׁקֶר תִּרְחָק", וּתְזַכֵּנִי בְּרַחֲמֶיךָ הָרַבִּים לִהְיוֹת אִישׁ אֱמֶת בְּכָל הָעִנְיָנִים; לְהִתְנַהֵג בְּדֶרֶךְ הָאֱמֶת, וּלְדַבֵּר אֱמֶת בִּלְבָבִי וְלֹא אֶטֶּה וְלֹא אָסוּר מִמֶּרְכַּז נְקֻדַּת הָאֱמֶת יָמִין וּשְׂמֹאל (ל״ת מ״ז)

~

לזכור חטאיו ושה' יתברך ידריכהו בדרך הישר

יְהִי רָצוֹן מִלְּפָנֶיךָ יְהֹוָה אֱלֹהֵינוּ וֵאלֹהֵי אֲבוֹתֵינוּ, שֶׁתַּעַזְרֵנִי בְּרַחֲמֶיךָ הָרַבִּים, וּתְזַכֵּנִי לְקַדֵּשׁ אֶת דִּבּוּר פִּי תָּמִיד, וְאֶזְכֶּה לְדַבֵּר תָּמִיד דִּבּוּרִים קְדוֹשִׁים הַרְבֵּה בְּכָל יוֹם וָיוֹם, שֶׁאֶזְכֶּה לְהַרְבּוֹת בְּלִמּוּד הַתּוֹרָה הַקְּדוֹשָׁה וּבִתְפִלּוֹת וּתְחִנּוֹת וּבַקָּשׁוֹת הַרְבֵּה בְּכָל יוֹם וָיוֹם, וְלֹא אַפְסִיק פִּי מִגִּרְסָא וְלִמּוּד וּתְפִלּוֹת וּבַקָּשׁוֹת וְשִׁירוֹת וְתִשְׁבָּחוֹת לְשִׁמְךָ הַגָּדוֹל וְהַקָּדוֹשׁ וְכָל הַיּוֹם תִּהְיֶה שִׂיחָתִי וְדִבּוּרִי בְּתוֹרָה וּתְפִלָּה, וְאֶזְכֶּה לְהִתְוַדּוּת וִדּוּי דְּבָרִים לְפָנֶיךָ בְּכָל יוֹם עַל כָּל מַה שֶּׁפָּגַמְתִּי נֶגְדְּךָ, וּלְפָרֵשׁ חֲטָאַי לְפָנֶיךָ בְּפֶה מָלֵא בְּפֵרוּשׁ וְאֶזְכֶּה לְהַרְבּוֹת בְּהִתְבּוֹדְדוּת תָּמִיד, עַד שֶׁהַדִּבּוּר דִּקְדֻשָּׁה זְכוֹר יִזְכְּרֵנִי לְטוֹבָה וִישִׁיבֵנִי אֵלֶיךָ בֶּאֱמֶת וּבְלֵב שָׁלֵם, בִּתְשׁוּבָה שְׁלֵמָה לְפָנֶיךָ: (ל"ת פ')

שה' יתברך יאיר עיניו בתורתו הקדושה

וְאֶזְכֶּה לְבַטֵּל עַצְמִי נֶגְדְּךָ בֶּאֱמֶת, וְלֹא יַעֲלֶה בְּלִבִּי וְדַעְתִּי שׁוּם צַד גֵּאוּת וְגַבְהוּת וּפְנִיּוּת בָּעוֹלָם, וְאֶזְכֶּה לַעֲנָוָה בֶּאֱמֶת לַאֲמִתּוֹ, וְתַעַזְרֵנִי וּתְזַכֵּנִי שֶׁיִּתְגַּדֵּל וְיִתְקַדֵּשׁ וְיִשְׁתַּבַּח כְּבוֹדְךָ הַגָּדוֹל עַל יָדִי, וּתְזַכֵּנִי לְדִבּוּרִים הַמְּאִירִים בַּתּוֹרָה, וְיָאִירוּ לִי דִּבּוּרֵי הַתּוֹרָה לָצֵאת מִפְּחִיתוּת וְשִׁפְלוּת מַדְרֵגָתִי הַפְּחוּתָה וּשְׁפָלָה מְאֹד, וְאֶזְכֶּה שֶׁיָּאִירוּ לִי דִּבּוּרֵי הַתּוֹרָה בְּכָל פַּעַם לְכָל הַמְּקוֹמוֹת שֶׁאֲנִי צָרִיךְ לַעֲשׂוֹת תְּשׁוּבָה, בְּאֹפֶן שֶׁאֶזְכֶּה לַעֲשׂוֹת תְּשׁוּבַת הַמִּשְׁקָל מַמָּשׁ עַל כָּל חֲטָאַי וַעֲווֹנוֹתַי וּפְשָׁעַי הַמְרֻבִּים, וְעַל כָּל הַפְּגָמִים שֶׁפָּגַמְתִּי בִּכְבוֹדְךָ הַגָּדוֹל יִתְבָּרַךְ מִנְּעוּרַי עַד עַתָּה וּתְזַכֵּנִי לְתַקֵּן הַכֹּל בְּחַיַּי, וְתַעַזְרֵנִי בְּכָל פַּעַם לַעֲלוֹת מִדַּרְגָּא לְדַרְגָּא: (ל"ת י"א)

התבודדות

[אָנָּא] זַכֵּנִי לְהַרְבּוֹת בְּהִתְבּוֹדְדוּת וְשִׂיחָה בֵּינִי לְבֵין קוֹנִי, וְאֶזְכֶּה לְקַיֵּם מִקְרָא שֶׁכָּתוּב: קוּמִי רֹנִּי בַלַּיְלָה לְרֹאשׁ אַשְׁמֻרוֹת שִׁפְכִי כַמַּיִם לִבֵּךְ נֹכַח פְּנֵי אֲדֹנָי. וְתַשְׁפִּיעַ לִי דִּבּוּרִים קְדוֹשִׁים שֶׁל הִתְעוֹרְרוּת הַלֵּב וְגַעְגּוּעִים וְכִסּוּפִים וְהִשְׁתּוֹקְקוּת דִּקְדֻשָּׁה עַד שֶׁאֶזְכֶּה לִבְכּוֹת בִּדְמָעוֹת הַרְבֵּה לְפָנֶיךָ כְּבֵן הַבּוֹכֶה לִפְנֵי אָבִיו. וְתַעַזְרֵנִי בִּשְׁעַת הִתְבּוֹדְדוּת וַאֲמִירַת הַתְּחִנּוֹת וּבַקָּשׁוֹת שֶׁאֶזְכֶּה לְהַרְחִיק אָז מֵעַצְמִי כָּל מִינֵי מַחֲשָׁבוֹת חוּץ שֶׁבָּעוֹלָם. (תפילות ותחנונים עמ' ע״ז)

⚜

וּתְזַכֵּנִי בְּרַחֲמֶיךָ הָרַבִּים אוֹתִי וְאֶת זַרְעִי וְאֶת זֶרַע זַרְעִי וְאֶת כָּל עַמְּךָ בֵּית יִשְׂרָאֵל שֶׁנִּזְכֶּה כָּל אֶחָד וְאֶחָד לְדַבֵּר בֵּינוֹ לְבֵין קוֹנוֹ וּנְעוֹרֵר לְבָבֵנוּ לְיִרְאַת שָׁמַיִם וְנִזְכֶּה תָּמִיד לְפָרֵשׁ שִׂיחָתֵנוּ לְפָנֶיךָ בְּכָל יוֹם וָיוֹם בַּלָּשׁוֹן שֶׁמְּדַבְּרִים בּוֹ, בְּרַחֲמִים וְתַחֲנוּנִים גְּדוֹלִים, וּבִדְבָרֵי רִצּוּיִים וּפִיּוּסִים הַרְבֵּה, וּבִטְעָנוֹת וַאֲמַתְלָאוֹת נְכוֹנוֹת, וּבְהִתְעוֹרְרוּת גָּדוֹל בֶּאֱמֶת, וּבְדִבְרֵי חֵן וְתַחֲנוּנִים, עַד שֶׁנִּזְכֶּה לְקַשֵּׁר לִבֵּנוּ אֶל הַנְּקֻדָּה הַקְּדוֹשָׁה שֶׁיֵּשׁ בָּנוּ שֶׁהִיא בְּחִינַת "צַדִּיק מוֹשֵׁל" וְנִזְכֶּה לְהַעְתִּיר הַרְבֵּה לְפָנֶיךָ, וּלְהַרְבּוֹת מְאֹד בְּכָל יוֹם וָיוֹם בְּשִׂיחָה זוֹ תְּפִלָּה, וְנִזְכֶּה לוֹמַר לְפָנֶיךָ בְּכָל יוֹם וָיוֹם כַּמָּה וְכַמָּה תְּחִנּוֹת וּבַקָּשׁוֹת וִוִדּוּיִים וּתְפִלּוֹת וְהַפְצָרוֹת וְנִתְחַזֵּק וְנִתְאַמֵּץ בִּתְפִלָּה וְתַחֲנוּנִים בְּכָל עֹז וְתַעֲצוּמוֹת וְאַל נִתֵּן דֳּמִי לָךְ עַד שֶׁתְּחָנֵּנוּ, נִקְרָא אֵלֶיךָ עַד שֶׁתַּעֲנֵנוּ, עַד שֶׁנְּעוֹרֵר רַחֲמֶיךָ הָאֲמִתִּיִּים עָלֵינוּ וְנִזְכֶּה לָנֶצַח אוֹתְךָ בִּתְפִלָּתֵנוּ וְתַחֲנוּנוֹתֵינוּ וְשִׂיחוֹתֵינוּ, שֶׁתָּשִׁיב פָּנֶיךָ אֵלֵינוּ וּתְרַחֲמֵנוּ, וּתְשִׁיבֵנוּ בִּתְשׁוּבָה שְׁלֵמָה לְפָנֶיךָ בֶּאֱמֶת בְּכָל לֵב וָנֶפֶשׁ: (ל״ת ל״ד)

⚜

להתפלל לה׳ שיבוא על האמת

רִבּוֹנוֹ שֶׁל עוֹלָם, זַכֵּנוּ לַעֲסֹק הַרְבֵּה בְּתוֹרָתְךָ הַקְּדוֹשָׁה בְּכָל יוֹם וָיוֹם, וְאֶזְכֶּה לִלְמֹד בַּסְּפָרִים הַרְבֵּה שֶׁנִּתְחַבְּרוּ עַל יְדֵי חֲכָמֶיךָ הַקְּדוֹשִׁים, וְתִתֶּן לִי חָכְמָה בִּינָה וָדַעַת, עַד אֲשֶׁר בְּכָל סֵפֶר וָסֵפֶר שֶׁאֶהְיֶה מְעַיֵּן וְלוֹמֵד בּוֹ, אֶזְכֶּה לְהָבִין הֵיטֵב כַּוָּנַת הַמְחַבֵּר בֶּאֱמֶת לַאֲמִתּוֹ וְלֹא אֶשְׁגֶּה בְּכַוָּנָתוֹ וְלֹא אֲפָרֵשׁ בּוֹ פֵּרוּשׁ זָר חַס וְשָׁלוֹם. (תפילות ותחנונים עמ׳ ס״ה)

※

וְהָאֵר עֵינֵינוּ בְּתוֹרָתֶךָ, וְזַכֵּנוּ לְהוֹצִיא לָאוֹר כָּל חֵלֶק פְּשָׁט רֶמֶז דְּרָשׁ וְסוֹד, הַשַּׁיָּכִים לְנַפְשֵׁנוּ רוּחֵנוּ וְנִשְׁמָתֵנוּ, וּלְחַדֵּשׁ חִדּוּשִׁים רַבִּים אֲמִתִּיִּים לַאֲמִתָּהּ שֶׁל תּוֹרָה. וְלֹא נִכָּשֵׁל בִּדְבַר הֲלָכָה, וְלֹא נֹאמַר עַל טָמֵא טָהוֹר וְלֹא עַל טָהוֹר טָמֵא, וְלֹא עַל מֻתָּר אָסוּר וְלֹא עַל אָסוּר מֻתָּר, וְלֹא לְזַכַּאי חַיָּב וְלֹא לְחַיָּב זַכַּאי. וְתַצִּילֵנוּ מִכָּל טָעוּת, וְאַל תַּצֵּל מִפִּינוּ דְּבַר אֱמֶת לְעוֹלָם. (אוצר תפלות ישראל ג, עמ׳ מ׳)

※

וַאֲנִי מַאֲמִין בֶּאֱמוּנָה שְׁלֵמָה, שֶׁאִם אִגַּע עַצְמִי בַּתּוֹרָה הַקְּדוֹשָׁה בְּוַדַּאי אֶמְצָא אוֹר הַנֶּעְלָם בָּהּ לִכְבוֹד שְׁמוֹ יִתְבָּרַךְ, וְתָאִיר חֶשְׁכִּי לִרְאוֹת וְלִמְצֹא דֶּרֶךְ הָאֱמֶת שֶׁאֵלֶךְ בּוֹ. וְהִנְנִי מְקַשֵּׁר נַפְשִׁי רוּחִי וְנִשְׁמָתִי עִם נִשְׁמַת כָּל הַתַּנָּאִים וְהָאֲמוֹרָאִים וְעִם נִשְׁמַת כָּל הַצַּדִּיקִים שֶׁעַל יָדָם גִּלִּית דִּבְרֵי תוֹרָתְךָ הַלָּלוּ, וְהִנְנִי מְקַשֵּׁר עַצְמִי עִם נִשְׁמַת צַדִּיק הַדּוֹר הַכּוֹלֵל נִשְׁמוֹת יִשְׂרָאֵל, וְעִם נִשְׁמַת הַצַּדִּיקִים הָאֲמִתִּיִּים הַנִּגְלִים וְהַנִּסְתָּרִים הַיּוֹדְעִים סוֹד הַלִּמּוּד לְיַחֵד שְׁמוֹתֶיךָ הַקְּדוֹשִׁים, וְעִם נִשְׁמַת כָּל תַּלְמִידֵי חֲכָמִים הָעוֹסְקִים בַּתּוֹרָה לִשְׁמָהּ וְעִם נִשְׁמוֹתֵיהֶם שֶׁל כָּל יִשְׂרָאֵל הַגְּדוֹלִים וְהַקְּטַנִּים. (אוצר תפלות ישראל ג, עמ׳ ל״ב)

※

תפילות להנהגות האדם

הנהגות האדם א

ללמוד גמרא ופוסקים באמת והכנה ללימוד

[רִבּוֹנוֹ שֶׁל עוֹלָם, אָנָּא] תַּעַזְרֵנִי בְּרַחֲמֶיךָ הָרַבִּים שֶׁאֶזְכֶּה לַעֲסֹק בְּסִפְרֵי הַפּוֹסְקִים בְּהַתְמָדָה גְדוֹלָה וְתַעַזְרֵנִי וְתוֹשִׁיעֵנִי לִלְמֹד הַרְבֵּה בְּכָל יוֹם וָיוֹם סִפְרֵי הַפּוֹסְקִים וְתִפְתַּח אֶת דַּעְתִּי, וְתָכִין אֶת לִבָּבִי, שֶׁאֶזְכֶּה לִלְמֹד בִּמְהִירוּת גָּדוֹל, וּלְהָבִין הַדִּין עַל בֻּרְיוֹ, וּלְבָרֵר וּלְלַבֵּן הַפְּסַק הֲלָכָה בְּכָל דִּינֵי הַתּוֹרָה בֶּאֱמֶת לַאֲמִתּוֹ וְאֶזְכֶּה לֵידַע הַהַכְרָעָה בֶּאֱמֶת, בֵּין כָּל בַּעֲלֵי הַמַּחֲלֹקֶת דִּקְדֻשָּׁה שֶׁמִּחֲלָקִים בְּדִינֵי הַתּוֹרָה וְאֶזְכֶּה לַעֲשׂוֹת שָׁלוֹם וְהַכְרָעָה בֵּינֵיהֶם וְעַל יְדֵי הַשָּׁלוֹם הַזֶּה יִמָּשֵׁךְ וְיִשְׁתַּלְשֵׁל שָׁלוֹם בְּכָל הָעוֹלָמוֹת, עַד שֶׁיִּתְפַּשֵּׁט הַשָּׁלוֹם גַּם בָּעוֹלָם הַזֶּה וְתָשִׂים שָׁלוֹם בֵּין כָּל עַמְּךָ יִשְׂרָאֵל לְעוֹלָם: (ל"ת ס"ב)

※

אוֹדֶה ה' מְאֹד אֲשֶׁר שָׂם חֶלְקִי מִיּוֹשְׁבֵי בֵּית הַמִּדְרָשׁ וְלֹא שָׂם חֶלְקִי מִיּוֹשְׁבֵי קְרָנוֹת. יְהִי שֵׁם ה' מְבֹרָךְ וּמְרוֹמָם עַל כָּל בְּרָכָה וּתְהִלָּה. וְאִלּוּ פִּי מָלֵא שִׁירָה כַּיָּם, לֹא אַסְפִּיק לְהַלֶּלְךָ, כִּי חַסְדְּךָ גָּדוֹל עָלַי. קָטֹנְתִּי מִכֹּל הַחֲסָדִים וּמִכָּל הָאֱמֶת אֲשֶׁר עָשִׂיתָ אֶת עַבְדֶּךָ. וּבְכֵן יְהִי רָצוֹן מִלְּפָנֶיךָ ה' אֱלֹהֵינוּ וֵאלֹהֵי אֲבוֹתֵינוּ, שֶׁכְּשֵׁם שֶׁחוֹנַנְתָּנוּ לִהְיוֹת חֶלְקֵנוּ מִיּוֹשְׁבֵי בֵּית הַמִּדְרָשׁ, כֵּן תְּחָנֵנוּ, אָבִינוּ אָב הָרַחֲמָן, הַמְרַחֵם, רַחֵם נָא עָלֵינוּ, וְתֵן בְּלִבֵּנוּ וּבְלֵב זַרְעֵנוּ בִּינָה לְהָבִין וּלְהַשְׂכִּיל, לִשְׁמֹעַ, לִלְמֹד וּלְלַמֵּד, לִשְׁמֹר וְלַעֲשׂוֹת וּלְקַיֵּם אֶת כָּל דִּבְרֵי תַלְמוּד תּוֹרָתֶךָ בְּאַהֲבָה. (אוצר תפלות ישראל ג, עמ' מ')

מַלְכִּי וֵאלֹהַי אֵלֶיךָ אֶתְפַּלָּל אָנָּא יְהֹוָה הוֹשִׁיעֵנִי בְּרַחֲמֶיךָ הָרַבִּים שֶׁאֶזְכֶּה לַעֲסֹק בְּדִבְרֵי תּוֹרָתְךָ לִשְׁמָהּ בְּהִתְמָדָה גְדוֹלָה וּבְתוֹרָתְךָ נֶהְגֶּה יוֹמָם וָלַיְלָה, וְתִהְיֶה עִמִּי תָּמִיד וּתְעַזְּרֵנִי וְתוֹשִׁיעֵנִי שֶׁלֹּא יִתְגַּשְּׁמוּ וְשֶׁלֹּא יִתְחַשְּׁכוּ דִּבְרֵי הַתּוֹרָה מִפִּי חַס וְשָׁלוֹם רַק אֶזְכֶּה לִלְמֹד תּוֹרָה בִּקְדֻשָּׁה וּבְטָהֳרָה גְּדוֹלָה לְבַטֵּל עַצְמִי וְכָל גַּשְׁמִיּוּתִי בִּשְׁעַת לִמּוּדִי, בְּאֹפֶן שֶׁאֶזְכֶּה לְהַרְגִּישׁ בְּלִבִּי וְדַעְתִּי הָעֲרֵבוּת וְהַנְּעִימוּת וְהָרוּחָנִיּוּת וְהַדַּקּוּת וְהָעֲמָקוּת שֶׁבְּתוֹרָתְךָ הַקְּדוֹשָׁה כִּי אַתָּה לְבַד יָדַעְתָּ עֹצֶם מְתִיקוּת הַנְּעִימוּת וְהָעֲרֵבוּת וְהָרוּחָנִיּוּת שֶׁל דִּבְרֵי תּוֹרָתְךָ הַקְּדוֹשָׁה הַטְּהוֹרָה וְהַתְּמִימָה, כְּמוֹ שֶׁנֶּאֱמַר: "הַנֶּחֱמָדִים מִזָּהָב וּמִפַּז רָב, וּמְתוּקִים מִדְּבַשׁ וְנֹפֶת צוּפִים": (ל"ת קי"א)

וּבְכֵן יְהִי רָצוֹן מִלְּפָנֶיךָ יְהוָה אֱלֹהֵינוּ וֵאלֹהֵי אֲבוֹתֵינוּ, שֶׁתַּעַזְרֵנִי וְתִשְׁמְרֵנִי וְתַצִּילֵנִי מִדִּבּוּרִים רָעִים וְלֹא אֶפְגַּם אֶת דִּבּוּר פִּי לְעוֹלָם וְלֹא יֵצֵא מִפִּי שׁוּם דִּבּוּר רַע עַל שׁוּם יִשְׂרָאֵל שֶׁבָּעוֹלָם, וְלֹא אֶחְקֹד אַחַר חוֹבוֹת בְּנֵי אָדָם, רַק תַּעַזְרֵנִי וְתַטֶּה אֶת לְבָבִי שֶׁאֶזְכֶּה לַחְקֹר תָּמִיד אַחַר כָּל זְכוּת וָטוֹב שֶׁאֶפְשָׁר לִמְצֹא בְּכָל אֶחָד וְאֶחָד מִיִּשְׂרָאֵל, אֲפִלּוּ בְּהַגְּרוּעַ שֶׁבַּגְּרוּעִים וְאֶזְכֶּה לְהִתְיַגֵּעַ וְלִטְרֹחַ אַחַר זֶה, לַחְתֹּר לִמְצֹא אֵיזֶה זְכוּת אֲפִלּוּ בְּהַפְּחוּת שֶׁבַּפְּחוּתִים וְתִהְיֶה עִמִּי תָּמִיד וְתַעַזְרֵנִי שֶׁיַּעֲלֶה בְּיָדִי שֶׁאֶזְכֶּה לִמְצֹא בָהֶם תָּמִיד צַד זְכוּת וָטוֹב וְאֶזְכֶּה לָדוּן אֶת כָּל אָדָם לְכַף זְכוּת תָּמִיד, וְתַצִּילֵנִי בְּרַחֲמֶיךָ הָרַבִּים מֵעָוֹן הַגָּדוֹל וְהֶחָמוּר מְאֹד, שֶׁהוּא עֲוֹן לָשׁוֹן־הָרַע וּרְכִילוּת הֶחָמוּר בְּיוֹתֵר, הַשָּׁקוּל כְּנֶגֶד שָׁלֹשׁ הָעֲבֵרוֹת הַגְּדוֹלִים שֶׁבַּתּוֹרָה, שֶׁהֵם עֲבוֹדָה זָרָה וְגִלּוּי עֲרָיוֹת וּשְׁפִיכוּת דָּמִים וַעֲוֹן לָשׁוֹן־הָרַע שָׁקוּל כְּנֶגֶד כֻּלָּם: (ל"ת ל"ח)

הַתְמָדָה

וּבְכֵן תְּזַכֵּנִי בְּרַחֲמֶיךָ הָרַבִּים, שֶׁאֶזְכֶּה לַעֲסֹק בְּתוֹרָתְךָ הַקְּדוֹשָׁה תָּמִיד יוֹמָם וָלַיְלָה, וְתִפְתַּח אֶת דַּעְתִּי וְתָאִיר עֵינַי בְּתוֹרָתֶךָ וְאֶזְכֶּה לִלְמֹד תּוֹרָתְךָ הַקְּדוֹשָׁה בְּשֵׂכֶל צַח וָזָךְ, וְאֶזְכֶּה לֵידַע וּלְהָבִין בִּמְהִירוּת גָּדוֹל בְּכָל מָקוֹם שֶׁאֲנִי לוֹמֵד וְלֹא יִהְיֶה כֹּחַ לְשׁוּם מְבַלְבֵּל לְבַלְבֵּל אֶת דַּעְתִּי, חַס וְשָׁלוֹם, בִּשְׁעַת לִמּוּדִי בְּשׁוּם בִּלְבּוּל שֶׁבָּעוֹלָם, הֵן מַחֲשָׁבוֹת חוּץ מַחֲשָׁבוֹת זָרוֹת מֵהַבְלֵי עוֹלָם, הֵן בִּלְבּוּלִים וְעִרְבּוּבִים וְעַקְמוּמִיּוֹת בְּעִנְיַן הַלִּמּוּד בְּעַצְמוֹ, מִכֻּלָּם תַּצִּיל אוֹתִי אָבִי שֶׁבַּשָּׁמַיִם בְּרַחֲמֶיךָ הָרַבִּים רַק אֶזְכֶּה לְהִתְגַּבֵּר בְּרַחֲמֶיךָ לְסַלֵּק וּלְבַטֵּל מֵעָלַי כָּל מִינֵי בִּלְבּוּלִים וְעַקְמוּמִיּוֹת שֶׁבָּעוֹלָם בִּשְׁעַת הַלִּמּוּד, וְאֶזְכֶּה לִלְמֹד הַרְבֵּה בִּמְהִירוּת גָּדוֹל, בְּשֵׂכֶל צַח וָזָךְ בֶּאֱמֶת, וְאֶזְכֶּה לְהַתְחִיל וְלִגְמֹר כָּל סִפְרֵי הַתּוֹרָה הַקְּדוֹשָׁה שֶׁבִּכְתָב וּבְעַל פֶּה, וּלְלַמֵּד אוֹתָם כַּמָּה פְּעָמִים: (ל"ת ט"ו)

לְדַרְכֵי הַקְּדֻשָּׁה בֶּאֱמֶת, וְתַעֲזְרֵנוּ שֶׁנִּהְיֶה עַז כַּנָּמֵר נֶגְדָּם לְנַצְּחָם וּלְהַשְׁפִּילָם עַד עָפָר, לְשַׁבְּרָם וּלְבַטְּלָם לְגַמְרֵי, וּתְזַכֵּנִי שֶׁאֶהְיֶה עַז וְחָזָק בַּעֲבוֹדָתְךָ תָּמִיד: (ל״ת כב)

~

חוּס וְחָנֵּנִי, וְרַחֵם עָלַי וְהוֹשִׁיעֵנִי, וְזַכֵּנִי לָעֵזוּת דִּקְדֻשָּׁה, שֶׁאֶזְכֶּה תָּמִיד בִּשְׁעַת הַתְּפִלָּה לְהִתְגַּבֵּר לְסַלֵּק הַבּוּשָׁה, שֶׁלֹּא אֵבוֹשׁ מִלְּפָנֶיךָ, וְאָעִיז פָּנַי לְבַקֵּשׁ אוֹתְךָ כָּל מִינֵי בַּקָּשׁוֹת גְּדוֹלוֹת שֶׁבָּעוֹלָם הַנּוֹגְעִים לַעֲבוֹדָתְךָ בֶּאֱמֶת, שֶׁתְּקָרְבֵנִי אֵלֶיךָ בְּכָל מִינֵי הִתְקָרְבוּת, וְתַעֲשֶׂה עִמִּי פִּלְאֵי פְלָאוֹת, לְהַעֲלוֹת אוֹתִי מִשְּׁפַל הַמַּדְרֵגָה הַתַּחְתּוֹנָה, לְרוּם הַמַּעֲלוֹת הַקְּדוֹשׁוֹת, וְאֶזְכֶּה לָבוֹא וּלְהַגִּיעַ מְהֵרָה לְכָל הַמַּדְרֵגוֹת הָעֶלְיוֹנוֹת שֶׁל הַקְּדֻשָּׁה, עַד שֶׁאֶזְכֶּה לְהַשִּׂיג אֱלֹהוּתְךָ בְּתַכְלִית מַדְרֵגָה הָעֶלְיוֹנָה, בְּמַדְרֵגַת נְבִיאִים אֲמִתִּיִּים וְצַדִּיקִים גְּדוֹלִים וְנוֹרָאִים, בְּמַדְרֵגַת בְּנֵי עֲלִיָּה: (ל״ת ל׳)

~

לשמור אמרי פיו

אָב הָרַחֲמָן, חוּס נָא וְזַכֵּנִי לְמִדַּת הַשְּׁתִיקָה, שֶׁאֶהְיֶה נִזְהָר מִלְּדַבֵּר אַף דִּבּוּרִים בְּטֵלִים, מִכָּל שֶׁכֵּן דִּבּוּרֵי אִסּוּר, חַס וְשָׁלוֹם. וְיַעֲמָד נָא לִי זְכוּתוֹ שֶׁל רַבָּן שִׁמְעוֹן בֶּן גַּמְלִיאֵל, וּזְכוּתוֹ שֶׁל רַבָּן יוֹחָנָן בֶּן זַכַּאי, וְרַבִּי מֵאִיר, וְרַב, וְרַב הוּנָא, וּזְכוּתוֹ שֶׁל רַבִּי יִצְחָק, וְרַבִּי יְהוּדָה בֶּן שׁוּשָׁן. הַצַּדִּיקִים הָאֵלּוּ הָיוּ נִזְהָרִים מְאֹד מְאֹד בְּמִדַּת הַשְּׁתִיקָה. גַּם אוֹתִי יְזַכֵּנִי ה׳ בָּהּ כָּל יָמַי, וְאָשִׂים מַחְסוֹם לְפִי זוּלַת בְּדִבְרֵי תּוֹרָה וְיִרְאָה וּתְפִלָּה. יִהְיוּ לְרָצוֹן אִמְרֵי פִי וְהֶגְיוֹן לִבִּי לְפָנֶיךָ, ה׳ צוּרִי וְגוֹאֲלִי.

(ספר משפט צדק אות ח׳)

~

צוֹפִיָּה הֲלִיכוֹת בֵּיתָהּ וְלֶחֶם עַצְלוּת לֹא תֹאכֵל. לֵךְ אֶל נְמָלָה [עָצֵל] רְאֵה דְרָכֶיהָ וַחֲכָם. רִבּוֹנוֹ שֶׁל עוֹלָם, עָזְרֵנִי וְזַכֵּנִי שֶׁאֶזְכֶּה לִזְרִיזוּת דִּקְדֻשָּׁה, וְכָל דָּבָר שֶׁבִּקְדֻשָּׁה אֶזְכֶּה לַעֲשׂוֹת בִּקְדֻשָּׁה בִּזְרִיזוּת גָּדוֹל, וְאַל אֶדְחֶה חַס וְשָׁלוֹם מִיּוֹם לְיוֹם כָּל דָּבָר שֶׁבִּקְדֻשָּׁה, וּבִפְרָט בְּעֵת שֶׁצָּרִיךְ אֲנִי לָקוּם מִשְּׁנָתִי, הֵן בַּלַּיְלָה הֵן בַּחֲצוֹת הֵן בַּבֹּקֶר, אֶזְכֶּה לָקוּם בִּזְרִיזוּת בִּקְדֻשָּׁה, וּלְקַיֵּם מַאֲמַר חֲכָמֵינוּ זִכְרוֹנָם לִבְרָכָה: יִתְגַּבֵּר כָּאֲרִי לַעֲמֹד בַּבֹּקֶר לַעֲבוֹדַת הַבּוֹרֵא יִתְבָּרַךְ שְׁמוֹ, וּכְמוֹ שֶׁאָמְרוּ רַבּוֹתֵינוּ זִכְרוֹנָם לִבְרָכָה: וּמִיָּד שֶׁיֵּעוֹר מִשְּׁנָתוֹ יָקוּם בִּזְרִיזוּת לַעֲבוֹדַת בּוֹרְאוֹ. רִבּוֹנוֹ שֶׁל עוֹלָם, עֵינֶיךָ הֲלֹא לֶאֱמוּנָה. זַכֵּנִי שֶׁעַל יְדֵי שֶׁאֶזְכֶּה לִזְרִיזוּת בִּקְדֻשָּׁה וְלָקוּם בַּבֹּקֶר בִּזְרִיזוּת, שֶׁאֶזְכֶּה לְגַדֵּל וּלְחַזֵּק אֶת הָאֱמוּנָה הַקְּדוֹשָׁה. וְאֶזְכֶּה עַל יְדֵי שֶׁאָקוּם מִן הַשֵּׁנָה בִּזְרִיזוּת, לְחַזֵּק אֶת עַצְמִי בָּאֱמוּנָה הַקְּדוֹשָׁה, כְּדֵי לִבְנוֹת וּלְגַדֵּל אֶת הָאֱמוּנָה וּלְהוֹדִיעַ אֱמוּנָתְךָ הַקְּדוֹשָׁה לְכָל בָּאֵי עוֹלָם, וְעַל יְדֵי זֶה אֶזְכֶּה לְהַמְלִיךְ אוֹתְךָ עַל כָּל אֵיבָרַי וְגִידַי וְעַל כָּל הָעוֹלָם כֻּלּוֹ.

(תפילות הבוקר עמ' ט')

בושה רעה

וְתַשְׁפִּיעַ עָלֵינוּ בְּרַחֲמֶיךָ הָרַבִּים דַּעַת דִּקְדֻשָּׁה, שֶׁאֶזְכֶּה לֵידַע אֵיךְ לְהִתְנַהֵג עִם הָעַזּוּת בְּאֹפֶן שֶׁלֹּא יִהְיֶה לִי שׁוּם עַזּוּת דְּסִטְרָא אָחֳרָא כְּלָל, וְלֹא אֶשְׁתַּמֵּשׁ עִם הָעַזּוּת כִּי אִם לִשְׁמְךָ וְלַעֲבוֹדָתְךָ בֶּאֱמֶת, וְתַצִּילֵנִי וּתְמַלְּטֵנִי מִדִּינָהּ שֶׁל גֵּיהִנָּם הַקָּשָׁה וּמַר מְאֹד הַמַּגִּיעַ לְעַזֵּי פָנִים, אֲשֶׁר הֵם נוֹפְלִים בְּגֵיהִנָּם בְּאֵין סוֹמֵךְ וּמַצִּיל חוּס וַחֲמֹל עָלַי בְּחֶמְלָתֶיךָ הָאֲמִתִּיִּים, חוּס וַחֲמֹל עָלַי וְתַצִּילֵנִי מִכָּל מִינֵי עַזּוּת דְּסִטְרָא אָחֳרָא מִכָּל מִינֵי עַזּוּת הַגּוּף, וּתְזַכֵּנִי לְעַזּוּת דִּקְדֻשָּׁה בֶּאֱמֶת לַעֲמֹד כְּנֶגֶד הָעַזֵּי פָנִים שֶׁבַּדּוֹר הָרוֹצִים לְרַחֵק מִדַּרְכֵי אֱמֶת אוֹ לְהַחֲלִישׁ דַּעְתָּם, חַס וְשָׁלוֹם, שֶׁל הָרוֹצִים לְהִתְקָרֵב

וִיהִי רָצוֹן מִלְּפָנֶיךָ, ה' אֱלֹהֵינוּ וֵאלֹהֵי אֲבוֹתֵינוּ, שֶׁתַּצִּילֵנוּ מִכָּל נִדְנוּד אִסּוּר, בִּפְרָט הַתָּלוּי בַּאֲכִילָה וּשְׁתִיָּה, וּמִכָּל חֳלִי, וּבִפְרָט הַבָּא עַל יְדֵי אֲכִילָה וּשְׁתִיָּה, וּתְזַכֵּנוּ לְבָרֵר וּלְהוֹצִיא לָאוֹר כָּל נִיצוֹצוֹת הַקְּדֻשָּׁה הַדְּבוּקִים בְּכָל אֲשֶׁר נֹאכַל וַאֲשֶׁר נִשְׁתֶּה, וְתַמְשִׁיךְ שֶׁפַע קְדֻשָּׁה וּבְרָכָה בְּכָל אֲשֶׁר נֹאכַל וַאֲשֶׁר נִשְׁתֶּה. (בית תפלה אות ג')

צעטיל קטן טז

עיקר עבודה לשבר את הטבע

זריזות

רִבּוֹנוֹ שֶׁל עוֹלָם אֱלֹהִים חַיִּים וּמֶלֶךְ עוֹלָם, שִׂמְחַת יִשְׂרָאֵל, רַחֵם עָלַי לְמַעַן שְׁמֶךָ, וְהַצִּילֵנִי מֵעֲצָבוֹת וּמֵעַצְלוּת אֲשֶׁר הֵם הָיוּ בְּעוֹכְרִי, וּבִטְּלוּ אוֹתִי הַרְבֵּה מִתּוֹרָה וּתְפִלָּה וּמִטּוֹב הַרְבֵּה, וֶהֱבִיאוּנִי לְמָה שֶׁהֱבִיאוּנִי כַּאֲשֶׁר הוֹדַעְתָּ לָנוּ עַל יְדֵי חֲכָמֶיךָ הַקְּדוֹשִׁים, שֶׁעִקַּר נְשִׁיכַת הַנָּחָשׁ הוּא עַצְבוּת וְעַצְלוּת רַחֲמָנָא לִצְלָן, רַחֵם עָלַי מָלֵא רַחֲמִים, וְהַצִּילֵנִי מֵעַתָּה מִנְּשִׁיכוּת הָאֵלֶּה תֶּן לִי חַיִּים וְאֶחְיֶה "שַׂמֵּחַ נֶפֶשׁ עַבְדֶּךָ כִּי אֵלֶיךָ יְהֹוָה אֶשָּׂא נַפְשִׁי תַּשְׁמִיעֵנִי שָׂשׂוֹן וְשִׂמְחָה תָּגֵלְנָה עֲצָמוֹת דִּכִּיתָ" זַכֵּנִי לְהִזְדָּרֵז בְּתוֹרָתְךָ וּבַעֲבוֹדָתְךָ תָּמִיד בִּזְרִיזוּת גָּדוֹל וּבְשִׂמְחָה רַבָּה וַעֲצוּמָה כָּרָאוּי לְהִזְדָּרֵז וְלִשְׂמֹחַ בַּעֲבוֹדָתְךָ וּבְתוֹרָתְךָ הַקְּדוֹשָׁה אֲשֶׁר הֵם חַיֵּינוּ וְאֹרֶךְ יָמֵינוּ בָּזֶה וּבַבָּא לָעַד וּלְנֶצַח, וְחוּץ מִזֶּה הַכֹּל הֶבֶל נִדָּף הֲבֵל הֲבָלִים אֵין בּוֹ מַמָּשׁ, "מַה יִּתְרוֹן לָאָדָם בְּכָל עֲמָלוֹ שֶׁיַּעֲמֹל תַּחַת הַשָּׁמֶשׁ" חוּץ מִתּוֹרָה וּתְפִלָּה וַעֲבוֹדָה: (ל"ת קכ"ח)

צעטיל קטן טו

תשובה לפני אכילה, ואכילה בקדושה

אָבִינוּ שֶׁבַּשָּׁמַיִם, עָזְרֵנוּ וְהוֹשִׁיעֵנוּ, שֶׁנִּזְכֶּה לְשַׁבֵּר מֵאִתָּנוּ תַּאֲוַת אֲכִילָה, וְנִזְכֶּה שֶׁתִּהְיֶה אֲכִילָתֵנוּ בְּצִמְצוּם, רַק כְּפִי הַהֶכְרֵחַ לְקִיּוּם הָאָדָם לְבַד, וְנִזְכֶּה לֶאֱכֹל בִּקְדֻשָּׁה וּבְטָהֳרָה לִשְׁמֶךָ לְבַד: (ספר קדושה - אוצר תפלות ישראל ג, עמ' רכ"א)

~

וּבְכֵן תְּזַכֵּנוּ בְּרַחֲמֶיךָ הָרַבִּים, שֶׁתִּהְיֶה אֲכִילָתֵנוּ בִּקְדֻשָּׁה וּבְטָהֳרָה בְּלִי שׁוּם תַּאֲוָה גַּשְׁמִיּוּת כְּלָל, וְתִתֶּן לָנוּ כֹּחַ לְעוֹרֵר הַתְּנוֹצְצוּת הָאוֹתִיּוֹת הַקְּדוֹשִׁים שֶׁל כ"ח אָתָוָן דְּמַעֲשֵׂה בְרֵאשִׁית שֶׁמְּלֻבָּשׁ בְּכָל דָּבָר שֶׁבָּעוֹלָם, עַד שֶׁכָּל אֲכִילָתֵנוּ וּשְׁתִיָּתֵנוּ וְכָל סְעֻדָּתֵנוּ וְתַעֲנוּגֵנוּ יִהְיֶה רַק מֵהִתְנוֹצְצוּת הָאוֹתִיּוֹת הַקְּדוֹשִׁים לְבַד שֶׁיֵּשׁ בְּאוֹתוֹ הַדָּבָר, שֶׁאָנוּ אוֹכְלִים וְשׁוֹתִים אוֹ מִתְעַנְּגִים מִמֶּנּוּ וְעַל יְדֵי זֶה נִזְכֶּה לְלֵב טוֹב, שֶׁלִּבִּי יִהְיֶה מֵאִיר בִּקְדֻשָּׁה גְדוֹלָה עַל יְדֵי שֶׁיִּזְכֶּה לֵהָנוֹת וְלָזוּן רַק מֵהִתְנוֹצְצוּת הָאוֹתִיּוֹת שֶׁל כֹּחַ מַעֲשֵׂה בְרֵאשִׁית שֶׁיֵּשׁ בְּכָל דָּבָר: (ל"ת י"ט) ~

וּתְזַכֵּנוּ לֶאֱכֹל בִּקְדֻשָּׁה וּבְטָהֳרָה גְדוֹלָה, וְנֹאכַל לְבַד לְקִיּוּם גּוּפֵנוּ, וְנְמַעֵט תַּאֲוַת טִבְעֵנוּ וְנִזְכֶּה לְהִסְתַּפֵּק בִּמְעַט אֲכִילָה, וְנִהְיֶה נִכְלָלִים בִּכְלַל הַצַּדִּיקִים הָאוֹכְלִים לְשֹׂבַע נַפְשָׁם הַקְּדוֹשָׁה לְבַד, כְּמוֹ שֶׁכָּתוּב: "צַדִּיק אֹכֵל לְשֹׂבַע נַפְשׁוֹ" וְתַעַזְרֵנוּ שֶׁתִּהְיֶה אֲכִילָתֵנוּ בִּקְדֻשָּׁה גְדוֹלָה כָּל כָּךְ, עַד שֶׁנִּזְכֶּה לְהַשְׂבִּיעַ בְּצַחְצָחוֹת נַפְשֵׁנוּ לְהִתְעַנֵּג עַל יְהֹוָה, לִשְׂבֹּעַ וּלְהִתְעַנֵּג בְּאוֹרוֹת הַצַּחְצָחוֹת הָעֶלְיוֹנוֹת, וְנִזְכֶּה "לַחֲזוֹת בְּנֹעַם יְהֹוָה וּלְבַקֵּר בְּהֵיכָלוֹ" וִיקֻיַּם בָּנוּ מִקְרָא שֶׁכָּתוּב: "וְנָחֲךָ יְהֹוָה תָּמִיד וְהִשְׂבִּיעַ בְּצַחְצָחוֹת נַפְשֶׁךָ", עַד שֶׁנִּזְכֶּה לְצַחְצֵחַ נַפְשֵׁנוּ וְרוּחֵנוּ וְנִשְׁמוֹתֵינוּ תָּמִיד בְּשֶׁבַע הַצַּחְצָחוֹת הָעֶלְיוֹנוֹת: (ל"ת תנינא ה')

צעטיל קטן יג

לספר למורה או לחבר

וּתְזַכֵּךְ נַפְשֵׁנוּ עַל יְדֵי לִמּוּד תּוֹרָתְךָ הַקְּדוֹשָׁה הַנִּמְשָׁלָה לָאֵשׁ, שֶׁנֶּאֱמַר: הֲלוֹא כֹה דְבָרִי כָּאֵשׁ. וּנְטַהֵר עַצְמֵנוּ מִכָּל סִיג וּפְגָם, מִבִּפְנִים וּמִבַּחוּץ, וְנִזְכֶּה לְזַכֵּךְ וּלְקַדֵּשׁ מֹחֵנוּ וְשִׂכְלֵנוּ, שֶׁלֹּא נַחֲשֹׁב הִרְהוּרִים בְּטֵלִים וּמַחֲשָׁבוֹת בְּטֵלוֹת, וְכָל שֶׁכֵּן שֶׁלֹּא נְהַרְהֵר הִרְהוּרִים אֲסוּרִים חַס וְשָׁלוֹם, וּתְקַדֵּשׁ וּתְטַהֵר אוֹתָנוּ עַד שֶׁנִּזְכֶּה לִהְיוֹת כִּסֵּא וּמֶרְכָּבָה לַשְּׁכִינָה הַקְּדוֹשָׁה. וּתְזַכֵּנוּ לִמְצֹא בְּתוֹרָתֵנוּ הַקְּדוֹשָׁה בְּכָל פַּעַם עֵצוֹת וְשִׂכְלִיּוֹת וּדְרָכִים חֲדָשִׁים אֲמִתִּיִּים לַעֲבוֹדָתֶךָ, יִתְבָּרַךְ שְׁמֶךָ, וְלִמְצֹא בָהּ סֵדֶר וְאֹפֶן תִּקּוּן נַפְשֵׁנוּ וְדַרְכֵי עֲבוֹדָתֶךָ, וְהַזְמֵן לָנוּ צַדִּיקִים וְעוֹבְדֵי הַשֵּׁם וַחֲבֵרִים טוֹבִים, לִלְמֹד וּלְקַבֵּל מֵהֶם דַּרְכֵי תּוֹרָתֶךָ וַעֲבוֹדָתְךָ הַקְּדוֹשָׁה הָאֲמִתִּיִּים, בְּלִי שׁוּם תַּעֲרוֹבוֹת אֵיזֶה שֶׁקֶר חָלִילָה. (אוצר תפלות ישראל ג, עמ' נ"ז)

רַחֵם עָלַי בַּעַל הָרַחֲמִים גְּדוֹל הָעֵצָה וְרַב הָעֲלִילָה, וְזַכֵּנִי לְקַבֵּל תָּמִיד כָּל הָעֵצוֹת מִצַּדִּיקֵי וּכְשֵׁרֵי הַדּוֹר הָאֲמִתִּיִּים, אֲשֶׁר כָּל עֲצוֹתֵיהֶם נִמְשָׁכוֹת מֵהַתּוֹרָה הַקְּדוֹשָׁה שֶׁקִּבְּלוּ מֵרַבּוֹתֵיהֶם הַצַּדִּיקִים הַקְּדוֹשִׁים הָאֲמִתִּיִּים, זַכֵּנוּ לְהִתְקָרֵב אֲלֵיהֶם בֶּאֱמֶת וּלְקַבֵּל מֵהֶם כָּל הָעֵצוֹת בְּכָל הַדְּבָרִים שֶׁבָּעוֹלָם, הֵן בַּעֲבוֹדוֹת יְהֹוָה וְהֵן בַּעֲבוֹדוֹת מַשָּׂא וּמַתָּן וּפַרְנָסָה, וְהֵן בִּשְׁאָרֵי עֲסָקִים, בְּכֻלָּם אֶשְׁאַל אֶת פִּיהֶם וְאֶזְכֶּה לֵהָנוֹת מֵהֶם עֵצָה וְתוּשִׁיָּה, וְיָאִירוּ בִי חָכְמָתָם הַקְּדוֹשָׁה, וְעַל יְדֵי זֶה יִהְיֶה נִמְשָׁךְ עָלַי חֶסֶד גָּדוֹל, וְיַמְתִּיקוּ וִיבַטְּלוּ מִמֶּנִּי כָּל הַדִּינִים שֶׁבָּעוֹלָם וְאֶזְכֶּה לִישׁוּעָה שְׁלֵמָה בְּכָל עֵת כְּמוֹ שֶׁכָּתוּב: "וּתְשׁוּעָה בְּרֹב יוֹעֵץ": (ל"ת קי"ז)

לַעֲלוֹת עַל דַּעְתִּי כְּלָל, בְּאֹפֶן שֶׁתִּהְיֶה תְפִלָּתִי זַכָּה וּנְכוֹנָה וּרְצוּיָה וּמְקֻבֶּלֶת לְפָנֶיךָ: (ל״ת תנינא מ״ג)

אמירת אמן

רִבּוֹנוֹ שֶׁל עוֹלָם, גָּלוּי וְיָדוּעַ לְפָנֶיךָ שֶׁאֲנִי בָּשָׂר וָדָם, וְאֵין בִּי כֹּחַ לְכַוֵּן כַּוָּנַת אָמֵן כָּרָאוּי. בְּכֵן יְהִי רָצוֹן מִלְּפָנֶיךָ, שֶׁתְּהֵא עוֹלָה כַּוָּנָה שֶׁלִּי עִם כַּוָּנַת אָמֵן כְּאוֹתָם הַשְּׂרִידִים הַיּוֹדְעִים לְכַוֵּן עֲנִיַּת אָמֵן כָּרָאוּי.
(אוצר תפילות ישראל ב, עמ' תקל״ה)

צעטיל קטן יב

יצייר שאיש עומד עליו

וְאֶזְכֶּה לְהִשְׁתּוֹקֵק וְלִכְסֹף כָּל כָּךְ לַעֲבוֹדָתְךָ בְּרָצוֹן וְהִשְׁתּוֹקְקוּת גָּדוֹל וְחָזָק, עַד אֲשֶׁר בְּכָל סֵפֶר וָסֵפֶר שֶׁאֶלְמַד וַאֲעַיֵּן בּוֹ, אֶזְכֶּה תֵּכֶף לִמְצֹא אֶת עַצְמִי, הַיְנוּ שֶׁאֶזְכֶּה לִרְאוֹת פְּחִיתוּתִי וְשִׁפְלוּתִי, וּלְקַבֵּל מוּסָר וְהִתְעוֹרְרוּת גָּדוֹל לַעֲבוֹדָתְךָ מִכָּל לִמּוּד וְלִמּוּד שֶׁאֶזְכֶּה לְעַיֵּן וְלִלְמֹד בְּכָל סֵפֶר וָסֵפֶר מֵהַסְּפָרִים הַקְּדוֹשִׁים, וְאֶזְכֶּה לְקַבֵּל מֵהֶם עֵצוֹת טוֹבוֹת וְהִתְעוֹרְרוּת וְהִתְחַזְּקוּת גָּדוֹל לַעֲבוֹדָתְךָ, בְּכָל עֵת וָעֵת כְּפִי בְּחִינָתִי וּמַדְרֵגָתִי וְאֵיכוּתִי וּמַהוּתִי, וּכְפִי הַסִּבּוֹת הָעוֹבְרִין עָלַי בְּכָל עֵת, וִיקֻיַּם בִּי מִקְרָא שֶׁכָּתוּב: אָז אָמַרְתִּי הִנֵּה בָאתִי בִּמְגִלַּת סֵפֶר כָּתוּב עָלָי. עָלַי דַּיְקָא, שֶׁיִּהְיֶה נֶחְשָׁב אֶצְלִי כָּל לִמּוּד וְלִמּוּד שֶׁאֶזְכֶּה לִלְמֹד בְּאֵיזֶה סֵפֶר, כְּאִלּוּ זֶה הַסֵּפֶר נִכְתַּב רַק בִּשְׁבִילִי וּמְדַבֵּר עִמִּי, כְּפִי מַה שֶּׁאֲנִי יוֹדֵעַ מַה שֶּׁעוֹבֵר עָלַי, וְאָז אֵדַע כִּי אֲנִי חָפֵץ וּמִשְׁתּוֹקֵק לַעֲשׂוֹת רְצוֹנְךָ בִּבְחִינַת: לַעֲשׂוֹת רְצוֹנְךָ אֱלֹהַי חָפָצְתִּי וְתוֹרָתְךָ בְּתוֹךְ מֵעָי. אָמֵן כֵּן יְהִי רָצוֹן. (תפילות ותחנונים עמ' כ״ו)

וּבְיִרְאָה וּבְאַהֲבָה. וְזַכֵּנוּ לְקַשֵּׁר מַחֲשַׁבְתֵּנוּ בְּדִבּוּרֵי הַתְּפִלָּה בְּקֶשֶׁר אַמִּיץ וְחָזָק, וְלֹא יֵצֵא שׁוּם דִּבּוּר מִפִּינוּ בְּלֹא כַוָּנָה, וְנִזְכֶּה לְהִתְפַּלֵּל תָּמִיד בִּמְסִירַת הַנֶּפֶשׁ, וְתִתֶּן לָנוּ כֹּחַ וּגְבוּרָה לְהִתְגַּבֵּר עַל כָּל הַמַּחֲשָׁבוֹת זָרוֹת לְהַכְנִיעָם וּלְגָרְשָׁם וּלְבַטְּלָם וּלְהָסִיחַ דַּעְתֵּנוּ מֵהֶם לְגַמְרֵי, וְיִהְיוּ מַחֲשְׁבוֹתֵינוּ קְדוֹשִׁים וּטְהוֹרִים תָּמִיד: (אוצר תפילות ישראל ב, עמ' תצ"ג)

וְאֶזְכֶּה לַעֲבוֹד אוֹתְךָ בֶּאֱמֶת וּבֶאֱמוּנָה שְׁלֵמָה וּבִתְמִימוּת גָּדוֹל, וְלַעֲסֹק בַּתּוֹרָה וּתְפִלָּה בְּכַוָּנָה גְדוֹלָה וַעֲצוּמָה וּלְהַכְנִיס כָּל כֹּחִי וְכָל מַחְשְׁבוֹת לִבִּי וְדַעְתִּי בְּתוֹךְ כָּל דִּבּוּר וְדִבּוּר שֶׁל הַתְּפִלָּה הַקְּדוֹשָׁה וְהַנּוֹרָאָה מְאֹד מְאֹד, וְאֵדַע וְאַאֲמִין בֶּאֱמוּנָה שְׁלֵמָה, כִּי מְלֹא כָל הָאָרֶץ כְּבוֹדֶךָ, וְאַתָּה עוֹמֵד עָלֵינוּ בִּשְׁעַת הַתְּפִלָּה, וְאַתָּה שׁוֹמֵעַ וּמַבִּיט וּמַאֲזִין וּמַקְשִׁיב כָּל דִּבּוּר וְדִבּוּר שֶׁל הַתְּפִלָּה, וְאֵדַע לִפְנֵי מִי אֲנִי עוֹמֵד, לִפְנֵי מֶלֶךְ מַלְכֵי הַמְּלָכִים הַקָּדוֹשׁ בָּרוּךְ הוּא, וְעַל יְדֵי זֶה יִמְשָׁךְ עָלַי יִרְאָה וְאֵימָה גְדוֹלָה מִפָּנֶיךָ, וְאֶזְכֶּה לְכַוֵּן הֵיטֵב הֵיטֵב בְּכָל דִּבּוּר וְדִבּוּר שֶׁל הַתְּפִלָּה וְלֹא אָסִיחַ אֶת דַּעְתִּי כְּלָל מִשּׁוּם דִּבּוּר שֶׁל הַתְּפִלָּה, וְלֹא אַתְחִיל לְהַטּוֹת דַּעְתִּי כְּלָל מִכַּוָּנַת פֵּרוּשׁ הַמִּלּוֹת שֶׁל הַתְּפִלָּה וְלֹא אֶחֱשֹׁב חַס וְשָׁלוֹם שׁוּם מַחֲשָׁבָה חִיצוֹנָה וְזָרָה כְּלָל בִּשְׁעַת הַתְּפִלָּה, רַק אֶזְכֶּה לְקַשֵּׁר מַחְשַׁבְתִּי בְּדִבּוּרֵי הַתְּפִלָּה בְּקֶשֶׁר אַמִּיץ וְחָזָק אֲשֶׁר לֹא יִנָּתֵק וְלֹא יֵהָרֵס לְעוֹלָם: (ל"ת פ"ד)

רַחֵם עָלַי לְמַעַן שְׁמֶךָ, וְהוֹשִׁיעֵנִי וְעָזְרֵנִי וְחַזְּקֵנִי וְאַמְּצֵנִי בְּכֹחֲךָ הַגָּדוֹל שֶׁאֶזְכֶּה לְהַכְנִיס כָּל הַכֹּחוֹת שֶׁבִּי בְּתוֹךְ הַתְּפִלָּה וְאֶתְפַּלֵּל לְפָנֶיךָ תְּפִלָּתִי תָּמִיד בְּכֹחַ גָּדוֹל, עַד שֶׁאֶזְכֶּה עַל יְדֵי זֶה לְבַטֵּל לְגַמְרֵי כָּל הַמַּחֲשָׁבוֹת שֶׁל גַּדְלוּת וּפְנִיּוּת וְכָל הַמַּחֲשָׁבוֹת זָרוֹת שֶׁבָּעוֹלָם, שֶׁלֹּא יִהְיֶה לָהֶם שׁוּם כֹּחַ לְבַלְבֵּל אֶת תְּפִלָּתִי חַס וְשָׁלוֹם, רַק אֶזְכֶּה לְגָרְשָׁם וּלְסַלְּקָם וּלְבַטְּלָם לְגַמְרֵי מֵעָלַי וּמֵעַל גְּבוּלִי שֶׁלֹּא יוּכְלוּ

אָנָּא יְהֹוָה, עָזְרֵנוּ שֶׁיִּהְיֶה נַעֲשֶׂה אֶצְלֵנוּ מִלִּמּוּד הַתּוֹרָה הַקְּדוֹשָׁה סַם חַיִּים, שֶׁנִּזְכֶּה עַל יְדֵי לִמּוּדֵנוּ לַחֲזֹר בִּתְשׁוּבָה שְׁלֵמָה לְפָנֶיךָ בֶּאֱמֶת וּלְחַדֵּשׁ כַּנֶּשֶׁר נְעוּרֵנוּ, לְחַדֵּשׁ יָמֵינוּ שֶׁעָבְרוּ בַּחֹשֶׁךְ גָּדוֹל, וּזְכוּת וְכֹחַ הַתּוֹרָה הַקְּדוֹשָׁה יָגֵן עָלֵינוּ, לְהַצִּילֵנוּ מֵעַתָּה מִכָּל מִינֵי חֲטָאִים וַעֲוֹנוֹת וּפְשָׁעִים וּמִכָּל מִינֵי פְּגָמִים שֶׁבָּעוֹלָם, בֵּין בְּעֵת שֶׁנַּעֲסֹק בָּהּ וּבֵין בְּעֵת שֶׁאָנוּ מֻכְרָחִים שֶׁלֹּא לַעֲסֹק בָּהּ, תָּמִיד יָגֵן עָלֵינוּ זְכוּת וְכֹחַ הַתּוֹרָה הַקְּדוֹשָׁה לְהַצִּילֵנוּ מִכָּל מִינֵי חֲטָאִים וּפְגָמִים שֶׁבָּעוֹלָם כְּמוֹ שֶׁהוֹדַעְתָּ לָנוּ עַל יְדֵי חֲכָמֶיךָ הַקְּדוֹשִׁים, שֶׁאָמְרוּ: 'אוֹרַיְתָא מַגִּינָא וּמַצְּלָה בֵּין בְּעִדָּנָא דְּעָסִיק בָּהּ וּבֵין בְּעִדָּנָא דְּלָא עָסִיק בָּהּ, וְנִזְכֶּה שֶׁיִּמָּשֵׁךְ עָלֵינוּ קְדֻשָּׁה וְטָהֳרָה עַל יְדֵי לִמּוּד הַתּוֹרָה הַקְּדוֹשָׁה, שֶׁנִּזְכֶּה מֵעַתָּה לְקַדֵּשׁ וּלְטַהֵר עַצְמֵנוּ בִּקְדֻשָּׁה גְּדוֹלָה כִּרְצוֹנְךָ הַטּוֹב: (ל"ת י"ב)

———⊸⊶⊷⊶⊷⊶———

צעטיל קטן יא

להתפלל בכוונה בכח ובקול

אָבִינוּ שֶׁבַּשָּׁמַיִם, לְפָנֶיךָ נִגְלָה הַכֹּל, וְאַתָּה יוֹדֵעַ עֹצֶם הַבִּלְבּוּלִים הָרַבִּים וְעִרְבּוּב הַדַּעַת שֶׁבָּא עָלֵינוּ בִּשְׁעַת הַתְּפִלָּה, וְאֵין לָנוּ עַל מִי לְהִשָּׁעֵן כִּי אִם עָלֶיךָ אָבִינוּ שֶׁבַּשָּׁמַיִם, חוּס וְרַחֵם עָלֵינוּ וְהוֹשִׁיעֵנוּ וְהַצִּילֵנוּ וּמַלְּטֵנוּ מִכָּל מִינֵי מַחֲשָׁבוֹת רָעוֹת וְהִרְהוּרִים רָעִים וְכָל מִינֵי בִּלְבּוּלִים וְעִרְבּוּב הַדַּעַת מֵעַתָּה וְעַד עוֹלָם. וְזַכֵּנוּ שֶׁתִּהְיֶה מַחֲשַׁבְתֵּנוּ זַכָּה וּנְקִיָּה וּקְדוֹשָׁה וּטְהוֹרָה תָּמִיד, וּבִפְרָט בִּשְׁעַת הַתְּפִלָּה נִזְכֶּה לְטַהֵר וּלְקַדֵּשׁ אֶת מַחֲשַׁבְתֵּנוּ בְּיוֹתֵר, עַד שֶׁלֹּא יַעֲלֶה וְלֹא יָבוֹא לְלִבֵּנוּ שׁוּם בִּלְבּוּל הַדַּעַת וְלֹא שׁוּם מַחֲשָׁבָה שֶׁאֵינָהּ מֵעִנְיַן הַתְּפִלָּה, וְלֹא תִדְמֶה עָלֵינוּ תְּפִלָּתֵנוּ כְּמַשּׂאוֹי חַס וְשָׁלוֹם, וְהוֹשִׁיעֵנוּ שֶׁנִּזְכֶּה לְהִתְפַּלֵּל לְפָנֶיךָ בְּכָל לֵב וָנֶפֶשׁ, בְּכַוָּנָה גְּדוֹלָה, בִּקְדֻשָּׁה וּבְטָהֳרָה

אֲמִירַת הַקִּינוֹת וְהַמִּזְמוֹרִים שֶׁל תִּקּוּן חֲצוֹת, וְאֶזְכֶּה לִבְלִי לְאָמְרָם עַל הֶעָבָר לְבַד, רַק אֶזְכֶּה לְכַוֵּן וְלִמְצֹא בָּהֶם כָּל מַה שֶּׁנַּעֲשָׂה עִמִּי עַכְשָׁו בִּפְרָטִיּוּת גַּם כֵּן. (תפילות ותחנונים עמ' ע"ט)

תשובה והמאור שבתורה יחזירנו למוטב

[רִבּוֹנוֹ שֶׁל עוֹלָם] הִנְנִי יָרֵא וְחָרֵד לְהַתְחִיל בְּלִמּוּד תּוֹרָה הַקְּדוֹשָׁה, כִּי פֶּה הַנִּפְגָּם בְּכָל מִינֵי פְגִימוֹת אֵיךְ יְדַבֵּר בַּתּוֹרָה הַקְּדוֹשָׁה. פֶּה דּוֹבֵר נְבָלָה אֵיךְ יְדַבֵּר בַּתּוֹרָה הַקְּדוֹשָׁה, עֵינַיִם הַנִּפְגָּמִים אֵיךְ יִסְתַּכְּלוּ בַּתּוֹרָה הַקְּדוֹשָׁה, אֹזֶן הַנִּפְגָּם בִּשְׁמִיעַת לְשׁוֹן הָרָע, וּבִשְׁאָר פְּגִימוֹת, אֵיךְ יִשְׁמַע בַּתּוֹרָה הַקְּדוֹשָׁה, רַעְיוֹן וּמַחֲשָׁבָה אֲשֶׁר נִטְמָא בְּהִרְהוּרִים רָעִים אֵיךְ יַחֲשֹׁב בַּתּוֹרָה הַקְּדוֹשָׁה, וְיָרֵאתִי אִם לֹא נֶאֱמַר עָלַי חַס וְשָׁלוֹם, וְלָרָשָׁע אָמַר אֱלֹהִים מַה לְּךָ לְסַפֵּר חֻקָּי וְגוֹ', זֶבַח רְשָׁעִים תּוֹעֵבָה. וְשֶׁמָּא, חַס וְשָׁלוֹם, אָבַד שִׂבְרִי וְתוֹחַלְתִּי מֵה', אַךְ לִבִּי אוֹמֵר לִי, מַה לְּךָ נִרְדָּם קוּם קְרָא אֶל אֱלֹהֶיךָ כִּי חָפֵץ חֶסֶד הוּא וְלֹא יַחְפֹּץ בְּמוֹת הַמֵּת כִּי אִם בְּשׁוּבוֹ מֵחַטָּאתוֹ וְחָי. וְלֹא עַל צִדְקוֹתַי אֲנִי מַפִּיל תַּחֲנוּנַי לְפָנֶיךָ ה', רַק עַל רַחֲמֶיךָ הַמְרֻבִּים, כִּי אֵל מֶלֶךְ מוֹחֵל וְסוֹלֵחַ אַתָּה וִימִינְךָ פְּשׁוּטָה לְקַבֵּל שָׁבִים. לָכֵן, יְהִי רָצוֹן מִלְּפָנֶיךָ ה' אֱלֹהַי וֵאלֹהֵי אֲבוֹתַי, שֶׁתִּתְחַתֵּר חֲתִירָה מִתַּחַת כִּסֵּא כְבוֹדֶךָ וּתְקַבֵּל אֶת תְּשׁוּבָתִי וּתְפִלָּתִי, וְתִמְחָל וְתִסְלַח לִי עַל כָּל פְּשָׁעִים וַחֲטָאִים שֶׁעָשִׂיתִי מֵעוֹדִי עַד הַיּוֹם הַזֶּה, בֵּין בְּגִלְגּוּל זֶה, בֵּין בְּגִלְגּוּל אַחֵר, וְאַל תְּשִׁיבֵנִי רֵיקָם מִלְּפָנֶיךָ, וּשְׁמַע תְּפִלָּתִי בְּרַחֲמֶיךָ הָרַבִּים, כִּי אַתָּה שׁוֹמֵעַ תְּפִלַּת כָּל פֶּה, וְשִׂימָה דִמְעָתִי בְנֹאדֶךָ. יִהְיוּ לְרָצוֹן אִמְרֵי פִי וְהֶגְיוֹן לִבִּי לְפָנֶיךָ, ה' צוּרִי וְגוֹאֲלִי: (תפלה למשה - אוצר תפלות ישראל ג, עמ' נ')

צעטיל קטן י

התמדת הלימוד ולא להפסיק באמצע הלימוד

וְעָזְרֵנוּ בְּרַחֲמֶיךָ, שֶׁנִּזְכֶּה לִלְמוֹד וְלַהֲגוֹת וּלְהַתְמִיד בְּתוֹרָתְךָ הַקְּדוֹשָׁה יוֹמָם וָלַיְלָה בִּקְדֻשָּׁה וּבְטָהֳרָה, אֲנַחְנוּ וְצֶאֱצָאֵינוּ וְצֶאֱצָאֵי צֶאֱצָאֵינוּ, וְלֹא תִשָּׁכַח הַתּוֹרָה מִפִּינוּ וּמִפִּי זַרְעֵנוּ לְעוֹלָם וִיקֻיַּם מִקְרָא שֶׁכָּתוּב: "וַאֲנִי זֹאת בְּרִיתִי אוֹתָם אָמַר יְהֹוָה, רוּחִי אֲשֶׁר עָלֶיךָ וּדְבָרַי אֲשֶׁר שַׂמְתִּי בְּפִיךָ, לֹא יָמוּשׁוּ מִפִּיךָ וּמִפִּי זַרְעֲךָ וּמִפִּי זֶרַע זַרְעֲךָ, אָמַר יְהֹוָה מֵעַתָּה וְעַד עוֹלָם": (ל"ת י"ב)

~

חצות

"זָכַרְתִּי בַלַּיְלָה שִׁמְךָ ה' וָאֶשְׁמְרָה פְּקוּדֶיךָ, חֲצוֹת לַיְלָה אָקוּם לְהוֹדוֹת לָךְ עַל מִשְׁפְּטֵי צִדְקֶךָ, קִדַּמְתִּי בַנֶּשֶׁף וָאֲשַׁוֵּעָה לִדְבָרְךָ יִחָלְתִּי. קִדְּמוּ עֵינַי אַשְׁמֻרוֹת לָשִׂיחַ בְּאִמְרָתֶךָ, קוֹלִי שָׁמְעָה אֶל תַּעְלֵם אָזְנְךָ לְרַוְחָתִי לְשַׁוְעָתִי". רִבּוֹנוֹ שֶׁל עוֹלָם, מָלֵא רַחֲמִים מָלֵא חֶסֶד, רַחֵם עָלַי וְזַכֵּנִי שֶׁאֶזְכֶּה לָקוּם בְּכָל לַיְלָה וָלַיְלָה בַּחֲצוֹת מַמָּשׁ, וְאֶזְכֶּה לְהִתְעוֹרֵר מִשְּׁנָתִי וּלְהִתְגַּבֵּר עַל יִצְרִי, לְהַתְחִיל לָשׁוּב בִּתְשׁוּבָה שְׁלֵמָה לְפָנֶיךָ, וּלְסַדֵּר תִּקּוּן חֲצוֹת בְּלֵב נִשְׁבָּר בֶּאֱמֶת וְלִקוֹנֵן עַל חֻרְבַּן בֵּית הַמִּקְדָשׁ, וְלִשְׁפֹּךְ לִבִּי כַּמַּיִם נֶגְדְּךָ עַל כָּל חֲטָאַי וּפְשָׁעַי שֶׁחָטָאתִי וּפָשַׁעְתִּי נֶגְדְּךָ מִנְּעוּרַי עַד הַיּוֹם הַזֶּה וְהֶאֱרַכְתִּי אֶת הַגָּלוּת עַל יְדֵי חֲטָאַי. וְאַתָּה תִּשְׁלַח לִי מִן הַשָּׁמַיִם דִּבְרֵי חֵן וְתַחֲנוּנִים שֶׁאֶזְכֶּה לִרְצוֹת וּלְפַיֵּס אוֹתְךָ וְאֶזְכֶּה לִמְצֹא בִּי גַּם כֵּן נְקֻדּוֹת טוֹבוֹת: (תפלות הבוקר עמ' ג')

~

וְזַכֵּנִי לוֹמַר בְּכָל יוֹם תִּקּוּן חֲצוֹת, וְאֶזְכֶּה לְפָרֵשׁ שִׂיחָתִי לְפָנֶיךָ עַל יְדֵי זֶה גַּם כֵּן, הַיְנוּ שֶׁאֶזְכֶּה לִמְצֹא אֶת עַצְמִי וְכָל אֲשֶׁר עִם לְבָבִי בְּתוֹךְ

וְלִשְׁמֹר וּלְקַיֵּם אוֹתָם, וּלְהַשְׁלִים תִּקּוּן נַפְשֵׁנוּ רוּחֵנוּ וְנִשְׁמָתֵנוּ בְּגִלְגּוּל זֶה, וְנִזְכֶּה לַחֲלוּקָא דְרַבָּנָן לֶעָתִיד לָבֹא. (בית תפלה אות ט׳)

וּתְזַכֵּנוּ לְקַיֵּם מִצְוַת צִיצִית כָּרָאוּי בְּכָל פְּרָטֶיהָ וְדִקְדּוּקֶיהָ וְכַוָּנוֹתֶיהָ, וְתַרְיָ"ג מִצְוֹת הַתְּלוּיִים בָּהּ, וְעַל יְדֵי כַּנְפֵי הַצִּיצִית הַקְּדוֹשִׁים תָּגֵן עָלֵינוּ וְתַצִּיל אוֹתָנוּ מִכָּל מִינֵי פְּגַם הַבְּרִית, וּתְזַכֵּנוּ לְהִתְקַדֵּשׁ בִּקְדֻשָּׁתְךָ תָּמִיד, וְעַל יְדֵי זֶה תַּצִּיל אוֹתָנוּ מֵעֲצַת הַנָּחָשׁ, מֵעֲצַת הַמְפַתִּים וְהַמְסִיתִים וְהַמַּדִּיחִים מִדֶּרֶךְ הָאֱמֶת, בְּכַוָּנָה לְהָרַע אוֹ שֶׁלֹּא בְּכַוָּנָה וְנִזְכֶּה לְקַבֵּל וּלְהַמְשִׁיךְ עָלֵינוּ אוֹר הַשֵּׂכֶל הָאֱמֶת שֶׁל צַדִּיקֵי אֱמֶת עַל יְדֵי שֶׁנִּזְכֶּה לְקַבֵּל וּלְקַיֵּם עֵצוֹת טוֹבוֹת וַאֲמִתִּיּוֹת שֶׁלָּהֶם וְעַל יְדֵי זֶה נִזְכֶּה לֶאֱמֶת וְלֹא יֵצֵא דְבַר שֶׁקֶר מִפִּינוּ לְעוֹלָם:
(ל״ת ז׳)

יְהִי רָצוֹן מִלְּפָנֶיךָ יְהוָֹה אֱלֹהַי וֵאלֹהֵי אֲבוֹתַי, שֶׁתְּעַזְּרֵנִי וְתוֹשִׁיעֵנִי בְּרַחֲמֶיךָ הָרַבִּים לִזְכּוֹת לְשִׂמְחָה גְּדוֹלָה בֶּאֱמֶת בַּעֲבוֹדָתְךָ, כְּמוֹ שֶׁכָּתוּב: "עִבְדוּ אֶת יְהוָֹה בְּשִׂמְחָה וְגִילוּ בִּרְעָדָה" וּתְזַכֵּנִי בְּרַחֲמֶיךָ הָרַבִּים לַעֲשׂוֹת כָּל הַמִּצְוֹת בְּשִׂמְחָה גְּדוֹלָה בֶּאֱמֶת, שֶׁיִּהְיֶה לִי שִׂמְחָה גְּדוֹלָה מֵהַמִּצְוָה בְּעַצְמָהּ, שֶׁאָגִיל וְאֶשְׂמַח מְאֹד בִּשְׁעַת עֲשִׂיַּת כָּל מִצְוָה וּמִצְוָה, בַּמֶּה שֶׁזָּכִיתִי בְּרַחֲמֶיךָ לַעֲשׂוֹת הַמִּצְוָה, וְכָל שִׂמְחָתִי יִהְיֶה רַק הַמִּצְוָה לְבַד לֹא בִּשְׁבִיל שְׂכַר עוֹלָם הַבָּא, מִכָּל שֶׁכֵּן וְכָל שֶׁכֵּן שֶׁלֹּא יַעֲלֶה בְּדַעְתִּי, חַס וְשָׁלוֹם פְּנִיּוֹת שֶׁל שְׁטוּת בִּשְׁבִיל בְּנֵי אָדָם אוֹ בִּשְׁבִיל עִסְקֵי עוֹלָם הַזֶּה, חַס וְשָׁלוֹם, רַק שֶׁאֶזְכֶּה לַעֲשׂוֹת כָּל הַמִּצְוֹת בְּשִׂמְחָה גְּדוֹלָה מֵהַמִּצְוָה בְּעַצְמָהּ וְיִהְיֶה כָּל הָעוֹלָם הַבָּא שֶׁלִּי בְּהַמִּצְוָה בְּעַצְמָהּ עַד שֶׁלֹּא אֶרְצֶה שׁוּם שְׂכַר עוֹלָם הַבָּא בִּשְׁבִיל הַמִּצְוָה, רַק שֶׁכָּל שְׂכָרִי יִהְיֶה שֶׁתְּזַכֵּנִי לַעֲשׂוֹת מִצְוָה אַחֶרֶת בִּשְׂכַר מִצְוָה זֹאת, כְּמוֹ שֶׁאָמְרוּ רַבּוֹתֵינוּ זִכְרוֹנָם לִבְרָכָה: שְׂכַר מִצְוָה מִצְוָה. (לקוטי תפילות חלק ראשון - תפילה ה)

הַבָּא עַל יְדֵי עֲוֹן לָשׁוֹן הָרָע חַס וְשָׁלוֹם, רַחֵם עָלֵינוּ לְמַעַן שְׁמֶךָ, וְעָזְרֵנוּ מֵעַתָּה לְתַקֵּן כָּל זֶה, וְתִשְׁמְרֵנוּ וְתַצִּילֵנוּ מֵעַתָּה מֵעֲוֹן לָשׁוֹן הָרָע הֶחָמוּר מְאֹד, וּמִכָּל מִינֵי פְּגַם הַדִּבּוּר, וְנִזְכֶּה לְקַדֵּשׁ אֶת דִּבּוּר פִּינוּ בְּכָל מִינֵי קְדֻשּׁוֹת: (ל"ת נ"ח)

⸻

צעטיל קטן ט

תֵּיכֶף וּמִיָּד כְּשֶׁיִּתְעוֹרֵר יֹאמַר "מוֹדֶה אֲנִי", וְיִשְׂמַח בְּקִיּוּמוֹ מִצְוַת נְטִילַת יָדַיִם וְצִיצִית

וְזַכֵּנוּ לִנְטִילַת יָדַיִם בְּכָל בֹּקֶר, עַד שֶׁנִּזְכֶּה לָשֵׂאת אֶת יָדֵינוּ אֶל לְבָבֵנוּ, אֶל אֵל שֶׁבַּשָּׁמָיִם. וַאֲקַיֵּם מִקְרָא שֶׁכָּתוּב: שְׂאוּ יְדֵיכֶם קֹדֶשׁ וּבָרְכוּ אֶת ה', שֶׁאֶזְכֶּה לְהָדִיס אֶת יָדַי וּלְטַהֲרָם, וּלְהַגְבִּיהָ כָּל הַכ"ח פְּרָקִין שֶׁל יָדַי אֶל הָרֹאשׁ שֶׁהוּא הַדַּעַת, לֵידַע שֶׁהַכֹּל בְּהַשְׁגָּחָתְךָ לְבַד וְאֵין שׁוּם דֶּרֶךְ הַטֶּבַע, וּלְהַכְנִיעַ וְלַעֲקֹר קְלִפַּת עֲמָלֵק יִמַּח שְׁמוֹ מִן הָעוֹלָם, שֶׁזֶּה עִקַּר הַכְנָעַת הַסִּטְרָא אָחֲרָא, שֶׁהֵם הָעַכּוּ"ם דְּעָלְמָא, שֶׁהַכֹּל הוּא בְּחִינַת קְלִפַּת עֲמָלֵק יִמַּח שְׁמוֹ, שֶׁהוּא מַמְשִׁיךְ חַס וְשָׁלוֹם כְּפִירוֹת בָּעוֹלָם. וְעַל יְדֵי נְטִילַת יָדַיִם נִזְכֶּה לְהַכְנִיעַ כָּל הַכְּפִירוֹת. (תפילות הבוקר עמ' מ"ג)

⸻

וִיהִי רָצוֹן מִלְּפָנֶיךָ, ה' אֱלֹהֵינוּ וֵאלֹהֵי אֲבוֹתֵינוּ, שֶׁתִּתְקַבֵּל בְּרַחֲמִים וּבְרָצוֹן מִצְוַת צִיצִית שֶׁאָנַחְנוּ מְקַיְּמִים, כְּאִלּוּ קִיַּמְנוּהָ בְּכָל פְּרָטֶיהָ וְתִקּוּנֶיהָ וְדִקְדּוּקֶיהָ, וּכְאִלּוּ נִתְכַּוֵּן בְּכָל הַכַּוָּנוֹת הָרְאוּיוֹת לְכַוֵּן, וּכְאִלּוּ קִיַּמְנוּ כָּל תרי"ג מִצְווֹת הַתְּלוּיוֹת בָּהּ. וּבְכֹחַ סְגֻלַּת מִצְוַת צִיצִית שֶׁאָנַחְנוּ נוֹתְנִים עַל אַרְבַּע כַּנְפוֹת כְּסוּתֵנוּ, נְפוּצוֹתֵינוּ קַבֵּץ מֵאַרְבַּע כַּנְפוֹת הָאָרֶץ, וְהַעֲלֵנוּ בְּשִׂמְחָה לְאַרְצֵנוּ. וְזַכֵּנוּ לִזְכֹּר כָּל מִצְווֹתֶיךָ,

צעטיל קטן ח

לקצר בדיבורו

רִבּוֹנוֹ שֶׁל עוֹלָם, יְהִי רָצוֹן מִלְפָנֶיךָ אֵל רַחוּם וְחַנּוּן, שֶׁתְּזַכֵּנִי הַיּוֹם וּבְכָל יוֹם לִשְׁמֹר פִּי וּלְשׁוֹנִי מִלָּשׁוֹן הָרַע וּרְכִילוּת וּמְקַבְּלָתָם, וְאֶהְיֶה זָהִיר מִלְּדַבֵּר אֲפִלּוּ עַל אִישׁ יְחִידִי, וְכָל שֶׁכֵּן מִלְּדַבֵּר לָשׁוֹן הָרַע עַל כְּלַל יִשְׂרָאֵל אוֹ חֵלֶק מֵהֶם, שֶׁעֲווֹנוֹ חָמוּר מְאֹד, וְכָל שֶׁכֵּן לְהִזָּהֵר מִלְּהִתְרָעֵם עַל מִדּוֹתָיו שֶׁל הַקָּדוֹשׁ בָּרוּךְ הוּא, שֶׁהוּא עָוֹן חָמוּר יוֹתֵר מִן הַכֹּל, וְלֹא לְדַבֵּר דִּבְרֵי שֶׁקֶר, חֲנֻפָּה, מַחֲלֹקֶת, כַּעַס, גַּאֲוָה, אוֹנָאַת דְּבָרִים, הַלְבָּנַת פָּנִים, לֵיצָנוּת, וְכָל דְּבָרִים אֲסוּרִים, וְלֹא לֵישֵׁב בֵּין לֵיצָנִים, וְלֹא לְהִתְגָּאוֹת וְלֹא לִכְעֹס אֲפִלּוּ בַּלֵּב, וְלֹא לַחֲשֹׁב רָעַת אִישׁ יִשְׂרָאֵל. וְזַכֵּנִי, שֶׁלֹּא לְדַבֵּר כִּי אִם דָּבָר הַצָּרִיךְ לְעִנְיְנֵי גוּפִי וְנַפְשִׁי, וְיִהְיוּ כָּל מַעֲשַׂי, דִּבּוּרַי וּמַחְשְׁבוֹתַי לְשֵׁם שָׁמַיִם. אָבִי שֶׁבַּשָּׁמַיִם, זַכֵּנִי הַיּוֹם וּבְכָל יוֹם לִשְׁמֹר אָזְנַי וְעֵינַי מִשְּׁמִיעַת וּקְרִיאַת לָשׁוֹן הָרַע וּרְכִילוּת, דִּבְרֵי מַחֲלֹקֶת, דְּבָרִים בְּטֵלִים, וְכָל דְּבָרִים אֲסוּרִים, וְכָל מַה שֶּׁשָּׁמַעְתִּי וְקָרָאתִי דְּבָרִים שֶׁלֹּא כִרְצוֹנֶךָ, עָזְרֵנִי נָא שֶׁיִּהְיוּ נִשְׁכָּחִים מִמֶּנִּי. וְזַכֵּנִי, שֶׁאֲפִלּוּ בְּשׁוֹגֵג וְשֶׁלֹּא בְּמִתְכַּוֵּן, וַאֲפִלּוּ עַל יְדֵי אֹנֶס, לֹא אֶשְׁמַע וְלֹא אֶקְרָא דָּבָר שֶׁאֵינוֹ הָגוּן, וְיִהְיוּ אָזְנַי וְעֵינַי מְקֻדָּשׁוֹת, שׁוֹמְעוֹת וְרוֹאוֹת כִּי אִם דְּבַר מִצְוָה (מהחפץ חיים זצ"ל - ספר עצה ותושיה אות ח')

~

אֱלֹהַי נְצוֹר לְשׁוֹנִי מֵרָע וּשְׂפָתַי מִדַּבֵּר מִרְמָה, וְתִהְיֶה בְּעֶזְרֵנוּ שֶׁלֹּא יַזִּיק לָנוּ פְּגַם הַדִּבּוּר וְהַלָּשׁוֹן הָרַע שֶׁל בְּנֵי הָעוֹלָם, שֶׁלֹּא נִהְיֶה נִלְכָּדִים בַּגְּאוֹנָם עַל יְדֵי חַטָּאת פִּיהֶם חַס וְשָׁלוֹם וּמֵעַתָּה תַּעֲזֹר לָנוּ וּלְכָל יִשְׂרָאֵל שֶׁנִּהְיֶה נִשְׁמָרִים מִפְּגַם הַדִּבּוּר, וְנִזְכֶּה כֻּלָּנוּ לְקַדֵּשׁ אֶת פִּינוּ תָּמִיד בִּקְדֻשָּׁה גְדוֹלָה, וְתִשְׁמְרֵנוּ מִגֵּאוּת וּגְדֻלּוֹת, וְתַעֲלֶה אֶת הַשְּׁכִינָה מִגָּלוּתָהּ אֲשֶׁר יָרְדָה בְּגָלוּת גָּדוֹל עַל יְדֵי פְּגַם הַגַּאֲוָה

וְתַחֲרוּת. רוּחַ מִינוּת. רוּחַ גַּסּוּת הָרוּחַ. רוּחַ שְׁמָדוֹת. כֻּלָּם יִתְרַחֲקוּ וְיִתְבָּעֲרוּ מִמֶּנִּי, אָמֵן נֶצַח סֶלָה וָעֶד. (שומר ישראל עמ' ש"כ)

צעטיל קטן ז

לבטל הסתכלות רעה

וְזַכֵּנוּ לִשְׁמֹר אֶת עֵינֵינוּ מִכָּל מִינֵי הִסְתַּכְּלוּת רָעִים רַחֲמָנָא לִיצְּלַן, רַק נִזְכֶּה לְהִסְתַּכֵּל בָּהֶם הִסְתַּכְּלוּת דִּקְדֻשָּׁה לְבַד, כִּי כְּבָר גִּלִּיתָ לָנוּ שֶׁהָעֵינַיִם שֶׁל יִשְׂרָאֵל הֵם דְּבָרִים עֶלְיוֹנִים גְּבוֹהִים וְרָמִים מְאֹד מְאֹד, וְהֵם רוֹאִים תָּמִיד דְּבָרִים גְּדוֹלִים וְנוֹרָאִים, וְאִם הָיָה הָאָדָם זוֹכֶה לְעֵינַיִם כְּשֵׁרִים הָיָה יוֹדֵעַ דְּבָרִים גְּדוֹלִים רַק מִמַּה שֶּׁעֵינָיו רוֹאוֹת, עַל כֵּן זַכֵּנוּ נָא לִשְׁמֹר אֶת עֵינֵינוּ וּלְקַדְּשָׁם בְּתַכְלִית הַקְּדֻשָּׁה, וְנִזְכֶּה לִרְאוֹת בָּהֶם דְּבָרִים נִפְלָאִים וְנוֹרָאִים. (תפילות ותחנונים עמ' נ"ט)

[אָנָּא ה'] תַּצִּילֵנִי מִפְּגַם הָרְאוּת, וּתְקַדֵּשׁ אֶת עֵינַי תָּמִיד וְלֹא אֶסְתַּכֵּל עוֹד בְּשׁוּם דְּבַר הַפּוֹגֵם אֶת הָרְאוּת, רַק אֶזְכֶּה לְהִסְתַּכֵּל בְּעֵינַי בְּתוֹרָתֶךָ, וּלְהִסְתַּכֵּל עַל צַדִּיקֶיךָ הָאֲמִתִּיִּים וְעַל כָּל הַדְּבָרִים הַמְקַדְּשִׁין אֶת הָעֵינַיִם, עַד שֶׁיִּהְיוּ עֵינַי קְדוֹשִׁים וּטְהוֹרִים תָּמִיד בֶּאֱמֶת לַאֲמִתּוֹ, וְאֶזְכֶּה לְתַקֵּן מְהֵרָה אֶת כָּל הַפְּגָמִים שֶׁפָּגַמְתִּי בְּעֵינַי, וְתַעַזְרֵנִי בְּרַחֲמֶיךָ וְתִשְׁמְרֵנִי מִקִּלְקוּל חוּשׁ הָרְאוּת חַס וְשָׁלוֹם, וְלֹא יִכְהֶה מְאוֹר עֵינַי לְעוֹלָם "וְגַם עַד זִקְנָה וְשֵׂיבָה אַל תַּעַזְבֵנִי" וְתִשְׁמֹר אֶת אוֹר עֵינַי תָּמִיד, לְמַעַן אֶזְכֶּה לַהֲגוֹת בְּתוֹרָתְךָ יוֹמָם וָלַיְלָה, וְלֹא אֶתֵּן שֵׁנָה לְעֵינַי וְלֹא יַגִּיעַ לִי עַל יְדֵי זֶה שׁוּם הֶזֵּק וּמִחוּשׁ לְעֵינַי וְיִהְיוּ עֵינַי מְאִירוֹת כַּשֶּׁמֶשׁ וְכַיָּרֵחַ: (ל"ת נ"א)

יִהְיֶה רַק בְּךָ וּבַעֲבוֹדָתֶךָ, וְנִזְכֶּה לִהְיוֹת זְרִיזִים בַּעֲבוֹדָתְךָ בְּתַכְלִית הַזְּרִיזוּת, וְלִהְיוֹת שְׂמֵחִים וְטוֹבֵי לֵב תָּמִיד שֶׁלֹּא תִּפֹּל עָלֵינוּ שׁוּם עֲצָלוּת וְעַצְבוּת לְעוֹלָם, רַק נְגִילָה וְנִשְׂמְחָה בָּךְ וְנִזְכֶּה לַעֲבֹד אֶת יְהֹוָה בְּשִׂמְחָה וּבְטוּב לֵבָב מֵרֹב כֹּל, וְלִהְיוֹת בְּשִׂמְחָה תָּמִיד: (ל"ת ד')

צעטיל קטן ו

לבטל מחשבה רעה

רִבּוֹנוֹ שֶׁל עוֹלָם, צוֹפֶה בְּעֶלְבּוֹן אֲנוּחִים, תִּיקַר נָא נַפְשִׁי הָאֻמְלָלָה בְּעֵינֶיךָ, וַחֲמֹל עָלַי בְּחֶמְלָתְךָ וַחֲנִינוֹתֶיךָ, וְעָזְרֵנִי וְסַיְּעֵנִי וְחַזְּקֵנִי וְאַמְּצֵנִי, וְקַדְּשֵׁנִי בִּקְדֻשָּׁתְךָ הָעֶלְיוֹנָה, שֶׁיִּמְשֹׁךְ עָלַי קְדֻשָּׁה וְטָהֳרָה מֵאִתְּךָ, בְּאֹפֶן שֶׁאֶזְכֶּה מֵעַתָּה לִשְׁמֹר עַצְמִי שֶׁלֹּא אַנִּיחַ לְכַנֵּס כְּלָל לְתוֹךְ מַחֲשַׁבְתִּי שׁוּם מַחֲשֶׁבֶת חוּץ שֶׁבָּעוֹלָם, וְלֹא שׁוּם בִּלְבּוּל הַדַּעַת וּמִכָּל שֶׁכֵּן וְכָל שֶׁכֵּן שֶׁלֹּא אֲהַרְהֵר בְּשׁוּם הִרְהוּר בָּעוֹלָם כְּלָל, רַק מַחֲשַׁבְתִּי תִּהְיֶה קְדוֹשָׁה תָּמִיד, זַכָּה וּנְקִיָּה מִכָּל סִיג וּפְסֹלֶת: (ל"ת ה')

קָרָאתִי בְכָל לֵב עֲנֵנִי יְיָ חֻקֶּיךָ אֶצֹּרָה: קְרָאתִיךָ הוֹשִׁיעֵנִי וְאֶשְׁמְרָה עֵדֹתֶיךָ: קִדַּמְתִּי בַנֶּשֶׁף וָאֲשַׁוֵּעָה לִדְבָרְךָ יִחָלְתִּי: קִדְּמוּ עֵינַי אַשְׁמֻרוֹת לָשִׂיחַ בְּאִמְרָתֶךָ: קוֹלִי שִׁמְעָה כְחַסְדֶּךָ יְיָ כְּמִשְׁפָּטֶךָ חַיֵּנִי: קָרְבוּ רֹדְפֵי זִמָּה מִתּוֹרָתְךָ רָחָקוּ: קָרוֹב אַתָּה יְיָ וְכָל מִצְוֹתֶיךָ אֱמֶת: קֶדֶם יָדַעְתִּי מֵעֵדֹתֶיךָ כִּי לְעוֹלָם יְסַדְתָּם: יְהִי רָצוֹן מִלְּפָנֶיךָ יְיָ אֱלֹהַי וֵאלֹהֵי אֲבוֹתַי, שֶׁתַּרְחִיק מִמֶּנִּי יֵצֶר הָרַע שֶׁל רוּחַ זְנוּנִים. רוּחַ מַחֲשָׁבוֹת רָעוֹת וְהִרְהוּרִים רָעִים. רוּחַ שְׂחוֹק. רוּחַ דְּבָרִים בְּטֵלִים. רוּחַ יְגוֹנוֹת. רוּחַ אֲנָחוֹת. רוּחַ שֶׁקֶר. רוּחַ תּוֹעָה. רוּחַ מַשְׁחִית. רוּחַ חַבָּלָה. רוּחַ קֶטֶב מְרִירִי. רוּחַ אֵשׁ שֶׁל עֲצָמוֹת. רוּחַ תַּזְזִית. רוּחַ טֻמְאָה. רוּחַ עִוְעִים. רוּחַ חֲצִיצִית. רוּחַ בָּא מִן הַנְּפִילִים. רוּחַ חֵמָה וָכַעַס. רוּחַ קִנְאָה

יָדַעְתִּי יְהֹוָה כִּי בַעַר אָנֹכִי, וַאֲנִי רֵיק וְחָסֵר מִכָּל אֵלּוּ הַדְּבָרִים, "כִּי בַעַר אָנֹכִי מֵאִישׁ וְלֹא בִינַת אָדָם לִי", וְאֵין לִי שׁוּם כֹּחַ וּגְבוּרָה בַּגּוּף וָנֶפֶשׁ, וּבֵיתִי רֵיקָן מֵעֲשִׁירוּת, וְאֵין בְּיָדִי לֹא חָכְמָה וְלֹא גְבוּרָה וְלֹא עֲשִׁירוּת גַּשְׁמִית וְלֹא עֲשִׁירוּת רוּחָנִית שֶׁל מַעֲשִׂים טוֹבִים. (ל"ת י"ד)

עצלות

וְאֶזְכֶּה עַל יְדֵי הַזְּרִיזוּת לְהַחֲיוֹת אֶת מֹחִי וְנִשְׁמָתִי, וּלְמַעֵט בְּשֵׁנָה שֶׁהוּא עַל יְדֵי עַצְלוּת, רַק אֶזְדָּרֵז בַּעֲבוֹדָתְךָ תָּמִיד, וְכָל מַה שֶּׁאוּכַל לַחְטֹף תּוֹרָה וְאֵיזֶה מִצְוָה, אֶזְכֶּה לַעֲשׂוֹתָהּ תֵּכֶף בְּלִי שׁוּם דְּחוּי וְעַצְלוּת כְּלָל. וְאֵדַע כִּי אֵין שׁוּם זְמַן כְּלָל, כִּי עִקַּר הַשְׁגָּחַת הַשֵּׁם יִתְבָּרַךְ הוּא עַל יְדֵי שֶׁיּוֹדְעִין שֶׁהַשֵּׁם יִתְבָּרַךְ הוּא לְמַעְלָה מִן הַזְּמַן וּמֵהַמָּקוֹם, וְהוּא מַשְׁגִּיחַ עַל כָּל הָעוֹלָם בְּהַשְׁגָּחָתוֹ יִתְבָּרַךְ וְאֵין שׁוּם דֶּרֶךְ הַטֶּבַע כְּלָל, וְעַל יְדֵי זֶה אֶזְכֶּה לְקִיּוּם הַדַּעַת וְהַמֹּחַ. וְעַל יְדֵי אֱמוּנָה שֶׁאַאֲמִין בְּכָל זֶה, אֶזְכֶּה שֶׁתַּעֲשֶׂה עִמָּנוּ נִסִּים וְנִפְלָאוֹת שֶׁלֹּא כְּדֶרֶךְ הַטֶּבַע כְּלָל, וּלְהַמְשִׁיךְ הַשְׁגָּחָתְךָ הַשְּׁלֵמָה מִבְּחִינַת עָלְמָא דְאָתֵי. (תפילות הבוקר עמ' מ"ח)

[אָנָּא ה'] שֶׁנִּזְכֶּה בְּרַחֲמֶיךָ וַחֲסָדֶיךָ הָרַבִּים לְהִתְקָרֵב לְצַדִּיקֵי אֱמֶת וְלִרְאוֹת אוֹר פְּנֵיהֶם הַמְּאִירִים, וְעַל יְדֵי זֶה תְּזַכֵּנוּ בְּרַחֲמֶיךָ הָרַבִּים לְהַצִּיל נַפְשֵׁנוּ הָאֻמְלָלָה מִן הַקּוֹצִים וּמִן הַפְּתָחִים שֶׁהֵם הַתַּאֲווֹת רָעוֹת וַעֲצָבוּת וְעַצְלוּת וְתוֹלְדוֹתֵיהֶם, וְעַל יְדֵי שֶׁתְּזַכֵּנוּ לִרְאוֹת פְּנֵי הַמְּאִירוֹת שֶׁל צַדִּיקֵי אֱמֶת וּלְהִתְקָרֵב אֲלֵיהֶם, עַל יְדֵי זֶה, תַּצִּיל נַפְשׁוֹתֵינוּ מִן הַמִּדּוֹת רָעוֹת הָאֵלּוּ, וְנִזְכֶּה בַּחֲסָדֶיךָ לְסַלֵּק וּלְשַׁבֵּר כָּל הַתַּאֲווֹת מֵאִתָּנוּ, שֶׁלֹּא יִהְיֶה לָנוּ שׁוּם תַּאֲוָה וּתְשׁוּקָה לְשׁוּם דָּבָר שֶׁבָּעוֹלָם כִּי-אִם אֵלֶיךָ, וְכָל תַּאֲוָתֵנוּ וּתְשׁוּקָתֵנוּ וְחֶפְצֵנוּ וּרְצוֹנֵנוּ

לְמַדְרֵגָה תַּעֲלֵנוּ, שֶׁנִּזְכֶּה לָבוֹא לְמַעֲלַת אֲבוֹתֵינוּ הַקְּדוֹשִׁים אַבְרָהָם יִצְחָק וְיַעֲקֹב, וּזְכוּתָם יַעֲמֹד לָנוּ שֶׁתִּשְׁמַע בְּקוֹל תְּפִלָּתֵנוּ שֶׁנִּהְיֶה תָּמִיד נֶעֱנִים בְּעֵת שֶׁנִּתְפַּלֵּל אֵלֶיךָ עָלֵינוּ אוֹ עַל שׁוּם אֶחָד מֵעַמְּךָ יִשְׂרָאֵל, עַל יָחִיד אוֹ עַל רַבִּים, וְתִשְׂמַח וְתִתְפָּאֵר בָּנוּ, וְנַעֲשֶׂה פְּרִי לְמַעְלָה וְשֹׁרֶשׁ לְמַטָּה: (מתפלת הרבי ר' אלימלך זצוק"ל)

⁂

וְיַחֵד לְבָבֵנוּ לְאַהֲבָה וּלְיִרְאָה אֶת שְׁמֶךָ, וְרִשְׁפֵּי הִתְעוֹרְדוּת אַהֲבָתְךָ וְיִרְאָתְךָ וְהִרְהוּרֵי תְּשׁוּבָה יַתְמִידוּ וְיִתְרַבּוּ בָּנוּ בְּלִי הֶפְסֵק, וְנִהְיֶה דְּבֵקִים בְּךָ תָּדִיר. וְזַכֵּנוּ לְהִתְרַחֵק מִכָּל הַמִּדּוֹת הָרָעוֹת וְהָאֲסוּרוֹת, וּבִפְרָט מֵהַגַּאֲוָה וְהַכַּעַס וְהַקַּפְּדָנוּת וְכָל גָּבְהַּ לֵב. וְנַכְנִיעַ מְעַט עָרְכֵּנוּ, וְנַפְשֵׁנוּ כֶּעָפָר לַכֹּל תִּהְיֶה, וּתְאַזְּרֵנוּ חַיִל לִשְׁמֹר לְפִינוּ מַחְסוֹם מֵחֲטֹא בִלְשׁוֹנֵנוּ. הַעֲבֵר עֵינֵינוּ מֵרְאוֹת שָׁוְא וְלִבַּב עִקֵּשׁ יָסוּר מִמֶּנּוּ, וְאַל יְעַרְבְּבוּנוּ מַחֲשָׁבוֹת זָרוֹת וְהִרְהוּרִים רָעִים, רַק נִהְיֶה דְּבֵקִים בְּךָ תָּדִיר. וּתְזַכֵּנוּ לְהִתְרַחֵק מִן הָעַצְלוּת וּמִן הָעַצְבוּת, וְנִהְיֶה שְׂמֵחִים בְּמִצְוֹתֶיךָ וּשְׂמֵחִים בְּחֶלְקֵנוּ, וְיִהְיֶה בִּטְחוֹנֵנוּ בְּךָ תָּדִיר, וְנִהְיֶה זְרִיזִים בַּעֲבוֹדָתֶךָ, וְתִהְיֶה עִם לְבָבֵנוּ בְּעֵת מַחֲשְׁבוֹתֵינוּ וְעִם פִּינוּ בְּעֵת דִּבּוּרֵנוּ וְעִם יָדֵינוּ בְּעֵת מַעֲבָדֵנוּ. וְתַקְּנֵנוּ מַלְכֵּנוּ בְּעֵצָה טוֹבָה מִלְּפָנֶיךָ, לְמַעַן נֵלֵךְ בְּדֶרֶךְ טוֹבִים וְאָרְחוֹת צַדִּיקִים נִשְׁמֹר, וְנַעֲשֶׂה הַטּוֹב וְהַיָּשָׁר בְּעֵינֵי אֱלֹהִים וְאָדָם. (בית תפלה אות ה')

⁂

[אָנָּא ה' זַכֵּנִי שֶׁאֶזְכֶּה] לִבְלִי לָסוּר מֵרְצוֹנְךָ וּמִמִּצְוֹתֶיךָ יָמִין וּשְׂמֹאל מֵעַתָּה וְעַד עוֹלָם וְאֶזְכֶּה בְּרַחֲמֶיךָ הָרַבִּים לְשַׁבֵּר וּלְבַטֵּל מִדַּת הַגַּאֲוָה בְּתַכְלִית, מֵעָלַי וּמֵעַל גְּבוּלִי, וְלֹא יַעֲלֶה בְּלִבִּי שׁוּם צַד גֵּאוּת וְגַבְהוּת בָּעוֹלָם כְּלָל מִכָּל הַדְּבָרִים שֶׁדֶּרֶךְ בְּנֵי אָדָם לְהִתְגַּדֵּל בָּהֶם הֵן בְּחָכְמָה וּמַעֲשִׂים טוֹבִים, וְהֵן בִּגְבוּרָה וְהֵן בַּעֲשִׁירוּת בַּכֹּל אֶזְכֶּה לִהְיוֹת עָנָו וְשָׁפָל בֶּאֱמֶת לְבַל אֶתְגָּאֶה וְאֶתְגַּדֵּל בָּהֶם כְּלָל אִם אָמְנָם

לְשֵׁם יִחוּד קֻדְשָׁא בְּרִיךְ הוּא וּשְׁכִינְתֵּיהּ בִּדְחִילוּ וּרְחִימוּ לְיַחֵד שֵׁם י"ה בּו"ה בְּיִחוּדָא שְׁלִים בְּשֵׁם כָּל יִשְׂרָאֵל הֲרֵינִי עוֹשֶׂה מִצְוָה זוֹ לְתַקֵּן אֶת שָׁרְשָׁהּ בְּמָקוֹם עֶלְיוֹן בְּשִׁעוּר קוֹמָה בְּכָל פְּרָטֶיהָ וְתִקּוּנֶיהָ וְדִקְדּוּקֶיהָ לַעֲשׂוֹת כַּוָּנַת יוֹצְרִי שֶׁצִּוַּנִי לַעֲשׂוֹת מִצְוָה זוֹ לָתֵת נַחַת רוּחַ וּלְהָקִים הַשְּׁכִינָה וּלְהָקִים סֻכַּת דָּוִד לְהַחֲזִיר עֲטָרָה לְיוֹשְׁנָהּ וְלִגְרוֹם שֶׁפַע וּבְרָכָה רַבָּה בְּכָל הָעוֹלָמוֹת וּלְתַקֵּן כָּל הַנִּיצוֹצוֹת שֶׁנָּפְלוּ תּוֹךְ הַקְּלִיפּוֹת בֵּין עַל יְדֵי וּבֵין עַל יְדֵי שְׁאָר עַמְּךָ יִשְׂרָאֵל וּלְתַקֵּן כָּל הַתַּרְיָ"ג מִצְוֹת הַכְּלוּלִים בְּמִצְוָה זוֹ לִגְרוֹם זִוּוּג בְּאַרְבַּע אוֹתִיּוֹת שֵׁם הַקּוֹדֶשׁ וּלְזַכֵּךְ נַפְשִׁי וְרוּחִי וְנִשְׁמָתִי שֶׁיִּהְיוּ רְאוּיִים לְעוֹרֵר מַיִן נוּקְבִין עַל יְדֵי מִצְוָה זֹאת. וְאַל יְעַכֵּב שׁוּם חֵטְא וְעָווֹן וְהִרְהוּר רַע אֶת הַמִּצְוָה הַזֹּאת וְתַעֲלֶה לְרָצוֹן לִפְנֵי מִי שֶׁצִּוָּה אוֹתָהּ לְעוֹרֵר אַהֲבַת דּוֹדִים. וִיזַכֶּה אוֹתָנוּ לְקַיֵּם מִצְוָה זֹאת בְּלֵב שָׁלֵם וַחֲשִׁיקוּת גָּדוֹל וּבְשִׂמְחָה גְדוֹלָה בְּלִי שׁוּם פְּנִיָּה וְגַסּוּת רוּחַ וְשׁוּם מַחֲשָׁבָה זָרָה וְלַעֲשׂוֹתָהּ בְּכָל דִּקְדּוּקֶיהָ כְּפִי דִין תּוֹרָתְךָ הַקְּדוֹשָׁה הַכֹּל כִּרְצוֹנְךָ הַטּוֹב. יִהְיוּ לְרָצוֹן אִמְרֵי פִי וְהֶגְיוֹן לִבִּי לְפָנֶיךָ יְיָ צוּרִי וְגוֹאֲלִי: (הובא בס' משפט צדק על תהלים)

צעטיל קטן ה

לבטל הרגלים של מדות רעות

גאוה

וְתִשְׁמְרֵנוּ מִן הַפְּנִיּוֹת וְהַגֵּאוּת וּמִן הַכַּעַס וְהַקַּפְּדָנוּת וְהָעַצְבוּת וְהָרְכִילוּת וּשְׁאָר מִדּוֹת רָעוֹת, וּמִכָּל דָּבָר הַמַּפְסִיד עֲבוֹדָתְךָ הַקְּדוֹשָׁה וְהַטְּהוֹרָה הַחֲבִיבָה עָלֵינוּ, וְתַשְׁפִּיעַ רוּחַ קָדְשְׁךָ עָלֵינוּ שֶׁנִּהְיֶה דְבֵקִים בָּךְ. וְשֶׁנִּשְׁתּוֹקֵק תָּמִיד אֵלֶיךָ יוֹתֵר וְיוֹתֵר, וּמִמַּדְרֵגָה

צעטיל קטן ד

לְשֵׁם יִחוּד קוּדְשָׁא בְּרִיךְ הוּא וְכוּ'

וּתְזַכֵּנוּ אָבִינוּ שֶׁבַּשָּׁמַיִם אֵל מָלֵא רַחֲמִים, שֶׁנְּיַחֵד אֶת לְבָבֵנוּ וּמַחְשְׁבוֹתֵינוּ וְדִבּוּרֵנוּ וּמַעֲשֵׂינוּ וְכָל תְּנוּעוֹתֵינוּ וְהַרְגָּשׁוֹתֵינוּ, הַיְדוּעוֹת לָנוּ וְשֶׁאֵינָן יְדוּעוֹת לָנוּ, הַנִּגְלוֹת וְהַנִּסְתָּרוֹת, שֶׁיְּהֵא הַכֹּל מְיֻחָד אֵלֶיךָ בֶּאֱמֶת וּבְתָמִים בְּלִי שׁוּם מַחֲשֶׁבֶת פְּסוּל חָלִילָה, וְטַהֵר לִבֵּנוּ וְקַדְּשֵׁנוּ, וּזְרֹק עָלֵינוּ מַיִם טְהוֹרִים וְטַהֲרֵנוּ בְּאַהֲבָתְךָ וּבְחֶמְלָתְךָ, וְתִטַּע אַהֲבָתְךָ וְיִרְאָתְךָ בְּלִבֵּנוּ תָּמִיד בְּלִי הֶפְסֵק רֶגַע, בְּכָל עֵת וּבְכָל זְמַן וּבְכָל מָקוֹם, בְּלֶכְתֵּנוּ וּבְשִׁבְתֵּנוּ, בְּשָׁכְבֵנוּ וּבְקוּמֵנוּ תְּבַעֵר תָּמִיד רוּחַ קָדְשְׁךָ בְּקִרְבֵּנוּ. וְנִשָּׁעֲנִים תָּמִיד בְּךָ וּבִגְדֻלָּתְךָ וּבְאַהֲבָתְךָ וּבְיִרְאָתְךָ. וּבְתוֹרָתְךָ שֶׁבִּכְתָב וְשֶׁבְּעַל פֶּה הַנִּגְלָה וְהַנִּסְתָּר וּבְמִצְוֹתֶיךָ, הַכֹּל לְיַחֵד שִׁמְךָ הַגִּבּוֹר וְהַנּוֹרָא: (מתפילת הרבי ר' אלימלך זצוק"ל)

~

לְשֵׁם יִחוּד קֻדְשָׁא בְּרִיךְ הוּא וּשְׁכִינְתֵּהּ בִּדְחִילוּ וּרְחִימוּ וּרְחִימוּ וּדְחִילוּ לְיַחֲדָא שֵׁם י"ה בּו"ה בְּיִחוּדָא שְׁלִים בְּשֵׁם כָּל יִשְׂרָאֵל. הֲרֵינִי מְקַבֵּל עָלַי אֱלֹהוּתוֹ יִתְבָּרֵךְ וְיִרְאָתוֹ וְאַהֲבָתוֹ, וְהִנְנִי עֶבֶד לְהַשֵּׁם יִתְבָּרֵךְ. וַהֲרֵינִי מְקַיֵּם מִצְוַת "וְאָהַבְתָּ לְרֵעֲךָ כָּמוֹךָ", וַהֲרֵינִי אוֹהֵב אֶת כָּל אָדָם מִיִּשְׂרָאֵל כְּנַפְשִׁי, וַהֲרֵינִי מְכַוֵּן לְקַיֵּם מִצְוַת תַּלְמוּד תּוֹרָה וּמִצְוַת צִיצִית וּתְפִלִּין, וַהֲרֵינִי מוּכָן לְקַיֵּם מִצְוַת קְרִיאַת שְׁמַע וּתְפִלַּת שַׁחֲרִית, הֵם וְהַמִּצְוֹת הַנִּגְלוֹת הַכְּלוּלוֹת בָּהֶם [וְכֵן כָּל הַמִּצְוֹת]. וַאֲנִי מְכַוֵּן בַּכֹּל לַעֲשׂוֹת נַחַת רוּחַ לְיוֹצְרֵנוּ שֶׁלֹּא עַל מְנָת לְקַבֵּל פְּרָס בְּשׁוּם צַד, וַאֲנִי מְכַוֵּן בַּכֹּל לְדַעַת רַשְׁבַּ"י הַקָּדוֹשׁ. וַהֲרֵינִי מְקַבֵּל עָלַי כָּל תַּרְיַ"ג מִצְוֹת דְּאוֹרַיְתָא וּמִצְוֹת דְּרַבָּנָן, הֵם וְעַנְפֵיהֶם, וְאַתָּה הָאֵל הַטּוֹב בְּרֹב רַחֲמֶיךָ תַּצִּילֵנוּ מִיֵּצֶר הָרָע וּתְזַכֵּנוּ לְעָבְדְּךָ בֶּאֱמֶת, כֵּן יְהִי רָצוֹן אָמֵן. וִיהִי נֹעַם אֲדֹנָי אֱלֹהֵינוּ עָלֵינוּ וּמַעֲשֵׂה יָדֵינוּ כּוֹנְנָה עָלֵינוּ וּמַעֲשֵׂה יָדֵינוּ כּוֹנְנֵהוּ: (כף אחת עמ' ר"כ)

צעטיל קטן ג

כוונת "ונקדשתי" כנזכר לעיל בשעת אכילה

וְעָזְרֵנוּ וּתְזַכֵּנוּ לְהִתְקַדֵּשׁ בִּקְדֻשָּׁה גְדוֹלָה, כָּרָאוּי לְיִשְׂרָאֵל עַמְּךָ הַקָּדוֹשׁ, אֲשֶׁר בָּהֶם בָּחַרְתָּ בְּאַהֲבָה, וְתִהְיֶה עִמָּנוּ תָּמִיד, וְתוֹשִׁיעֵנוּ וְתַעְזְרֵנוּ, שֶׁנִּזְכֶּה לְקַדֵּשׁ עַצְמֵנוּ בַּמֻּתָּר לָנוּ. וְנִזְכֶּה לְשַׁבֵּר נֶפֶשׁ הַמִּתְאַוָּה שֶׁבְּקִרְבֵּנוּ. וְנִזְכֶּה לַעֲלוֹת בְּכָל פַּעַם מִקְּדֻשָּׁה לִקְדֻשָּׁה עֶלְיוֹנָה, עַד שֶׁנִּזְכֶּה לְהִכָּלֵל בִּקְדֻשָּׁתְךָ הָעֶלְיוֹנָה, כִּרְצוֹנְךָ הַטּוֹב, בֶּאֱמֶת. (ספר קדושה - אוצר תפלות ישראל ג, עמ' רכ"א)

~

הֲרֵינִי בָא לֶאֱכֹל וְלִשְׁתּוֹת, כְּדֵי שֶׁיְּהֵא גוּפִי בָּרִיא וְחָזָק לַעֲבוֹדָתוֹ יִתְבָּרֵךְ שְׁמוֹ, וַאֲנִי מוּכָן לְקַיֵּם מִצְוַת לְבָרֵךְ בִּרְכוֹת הַנֶּהֱנִין, תְּחִלָּה וָסוֹף, עַל כָּל מַה שֶּׁאֹכַל וְאֶשְׁתֶּה, וּכְשֶׁאֹכַל פַּת, לְקַיֵּם מִצְוַת נְטִילַת יָדַיִם וּבִרְכָתָהּ, וּמִצְוַת לְבָרֵךְ בִּרְכַּת הַמּוֹצִיא וְלִטְבֹּל פְּרוּסַת הַמּוֹצִיא בְּמֶלַח שָׁלֹשׁ פְּעָמִים, וְלוֹמַר דִּבְרֵי תוֹרָה עַל הַשֻּׁלְחָן, וְלִטֹּל מַיִם אַחֲרוֹנִים, וּלְבָרֵךְ בִּרְכַּת הַמָּזוֹן, הַכֹּל כַּאֲשֶׁר לַכֹּל לַעֲשׂוֹת נַחַת רוּחַ לְיוֹצְרֵנוּ וּלְתַקֵּן הַדְּבָרִים בְּשָׁרְשָׁם לְמַעְלָה בַּמָּקוֹם עֶלְיוֹן. וִיהִי נֹעַם אֲדֹנָי אֱלֹהֵינוּ עָלֵינוּ, וּמַעֲשֵׂה יָדֵינוּ כּוֹנְנָה עָלֵינוּ, וּמַעֲשֵׂה יָדֵינוּ כּוֹנְנֵהוּ. (בית תפלה אות ג')

~

יְהִי רָצוֹן מִלְּפָנֶיךָ יְהֹוָה אֱלֹהַי וֵאלֹהֵי אֲבוֹתַי, שֶׁתִּהְיֶה בְּעֶזְרִי וְתוֹשִׁיעֵנִי בְּרַחֲמֶיךָ הָרַבִּים וּבַחֲסָדֶיךָ הָעֲצוּמִים, וּתְזַכֵּנִי לְשַׁבֵּר תַּאֲוַת אֲכִילָה לְגַמְרֵי, שֶׁאֶזְכֶּה שֶׁתִּהְיֶה אֲכִילָתִי וּשְׁתִיָּתִי בִּקְדֻשָּׁה וּבְטָהֳרָה גְדוֹלָה, בְּעִתּוֹ וּבִזְמַנּוֹ "בַּמִּדָּה וּבַמִּשְׁקָל וּבַמְּשׂוּרָה", כִּרְצוֹנְךָ הַטּוֹב בֶּאֱמֶת וְאֶזְכֶּה לְהַמְשִׁיךְ עָלַי תָּמִיד הַיִּרְאָה הַקְּדוֹשָׁה הַנִּגֶּשֶׁת וּבָאָה אֶל הָאָדָם לְעֵת הָאֹכֶל דַּיְקָא וְאֵשֵׁב עַל הַשֻּׁלְחָן בִּשְׁעַת סְעוּדָה בְּאֵימָה וּבְיִרְאָה גְדוֹלָה מִפָּנֶיךָ תָּמִיד. (ל"ת תנינא ל"ח)

צעטיל קטן ב

כונה "ונקדשתי" כנזכר לעיל בקריאת שמע ושמונה עשרה

וְעָזְרֵנִי וְהוֹשִׁיעֵנִי בְּרַחֲמֶיךָ הָרַבִּים שֶׁאֶזְכֶּה תָּמִיד לִמְסֹר נַפְשִׁי עַל קִדּוּשׁ הַשֵּׁם בֶּאֱמֶת, וּבִפְרָט בִּשְׁעַת קְרִיאַת שְׁמַע וּתְפִלָּה, שֶׁאֶזְכֶּה תָּמִיד לְהִתְפַּלֵּל וְלוֹמַר קְרִיאַת שְׁמַע בִּמְסִירַת נֶפֶשׁ בֶּאֱמֶת, וְאֶזְכֶּה לְקַבֵּל בְּדַעְתִּי בְּרָצוֹן חָזָק בֶּאֱמֶת לִמְסֹר נַפְשִׁי לָמוּת עַל קִדּוּשׁ הַשֵּׁם, לְהִתְלַהֵב בְּשַׁלְהוֹבִין דִּרְחִימוּתָא וּלְהִתְגַּבֵּר עַל יִצְרִי לִמְסֹר כָּל גּוּפִי וְנַפְשִׁי וּמְאֹדִי בִּשְׁבִיל לְקַדֵּשׁ שִׁמְךָ הַגָּדוֹל וְהַקָּדוֹשׁ וְהַנּוֹרָא. (ל"ת צ"ה)

༄

רִבּוֹנוֹ שֶׁל עוֹלָם, מַסְוֵה הַבּוּשָׁה עַל פָּנַי לְבַקֵּשׁ מִמְּךָ גְּדוֹלוֹת כָּאֵלֶּה, כִּי עֲדַיִן לֹא זָכִיתִי מֵעוֹלָם לִישׁוֹן בִּקְדֻשָּׁה וְלִקְרוֹת קְרִיאַת שְׁמַע שֶׁעַל הַמִּטָּה בִּקְדֻשָּׁה וּבְטָהֳרָה, וְהַמַּחֲשָׁבוֹת רָעוֹת עוֹלִים עַל לִבִּי לְהַדִּיחֵנִי חַס וְשָׁלוֹם מִן הַקְּדֻשָּׁה. עַל כֵּן רַחֵם עָלַי וְתֶן לִי בְּמַתְּנַת חִנָּם קְדֻשָּׁתְךָ הָעֲצוּמָה, וְקַדֵּשׁ אֶת מֹחִי בִּקְדֻשָּׁה, שֶׁאֶזְכֶּה לִישׁוֹן תָּמִיד מִתּוֹךְ דִּבְרֵי תוֹרָתְךָ הַקְּדוֹשָׁה, וְלַחְשֹׁב בְּעֵת שֶׁאֶרְצֶה לִישׁוֹן תָּמִיד דִּבְרֵי קְדֻשָּׁה וְטָהֳרָה. וְאֶזְכֶּה לָשׁוּב קֹדֶם הַשֵּׁנָה עַל כָּל מַעֲשַׂי וּבִפְרָט עַל כָּל מַה שֶּׁפָּגַמְתִּי נֶגְדְּךָ בְּאוֹתוֹ הַיּוֹם, וְלִקְרוֹת קְרִיאַת שְׁמַע בִּקְדֻשָּׁה, וְלִמְסֹר נַפְשִׁי בִּמְסִירוּת נֶפֶשׁ בֶּאֱמֶת בִּשְׁבִיל קְדֻשַּׁת שִׁמְךָ, וּלְבַטֵּל אֶת עַצְמִי וְלִסְתֹּם עֵינַי לְגַמְרֵי מֵחֵיזוּ דְּהַאי עָלְמָא, וּלְאִדַּבְּקָא מַחְשַׁבְתִּי בְּעָלְמָא דְּאָתֵי שֶׁהִיא הַתַּכְלִית הָאַחֲרוֹן, שֶׁאֵדַע שֶׁכֻּלּוֹ טוֹב, עַד שֶׁיִּתְבַּטְּלוּ מֵעָלַי כָּל הַתַּאֲווֹת וְהַבִּלְבּוּלִים וְהַצָּרוֹת וְהַיִּסּוּרִים, וְאֶזְכֶּה לְבַטֵּל כָּל הַדִּינִין מִכָּל הָעוֹלָם וְיִהְיֶה רַק טוֹב, וִיקֻיַּם בִּי מִקְרָא שֶׁכָּתוּב: אִם תִּשְׁכַּב לֹא תִפְחָד וְשָׁכַבְתָּ וְעָרְבָה שְׁנָתֶךָ. בְּטוּב אָלִין אָקִיץ בְּרַחֲמִים. (תפילות הבוקר עמ' ס"א)

תפילות על הצעטיל קטן

צעטיל קטן א

ונקדשתי בתוך בני ישראל

[רִבּוֹנוֹ שֶׁל עוֹלָם] וְתַעֲזְרֵנִי בְּכֹחֲךָ הַגָּדוֹל וְרַחֲמֶיךָ הָרַבִּים שֶׁאֶזְכֶּה לְחַזֵּק אֶת מַחֲשַׁבְתִּי בְּעִנְיַן הַמְסִירַת נֶפֶשׁ בֶּאֱמֶת בְּמַחֲשָׁבָה חֲזָקָה וְתַקִּיפָה בְּכָל הַכֹּחוֹת שֶׁיֵּשׁ בְּמַחֲשָׁבָה בִּפְנִימִיּוּת וְחִיצוֹנִיּוּת, וּלְצַיֵּר בְּמַחֲשַׁבְתִּי כָּל הַמִּיתוֹת וְהָעִנּוּיִים בְּצִיּוּר גָּמוּר, בְּמַחֲשָׁבָה חֲזָקָה וְתַקִּיפָה, בְּבִטּוּל כָּל הַהַרְגָּשׁוֹת עַד שֶׁאַרְגִּישׁ בְּמַחֲשַׁבְתִּי וּמוֹחִי צַעַר הַמִּיתָה וְהָעִנּוּיִים מַמָּשׁ כְּאִלּוּ מְמִיתִים וּמְיַסְּרִים אוֹתִי בְּמִיתוֹת וְיִסּוּרִים אֵלּוּ מַמָּשׁ בִּשְׁבִיל קְדֻשַּׁת שִׁמְךָ הַגָּדוֹל וְהַקָּדוֹשׁ, עַד שֶׁכִּמְעַט תֵּצֵא נַפְשִׁי חַס וְשָׁלוֹם וְלֹא יִהְיֶה שׁוּם חִלּוּק אֶצְלִי בֵּין יִסּוּרֵי הַמִּיתָה מַמָּשׁ, וּבֵין יִסּוּרֵי הַצִּיּוּר בְּמַחֲשָׁבָה וְהַקַּבָּלָה בַּלֵּב, עַד שֶׁאֶהְיֶה מֻכְרָח לְהִתְגַּבֵּר לְהַפְסִיק הַמַּחֲשָׁבָה מְעַט, בְּעֵת שֶׁאֶרְאֶה וְאָבִין שֶׁקָּרוֹב שֶׁתֵּצֵא נַפְשִׁי מַמָּשׁ חַס וְשָׁלוֹם, כְּדֵי שֶׁלֹּא אָמוּת בְּלֹא עִתִּי חַס וְשָׁלוֹם, וְאַתָּה תַּעֲזֹר וְתוֹשִׁיעַ לִי וּתְיַסְּרֵנִי וּתְלַמְּדֵנִי לְהִתְנַהֵג בָּזֶה כִּרְצוֹנְךָ הַטּוֹב בֶּאֱמֶת, לְקַבֵּל הַמְסִירַת נֶפֶשׁ בְּאַהֲבָה בֶּאֱמֶת בִּשְׁבִיל קְדֻשַּׁת הַשֵּׁם, וּלְצַיֵּר בְּמַחֲשַׁבְתִּי הַמִּיתָה וְהַיִּסּוּרִים בְּמַחֲשָׁבָה חֲזָקָה כָּל כָּךְ עַד שֶׁאַרְגִּישׁ צַעַר הַמִּיתָה וְהַיִּסּוּרִים מַמָּשׁ, וּלְהַנִּיחַ בְּסוֹף הַמַּחֲשָׁבָה לְהַפְסִיקָהּ מְעַט מִצִּיּוּר הַחָזָק שֶׁל יִסּוּרֵי הַמִּיתָה בְּעֵת שֶׁיִּהְיֶה הַדָּבָר קָרוֹב שֶׁתֵּצֵא נַפְשִׁי לְגַמְרֵי, כִּי אֵין זֶה רְצוֹנְךָ לְסַלֵּק הַנֶּפֶשׁ קֹדֶם הַזְּמַן חַס וְשָׁלוֹם: (ל״ת פ״ז)

תפילת התלמוד תורה
מספר שערי ציון

הִנְנִי רוֹצֶה לִלְמֹד שֶׁיְבִיאֵנִי הַתַּלְמוּד לִידֵי מַעֲשֶׂה וְלִידֵי מִדּוֹת יְשָׁרוֹת וְלִידֵי יְדִיעוֹת הַתּוֹרָה לְשֵׁם יִחוּד קוּבּ"ה וּשְׁכִנְתֵּי' בִּדְחִילוּ וּרְחִימוּ וּרְחִימוּ וּדְחִילוּ לְיַחֲדָא שֵׁם י"ה בְּו"ה בְּיִחוּדָא שְׁלִים בְּשֵׁם כָּל יִשְׂרָאֵל וּלְאוּקְמָא שְׁכִינְתָּא מֵעַפְרָא וִיהִי רָצוֹן מִלְפָנֶיךָ יְהֹוָה אֱלֹהַי וֵאלֹהֵי אֲבוֹתַי שֶׁתְּזַכֵּךְ רוּחֵינוּ וְנַפְשֵׁינוּ. וִיהִי נֹעַם אֲדֹנָי אֱלֹהֵינוּ עָלֵינוּ וּמַעֲשֵׂה יָדֵינוּ כּוֹנְנָה עָלֵינוּ וּמַעֲשֵׂה יָדֵינוּ כּוֹנְנֵהוּ:

תפילת השב להחסיד רבינו יונה ז"ל

אָנָּא הַשֵּׁם חָטָאתִי עָוִיתִי פָּשַׁעְתִּי כָּזֹאת וְכָזֹאת עָשִׂיתִי מִיּוֹם הֱיוֹתִי עַל הָאֲדָמָה עַד הַיּוֹם הַזֶּה. וְעַתָּה נְשָׂאַנִי לִבִּי וְנָדְבָה אוֹתִי רוּחִי לָשׁוּב אֵלֶיךָ בֶּאֱמֶת וּבְלֵב טוֹב וְשָׁלֵם, בְּכָל לִבִּי וְנַפְשִׁי וּמְאֹדִי, וְלִהְיוֹת מוֹדֶה וְעוֹזֵב לְהַשְׁלִיךְ מֵעָלַי כָּל פְּשָׁעַי וְלַעֲשׂוֹת לִי לֵב חָדָשׁ וְרוּחַ חֲדָשָׁה וְלִהְיוֹת זָרִיז וְזָהִיר בְּיִרְאָתֶךָ. וְאַתָּה יְהוָה אֱלֹהַי הַפּוֹתֵחַ יָד בִּתְשׁוּבָה וּמְסַיֵּעַ לַבָּאִים לְטַהֵר, פְּתַח יָדְךָ וְקַבְּלֵנִי בִּתְשׁוּבָה שְׁלֵמָה לְפָנֶיךָ, וְסַיְּעֵנִי לְהִתְחַזֵּק בְּיִרְאָתֶךָ, וְעָזְרֵנִי נֶגֶד הַשָּׂטָן הַנִּלְחָם בִּי בְּתַחְבּוּלָה וּמְבַקֵּשׁ נַפְשִׁי לַהֲמִיתֵנִי לְבִלְתִּי יִמְשׁוֹל בִּי. וְהַרְחִיקֵהוּ מֵרמ"ח אֵיבָרִים שֶׁבִּי, וְתַשְׁלִיכֵהוּ בִּמְצוּלוֹת יָם, וְתִגְעַר בּוֹ לְבִלְתִּי יַעֲמֹד עַל יְמִינִי לְשִׂטְנֵנִי. וְעָשִׂיתָ אֵת אֲשֶׁר אֵלֵךְ בְּחֻקֶּיךָ, וַהֲסִירוֹת לֵב הָאֶבֶן מִקִּרְבִּי, וְנָתַתָּ לִי לֵב בָּשָׂר. אָנָּא יְהוָה אֱלֹהַי, שְׁמַע אֶל תְּפִלַּת עַבְדְּךָ וְאֶל תַּחֲנוּנָיו, וְקַבֵּל תְּשׁוּבָתִי, וְאַל יְעַכֵּב שׁוּם חֵטְא וְעָוֹן אֶת תְּפִלָּתִי וּתְשׁוּבָתִי. וִיהִי לְפָנֶיךָ לִפְנֵי כִסֵּא כְבוֹדְךָ מֵלִיצֵי יֹשֶׁר לְהָלִיץ בַּעֲדִי לְהַכְנֵס תְּפִלָּתִי לְפָנֶיךָ. וְאִם בַּחֲטָאַי הָרַב וְעָצוּם אֵין לִי מֵלִיץ יֹשֶׁר, חֲתֹר לִי אַתָּה מִתַּחַת כִּסֵּא כְבוֹדְךָ וְקַבֵּל תְּשׁוּבָתִי וְלֹא אָשׁוּב רֵיקָם מִלְּפָנֶיךָ כִּי אַתָּה שׁוֹמֵעַ תְּפִלָּה:

תפילת השל"ה על מסירת נפש

אַתָּה קָדוֹשׁ וְשִׁמְךָ קָדוֹשׁ, וּקְדוֹשִׁים מְקֻדְּשֵׁי יִשְׂרָאֵל הִקְדִּישׁוּ וְקִדְּשׁוּ וְיַקְדִּישׁוּ שְׁמֶךָ, לִסְבֹּל סְקִילָה שְׂרֵפָה הֶרֶג וָחֶנֶק וּבְכָל עִנּוּיִים קָשִׁים וּמָרִים, בַּעֲבוּר קְדֻשַּׁת שְׁמֶךָ וּבַעֲבוּר הַצָּלַת אֻמָּה יִשְׂרָאֵל. אָנָּא הָאֵל הַקָּדוֹשׁ, בְּאִם יִהְיֶה רְצוֹנְךָ לְהָבִיא אֵלַי נִסָּיוֹן, קַדְּשֵׁנִי וְטַהֲרֵנִי, וְתֵן בְּמַחְשַׁבְתִּי וּבְפִי לְקַדֵּשׁ אֶת שִׁמְךָ בָּרַבִּים, כְּמוֹ שֶׁעָשׂוּ הַקְּדוֹשִׁים עֲשָׂרָה הֲרוּגֵי מַלְכוּת וַאֲלָפִים וּרְבָבוֹת מְקֻדְּשֵׁי יִשְׂרָאֵל, כִּי אַתָּה ה' אֱלֹהֵינוּ ה' אֶחָד הָאֲמִתִּי. וּבַעֲבוּר תּוֹרָתְךָ הַקְּדוֹשָׁה תּוֹרַת אֱמֶת שֶׁהִיא אַחֲרִית וְנִצְחִיִּית, וּבַעֲבוּר עַמְּךָ יִשְׂרָאֵל גּוֹי אֶחָד בָּאָרֶץ גּוֹי קָדוֹשׁ וְטָהוֹר, עֲנֵנִי ה' עֲנֵנִי, וְיִתְגַּלְגֵּל קְדֻשָּׁה עַל יָדִי.

דַּיָּן אֱמֶת וְשׁוֹפֵט צֶדֶק, לִמְּדוּנִי חֲכָמֵינוּ ז"ל: הַמּוֹסֵר אֶת עַצְמוֹ בְּלֵב שָׁלֵם לְקַדֵּשׁ שְׁמֶךָ, אָז אֵין מַרְגִּישׁ הַצַּעַר הַגָּדוֹל. אָמְנָם, אִי אֶפְשָׁר בְּתַקָּנַת חֲכָמִים הַנִּזְכָּר לְעֵיל, יִהְיֶה מַה שֶּׁיִּהְיֶה, רַק הָיָה תִהְיֶה עִמָּדִי שֶׁלֹּא יְעַכְּבֵנִי הַצַּעַר מִלִּהְיוֹת מַחְשְׁבוֹתַי דְּבוּקָה בָּךְ, וְאֶהְיֶה שָׂמֵחַ בְּלִבִּי בְּעֵת הַיִּסּוּרִין, וְתוֹסִיף בְּפִי כֹּחַ הַדִּבּוּר לְדַבֵּר וּלְקַדֵּשׁ בְּחָכְמָה וּבִתְבוּנָה וּבְדַעַת בָּרַבִּים - גָּלוּי וּמְפֻרְסָם לַכֹּל, וְנַקֵּנִי מֵחֲטָאַי וַעֲוֹנוֹתַי וּפְשָׁעַי, וְתֵן חֶלְקִי עִם הַקְּדוֹשִׁים הַדְּבֵקִים בִּקְדֻשָּׁתֶךָ.

"יִהְיוּ לְרָצוֹן אִמְרֵי פִי וְהֶגְיוֹן לִבִּי לְפָנֶיךָ ה' צוּרִי וְגוֹאֲלִי".

עָלֵינוּ, וְתַשְׁפִּיעַ רוּחַ קָדְשְׁךָ עָלֵינוּ שֶׁנִּהְיֶה דְבֵקִים בָּךְ. וְשֶׁנִּשְׁתּוֹקֵק תָּמִיד אֵלֶיךָ יוֹתֵר וְיוֹתֵר, וּמִמַּדְרֵגָה לְמַדְרֵגָה תַּעֲלֵנוּ, שֶׁנִּזְכֶּה לָבוֹא לְמַעֲלַת אֲבוֹתֵינוּ הַקְּדוֹשִׁים אַבְרָהָם יִצְחָק וְיַעֲקֹב, וּזְכוּתָם יַעֲמָד לָנוּ שֶׁתִּשְׁמַע בְּקוֹל תְּפִלָּתֵנוּ שֶׁנִּהְיֶה תָּמִיד נַעֲנִים בְּעֵת שֶׁנִּתְפַּלֵּל אֵלֶיךָ עָלֵינוּ אוֹ עַל שׁוּם אֶחָד מֵעַמְּךָ יִשְׂרָאֵל, עַל יָחִיד אוֹ עַל רַבִּים, וְתִשְׂמַח וְתִתְפָּאֵר בָּנוּ, וְנַעֲשֶׂה פְרִי לְמַעְלָה וְשֹׁרֶשׁ לְמַטָּה: וְאַל תִּזְכָּר לָנוּ חֲטָאתֵינוּ וּבִפְרָט חַטֹּאת נְעוּרֵינוּ, כְּמַאֲמַר דָּוִד הַמֶּלֶךְ עָלָיו הַשָּׁלוֹם חַטֹּאת נְעוּרַי וּפְשָׁעַי אַל תִּזְכֹּר, וְתַהֲפֹךְ עֲוֹנוֹתֵינוּ וּפְשָׁעֵינוּ לִזְכֻיּוֹת, וְתַשְׁפִּיעַ עָלֵינוּ מֵעוֹלָם הַתְּשׁוּבָה תָּמִיד הִרְהוּר לָשׁוּב אֵלֶיךָ וּלְתַקֵּן אֶת אֲשֶׁר פָּגַמְנוּ בְּשֵׁמוֹתֶיךָ הַקְּדוֹשִׁים וְהַטְּהוֹרִים: וְתַצִּילֵנוּ מִקִּנְאַת אִישׁ מֵרֵעֵהוּ וְלֹא יַעֲלֶה קִנְאַת אָדָם עַל לִבֵּנוּ וְלֹא קִנְאָתֵנוּ עַל אֲחֵרִים, אַדְּרַבָּה, תֵּן בְּלִבֵּנוּ שֶׁנִּרְאֶה כָּל אֶחָד מַעֲלַת חֲבֵרֵינוּ וְלֹא חֶסְרוֹנָם, וְשֶׁנְּדַבֵּר כָּל אֶחָד אֶת חֲבֵרוֹ בַּדֶּרֶךְ הַיָּשָׁר וְהָרָצוּי לְפָנֶיךָ, וְאַל יַעֲלֶה שׁוּם שִׂנְאָה מֵאֶחָד עַל חֲבֵרוֹ חָלִילָה: וּתְחַזֵּק הִתְקַשְּׁרוּתֵנוּ בְּאַהֲבָה אֵלֶיךָ, כַּאֲשֶׁר גָּלוּי וְיָדוּעַ לְפָנֶיךָ. שֶׁיְּהֵא הַכֹּל נַחַת רוּחַ אֵלֶיךָ, וְזֶה עִקַּר כַּוָּנָתֵנוּ. וְאִם אֵין לָנוּ שֵׂכֶל לְכַוֵּן אֶת לְבָבֵנוּ אֵלֶיךָ, אַתָּה תְלַמְּדֵנוּ אֲשֶׁר נֵדַע בֶּאֱמֶת כַּוָּנַת רְצוֹנְךָ הַטּוֹב: וְעַל כָּל זֹאת מִתְחַנְּנִים אֲנַחְנוּ לְפָנֶיךָ אֵל מָלֵא רַחֲמִים שֶׁתְּקַבֵּל אֶת תְּפִלָּתֵנוּ בְּרַחֲמִים וּבְרָצוֹן, אָמֵן כֵּן יְהִי רָצוֹן:

תְּעוֹרֵר נָא עָלֵינוּ רַחֲמֶיךָ וַחֲסָדֶיךָ הַגְּדוֹלִים וְהַמְרֻבִּים לְגָרֵשׁ וּלְבַעֵר אֶת יִצְרֵנוּ הָרָע מִקִּרְבֵּנוּ, וְתִגְעַר בּוֹ שֶׁיָּסוּר וְיֵלֵךְ מֵאִתָּנוּ, וְאַל יָסִית אוֹתָנוּ לְהַדִּיחֵנוּ מֵעֲבוֹדָתְךָ חָלִילָה. וְאַל יַעֲלֶה בְלִבֵּנוּ שׁוּם מַחֲשָׁבָה רָעָה חָלִילָה הֵן בְּהָקִיץ הֵן בַּחֲלוֹם. בִּפְרָט בְּעֵת שֶׁאֲנַחְנוּ עוֹמְדִים בִּתְפִלָּה לְפָנֶיךָ, אוֹ בְּשָׁעָה שֶׁאֲנַחְנוּ לוֹמְדִים תּוֹרָתֶךָ. וּבְשָׁעָה שֶׁאֲנַחְנוּ עוֹסְקִים בְּמִצְוֹתֶיךָ, תְּהֵא מַחְשְׁבוֹתֵינוּ זַכָּה צְלוּלָה וּבְרוּרָה וַחֲזָקָה, בֶּאֱמֶת וּבְלֵבָב שָׁלֵם כִּרְצוֹנְךָ הַטּוֹב עִמָּנוּ: וּתְעוֹרֵר לְבָבֵנוּ וּלְבַב כָּל יִשְׂרָאֵל עַמֶּךָ, וּלְבַב כָּל הַנִּלְוִים אֵלֵינוּ, וּלְבַב כָּל הַחֲפֵצִים בְּחֶבְרָתֵנוּ, לְיַחֶדְךָ בֶּאֱמֶת וּבְאַהֲבָה. לְעָבְדְּךָ עֲבוֹדָה הַיְשָׁרָה, הַמְקֻבֶּלֶת לִפְנֵי כִסֵּא כְבוֹדֶךָ. וְתִקְבַּע אֱמוּנָתְךָ בְּלִבֵּנוּ תָּמִיד בְּלִי הֶפְסֵק, וּתְהֵא אֱמוּנָתְךָ קְשׁוּרָה בְּלִבֵּנוּ כְּיָתֵד שֶׁלֹּא תִמּוֹט, וְתַעֲבִיר מֵעָלֵינוּ כָּל הַמָּסַכִּים הַמַּבְדִּילִים בֵּינֵינוּ לְבִינְךָ אָבִינוּ שֶׁבַּשָּׁמַיִם. וְתַצִּילֵנוּ מִכָּל מִכְשׁוֹל וּטְעוּת, אַל תַּעַזְבֵנוּ וְאַל תִּטְּשֵׁנוּ וְאַל תַּכְלִימֵנוּ, וּתְהֵא עִם פִּינוּ בְּעֵת הַטִּיפֵנוּ, וְעִם יָדֵינוּ בְּעֵת מַעֲבָדֵינוּ, וְעִם לִבֵּנוּ בְּעֵת מַחְשְׁבוֹתֵינוּ: וּתְזַכֵּנוּ אָבִינוּ שֶׁבַּשָּׁמַיִם אֵל מָלֵא רַחֲמִים, שֶׁנְּיַחֵד אֶת לִבֵּנוּ וּמַחְשְׁבוֹתֵינוּ וְדִבּוּרֵנוּ וּמַעֲשֵׂינוּ וְכָל תְּנוּעוֹתֵינוּ וְהַרְגְּשׁוֹתֵינוּ, הַיְדוּעוֹת לָנוּ וְשֶׁאֵינָן יְדוּעוֹת לָנוּ, הַנִּגְלוֹת וְהַנִּסְתָּרוֹת, שֶׁיְּהֵא הַכֹּל מְיֻחָד אֵלֶיךָ בֶּאֱמֶת וּבְתָמִים בְּלִי שׁוּם מַחֲשֶׁבֶת פְּסוּל חָלִילָה, וְטַהֵר לִבֵּנוּ וְקַדְּשֵׁנוּ, וּזְרֹק עָלֵינוּ מַיִם טְהוֹרִים וְטַהֲרֵנוּ בְּאַהֲבָתְךָ וּבְחֶמְלָתְךָ, וְתִטַּע אַהֲבָתְךָ וְיִרְאָתְךָ בְּלִבֵּנוּ תָּמִיד בְּלִי הֶפְסֵק, בְּכָל עֵת וּבְכָל זְמַן וּבְכָל מָקוֹם, בְּלֶכְתֵּנוּ וּבְשָׁכְבֵּנוּ וּבְשָׁכְבֵנוּ וּבְקוּמֵנוּ תְּבַעֵר תָּמִיד רוּחַ קָדְשְׁךָ בְּקִרְבֵּנוּ. וְנַשְׂגְּעֶנִים תָּמִיד בָּךְ וּבִגְדֻלָּתְךָ וּבְאַהֲבָתְךָ וּבְיִרְאָתְךָ. וּבְתוֹרָתְךָ שֶׁבִּכְתָב וְשֶׁבְּעַל פֶּה הַנִּגְלֶה וְהַנִּסְתָּר וּבְמִצְוֹתֶיךָ, הַכֹּל לְיַחֵד שִׁמְךָ הַגִּבּוֹר וְהַנּוֹרָא: וְתִשְׁמְרֵנוּ מִן הַפְּנִיּוֹת וְהַגַּאֲוֹת וּמִן הַכַּעַס וְהַקַּפְּדָנוּת וְהָעַצְבוּת וְהָרְכִילוּת וּשְׁאָר מִדּוֹת רָעוֹת, וּמִכָּל דָּבָר הַמַּפְסִיד עֲבוֹדָתְךָ הַקְּדוֹשָׁה וְהַטְּהוֹרָה הַחֲבִיבָה

תפילה מרבי אלימלך זצוק"ל

יְהִי רָצוֹן מִלְּפָנֶיךָ ה' אֱלֹהֵינוּ וֵאלֹהֵי אֲבוֹתֵינוּ שׁוֹמֵעַ קוֹל שַׁוְעַת עֲתִירוֹת. וּמַאֲזִין לְקוֹל תְּפִלַּת עַמּוֹ יִשְׂרָאֵל בְּרַחֲמִים. שֶׁתָּכִין לִבֵּנוּ וּתְכוֹנֵן מַחְשְׁבוֹתֵינוּ וּתְשַׁגֵּר תְּפִלָּתֵנוּ בְּפִינוּ. וְתַקְשִׁיב אָזְנֶיךָ לִשְׁמֹעַ בְּקוֹל תְּפִלַּת עֲבָדֶיךָ הַמִּתְחַנְּנִים אֵלֶיךָ בְּקוֹל שַׁוְעָה וְרוּחַ נִשְׁבָּרָה: וְאַתָּה אֵל רַחוּם בְּרַחֲמֶיךָ הָרַבִּים וּבַחֲסָדֶיךָ הַגְּדוֹלִים. תִּמְחוֹל וְתִסְלַח וּתְכַפֵּר לָנוּ וּלְכָל עַמְּךָ בֵּית יִשְׂרָאֵל. אֶת כָּל מַה שֶּׁחָטָאנוּ וְהֶעֱוִינוּ וְהִרְשַׁעְנוּ וּפָשַׁעְנוּ לְפָנֶיךָ, כִּי גָלוּי וְיָדוּעַ לְפָנֶיךָ כִּי לֹא בְּמֶרֶד וּבְמַעַל חָלִילָה וְחָלִילָה מָרִינוּ אֶת פִּיךָ וְדִבְרֵי תוֹרָתֶךָ וּמִצְוֹתֶיךָ. כִּי אִם מֵרֹב הַיֵּצֶר הַבּוֹעֵר בְּקִרְבֵּנוּ תָּמִיד. לֹא יָנוּחַ וְלֹא יִשְׁקֹט עַד אֲשֶׁר מְבִיאֵנוּ אֶל תַּאֲוֹת הָעוֹלָם הַשָּׁפָל הַזֶּה וְאֶל הֲבָלָיו. וּמְבַלְבֵּל אֶת מַחְשְׁבוֹתֵינוּ תָּמִיד, אֲפִלּוּ בְּשָׁעָה שֶׁאֲנַחְנוּ עוֹמְדִים לְהִתְפַּלֵּל לְפָנֶיךָ וּלְבַקֵּשׁ עַל נַפְשֵׁנוּ. הוּא מְבַלְבֵּל אֶת תְּפִלָּתֵנוּ וְאֶת מַחְשְׁבוֹתֵינוּ תָּמִיד בְּתַחְבּוּלוֹתָיו, וְאֵין אָנוּ יְכוֹלִים לַעֲמֹד נֶגְדּוֹ. כִּי נֶחֱלַשׁ שִׂכְלֵנוּ וּמֹחֵנוּ וְלִבֵּנוּ עַד מְאֹד. וְכָשַׁל כֹּחַ הַסַּבָּל מֵרֹב הַצָּרוֹת וְהַתְּלָאוֹת וְטִרְדַּת הַזְּמַן: לָכֵן אַתָּה אֵל רַחוּם וְחַנּוּן. עֲשֵׂה עִמָּנוּ כְּמוֹ שֶׁהִבְטַחְתָּנוּ עַל יְדֵי נֶאֱמַן בֵּיתֶךָ. וְחַנֹּתִי אֶת אֲשֶׁר אָחֹן וְרִחַמְתִּי אֶת אֲשֶׁר אֲרַחֵם, וְאָמְרוּ חֲכָמֵינוּ זִכְרוֹנָם לִבְרָכָה. אַף עַל פִּי שֶׁאֵינוֹ הָגוּן וְאֵינוֹ כְדַאי, כִּי כֵן דַּרְכְּךָ לְהֵיטִיב לָרָעִים וְלַטּוֹבִים, כִּי גָלוּי וְיָדוּעַ לְפָנֶיךָ אַנְקָתֵנוּ וְצַעֲרֵנוּ וְשִׂיחֵנוּ עַל אֲשֶׁר אֵין אָנוּ יְכוֹלִים לְקָרֵב עַצְמֵנוּ לַעֲבוֹדָתֶךָ. וּלְדַבֵּק לִבֵּנוּ בְּךָ בֶּאֱמֶת וּבְתָמִים, אֲהָהּ עַל נַפְשֵׁנוּ, אוֹי עָלֵינוּ מְאֹד, אָבִינוּ שֶׁבַּשָּׁמַיִם: וְעַתָּה

B. Y. HEIMLICH
Rabbi in Congregation
EDAH HACHAREDIT
4 Shomrei Amunim St.
JERUSALEM
Tel. (02) 582-8885

ברך יהודה הלוי היימליך
רב ומו"צ בהעדה החרדית
רחוב שומרי אמונים 4
בעה"ק ירושלים תובב"א
טל. 582-8885 (02)

ב"ה, ג' ניסן תשס"ב לסדר ודיבר ירושלים תודכ"א

הנני בזה לברכת הגאון לכתרים דיבי הרה"ג לגאון יקירו ירא וחשך הרב החסיב מוהר"ר אליעזר ראזענפעלד שליט"א אשר הוציא לאור דברי הבצל"ח קטן והנהגות ישרות אקדוש אלוקי רב"ד עוצם אמונתו צל"א, וגם ספר האמונה וההשגחה שהוא יסוד נעלה בבנו, ובדיקי הגבורות דחיעק והוובה השם ועובדות והנהגות ישרות מהצדיקים הקדושים המאהירים לבזרית בני ישראל לקדבם אל השם.

ובזה רחב לנו דבר בזה להוציאו אור עמירם דבה לזכות מלאית גדאית אמונה של יראי אלקים הרה"ח ר' אליעזר אשר שליט"א לעלות אותיות התורה המדקקים את ה' שנובדים דעה לו של הם יהיו מאובר לו.

ע"ב אמינא איישר לחילא שזכה עוד ישבוב עד"ועיתו חיבה לבבות לו בני ישראל הקדושים להאהיד לבם לדרכי ההורא הבצל"ח תורה ולהאהבירה עמוק בריוג לוגא ויוהרא אלצא עמון היתהב הגאות והם הקדושה עדי עלה לקדוץ לפינו דית המקדש ויגאל עם מן הגלותים ונגן הבסתים במהרה דידן אמן.

ובע"ח באוהבו לעצן כבוב תורתינו הק' ולועביה
ברך יהודה הלוי היימליך

מכתב ברכה

בס"ד, כ"ג שבט תשס"ט

הנני לברך את ידידנו היקר הרב **אליעזר שאול זיסמאן** שליט"א

אשר רחש לבו דבר טוב לזכות את הרבים להוציא לאור עולם את ה"צעטיל קטן" מרבנו הקדוש בעל נועם אלימלך זצ"ל עם ריכוז תפילות נפלאות ונוראות ע"י חסידי עליון שרפי קודש אשר כל דברים גחלי אש יוקדת שלהבת י–ה.

תפילות אלו מלהיבות לב האומרן והם דברים הנצרכים לכל אחד, למען אשר ילך בדרך העולה בית א–ל. וגם צירף ליקוט נפלא מספרים הקדושים בעניינים השייכים להמובא בה"צעטיל קטן" דבר דבור על אופניו, ואשר המחבר שליט"א ידע לאוספם בחכמה ולסדרם אחת לאחת ולא נצרכה אלא לברכה.

יה"ר שהחפץ בידו יצליח, ויזכה להפיץ את ספרו **המלוכה והממשלה** בכל קצוות תבל, ויהיה בזה נחת רוח לפני בורא עולם אמן.

כעתירת מוקירו:
יעקב שכנזי

RABBI ARON DAVID NEUSTADT	אהרן דוד ניישטאדט
RAV OF CONG ; KHAL CHASIDIM	רב דק"ק "קהל חסידים" נוה יעקב
DAYAN OF BEIS DIN GIVAT SHAUL	וחבר בית דין ממונות גבעת שאול
29 ZEVIN ST. JERUSALEM	רח' זוין 29 פעיה"ק ירושלים תובב"א

ב"ה ראש חודש תמוז התשע"ה לפ"ג

הנה דבר שפתיים הוא אך למותר להאריך בשבח חשיבות עריכת אזניים לתורתו של הרב הקדוש איש אלוקים הרבי רבי אלימלך מליזענסק זיעוכ"י, ומי זה יבוא אחר המלך, אמנם בואו ונחזיק טובה להאי גברא רבא ויקירא הרב הגה"ח **רבי אליעזר שאול זיסמן שליט"א** שזכה לעסוק בבירור מקחו של צדיק והוציא לאור חיבור על **הצעטיל קטן** בשם **המלוכה והממשלה** סובב הולך בלקיטת ציצים ופרחים ואמרים יקרים על הצעטיל קטן ועוד, אלו הדברים אשר יעשה האדם וחי בהם.

והכל אשר לכול עשה יפה בעטו עט סופר מהיר, וזכה להוציא מתחת ידו דבר נאה ומתוק, בעריכה נאה ומאירת עיניים, בסגנון צח ושווה לכל נפש, **ועתה רחש לבו דבר טוב להוציא ספר זה גם בשפה האנגלית ע"י איש יקר ומהיר במלאכתו הרה"ח רבי אליעזר שארר שליט"א** וכבר זכה להוציא כמה חיבורים יקרים בשפה זו.

ואיתמחי גברא ה"ה **הרב זיסמן** שיחי', שכבר זכה להוציא מתח"י כמה חיבורים חשובים, שנתקבלו בחיבה ועלו לרצון על שולחן מלכים, מאן מלכי רבנן. ועוד ידו נטויה בעז"ה.

אשר על כן גם אני מצטרף בדברי ברכה, שיזכה להמשיך בפעליו הברוכים ויפוצו מעיינותיו חוצה להגדיל תורה ולהאדירה ויהא שם שמים מתאהב ומתקדש על ידו, מתוך שמחה ובריאות אורך ימים ושנים טובות.

ובזכות לימוד התורה הקדושה, נזכה לכל הייעודים הטובים, ובכל הברכות הכתובות בתורה ובנביאים ובכתובים, להיוושע בכל העניינים לטובה, ונזכה לביאת גואל צדק ולבניין בית מקדשנו ותפארתנו במהרה בימינו אמן.

חיים אורי בריזל
ר"מ בישיבת "שער השמים"
ללימוד תורת הנגלה והנסתר
פעיה"ק ירושלם תובב"א
רח' מצפה רש"פ 6 בית שמש

בס"ד   יום חודש שניתן בו תורה לישראל ה' תשע"ג

הן חזיתי איש מהיר במלאכתו האי גברא יקירא, ידידי הרה"ח ר' **אליעזר שאול זיסמן** שליט"א, אשר הוציא לאור עולם את פרי עמלו בספר הנפלא "המלוכה והממשלה" בו קיבץ וליקט פנינים ואמרות טהורות, הסובב על ה"צעטיל קטן" שחיבר זקני איש אלקים הרה"ק הרבי ר' אלימלך מליזענסק זיע"א, והרחיב את היריעה כאשר הוסיף עליהם ליקוט עובדות והנהגות ישרות, ותפילות יקרות מגדולי וצדיקי הדורות על ענינים אלו, לעורר לבבות בני ישראל לאבינו שבשמים.

ועתה רחש לבו דבר טוב לתרגמו ללועזות בלעז בלשון הענגליש שיזכו גם הם לטעום מנועב זיו קדושתו וטהרתו של הרה"ק מליזענסק זיע"א ולהבנים חיות בעצמותיהם וכבר הוסמ"ך גברא ע"ז.

ע"כ אף ידי תיכון עמו והנני לברכו שחפץ ד' בידו יצליח להוציאו לאור עולם, ויתרבה הדעת באור החסידות ויפוצו מעיינותיו חוצה, וזכות רביה"ק וזכות הרבים יהא מסייעתו להרב המחבר שליט"א להתברך בכל מילי דמיטב, ונזכה שאור חדש על ציון תאיר בבנין בית מקדשינו ותפארתינו בביאת משיח צדקנו בב"א.

הכו"ח למען ז"התורה ולומדיה

חיים אורי בריזל

יעקב מאיר שטרן
מו"צ בבי"ד דמרן הגר"ש ואזנר שליט"א
וחבר הבד"ץ דקרית ויזניץ
מח"ס משנת הסופר ואמרי יעקב
קהילות יעקב – בני ברק

בס"ד כ"ב אב תשס"ו

תחזקנה ידיו הטהורות של כבוד הרה"ח ר' **אליעזר שאול זיסמאן** לאוי"ט מעיה"ק ירושלים ת"ו שמדפיס חיבורו **המלוכה והממשלה** שהוא ליקוט יקר מאד מגדולי וצדיקי הדורות בחיזוק עבודה שבלב ובכלל עבודת ד' והדברים חוצבים להבות אש וגחלים בוערים המלהיבים את האדם ונותנים חיזוק גדול ובפרט חשיבות מיוחדת הוא הדבר שקבע את הדברים סביב הצעטיל קטן והנהגות ישרות ותפלת רבינו קודש הקדשים הרבי ר' אלימלך מליזענסק זצוק"ל.

ויהי רצון שזכות הרבי ר' אלימלך יעמוד לנו להתחזק בעמוד התפלה ובמהרה נושע בכלל ובפרט ונזכה לראות בישועתן של ישראל בהתגלות אורו של משיח בב"א.

נאום יעקב
מאיר שטרן

מתתיהו דייטש
רב שכונת רמת שלמה
דומ"צ העדה החרדית
עיה"ק ירושלים תובב"א
מחה"ס שו"ת "נתיבות אדם"

בס"ד, תמוז תשע"ה, פעיה"קת"ו.

הן כל יקר ראתה עיני ספר המלוכה והממשלה, והוא מעשי ידיו להתפאר של ידידי הרה"ג החסיד המפואר ירא ושלם ולן בעומקה של תורה מוה"ר אליעזר שאול זיסמן שליט"א מפעיה"קת"ו - אשר חפץ ה' בידו הצליח לבנות בנין שלם מהני מילי מעלייתא אמרות טהורות והנהגות קודש מגדולי וצדיקי הדורות, וכן הוסיף סיפורים ועובדות מגאו"צ הדורות זי"ע, וכפליים לתושיה מאמרים בגודל מעלת התפלה, והכל בנה מצורף לטהור סביב הולך הצעטיל קטן והנהגות האדם שחיבר רבן ומאורן של ישראל זקן ק"ק אור העולם הרבי רבי אלימלך מליזענסק זי"ע בעל נועם אלימלך - וכבר בהשקפה לטובה נראה שהרהמ"ח שליט"א השכיל בס"ד לאצור אוצר בלום של דברי תורה ויראה המעוררין את הלב לעבודת הבית"ש, ולתיקון המדות כראוי. והכל ערוך ומסודר באופן נפלא למען ירוץ בו הקורא, וניכר עמלו ויגיעתו להוציא התח"י דבר נאה ומתוקן - וכבר פקיע שמי' לתהלה כאשר הופיע הספר במהדורא קמאי ורבים וטובים גדולים יראי ה' וחושבי שמו יתברך שותים בצמא את הדברים המאירים והמללים ומשבחים את המחבר שליט"א על האור הנפלא אשר שם לפניהם בהאי ספרא יקירא, ואין גומרים עליו את ההלל, אשרי חלקו ועמלו.

ואשר על כן שמחתי לשמוע כי עומד להוציא מהדורא בתרא לזיכוי הרבים, ואמינא לפעלא טבא אישר כוחו וחילו לאורייתא - ויבואו רבים ויביאו הברכה לתוך ביתם כי ישמחו וידינו ויתבשמו נפשם ונשמתם מהני דיבורי קודש לעורר ולהתעורר לאהבת ה' ויראתו יתברך, ולהתחזק בתורה ותפלה ויראת שמים ותיקון המדות, וטוב להם בזה ובבא.

וזכות האי צדיק קדוש ונשגב הרר"א זי"ע תגן בעדו ובעד כב"י להיוושע בכל הישועות ברוחניות ובגשמיות, אורך ימים ושנות חיים, ללמוד וללמד לשמור ולעשות ולקיים את כל מצוות השי"ת מתוך שפע נחת והרחבה וטו"ס בשמחה ובטוב לבב אכי"ר.

ה

Rabbi Y.M. Morgenstern Rosh Hayeshiva of "Toras Chochom" Jerusalem	יצחק מאיר מורגנשטערן ראש ישיבת "תורת חכם" לתורת הנגלה והנסתר פעיה"ק ירושלים תותבב"א

ב"ה

עש"ק ... סיון התשע"ב לפ"ק

הנה הראה לפני מהדו' לומדי בית מדרשנו מיקירי קרתא דשפרא כש"ת
כמוהר"ר אליעזר שאול זיסמאן שליט"א, אשר כבר נתפרסם בשער בת רבים
בספרי השלום והמשלה אשר הלך סביב לזכרו קטן של הספה"ק הרבה
ד' אלימלך מליזענסק זי"ע והפלא בעמקי עומקות וכן הלאה וכל קושיות וחדר
זה המעיין לעבודת ה' ומשה בדרך שלו, ועתה מבקש לתרגם בלשון לעז
העולם, ובאמת אין מדרכינו להסכים על הדפסות מספרים בלשון זה מפני
הענין, אלא לתלמידו הישר בדרכו ברכות, על כן עוד ... שובה למרכזו שם
את ענין הישיבה בקדושה שאין מושג לשון הקודש ... בזכות רבותינו
אלו יצא שיפיץ הזה בלשון אחרת, והגה ... עליו ...
בהם שבם ... ויהי ... למעלה ... בספרו ...
אשר הקדושה ... ויפוצו מעיינותיו חוצה עד שיבוא ...
המקוה ... והגאולה השלמה במהרה בימינו אמן

הכו"ח ...

הק' יצחק מאיר מורגנשטערן

שמעון נתן נטע בידרמן
רח' ברוייאר 27 בני ברק

בס"ד כ"ג שבט תשס"ט

הנה האברך היקר הרה"ח **אליעזר שאול זיסמאן** הי"ו מעיה"ק ירושלים ת"ו הולך ומדפיס ספר **המלוכה והממשלה**, הסובב על הצעטיל קטן והנהגות ישרות ותפילת הרה"ק הרבי ר' אלימלך מליזענסק זיע"א, גם הוסיף והרחיב היריעה בעובדות והנהגות ישרות מגדולי וצדיקי עולם, לעורר לבבות בני ישראל ולהמשיכם לתורה ויראת ה' טהורה ותיקון המידות.

וכבר אמרו רז"ל אין עושין נפשות לצדיקים דבריהם הן הן זכרונם, ודבריהם כגחלי אש לשעה ולדורות.

ויה"ר ויזכה להגדיל תורה ולהאדירה לתועלת הכלל והפרט, וזכותו הגדולה של הרבי ר' אלימלך יגן בעדינו וימליץ טוב עלינו ועל כל ישראל להפקד בדבר ישועה ורחמים בכלל ובפרט ולביאת גואל צדק בב"א.

תוכן

ג	המלצות
יא	תפילה מרבי אלימלך זצוק״ל
יד	תפילה השל״ה הקדוש על מסירות נפש
טו	תפילה השב להחסיד רבינו יונה ז״ל
טז	תפילה התלמוד תורה מספר שערי ציון
יז	תפילות על הצעטיל קטן
מא	תפילות על ספר הנהגות האדם